Practical MATLAB and Python

A comparative approach to problem-solving to code like a pro

Dr. Mamta Kapoor

Dr. Geeta Arora

bpb

www.bpbonline.com

First Edition 2026

Copyright © BPB Publications, India

ISBN: 978-93-65891-263

LIMITS OF LIABILITY AND DISCLAIMER OF WARRANTY

To View Complete
BPB Publications Catalogue
Scan the QR Code:

www.bpbonline.com

Dedicated to

This book is dedicated to Almighty God for giving me the strength that illuminated every step of this journey. Furthermore, it is dedicated to my beloved parents, whose blessings, love, and sacrifices have been the foundation for the creation of this work.

- Dr. Mamta Kapoor

This book is dedicated to the Divine Power that has blessed me with a family whose love, care, and support have empowered me to chase my aspirations and realize my potential.

- Dr. Geeta Arora

About the Authors

- **Dr. Mamta Kapoor** is a mathematician and researcher. Her research areas are numerical approximation of linear and non-linear partial differential equations, semi-analytical solution of fractional partial differential equations, fractional calculus, fuzzy calculus, scientific computing, numerical analysis, and fluid mechanics. She has 58 research publications in national/international journals of repute (Scopus indexed). Along with this research, she has a number of certifications in data science due to her deep interest in this field. Some of the related certifications are: Professional Certificate Course in data science from E & ICT Academy, IIT Kanpur; Advanced Certification in applied data science, Machine Learning & IoT organized by E & ICT Academy, Indian Institute of Technology, Guwahati; etc.

- **Dr. Geeta Arora** is a mathematician and researcher. She earned her Ph.D. in mathematics from IIT Roorkee in 2011. Her research focuses on the development of numerical methods and statistics, with specific interests in computational techniques, numerical analysis, partial differential equations, working with collocation methods, differential quadrature techniques, wavelets, and radial basis functions. She has a substantial publication record, including around 85 research papers (Scopus indexed) in international and national journals. Additionally, she has authored 15 book chapters, written books on Vedic Mathematics and Essential Statistics, and edited several books on numerical methods. She has also conducted various short-term courses and workshops on MATLAB programming and applications, along with Vedic Mathematics.

About the Reviewers

❖ **Vishi Singh Bhatia** is a seasoned IT professional with a master's in information technology with over 17 years of IT experience spanning roles such as software developer, business analyst, functional lead, and architect, primarily within the healthcare insurance and pharmacy domain.

Recognized among the top 1% mentors on Topmate and honored with the People's Choice Award. He has served as a judge for prestigious technical awards, including the Globee Awards and Claro, as well as for international conferences such as the 8th International Conference on Intelligent Computing and Communication and the 2025 International Conference on applied artificial intelligence and innovation. Additionally, he has contributed as a reviewer for multiple books.

He has a proven track record of leading cross-functional teams across global locations, and driving large-scale transformation programs for Fortune 500 clients. Vishi has extensive experience in legacy modernization initiatives, successfully executing projects that integrate AI and cloud technologies. He is currently working at Tata Consultancy Services Limited and is part of the healthcare unit, where he is helping Fortune 500 companies undergo their digital transformation.

Certifications and affiliations: IEEE Senior Member, ACM, AAAI, judge in various hackathons and technical awards, PMP Certified and PMP Mentor, CSM, Azure Certified, ITIL, ISTQB, AHIP (Parts A & B).

❖ **Gowtham** is a seasoned AI professional with over 14 years of industry experience, transitioning from a data scientist to a lead AI engineer. He brings deep expertise across diverse domains, including healthcare, fintech, life sciences, and the automobile industry.

He has architected and delivered a wide range of data science solutions — from health insurance claim processing and claim amount forecasting to privacy-focused applications in fintech, leveraging computer vision and NLP for KYC document verification. In life sciences, he has designed and deployed generative AI solutions using LangChain, LangGraph, MCP, and OpenAI models — integrated with modern vector databases such as Qdrant and Weaviate — to assist in selecting the right candidates for clinical trials and driving advanced research insights.

Currently, he is working in the automobile sector as a lead AI engineer, where he applies GenAI, MCP, and vector database–driven solutions to transform warranty-related claims processing and optimize operational efficiency. His work spans developing and deploying innovative AI systems powered by Python and Rust that leverage **retrieval-augmented generation** (**RAG**) and multi-agent workflows to address complex real-world problems at scale.

He is passionate about applying AI responsibly and at scale, helping organizations reimagine processes, unlock business value, and maximize their technological investments.

Acknowledgements

First and foremost, we are profoundly grateful to our families for their unwavering support, encouragement, and understanding throughout this journey. Their love and motivation have been a constant source of strength and inspiration.

We extend our heartfelt thanks to BPB Publications for their expert guidance and continued support in transforming this manuscript into a published work. Their professionalism and assistance were invaluable in navigating the various stages of the publication process.

We also wish to acknowledge the contributions of the technical reviewers and editors whose thoughtful feedback and insights played a crucial role in refining and enhancing the quality of this book.

Finally, we are thankful to our readers for their interest and trust in our work. Your encouragement is deeply valued and continues to inspire us.

To all who have contributed in any way to the completion of this book—your efforts and support are sincerely appreciated.

Preface

Writing efficient and structured code has emerged as an essential skill across different domains such as engineering, scientific computing, data analysis, data science, machine learning, mathematical modeling, and research fields. Among several tools available, MATLAB and Python are noted as the two widely adopted programming languages, each with its own strengths and applications.

This book is created to develop a common understanding of these two languages among readers. It provides a learning guide as well as a practical reference for the students, educators, researchers, data analysts, data scientists, and professionals who wish to gain proficiency in these two languages and to enhance their coding skills as well.

Initiating with the basic concepts, this book covers a wide range of topics, including variables, data types, control structures, functions, data handling, plotting, and advanced topics such as signal and image processing. Each chapter provides the key functionalities in MATLAB and Python with comparative examples. This side-by-side comparison will help readers identify the syntax differences, conceptual similarities, and distinct strengths. Real-world applications and practice exercises are incorporated to reinforce the learning process and to bridge the gap between theory and practice.

Whether you are a beginner who is exploring the programming scope in scientific domains or an experienced professional, this book is designed to enhance your coding and problem-solving skills. By the end of this journey, readers will gain the ability to make suitable choices in tool selection and apply their coding skills in different domains, including data analysis, data science, scientific computing, etc.

Chapter 1: Introduction to MATLAB and Python- This chapter provides a basic introduction to the languages MATLAB and Python. By the end of this chapter, you will have an understanding of the key differences and strengths of MATLAB and Python. Moreover, you will learn how to set up and navigate the respective programming environments. Apart from this, you will gain familiarity with fundamental operations, data structures, and functions in both languages.

Chapter 2: MATLAB and Python Variables and Data Types- A thorough explanation of the variables and data types in MATLAB and Python, is given this chapter, respectively. This chapter covers a number of topics, including how to define variables in MATLAB, how to use arrays and matrices in MATLAB, and how to use strings and structures in MATLAB. Several subjects are introduced in relation to Python, such as declaring variables, data types, and strings, lists, tuples, dictionaries, and sets. Additionally, a comparison of Python and MATLAB is given through a number of examples. You may practice the topics they have learnt by completing the assignment at the end of the chapter.

Chapter 3: Basic Operations in MATLAB and Python Languages- We will examine the basic functions and operations of two potent programming languages—Python and MATLAB—in this chapter. Engineers and scientists like MATLAB because of its well-known prowess in numerical computations, especially in arithmetic and matrix operations. We will examine how well it can execute logical operations, sophisticated matrix manipulations, and fundamental arithmetic operations—all of which are critical for data analysis and algorithm creation. However, Python, which is well-known for its ease of use and adaptability, has a wide range of features, such as list operations, string manipulation, arithmetic operations, and several built-in functions that make it appropriate for data processing and general-purpose programming. By comprehending these fundamental ideas in Python and MATLAB, readers will acquire a deep knowledge of the concept.

Chapter 4: Control Flow and Structures in MATLAB and Python- The fundamental ideas of control flow and structures in MATLAB and Python, two popular programming languages in data analysis, engineering, and scientific computing, will be covered in this chapter. Readers who understand control flow will be able to write more effective programs that can repeat tasks and make judgments under certain circumstances.

This chapter is organized into three primary sections, the first two of which concentrate on the Python and MATLAB languages, respectively, while the third portion deals with popular instances of each. You will study loops and conditional expressions in the MATLAB portion. You may examine related ideas in the Python portion, but with some syntactic variations. Python implements decision-making logic via conditional expressions.

Chapter 5: Functions and Scripts in MATLAB and Python- You will learn how to create and utilize functions and scripts in MATLAB and Python, two robust programming languages that are frequently used in data analysis and scientific computing, in this chapter. You will discover how to use the function keyword in MATLAB to define reusable functions in distinct files, enabling modular and well-structured code. MATLAB scripts, which are collections of commands that are executed one after the other and are perfect for automating repetitive activities, are also covered in this chapter. You will also find anonymous functions made with the @ symbol, which offers a rapid method of defining basic, one-line functions without requiring a separate file. The def keyword will be used to define functions in the Python section, allowing for organized and reusable code blocks. Additionally, you will study lambda functions, which are concise and anonymous.

Chapter 6: Data Handling in MATLAB- In order to assist users in managing data for analysis, calculation, and visualization, this chapter provides a thorough overview of MATLAB's data handling features. Text files, spreadsheets, and binary files are just a few of the many sources of data that may be read and written using the powerful array of tools that MATLAB offers. Additionally, it allows import/export procedures for picture and audio files as well as formats like .csv, .xls, and .mat. Anyone working with experimental measurements, simulation findings, or system inputs and outputs has to understand these procedures. Beginning with basic I/O methods like fopen, fprintf, and fread, this chapter progresses to high-level functions like readtable and writetable that are utilized for tabular data. Additionally, it offers information on best practices, data cleaning methods, and real-world use cases.

Chapter 7: Data Handling in MATLAB and Python- You will study fundamental Python file handling strategies in this chapter, with an emphasis on using built-in functions like open, read, write, and close to carry out file operations. Data persistence and manipulation are made possible by these functions, which make it possible to read from and write to files efficiently. This chapter also explores working with common data types, including CSV and JSON. The CSV module in Python will teach readers how to read from and write to CSV files, which are frequently used to store tabular data. To manage JSON files, a popular format for data transmission, the json module will be presented. You will have the ability to handle files and process data in a variety of formats at the end of this chapter.

Chapter 8: Plotting and Visualization in MATLAB- This chapter aims to give readers the hands-on skills they need to design and modify different kinds of plots in MATLAB for practical uses. You may efficiently visualize data by mastering fundamental 2D charting functions like plot, bar, and scatter. In order to improve plot clarity and presentation, this chapter discusses customization approaches, such as adding titles, labels, and legends, and changing line styles. Additionally, you will learn how to display complex data in three dimensions by utilizing functions like plot3, surf, and mesh in 3D plotting. The chapter concludes by introducing specialized plots like polar plots, heatmaps, and histograms, which expand your capacity to evaluate and present data in a variety of fields, including science, engineering, finance, and data analytics.

Chapter 9: Plotting and Visualization in Python- In this chapter, MATLAB's plotting features are systematically compared with a thorough tutorial on data visualization approaches in Python. Beginning with an overview of Python's visualization ecosystem and its major libraries—Matplotlib for simple plotting, Seaborn for statistical graphics, and Plotly for interactive visualizations—the content is organized to guide users from fundamental ideas to sophisticated applications. After that, this chapter moves on to more fundamental charting methods, showing how to make and modify a variety of chart types, such as line plots, bar charts, scatter plots, and histograms. Advanced modification options to improve plot clarity and visual appeal are covered in detail in a separate section. A significant part of this chapter is the comparison analysis, in which we will compare how Python and MATLAB implement visualization tasks side by side.

Chapter 10: Working with Data in MATLAB and Python- With an emphasis on practical applications, this chapter aims to give readers the fundamental knowledge and abilities they need to handle, analyze, and preprocess data in MATLAB and Python. Readers will discover how to effectively index, slice, and reshape datasets by investigating data manipulation techniques. These abilities are essential for jobs like processing financial records or cleaning sensor data in engineering. Additionally, statistical functions are covered in the chapter, allowing users to calculate metrics like mean, standard deviation, and correlation—all of which are essential in domains like market trend analysis and biological research (e.g., evaluating data from clinical trials).

Chapter 11: Signal and Image Processing in MATLAB and Python- In this chapter, methods for image and signal processing in MATLAB and Python environments are examined. MATLAB and Python are important in domains like computer vision, audio analysis, and telecommunications because they offer powerful tools and frameworks for processing signals and images. A comparative analysis of MATLAB and Python programs with examples, MATLAB-based material with examples, and Python-based content with examples comprise this chapter.

Chapter 12: Case Studies in MATLAB and Python- This chapter aims to present practical, real-world case studies that demonstrate how MATLAB and Python can be applied to solve complex problems across various domains, including engineering, finance, signal processing, and data science. Through interactive, hands-on examples, readers will learn to perform numerical computations, data analysis, and visualization in both programming environments. The chapter is designed to build problem-solving capabilities by walking through industry-relevant scenarios such as signal filtering, image processing, financial forecasting, and statistical evaluation. By engaging with these examples, readers will enhance their ability to convert theoretical knowledge into working code, streamline workflows, and make informed decisions when choosing between MATLAB and Python for specific applications. The chapter also highlights best practices in algorithm design, debugging strategies, and performance assessment, empowering readers with the skills needed to effectively address real-world challenges.

Code Bundle and Coloured Images

Please follow the link to download the
Code Bundle and the *Coloured Images* of the book:

https://rebrand.ly/4a1c95

The code bundle for the book is also hosted on GitHub at
https://github.com/bpbpublications/Practical-MATLAB-and-Python.
In case there's an update to the code, it will be updated on the existing GitHub repository.
We have code bundles from our rich catalogue of books and videos available at
https://github.com/bpbpublications. Check them out!

Errata

We take immense pride in our work at BPB Publications and follow best practices to ensure the accuracy of our content to provide an indulging reading experience to our subscribers. Our readers are our mirrors, and we use their inputs to reflect and improve upon human errors, if any, that may have occurred during the publishing processes involved. To let us maintain the quality and help us reach out to any readers who might be having difficulties due to any unforeseen errors, please write to us at: errata@bpbonline.com

Your support, suggestions and feedback are highly appreciated by the BPB Publications' Family.

At www.bpbonline.com, you can also read a collection of free technical articles, sign up for a range of free newsletters, and receive exclusive discounts and offers on BPB books and eBooks. You can check our social media handles below:

Instagram

Facebook

Linkedin

YouTube

Get in touch with us at: business@bpbonline.com for more details.

Piracy

If you come across any illegal copies of our works in any form on the internet, we would be grateful if you would provide us with the location address or website name. Please contact us at business@bpbonline.com with a link to the material.

If you are interested in becoming an author

If there is a topic that you have expertise in, and you are interested in either writing or contributing to a book, please visit www.bpbonline.com. We have worked with thousands of developers and tech professionals, just like you, to help them share their insights with the global tech community. You can make a general application, apply for a specific hot topic that we are recruiting an author for, or submit your own idea.

Reviews

Please leave a review. Once you have read and used this book, why not leave a review on the site that you purchased it from? Potential readers can then see and use your unbiased opinion to make purchase decisions. We at BPB can understand what you think about our products, and our authors can see your feedback on their book. Thank you!

For more information about BPB, please visit www.bpbonline.com.

Join our Discord space

Join our Discord workspace for latest updates, offers, tech happenings around the world, new releases, and sessions with the authors:

https://discord.bpbonline.com

Table of Contents

CHAPTER 1
Introduction to MATLAB and Python

Introduction

In today's data-driven world, computational tools play a crucial role in scientific research, engineering, and data analysis. Two of the most widely used programming environments for numerical computing and algorithm development are **Matrix Laboratory** (**MATLAB**) and Python. While MATLAB has long been a primary tool in engineering and academia due to its powerful matrix operations and specialized toolboxes, Python has emerged as a versatile, open-source alternative with extensive libraries for scientific computing, machine learning, and automation. This chapter provides a comprehensive introduction to both MATLAB and Python, covering their core features, environments, and basic syntax.

Structure

This chapter contains the following topics:

- 1.1.MATLAB
- 1.2 Python
- 1.3 Comparison between MATLAB and Python

Objectives

By the end of this chapter, you will understand the key differences and strengths of MATLAB and Python and learn how to set up and navigate their respective programming environments.

You will also gain familiarity with fundamental operations, data structures, and functions in both languages and be prepared to apply these tools in mathematical modeling, data analysis, and algorithm development.

Whether you are an engineer, scientist, or programmer, mastering these languages will enhance your ability to solve complex computational problems efficiently.

1.1 MATLAB

Matrix Laboratory (MATLAB) is a high-performance numerical computing environment developed by MathWorks. It provides an interactive platform for algorithm development, data visualization, data analysis, and numerical computation. MATLAB is widely used in academia and industries such as engineering, physics, finance, and bioinformatics due to its powerful toolboxes and ease of use.

Some key features of MATLAB are:

- **Matrix-based computing**: Optimized for vector and matrix operations.

- **Rich library of functions**: Built-in mathematical, statistical, and engineering functions.

- **Toolboxes**: Specialized add-ons for signal processing, control systems, deep learning, and more.

- **Interactive graphics**: High-quality 2D/3D plotting and visualization tools.

- **Integration capabilities**: Supports interfacing with C/C++, Java, Python, and Fortran.

1.1.1 MATLAB environment

When you launch MATLAB, you interact with the following key components:

- **Command Window**: The Command Window in MATLAB is the primary interface where users can execute commands, perform calculations, and interact with the MATLAB environment in real time. It functions like an interactive shell, allowing users to enter expressions and immediately see the output. This is particularly useful for quick computations, debugging, and testing small code snippets without creating a script or function file. The Command Window also displays error messages, warnings, and outputs from scripts or functions. It supports command history, so previous commands can be accessed and reused easily. Overall, the Command Window is an essential component of MATLAB's workflow, enabling rapid experimentation and immediate feedback during numerical computations and programming.

  o It is used to enter commands and execute scripts.

  o Example: Typing 5 + 3 and pressing *Enter* displays ans = 8.

- **Workspace**: The Workspace in MATLAB is a dynamic area that displays all the variables currently in memory during a MATLAB session. It provides a convenient way to view, inspect, and manage variables, including their names, sizes, types, and values. Users can interact with the Workspace through the graphical interface or programmatically using commands like who, whos, and clear. This feature is especially useful for monitoring data during computation, debugging, and understanding how variables change over time. The Workspace complements the Command Window by allowing users to keep track of their data and results visually, making it an integral part of MATLAB's environment for efficient data handling and analysis.

  o It lists all variables currently stored in memory.

  o It shows variable names, values, and data types.

- **Current Folder**: The Current Folder panel in MATLAB displays the contents of the directory (folder) that MATLAB is currently accessing. It allows users to easily navigate the file system, open files, run scripts, and manage data files directly within the MATLAB environment. The Current Folder is important because MATLAB only has direct access to files located in this directory or on its path. Users can change the current folder using the navigation bar or commands like cd. Having quick access to project files, scripts, functions, and data sets makes the Current Folder panel a vital part of the MATLAB workflow, enhancing productivity and file organization.

o It displays files and scripts in the working directory.

o MATLAB executes files from this location.

- **Editor**: The Editor in MATLAB is a built-in text editor designed specifically for writing, editing, and debugging scripts, functions, and other code files. It offers features such as syntax highlighting, automatic indentation, code folding, and error checking, which help streamline the coding process. The Editor also provides tools for setting breakpoints, running sections of code, and stepping through code during debugging. Unlike the Command Window, which is used for executing individual commands interactively, the Editor is ideal for writing longer and more structured programs that can be saved and reused. It supports multiple tabs and integration with version control systems, making it a powerful tool for developing and maintaining complex MATLAB applications.

  o It is used to write, debug, and save MATLAB scripts (`.m` files).

  o It supports syntax highlighting and automatic indentation.

- **Toolboxes**: Toolboxes in MATLAB are specialized collections of functions, classes, and Simulink blocks that extend MATLAB's core capabilities to specific application areas. Each toolbox is designed to support tasks in a particular domain, such as signal processing, image processing, machine learning, control systems, optimization, and more. These toolboxes are developed and maintained by MathWorks and provide professionally developed algorithms, ready-to-use functions, and extensive documentation and examples. Toolboxes make it easier for users to perform complex operations without having to build everything from scratch. Since they are modular, users can install only the toolboxes relevant to their work, making MATLAB a flexible and scalable environment for both academic and industrial applications.

  o Extend MATLAB's functionality (e.g., Image Processing Toolbox, Simulink).

  Different types of toolboxes can be explored at the following link: **https://www.mathworks.com/products.html**

1.1.2 Basic syntax and operations

Variables and data types: In MATLAB, variables are used to store data values, and they are created automatically when a value is assigned using the equal sign (`=`). MATLAB is designed for matrix and numerical computation, so all variables are, by default, stored as matrices or arrays, even if they contain a single number. MATLAB is dynamically typed, meaning that you do not need to declare a variable's type before using it. Common data types in MATLAB include numeric types (`double`, `single`, `int8`, `int16`, etc.), character arrays and strings (`char`, `string`), logicals (`true`, `false`), cell arrays, structures (`struct`), and tables. MATLAB's powerful handling of arrays and data types allows users to perform complex mathematical and data manipulation tasks with simple and concise syntax. Understanding variables and data types is essential for writing efficient and error-free MATLAB programs. MATLAB is dynamically typed (no explicit declaration needed).

Some common data types are as follows:

- **Numeric**: `double`, `int8`, `single`
- **Logical**: `true/false`
- **Character**: `'Hello'`
- **Cell arrays**: `{1, 'text', [3 4]}`

Example 1.1: [Numeric (Default double)]:

```
a = 5.25;          % 'a' is stored as a double by default
class(a)           % Returns: 'double'
```

Example 1.2: [Integer data types (int8, int16, etc.)]

```
b = int8(127);        % Assign an 8-bit signed integer
class(b)              % Returns: 'int8'
```

Example 1.3: [Single precision floating point]:

```
c = single(3.14);    % Converts to single precision
class(c)              % Returns: 'single'
```

Example 1.4: [Logical values (true/false)]:

```
d = true;            % Logical variable
e = (5 > 10);        % Evaluates to false
class(e)             % Returns: 'logical'
```

Example 1.5: [Character array (String using single quotes)]:

```
greeting = 'Hello, MATLAB';   % Character array
class(greeting)               % Returns: 'char'
```

Example 1.6: String data type (introduced in newer MATLAB versions):

```
name = "Quantum";             % String scalar
class(name)                   % Returns: 'string'
```

Example 1.7: Cell array with mixed data types:

```
myCell = {1, 'MATLAB', [2 3 4]};    % Cell array containing number, string, and array
class(myCell)                       % Returns: 'cell'
```

Example 1.8: Accessing elements of a cell array:

```
element = myCell{2};         % Accesses 'MATLAB'
class(element)               % Returns: 'char'
```

Example 1.9: Creating logical array from condition:

```
A = [1, 2, 3, 4, 5];
logicalA = A > 3;            % Returns [0 0 0 1 1]
class(logicalA)              % Returns: 'logical'
```

Example 1.10: Combining types in a structure:

```
student.name = 'Alice';
student.age = int8(22);
student.passed = true;
student.grades = [85, 90, 78];
% Use 'class' function on a field
class(student.age)           % Returns: 'int8'
```

Example 1.11: MATLAB's array structures for row vectors, column vectors, and matrices:

```
a = 10;          % Scalar
b = [1 2 3];     % Row vector
c = [1; 2; 3];   % Column vector
d = rand(3,3);   % 3x3 random matrix
```

Arithmetic operations

In MATLAB, arithmetic operations are fundamental and are performed using standard operators such as addition (+), subtraction (-), multiplication (*), division (/ for right division and \ for left division), element-wise multiplication (.*), element-wise division (./, .\), and exponentiation (^ for matrix power and .^ for element-wise power), which are detailed in the following table. MATLAB is inherently designed for matrix and vector computations, so these operations can be applied to scalars, vectors, matrices, and higher-dimensional arrays. Element-wise operators are particularly important when performing operations on corresponding elements of arrays. MATLAB follows standard operator precedence rules, and parentheses can be used to change the order of evaluation. Mastery of arithmetic operations in MATLAB is essential for performing calculations, implementing algorithms, and developing simulations in engineering, science, and applied mathematics.

Operation	Syntax	Example
Addition	+	5 + 3 → 8
Subtraction	-	7 - 2 → 5
Multiplication	*	4 * 6 → 24
Division	/	10 / 2 → 5
Exponentiation	^	2^3 → 8

Table 1.1: Basic arithmetic operations in MATLAB

Vectorized addition:

```
A = [1, 2, 3];
B = [4, 5, 6];
C = A + B;          % Element-wise addition → [5, 7, 9]
```

Matrix multiplication:

```
M1 = [1 2; 3 4];
M2 = [5; 6];
result = M1 * M2;  % Matrix multiplication → [17; 39]
```

Scalar division:

```
totalMarks = 450;
subjects = 5;
average = totalMarks / subjects;   % → 90
```

Element-wise operations (for arrays):

```
A = [1 2; 3 4];
B = [5 6; 7 8];
C = A .* B;  % Element-wise multiplication → [5 12; 21 32]
```

Functions and scripts

In MATLAB, both scripts and functions are types of program files that contain sequences of MATLAB commands. While they may appear similar at first instance, they serve distinct purposes and differ in terms of how they handle input/output, variable scope, and reusability.

Functions

A function in MATLAB is a more structured and modular type of program file that allows for input arguments and output results. Functions operate in their own local workspace, which means variables inside the function do not interfere with variables in the base workspace unless explicitly passed in or out. This makes functions ideal for performing specific tasks repeatedly or with varying data.

Characteristics of functions:

- It is defined using the function keyword.
- It accepts input arguments and returns output values.
- It has their own isolated variable workspace.
- It supports modular, reusable programming practices.

Syntax:

```
function [output1, output2, ...] = functionName(input1, input2, ...)
    % Function body
end
```

Let us look at the following types of functions:

- **Built-in functions**: MATLAB provides a wide range of built-in functions that simplify mathematical, statistical, and engineering computations. These functions are optimized, pre-defined operations that can be applied directly to scalars, vectors, matrices, and higher-dimensional arrays. Whether you are performing basic arithmetic or complex scientific analysis, built-in functions in MATLAB help streamline your code and enhance performance. Functions like **sin()**, **cos()**, and **sqrt()** are used for mathematical operations, while **mean()** and **max()** are commonly used for data analysis:

  - **sin() – Sine of an angle (in radians):**
    ```
    angle = pi / 6;            % 30 degrees in radians
    sineValue = sin(angle);    % Returns 0.5
    ```

  - **cos() – Cosine of an angle (in radians):**
    ```
    theta = pi / 3;            % 60 degrees in radians
    cosValue = cos(theta);     % Returns 0.5
    ```

  - **sqrt() – Square root calculation:**
    ```
    distance = 25;
    rootValue = sqrt(distance);   % Returns 5
    ```

  - **mean() – Average of an array:**
    ```
    scores = [88, 92, 79, 85, 90];
    averageScore = mean(scores);  % Returns 86.8
    ```

  - **max() – Maximum element in an array:**
    ```
    temperatures = [22.5, 27.8, 25.1, 30.0, 28.4];
    maxTemp = max(temperatures);  % Returns 30.0
    ```

- **User-defined functions:**
  ```
  function y = square(x)
      y = x^2;
  end
  ```

Scripts

A sequence of commands saved in **.m** files. A script is a simple program file that contains a sequence of MATLAB commands. It operates in the base workspace, meaning any variables created or modified in the script are accessible after the script finishes running. Scripts are typically used for performing a series of calculations, visualizations, or simulations where data is already available in the workspace or defined within the script itself.

Characteristics of scripts:

- It does not accept input or return output explicitly.
- It shares the same workspace as the base MATLAB environment.
- It is ideal for quick analysis or when working with existing data.

Key differences between scripts and functions in MATLAB:

Feature	Script	Function
Input arguments	No	Yes
Output arguments	No	Yes
Workspace	Base workspace	Local workspace
Reusability	Limited	High
Best used for	Simple tasks, quick computations	Modular, repeatable tasks

Table 1.2: Main differences between scripts and functions in MATLAB

A function or a script in MATLAB can be used in the following ways:

- Use scripts when working interactively or when prototyping with known data.
- Use functions when you need to encapsulate a task that might be reused, or when you want to pass specific inputs and get well-defined outputs.

Example 1.12: Steps to run a script in MATLAB:

1. **Script name**: `circle_area.m`

   ```
   radius = 5;
   area = pi * radius^2;
   disp(['The area of the circle is: ', num2str(area)]);
   ```

2. **How to run**:

   a. Save the file as circle_area.m in your MATLAB working directory.

   b. In the Command Window, type:

      `circle_area`

3. **Output**:

   `The area of the circle is: 78.54`

1.2 Python

Python is a general-purpose, interpreted, high-level programming language known for its simplicity and readability. It is widely used in:

- Scientific computing (NumPy, SciPy)
- Data analysis (Pandas)
- Machine learning (Scikit-learn, TensorFlow)
- Web development (Django, Flask)

Reasons to use Python:

- Easy-to-read syntax
- Extensive standard library
- Strong community support
- Cross-platform compatibility

1.2.1 Setting up the environment

Before exploring Python programming, it is essential to set up a proper development environment to ensure smooth and efficient coding. A well-configured environment helps manage packages, run scripts, debug code, and visualize data with ease.

Setting up the Python environment typically involves installing Python itself, choosing an appropriate code editor or **integrated development environment (IDE)**, and configuring tools like pip for package management:

1. **Installing Python**: To install Python, visit the official website **python.org** and download the latest stable version compatible with your operating system (Windows, macOS, or Linux). The installation package includes the Python interpreter, the standard library, and an IDE. During installation on Windows, make sure to check the box **"Add Python to PATH"** to enable command-line access. Alternatively, many users prefer installing Anaconda (it is space-heavy and requires several gigabytes of disk space), a popular distribution that bundles Python with essential scientific libraries (like NumPy, pandas, and Matplotlib) and tools such as Jupyter Notebook. This method is especially recommended for data science, machine learning, and academic applications.

   a. Download from **python.org**.

   b. Verify installation:

   ```
   python --version  # Checks installed version
   ```

2. **Choosing an IDE/editor**: Choosing the right IDE or code editor is essential for enhancing productivity, debugging efficiency, and ease of coding in Python. The following are commonly used IDEs and editors, along with their features and recommended use cases:

   - **Integrated development and learning environment (IDLE)**: IDLE is Python's default lightweight IDE that comes bundled with the standard Python installation. It provides a simple interface with a built-in shell, editor, and debugger, making it ideal for beginners to write, test, and run Python code easily.

     Characteristics:

       o   It comes bundled with a standard Python installation.

       o   It is simple and lightweight.

       o   It includes a shell and basic text editor with syntax highlighting.

     When to use: It is ideal for beginners and small scripts. Great for quick testing or learning Python basics.

   - **Jupyter Notebook**: Jupyter Notebook is an open-source, web-based interactive environment that allows users to write and execute Python code alongside rich text elements like equations, visualizations, and markdown. It is widely used in data science, machine learning, and academic research for creating reproducible and well-documented workflows.

     Characteristics:

       o   It is web-based interface for writing live code, visualizations, and narrative text (Markdown).

o It is excellent support for data science workflows and interactive analysis.

o It is popular to share reproducible research and teaching.

When to use: It is best for data analysis, machine learning, academic work, and prototyping.

- **PyCharm**: PyCharm is a powerful, full-featured Python IDE developed by JetBrains, designed for professional software development. It offers intelligent code completion, debugging tools, version control integration, and support for web frameworks and scientific libraries, making it ideal for large-scale and complex Python projects. PyCharm is especially useful for debugging large programs and offers advanced features and solutions that are not mainly found in free, open-source IDEs.

Characteristics:

o It is a full-featured IDE by JetBrains (Community and Professional editions).

o It offers intelligent code completion, debugging tools, version control, and virtual environment integration.

When to use: It is ideal for large-scale projects, software development, and professional Python programming.

- **Visual Studio Code (VS Code)**: It is a lightweight, open-source code editor developed by Microsoft that supports multiple programming languages, including Python. With its rich ecosystem of extensions (like the Python extension), integrated terminal, and debugging tools, VS Code is highly customizable and suitable for both beginners and experienced developers.

Characteristics:

o It is a lightweight yet powerful open-source editor by Microsoft.

o It is extensible with plugins (Python, Jupyter, Git, etc.).

o It is an integrated terminal and supports for debugging.

When to use: It is great for both beginners and advanced users who want a customizable environment for general-purpose programming.

- **Scientific Python Development Environment (Spyder)**: Spyder is an open-source IDE designed specifically for scientific computing and data analysis in Python. It features a MATLAB-like interface with an integrated editor, console, variable explorer, and plotting tools, making it ideal for researchers, engineers, and scientists working on numerical and analytical tasks.

Characteristics:

o It is tailored for scientific computing and data analysis.

o It resembles MATLAB in layout (editor, variable explorer, plot viewer).

o It is often included in the Anaconda distribution.

When to use: It is preferred in academic and research settings involving numerical and scientific computations.

- **Thonny**: Thonny is a beginner-friendly Python IDE designed for teaching and learning programming. It features a simple interface, built-in debugger, and easy-to-understand variable visualization, making it ideal for students and those new to Python.

Characteristics:

o It is a beginner-friendly IDE with a simple UI and step-by-step debugging.

o It is designed specifically for educational purposes.

When to use: It is excellent for students and first-time programmers learning Python.

- **Atom and Sublime Text**: Atom and Sublime Text are lightweight, fast, and highly customizable text editors that support Python programming through community-supported plugins. While Atom is open-source and known for its collaborative features, Sublime Text is valued for its speed and elegant user interface. Both are ideal for quick scripting, editing, and general-purpose development.

Characteristics:

o It is a lightweight text editor with Python support via plugins.

o It is fast and customizable, with basic features for coding.

When to use: It is useful for quick edits, scripting, or when working on minimal setups.

A summary of their features is shown in the following table:

IDE/Editor	Best for
IDLE	Beginners, quick testing
Jupyter	Data science, prototyping, teaching
PyCharm	Large-scale software development
VS Code	Customizable coding across projects
Spyder	Scientific and numerical computing
Thonny	Learning and teaching Python
Atom/Sublime	Lightweight scripting, general-purpose use

Table 1.3: Details of IDE/editor in Python and best usage

3. **Package management with pip**: `pip` is the standard package manager for Python and is used to install, upgrade, and manage external Python libraries that are not part of the standard library. The name pip stands for Pip Installs Packages or Pip Installs Python, and it allows users to easily access a vast ecosystem of third-party tools and libraries hosted on the **Python Package Index (PyPI)**.

Key features of pip:

- It allows the installation of packages from PyPI and other repositories.
- It supports version control (installing specific versions).
- It enables easy uninstallation and upgrading of packages.
- It works seamlessly with virtual environments for isolated project dependencies.

Some basic pip commands are as follows:

1. **Install a package**: `pip install numpy`
2. **Install a specific version**: `pip install pandas==1.5.3`
3. **Upgrade a package**: `pip install --upgrade matplotlib`
4. **Uninstall a package**: `pip uninstall scipy`
5. **List installed packages**: `pip list`

1.2.2 Basic syntax and operations

Python is known for its clean, readable syntax that closely resembles the English language, making it an excellent choice for beginners. Indentation is a key feature in Python, used to define blocks of code instead of curly braces as in many other languages. Basic operations in Python include arithmetic operations like addition (+), subtraction (-), multiplication (*), division (/), and modulus (%). Variables are dynamically typed, meaning you do not need to declare their data type explicitly. Python also supports string manipulation, list operations, and logical expressions with ease. This simplicity and flexibility make Python a powerful tool for a wide range of programming tasks.

Variables and data types

In Python, variables are used to store data that can be referenced and manipulated throughout a program. A variable is essentially a named location in memory that holds a value, and it is created the moment a value is assigned to it using the assignment operator (=). Python is dynamically typed, which means you do not need to declare the type of a variable explicitly—the interpreter automatically infers it based on the assigned value.

Data types in Python define the kind of value a variable can hold, and they are broadly categorized into built-in types such as numeric types (**int**, **float**, **complex**), sequence types (**str**, **list**, **tuple**), mapping types (**dict**), set types (**set**, **frozenset**), Boolean type (**bool**), and others like **NoneType**. Understanding how variables and data types work is fundamental in Python, as they influence how data is stored, accessed, and manipulated within a program.

Python supports dynamic typing:

```
x = 10          # Integer
y = 3.14        # Float
name = "Python" # String
is_true = True  # Boolean
```

Arithmetic operations

Arithmetic operations in Python allow you to perform basic mathematical calculations using operators. Python supports a range of arithmetic operators, such as addition (+), subtraction (-), multiplication (*), division (/), floor division (//), modulus (%), and exponentiation (**). These operators can be used with numeric data types like integers and floats. For example, 5 + 3 will yield 8, while 10 / 4 will return 2.5, and 10 // 4 will return 2 (discarding the decimal part). Python follows standard mathematical precedence rules (also known as PEMDAS) to evaluate expressions. The following operations form the basis of most computations in Python and are widely used in everything from simple scripts to complex data processing and scientific computing:

Operation	Syntax	Example
Addition	+	5 + 3 = 8
Subtraction	-	7 - 2 = 5
Multiplication	*	4 * 6 = 24
Division	/	10 / 3 = 3.333
Exponentiation	**	2**3 = 8

Table 1.4: Arithmetic operations in Python

Lists, tuples, and dictionaries

In Python, lists, tuples, and dictionaries are fundamental data structures used to store collections of data.

A list is an ordered, mutable (changeable) collection of items, defined using square brackets **[]**, and can hold elements of different data types. For example, **my_list = [1, "apple", 3.14]** is a valid list.

A tuple is similar to a list but is immutable, meaning its elements cannot be changed after creation. Tuples are defined using parentheses **()**, such as **my_tuple = (1, "banana", 2.71)**.

Dictionaries, on the other hand, are unordered collections of key-value pairs, defined using curly braces **{}**. Each value in a dictionary is accessed via its corresponding key, for example: **my_dict = {"name": "Alice", "age": 25}**.

Lists and tuples are typically used for storing sequences of data, while dictionaries are ideal for representing relationships or structured data with labels. These structures are essential for data organization and manipulation in Python programming:

```
my_list = [1, 2, 3]         # Mutable
my_tuple = (1, 2, 3)        # Immutable
my_dict = {"a": 1, "b": 2}  # Key-value pairs
```

Functions

In Python, functions are reusable blocks of code that perform a specific task when called. They help in organizing code into modular, manageable pieces, improving readability, and reducing redundancy. Functions are defined using the **def** keyword followed by the function name and parentheses, which may include parameters. For example, **def greet(name)**: defines a function that takes one parameter. The code inside the function is indented and runs only when the function is called. Functions can return values using the return statement or perform actions without returning anything. Python also supports built-in functions (like **len()**, **sum()**, **print()**), as well as user-defined functions. Additionally, advanced features such as default arguments, keyword arguments, variable-length arguments (***args**, ****kwargs**), and **lambda** (anonymous) functions enhance their flexibility. Functions are central to write clean, efficient, and maintainable Python code:

```
def greet(name):
    return f"Hello, {name}!"
print(greet("Alice"))  # Output: Hello, Alice!
```

NumPy for numerical computing

Numerical Python (**NumPy**) is a powerful open-source library in Python that is essential for numerical computing and data analysis. It provides support for large, multi-dimensional arrays and matrices, along with a collection of mathematical functions to operate on them efficiently. Unlike regular Python lists, NumPy arrays (**ndarray**) are more compact, faster, and support vectorized operations, which means operations can be applied on entire arrays without explicit loops. NumPy also includes tools for linear algebra, Fourier transforms, random number generation, and integration with C/C++ code. Due to its performance and versatility, NumPy is a foundational package in the scientific Python ecosystem and is widely used in data science, machine learning, and engineering applications:

```
import numpy as np
A = np.array([1, 2, 3])  # Creates a NumPy array
B = np.array([[1, 2], [3, 4]])
print(B * 2)  # Element-wise multiplication
```

1.3 Comparison between MATLAB and Python

MATLAB and Python are both widely used programming languages in scientific computing, engineering, and data analysis, but they differ significantly in terms of structure, usage, and community support. MATLAB is a proprietary language developed by MathWorks, specifically designed for matrix operations, numerical analysis, and visualization. It offers an IDE with built-in toolboxes tailored for fields such as control systems, signal processing, and computational mechanics. Its syntax is simple for mathematical modeling, making it particularly user-friendly for engineers and domain experts. On the other hand, Python is an open-source, general-purpose programming language that has gained immense popularity due to its readability, versatility, and rich ecosystem of libraries like NumPy, SciPy, Pandas, Matplotlib, and TensorFlow.

Unlike MATLAB, Python is not limited to numerical computing and can be used for web development, automation, machine learning, and more. While MATLAB excels in tool integration and GUI-based applications, Python offers more flexibility, a larger community, and cost-effectiveness since it is free and open-source. Ultimately, the choice between MATLAB and Python depends on specific project needs, cost considerations, and the user's familiarity with programming, as shown in the following table:

Feature	MATLAB	Python
Primary use	Numerical computing, engineering	General-purpose, scientific computing
Syntax	Matrix-oriented, proprietary	Readable, open-source
Cost	Paid (free for students)	Free
Libraries	Toolboxes (e.g., Signal Processing)	NumPy, SciPy, Pandas
Speed	Fast for matrix operations	Slower (unless using optimized libraries)
Community	Strong in engineering	Large open-source community

Table 1.5: Basic comparison between MATLAB and Python

Let us look at some key takeaways:

- MATLAB is optimized for numerical simulations, control systems, and signal processing, making it ideal for engineers and researchers.

- Python is a general-purpose language with strong scientific computing support, widely used in AI, data analysis, and web development.

- Both languages have distinct advantages; MATLAB's simplicity in matrix operations vs. Python's versatility and open-source nature.

Conclusion

This chapter introduced the foundational concepts of MATLAB and Python, two powerful languages for numerical computing and algorithm development. MATLAB excels in matrix-based computations and offers specialized toolboxes for engineering applications, while Python provides a flexible, open-source ecosystem with extensive libraries for data science, machine learning, and automation.

By understanding the basics covered in this chapter, you are now ready to explore more advanced topics and apply these tools to real-world problems. Whether you choose MATLAB, Python, or both, these languages will serve as essential tools in your computational toolkit. In the next chapter, we will explore MATLAB and Python variables and data types.

Exercises

1. Write a MATLAB command to create a row vector of the first five natural numbers.

2. Use MATLAB to generate a 4×4 matrix of random numbers between 0 and 1.

3. Describe the purpose of the MATLAB Command Window, Workspace, and Editor with examples.

4. Write a script in MATLAB to calculate the square root of each element in a vector [4 9 16 25].

5. Use MATLAB to create a 3×3 identity matrix. Explain what this matrix represents.

6. Perform matrix multiplication between two 2×2 matrices in MATLAB and display the result.

7. Explain how the MATLAB environment helps you debug a syntax error.

8. Write a MATLAB command to plot the sine function for values from 0 to 2π.

9. Use the mean() and max() functions to analyze a given vector of data.

10. Describe how MATLAB handles variables and data types during execution.

11. Write a MATLAB program that uses loops and conditional statements to check for even numbers in an array.

12. Demonstrate how to use the MATLAB help command to learn about the rand function.

13. Install Python and write a simple script that prints "Hello, Python World!.

14. Explain the difference between a list and a tuple in Python with examples.

15. Write Python code to calculate the square of numbers from 1 to 10 using a loop.

16. Create a Python dictionary that stores the names and marks of three students, and print the student with the highest marks.

17. Describe the process of setting up Python using an IDE like PyCharm or Jupyter Notebook.

18. Use Python to generate a list of even numbers from 1 to 20 using list comprehension.

19. Write a Python function that takes two numbers as arguments and returns their sum and product.

20. Demonstrate the use of import math in Python and calculate the cosine of 45 degrees.

21. Write a program in Python that checks if a number entered by the user is positive, negative, or zero.

22. How does Python handle indentation? Write a code block that uses if-else logic with proper indentation.

23. Use Python to convert a temperature from Celsius to Fahrenheit.

24. Compare how MATLAB and Python handle array indexing using a small example.

25. Write Python code to read user input, convert it to an integer, and print its square.

Join our Discord space

Join our Discord workspace for latest updates, offers, tech happenings around the world, new releases, and sessions with the authors:

https://discord.bpbonline.com

CHAPTER 2
MATLAB and Python Variables and Data Types

Introduction

The present section provides a detailed discussion about the variables and data types in MATLAB and Python, respectively. Several aspects are discussed in this chapter, such as defining variables in MATLAB, arrays/ matrices in MATLAB, and strings/structures in MATLAB. Regarding Python, various topics are introduced, like defining variables in Python, data types in Python, string/list/tuple/dictionary/set in Python. Moreover, a comparison between MATLAB and Python is also provided via several examples. At the end of the chapter, an exercise is provided for the readers to practice the learned concepts.

Structure

In this chapter, we will learn about the following topics:

- 2.1 MATLAB
- 2.2 Python
- 2.3 Comparison of examples via MATLAB and Python

Objectives

The main objective of this chapter is to create a proper understanding of MATLAB and Python concepts among readers, so that on the basis of this deep understanding, a comparative study between MATLAB and Python problems can be tackled.

2.1 MATLAB

The basics of MATLAB are discussed in this section, along with the solved examples. How to define the variables and deal with matrices, arrays, etc., is also mentioned in this section.

2.1.1 Defining variables in MATLAB

In MATLAB, a variable is a symbolic name used to store data for computation and analysis. One of MATLAB's strengths is its dynamically typed nature, meaning that you do not need to declare a variable's type explicitly before assigning a value to it. This allows for flexible and rapid prototyping, especially in mathematical and engineering applications.

2.1.2 Creating variables

To define a variable in MATLAB, assign it a value using the equals sign (=). For example, refer to the following *Table 2.1* and *Table 2.2*:

```
radius = 5
% Scalar variable
numbers = [10 20 30 40]
% Vector
A = [1 2 3; 4 5 6; 7 8 9]
% Matrix
area = pi * radius^2
% Perform a calculation using variables
```

```
Output
radius =
     5
numbers =
    10    20    30    40
A =
     1     2     3
     4     5     6
     7     8     9
area =
   78.5398
```

Table 2.1: Assigning different variables in MATLAB

```
x = 10
% Assigns integer 10 to the variable x
y = 5.5
% Assigns floating-point number 5.5 to the variable y
z = 'Hello, MATLAB!'
% Assigns string to the variable z
```

```
Output
x =
    10
y =
    5.5000
z =
Hello, MATLAB!
```

Table 2.2: Assigning variables in MATLAB

2.1.3 Displaying variables

You can view the contents of a variable by simply typing its name in the Command Window or by using the disp function, as shown in the following table:

```
x = 10;
% Assigns integer 10 to the variable x
y = 5.5;
% Assigns floating-point number 5.5 to the variable y
z = 'Hello, MATLAB!';
% Assigns string to the variable z
disp(x);      % Displays value of x
disp(y);      % Displays value of y
disp(z);      % Displays value of z
```

```
Output
10
5.5000
Hello, MATLAB!
```

Table 2.3: Displaying variables in MATLAB

The variable naming rules are as follows:

- Variable names must start with a letter, followed by letters, digits, or underscores.
- MATLAB is case-sensitive, so Var and var are different variables.
- Avoid using MATLAB function names (for example, sum, mean) as variable names to prevent conflicts.

2.1.4 Data types in MATLAB

MATLAB provides various data types to handle different types of data effectively. Some primary data types commonly used in MATLAB are as follows:

- **Numeric types**: MATLAB supports multiple numeric data types, including:

  o **Double precision (double)**: Default numeric type in MATLAB. It is the default type for most calculations in MATLAB. Use when high numerical accuracy is needed, such as in scientific computations, simulations, and engineering models.

  o **Single precision (single)**: Uses less memory than double. It uses half the memory of double. Ideal when working with large datasets, or when performance/memory efficiency is more important than precision, e.g., in real-time applications or GPU computations.

  o **Integer types (int8, int16, int32, int64)**: Stores integer values with varying byte sizes. It is used for storing whole numbers with minimal memory. It is often applied in image processing, data acquisition, or embedded systems, where data size and precision are controlled.

| ```
a = 10.5;      % Double precision (default)
b = single(3.7);    % Single precision
c = int16(10);     % 16-bit integer
``` | **Output**<br><br>a =<br>    10.5000<br>b =<br>    3.7000<br>c =<br>    10 |

Table 2.4: Datatypes in MATLAB

- **Logical type**: The logical data type in MATLAB represents Boolean values true and false. Logical data is essential for conditions and control statements:

| ```
x = 5
isPositive = (x > 0)
% Returns 1 if x is greater than 0
isNegative = (x < 0)
% Returns 0 if x is not less than 0
``` | **Output**<br><br>x =<br>    5<br>isPositive =<br>    1<br>isNegative =<br>    0 |

Table 2.5: Logical datatype in MATLAB

2.1.5 Arrays and matrices

Arrays and matrices are central to MATLAB's data structure capabilities, especially for scientific and engineering calculations. Different concepts are discussed such as, 1D array, 2D array, matrix operations, etc.:

- **1D arrays (Vectors)**: A 1D array or vector in MATLAB is a list of values. You can define row or column vectors, as shown in the following table:

rowVector = [1, 2, 3, 4]
% Row vector
columnVector = [1; 2; 3; 4]
% Column vector
	Output
	rowVector =
	   1 2 3 4
	columnVector =
	  1
	  2
	  3
	  4

Table 2.6: Row and column vector in MATLAB

- **2D arrays (Matrices)**: Matrices are 2D arrays and the fundamental data structure in MATLAB. Let us look at how 2D arrays are defined via the following:

A = [1, 2, 3; 4, 5, 6; 7, 8, 9]
% 3x3 matrix
B = [1 2 3; 4 5 6; 7 8 9]
% Another way to define the same matrix
	Output
	A =
	   1 2 3
	   4 5 6
	   7 8 9
	B =
	   1 2 3
	   4 5 6
	   7 8 9

Table 2.7: 2D array in MATLAB

Matrix operations

MATLAB includes various built-in operations for working with matrices, which are as follows:

- **Element-wise operations**: Use the `.*` operator to multiply corresponding elements.
- **Matrix multiplication**: Use `*` for matrix multiplication (following linear algebra rules).
- **Transpose**: Use the apostrophe (`'`) to transpose a matrix:

A = [1, 2, 3; 4, 5, 6; 7, 8, 9];
B = [2, 2, 3; 5, 5, 6; 7, 7, 8];
C = A * B
% Matrix multiplication
D = A .* B
% Element-wise multiplication
A_T = A'
% Transpose of matrix A
	Output
	C =
	  33 33 39
	  75 75 90
	 117 117 141
	D =
	   2 4 9
	  20 25 36
	  49 56 72
	A_T =
	   1 4 7
	   2 5 8
	   3 6 9

Table 2.8: Matrix operations in MATLAB

2.1.6 Strings

Strings are sequences of characters enclosed in single quotes (') or, in newer MATLAB versions, double quotes ("). MATLAB supports both character arrays and string arrays, although string arrays are more flexible for text manipulation. The difference between the two is explained in the following table:

If double quotes ("") are not working in your MATLAB, it is likely due to your MATLAB version being older than **R2016b**, as support for the **string** data type was introduced in MATLAB **R2016b**.

In older versions of MATLAB (before R2016b):

- Strings ("") are not supported.

- You must use character arrays (' ') to represent text.

Feature	Character array ('text')	String array ("text")
Introduced in	Available in all versions	R2016b and later
Quote used	Single quote ' '	Double quote " "
Text manipulation	Limited functionality	More built-in methods
Recommended for new code	Not preferred	Yes, preferred from R2016b+

Table 2.9: Difference between character array and string array

You can define a string or character array as follows:

charArray = 'Hello' % Character array	Output charArray = Hello

Table 2.10: String in MATLAB

String operations

MATLAB provides various functions for manipulating strings, which are as follows:

- **Concatenation**: Use **strcat** to join strings.

- **Search**: Use **strfind** to find substrings within strings.

Comparison: Use **strcmp** or **strcmpi** (case-insensitive).

Replacement: Use strrep to replace parts of a string. Via the **strrep** function, any specific part of string can be replaced.

str1 = 'Hello'; str2 = 'World'; str3 = strcat(str1, str2) % Concatenates strings index = strfind(str3, 'World') % Finds "World" in str3 newStr = strrep(str3, 'World', 'MATLAB') % Replaces "World" with "MATLAB"	Output str1 = Hello str2 = World str3 = HelloWorld index = 6 newStr = HelloMATLAB

Table 2.11: String operations in MATLAB

2.1.7 Cell arrays

Cell arrays are containers that allow you to store data of varying types and sizes. Unlike standard arrays, cell arrays can hold strings, numbers, matrices, and even other cell arrays, making them useful for complex data sets.

To create a cell array, use curly braces {}:

`C = {1, 2, 3; 'text', [4, 5], true}`	**Output**
	
	 C =
	
	         [1] [2] [3]
	   'text' [1x2 double] [1]

Table 2.12: Cell arrays in MATLAB

You can access cell elements using curly braces {} for the content and parentheses () for sub-cells:

`C = {1, 2, 3; 'text', [4, 5], true}`
 `val = C{1,2}`
 `% Accesses the element in row 1, column 2`
 `subCell = C(1,:)`
 `% Accesses all elements in row 1 as a sub-cell array`
	Output
	
	 val =
	     2
	 subCell =
	     [1] [2] [3]

Table 2.13: Accessing cell element in MATLAB

2.1.8 Structures

Structures are another flexible data type in MATLAB. They store data in fields, each of which can contain any type of data, including arrays, strings, or other structures. Structures are particularly useful for organizing related data in a meaningful way.

Creating structures: Define a structure by specifying field names and assigning values:

`student.name = 'John Doe'`
 	
 `student.age = 21`
 	
 `student.scores = [95, 88, 92]`
	Output
	 student =
	     name: 'John Doe'
	 student =
	     name: 'John Doe'
	     age: 21
	 student =
	     name: 'John Doe'
	     age: 21
	     scores: [95 88 92]

Table 2.14: Structure in MATLAB

Accessing and modifying structure fields: Use the dot notation (**.**) to access fields:

```name = student.name```
```% Accesses the 'name' field```
```student.age = 22```
```% Updates the 'age' field```
	Output
	```name =```
	```John Doe```
	```student =```
	``` name: 'John Doe'```
	``` age: 22```
	``` scores: [95 88 92]```

Table 2.15: Accessing and modifying structure fields in MATLAB

Nested structures and arrays of structures: Structures can contain other structures, allowing nested data organization. MATLAB also supports arrays of structures for organizing multiple similar entities:

```class(1).student = 'Alice'```
```class(2).student = 'Bob'```
```class(1).grade = 85```
```class(2).grade = 90```
	Output
	```class =```
	``` student: 'Alice'```
	```class =```
	```1x2 struct array with fields:```
	``` student```
	```class =```
	```1x2 struct array with fields:```
	``` student```
	``` grade```
	```class =```
	```1x2 struct array with fields:```
	``` student```
	``` grade```

Table 2.16: Class in MATLAB

MATLAB offers functions for working with structures, which are as follows:

- **isfield**: Checks if a structure has a specific field.

- **fieldnames**: Lists all field names in a structure.

- **rmfield**: Removes a field from a structure:

```student.name = 'John Doe';```
```student.age = 21;```
```student.scores = [95, 88, 92];```
```fields = fieldnames(student)```
```% Returns {'name', 'age', 'scores'}```
```hasGrade = isfield(student, 'grade')```
```% Checks if 'grade' field exists```
```student = rmfield(student, 'age')```
```% Removes the 'age' field```
	Output
	```fields =```
	``` 'name'```
	``` 'age'```
	``` 'scores'```
	```hasGrade =```
	``` 0```
	```student =```
	``` name: 'John Doe'```
	``` scores: [95 88 92]```

Table 2.17: Working with structure in MATLAB

2.2 Python

Python is a versatile, high-level programming language widely used in fields such as data science, web development, automation, and artificial intelligence. In contrast to MATLAB's matrix-centric design, Python is a general-purpose language with a strong emphasis on readability and simplicity. This section introduces how to define variables and understand the fundamental data types in Python. Gaining proficiency with these types, such as integers, floats, strings, lists, tuples, dictionaries, and sets will significantly enhance your ability to write clean, efficient, and robust Python programs.

2.2.1 Defining variables in Python

In Python, a variable is a reserved memory location used to store values. Python is a dynamically typed language, meaning you do not need to declare a variable's type before assigning it a value.

To define a variable in Python, assign it a value with the equals sign (=):

```python
x = 10
# Assigns the integer 10 to the variable x
y = 5.5
# Assigns the float 5.5 to the variable y
name = 'Alice'
# Assigns a string to the variable name
```

Table 2.18: Defining a variable in Python

Use the **print()** function to display variable values:

	Output

`print(x)`
`# Outputs 10`
`print(y)`
`# Outputs 5.5`
`print(name)`
`# Outputs Alice`
	`10`
	`5.5`
	`Alice`

Table 2.19: Print function in Python

Some variable naming rules are as follows:

- Variable names must start with a letter or an underscore (_).
- Names are case-sensitive, so **Var** and **var** are different.
- Python uses **snake_case** for variable naming, such as **my_variable_name**.

You can check a variable's type using the **type()** function, as shown in the following table:

	Output

`x = 10`
`y = 5.5`
`name = 'Alice'`
`print(type(x))`
`# Outputs <class 'int'>`
`print(type(y))`
`# Outputs <class 'float'>`
`print(type(name))`
`# Outputs <class 'str'>`
	`<class 'int'>`
	`<class 'float'>`
	`<class 'str'>`

Table 2.20: Variable type in Python

2.2.2 Data types in Python

Python has several built-in data types, allowing you to handle numbers, sequences, mappings, and other data structures efficiently. Various data types are mention in this section such as integer and floats. Moreover, arithmetic operations are also mentioned.

2.2.3 Integers

Integers (`int`) represent whole numbers, positive or negative, with no decimal point. Python integers have unlimited precision, meaning they can grow as large as memory allows.

	Output
a = 10 b = -3 print(type(a)) # Outputs <class 'int'>	<class 'int'>

Table 2.21: Data type in Python

Floats represent real numbers and include a decimal point. Floats are essential for precise numerical calculations.

	Output
pi = 3.14159 g = -9.8 print(type(pi)) # Outputs <class 'float'>	<class 'float'>

Table 2.22: Data type in Python

2.2.4 Arithmetic operations

Python supports common arithmetic operations with integers and floats, like the following:

- **Addition**: +

- **Subtraction**: -

- **Multiplication**: *

- **Division**: /

- **Exponentiation**: **

- **Modulus**: % (remainder after division):

	Output
a = 10 b = -3 sum_result = a + b product = a * pi power = 2 ** 3 # 2 to the power of 3 print(sum_result, product, power)	7 31.4159 8

Table 2.23: Arithmetic operations in MATLAB

You can convert between int and float types as needed:

	Output
| ```python
x = 10
# Integer
print(x)
y = float(x)
# Converts x to a float (10.0)
print(y)
z = int(y)
# Converts y back to an integer (10)
print(z)
``` | 10<br><br>10.0<br><br>10 |

Table 2.24: Conversion of datatypes in Python

2.2.5 Strings

Strings represent sequences of characters. They are enclosed in single quotes (') or double quotes ("), with triple quotes (''' or """) used for multi-line strings.

	Output
| ```python
greeting = "Hello, World!"
print(greeting)
quote = 'Python is awesome'
print(quote)
multi_line_text = """This is a
multi-line string"""
print(multi_line_text)
``` | Hello, World!<br><br>Python is awesome<br><br>This is a<br><br>multi-line string |

Table 2.25: String in Python

Python supports a wide array of operations with strings, which are as follows:

- **Concatenation**: Combine strings using +.

- **Repetition**: Repeat strings using *.

- **Indexing and slicing**: Access specific characters or substrings.

  Note: **In slicing [7:12] up to 11 characters will be considered.**

	Output
| ```python
greeting = "Hello, World!"
quote = 'Python is awesome'
hello_world = greeting + " " + quote
print(hello_world)
repeat_text = greeting * 2
print(repeat_text)
first_char = greeting[0]
print(first_char)
# First character ('H')
substring = greeting[7:12]
print(substring)
# Slice ('World')
``` | Hello, World! Python is awesome<br><br>Hello, World!Hello, World!<br><br>H<br><br>World |

Table 2.26: Concatenation, repetition, indexing, and slicing in Python
```

Common string methods

Python provides several built-in methods for efficient string manipulation. The **.upper()** and **.lower()** methods convert text to uppercase and lowercase, respectively, while **.strip()** removes any leading or trailing whitespace; useful for cleaning input data. The **.replace()** method allows substitution of specific substrings within a string, and **.find()** helps locate the position of a substring. These methods are essential for tasks including text cleaning, formatting, and analysis.

Python has the following built-in methods for string manipulation:

- **.upper() and .lower()**: Convert to uppercase or lowercase.

- **.strip()**: Remove whitespace from the beginning and end.

- **.replace()**: Replace occurrences of a substring.

- **.find()**: Find the position of a substring:

```text = " Hello Python "```
 ```print(text)```
 ```text_upper = text.upper()```
 ```print(text_upper)```
 ```text_stripped = text.strip()```
 ```print(text_stripped)```
 ```new_text = text.replace("Hello", "Hi")```
 ```print(new_text)```
 ```index = text.find("Python")```
 ```print(index)```
	Output
	 ```Hello Python```
	 ``` HELLO PYTHON```
	 ```Hello Python```
	 ``` Hi Python```
	 ```7```

Table 2.27: Common string methods in Python

Escape characters

The following escape characters allow special formatting within strings:

- **\n**: New line

- **\t**: Tab

- ****: Backslash

```
path = "C:\\Users\\Username"
# Windows file path
formatted_text = "Hello\nWorld"
# New line in string
```

Table 2.28: escape characters in Python

2.2.6 Lists

Let us look at the definition and characteristics of lists.

In programming, a list is a data structure that stores an ordered collection of items, which can be of various types, such as numbers, strings, or even other lists. Lists are dynamic, meaning they can grow or shrink in size as needed, and they allow for duplicate values. Each item in a list is stored at a specific index, with indexing usually starting from zero.

Some key characteristics of lists are:

- **Ordered**: The elements have a specific order based on the position at which they were added.

- **Mutable**: Lists can be modified after creation by adding, removing, or updating elements.

- **Heterogeneous**: Lists can contain elements of different types (e.g., integers, strings, floats).

- **Indexable**: Items can be accessed and manipulated using their index.

2.2.7 Use cases and importance in data handling

Lists are integral to data handling and manipulation across various domains for several reasons:

- **Data storage and organization**: Lists enable efficient organization of data, such as storing a series of measurements, user inputs, or records in a predictable and accessible format.

- **Iteration and aggregation**: Lists facilitate looping or iterating through elements, which is crucial in tasks like data processing, transformation, and aggregation.

- **Flexible**: Lists can change in size, making them suitable for scenarios where data volume is unknown in advance or varies dynamically (e.g., reading data from user input or a file).

- **Efficient access and modification**: Lists provide efficient access and modification of data using indexing, which is valuable for algorithms that require frequent data retrieval and updates.

- **Data analysis**: Lists are often used in data analysis, especially in programming languages like Python, where they act as the foundational data structure in libraries, such as Pandas and NumPy.

Creating lists

Basic list creation: To create a basic list, you simply enclose your data elements within square brackets **[ ]**, separated by commas. Lists can contain any data type, and elements do not have to be of the same type.

# Example of basic list creation 	
numbers = [1, 2, 3, 4, 5]
mixed_list = [1, "apple", 3.5, True]
	Output
	[1, 2, 3, 4, 5]
	[1, 'apple', 3.5, True]

Table 2.29: List creation in Python

Using range() to generate lists: The **range()** function is a convenient way to generate a sequence of numbers. When combined with the **list()** function, it creates a list of integers from a specified start to end, with an optional step.

# Generating a list of numbers from 0 to 9 	
numbers = list(range(10))
print(numbers)
	Output
	[0, 1, 2, 3, 4, 5, 6, 7, 8, 9]

# Generating a list with a custom start, stop, and step even_numbers = list(range(2, 20, 2)) print(even_numbers)	Output [2, 4, 6, 8, 10, 12, 14, 16, 18]

Table 2.30: Range function in Python

List comprehension basics: List comprehension is a powerful feature in Python that enables you to create lists concisely, as shown in *Tables 2.31* and *2.32*. It is an elegant way to transform and filter elements in a list in a single line of code.

```
# The basic syntax for list comprehension is:
new_list = [expression for item in iterable if condition]
```

Table 2.31: *List comprehension basics in Python*

`# Creating a list of squares using list comprehension`
`squares = [x ** 2 for x in range(10)]`
`print(squares)`
	Output
	
	`[0, 1, 4, 9, 16, 25, 36, 49, 64, 81]`

`# Creating a list of even numbers with list comprehension`
`evens = [x for x in range(10) if x % 2 == 0]`
`print(evens)`
	Output
	
	`[0, 2, 4, 6, 8]`

Table 2.32: *List comprehension basics in Python*

Accessing list elements

Indexing and slicing: In Python, lists are zero-indexed, meaning the first element is accessed using index 0, the second element with index 1, and so on. You can also retrieve a subset of elements (a slice) using a start and stop index.

`# Sample list`
`fruits = ["apple", "banana", "cherry", "date", "elderberry"]`
`# Accessing elements by index`
`print(fruits[0])`
`print(fruits[2])`
	Output
	
	`apple`
	
	`cherry`

`# Sample list`
`fruits = ["apple", "banana", "cherry", "date", "elderberry"]`
`# Slicing the list`
`print(fruits[1:4])`
`print(fruits[:3])`
`print(fruits[2:])`
	Output
	
	`['banana', 'cherry', 'date']`
	
	`['apple', 'banana', 'cherry']`
	
	`['cherry', 'date', 'elderberry']`

Table 2.33: *Access of the list elements in Python*

Negative indexing allows you to access elements starting from the end of the list. For instance, **-1** refers to the last element, **-2** to the second-last, and so on.

`# Accessing elements from the end of the list`
`fruits = ["apple", "banana", "cherry", "date", "elderberry"]`
`print(fruits[-1])`
`print(fruits[-3])`
	Output
	
	`elderberry`
	
	`cherry`

`# Slicing with negative indices`
`print(fruits[-3:])`
`print(fruits[:-2])`
	Output
	
	`['cherry', 'date', 'elderberry']`
	
	`['apple', 'banana', 'cherry']`

Table 2.34: *Access of the list elements in Python*

Lists can contain other lists as elements, which are known as nested lists. To access elements within a nested list, you use multiple indexing levels.

```# Sample nested list nested_list = [["apple", "banana"], ["carrot", "date"], ["eggplant", "fig"]] # Accessing elements in a nested list print(nested_list[0]) print(nested_list[1][0]) print(nested_list[2][1])```	**Output** ['apple', 'banana'] carrot fig
```# Sample nested list nested_list = [["apple", "banana"], ["carrot", "date"], ["eggplant", "fig"]] # Modifying an element in a nested list nested_list[0][1] = "blueberry" print(nested_list)```	**Output** [['apple', 'blueberry'], ['carrot', 'date'], ['eggplant', 'fig']]

Table 2.35: Nested list in Python

Modifying lists

Let us learn how to modify the elements of a list. Under such aspect, different functions are explained such as, **append()**, **insert()**, **extend()**, **remove()**, **pop()**, **clear()**, etc.

- **Adding elements**:

  o **append()**: Adds a single element to the end of the list.

```fruits = ["apple", "banana"] fruits.append("cherry") print(fruits)```	**Output** ['apple', 'banana', 'cherry']

Table 2.36: Appending in list in Python

  o **insert()**: Adds an element at a specified index in the list.

```fruits = ["apple", "banana", "cherry"] fruits.insert(1, "blueberry") print(fruits)```	**Output** ['apple', 'blueberry', 'banana', 'cherry']

Table 2.37: Insertion of element into a list in Python

  o **extend()**: Adds all elements of an iterable (e.g., another list) to the end of the list.

```fruits = ["apple","blueberry", "banana", "cherry"] fruits.extend(["date", "elderberry"]) print(fruits)```	**Output** ['apple', 'blueberry', 'banana', 'cherry', 'date', 'elderberry']

Table 2.38: Extension of element of list in Python

- **Removing elements**:
  - o **remove()**: Removes the first occurrence of a specified element from the list. If the element is not found, it raises an error.

```python fruits = ["apple","blueberry", "banana", "cherry","date", "elderberry"] fruits.remove("banana") print(fruits)```	**Output** ['apple', 'blueberry', 'cherry', 'date', 'elderberry']

Table 2.39: *Removal of list element in Python*

  - o **pop()**: Removes and returns the element at a specified index. If no index is specified, it removes the last element.

```python fruits = ["apple","blueberry", "cherry","date", "elderberry"] fruits.pop(1) # Removes element at index 1 print(fruits)```	**Output** ['apple', 'cherry', 'date', 'elderberry']

``python
last_fruit = fruits.pop()
# Removes and returns the last element 	
print(last_fruit)
print(fruits)```
	Output
	  elderberry
	
	['apple', 'cherry', 'date']

Table 2.40: *Pop function in Python*

  - o **clear()**: Removes all elements from the list, making it an empty list.

```python fruits = ["apple","cherry","date"] fruits.clear() print(fruits)```	**Output** []

Table 2.41: *Clear function in Python*

- **Updating elements at specific positions**: To update an element at a specific index, simply use indexing to access the element and assign it a new value.

``python
# Sample list 	
fruits = ["apple", "banana", "cherry"]
# Updating an element at a specific index 	
fruits[1] = "blueberry"
print(fruits)```
	Output
	['apple', 'blueberry',
	'cherry']

```python # Updating multiple elements by slicing fruits[0:2] = ["avocado", "blackberry"] print(fruits)```	**Output** ['avocado', 'blackberry', 'cherry']

Table 2.42: *Updating list element in Python*

List operations

List operations are of various types such as concatenation and repetition. Membership can also be tested via membership checks in Python:

- **Concatenation and repetition**:

    o **Concatenation (+)**: Combines two lists into a single list.

`list1 = [1, 2, 3]`	**Output**
`list2 = [4, 5, 6]`	`[1, 2, 3, 4, 5, 6]`
`combined = list1 + list2`	
`print(combined)`	

    Table 2.43: List concatenation in Python

    o **Repetition (*)**: Repeats the elements of a list a specified number of times.

`numbers = [0, 1]`	**Output**
`repeated = numbers * 3`	`[0, 1, 0, 1, 0, 1]`
`print(repeated)`	

    Table 2.44: Repetition in Python for list elements

- **Membership check using in and not in**:

    o **in**: Checks if an element is present in the list.

`fruits = ["apple", "banana", "cherry"]`	**Output**
`print("apple" in fruits)`	**True**
`print("date" in fruits)`	**False**

    Table 2.45: Membership check in Python

    o **not in**: Checks if an element is not present in the list.

`fruits = ["apple", "banana", "cherry"]`	**Output**
`print("date" not in fruits)`	**True**

    Table 2.46: Membership check in Python

- **Sorting, reversing, and finding the length of a list**:

    o **sort() and sorted()**: Sorts the elements of a list in ascending order by default. **sort()** modifies the original list, while **sorted()** returns a new sorted list.

`numbers = [3, 1, 4, 1, 5]`	**Output**
`numbers.sort()`	`[1, 1, 3, 4, 5]`
`# Sorts in place`	
`print(numbers)`	

	Output

`# Using sorted() to create a new sorted list`
`original = [3, 1, 4, 1, 5]`
`sorted_numbers = sorted(original)`
`print(original)`
`print(sorted_numbers)`
	[3, 1, 4, 1, 5]
	
	[1, 1, 3, 4, 5]

Table 2.47: Sorting in Python

o **reverse() and reversed()**: Reverses the order of elements in the list.

reverse() modifies the original list, while **reversed()** returns an iterator with the reversed order.

	Output

`numbers = [1, 2, 3, 4]`
`numbers.reverse()`
`# Reverses in place`
`print(numbers)`
	[4, 3, 2, 1]

`# Using reversed() to get a reversed list without modifying the original`
`original = [1, 2, 3, 4]`
`reversed_numbers = list(reversed(original))`
`print(original)`
`print(reversed_numbers)`
	Output
	[1, 2, 3, 4]
	
	[4, 3, 2, 1]

Table 2.48: Reverse and reversed functions in Python

o **len()**: Returns the number of elements in a list.

	Output
`fruits = ["apple", "banana", "cherry"]` `print(len(fruits))`	**3**

Table 2.49: Len function in Python

Let us look at some common list methods and functions:

- **Basic functions**: min(), max()

  o **min()**: Returns the smallest element in the list.

	Output
`numbers = [1, 2, 3, 4]` `print(min(numbers))`	**1**

Table 2.50: Common list methods in Python

  o **max()**: Returns the largest element in the list.

	Output
`numbers = [1, 2, 3, 4]` `print(max(numbers))`	**4**

Table 2.51: Common list methods in Python

- **Counting and indexing:** `count()`, `index()`

  o **count()**: Returns the number of occurrences of a specified element in the list.

numbers = [1, 2, 2, 3, 4, 2] print(numbers.count(2))	Output 3

Table 2.52: Common list methods in Python

  o **index()**: Returns the index of the first occurrence of a specified element. Raises a **ValueError** if the element is not found.

numbers = [1, 2, 2, 3, 4, 2] print(numbers.index(3))	Output 3 (index of the first occurrence of 3)

Table 2.53: Common list methods in Python

Types of lists (2D lists)

In Python, 2D lists (or lists of lists) are commonly used to represent structures like matrices or tables where data is organized in rows and columns.

- **Creating a 2D list**: A 2D list is simply a list where each element is itself a list. Here is an example that creates a 2D list with 3 rows and 3 columns.

# Creating a 3x3 matrix 	
matrix = [[1, 2, 3],
    [4, 5, 6],
    [7, 8, 9]]
print(matrix)
	Output
	[[1, 2, 3], [4, 5, 6], [7, 8, 9]]

Table 2.54: 2D list in Python

- **Accessing elements in a 2D list**: To access elements in a 2D list, you use two indices: the first for the row and the second for the column.

# Accessing elements in the matrix 	
print(matrix[0][0])
print(matrix[1][2])
print(matrix[2][1])
	Output
	1
	6
	8

Table 2.55: Access of element in 2D list in Python

- **Modifying elements in a 2D list**: You can modify elements in a 2D list by directly accessing them with their row and column indices.

# Modifying an element 	
matrix[0][1] = 20
print(matrix)
	Output
	[[1, 20, 3], [4, 5, 6], [7, 8, 9]]

Table 2.56: Modifying element in 2D list in Python

2.2.8 Matrix representation and basic operations

Matrices is a well-known concept which is essential in Python as well. There exist different concepts in this regard, such as how to create an identity matrix, and how to add two matrices in Python:

Creating a 2x2 identity matrix:

`identity_matrix = [[1, 0], [0, 1]]` `print(identity_matrix)`	**Output** `[[1, 0], [0, 1]]`

Table 2.57: Identity matrix in Python

Adding two matrices: You can add two matrices by adding corresponding elements in each row and column.

`matrix_a = [[1, 2], [3, 4]]`
`matrix_b = [[5, 6], [7, 8]]`
`# Initializing an empty matrix to store the result`
`result = [ [0, 0], [0, 0]]`
 	
`# Adding matrices element-wise`
`for i in range(len(matrix_a)):`
`    for j in range(len(matrix_a[0])):`
`        result[i][j] = matrix_a[i][j] + matrix_b[i][j]`
`print(result)`
	Output
	
	`[[6, 8], [10, 12]]`

Table 2.58: Matrix addition in Python

2.2.9 Tuples

A tuple is a built-in data structure in Python that allows you to store a collection of items in a single variable. Like lists, tuples can contain multiple data types, including integers, strings, lists, and even other tuples. However, tuples are often used when the data stored in the collection should not be changed throughout the program.

The definition and characteristics of tuples are:

- **Immutable**: Tuples are immutable, meaning that once a tuple is created, its elements cannot be modified, added, or removed.

- **Ordered**: Elements within a tuple have a defined order, which means that indexing and slicing operations are possible.

- **Heterogeneous elements**: Tuples can store elements of different data types (e.g., integers, strings, other tuples).

- **Fixed size**: Since tuples are immutable, they have a fixed size after their creation.

Syntax: A tuple is created by placing elements inside parentheses **()** and separating them with commas:

`my_tuple = (1, "apple", 3.14)` `print(my_tuple)`	**Output** `(1, 'apple', 3.14)`

Table 2.59: Tuple in Python

Creating tuples

Tuples in Python are easy to create and offer a simple, efficient way to store ordered data. Here is an overview of basic tuple creation, special cases for single-element tuples, and how to unpack tuples for multiple assignments:

- **Basic tuple creation**: To create a tuple, place a series of values separated by commas inside parentheses (). Tuples can contain any data type, including other tuples.

```# Creating a tuple with multiple elements my_tuple = (1, "apple", 3.14, True) print(my_tuple) # Nested tuple nested_tuple = (1, ("a", "b"), 3) print(nested_tuple)```	**Output** (1, 'apple', 3.14, True) (1, ('a', 'b'), 3)

Table 2.60: Tuple creation in Python

- **Single-element tuples and comma usage**: A single-element tuple needs special syntax to distinguish it from a regular value enclosed in parentheses. For a single-element tuple, add a trailing comma after the element.

```# Without the comma, Python interprets this as an integer in parentheses not_a_tuple = (5)```	**Output** 5
```# Adding a comma makes it a tuple single_element_tuple = (5,) print(single_element_tuple)```	**Output** (5,)

Table 2.61: Tuple creation in Python

- **Tuple unpacking and multiple assignments**: Tuple unpacking allows you to assign values from a tuple to multiple variables in a single line. This feature makes it easy to work with tuples that contain related data.

```# Basic tuple unpacking person_info = ("Alice", 30, "Engineer") name, age, profession = person_info # Result print(name) print(age) print(profession)```	**Output** Alice 30 Engineer

Table 2.62: Tuple creation in Python

Tuple unpacking can also be useful for swapping values without using a temporary variable:

```x = 5 y = 10 x, y = y, x # Swaps values of x and y print(x) print(y)```	**Output** 10 5

Table 2.63: Tuple unpacking in Python

Accessing tuple elements

Tuples support indexing and slicing, similar to lists, allowing access to individual elements or subparts of a tuple. They also enable accessing elements within nested tuples:

- **Indexing tuples**: You can access individual elements of a tuple using square brackets **[ ]** with an index value. Indexing in tuples (like in most programming languages) starts at 0, where 0 is the first element, 1 is the second, and so on.

my_tuple = ("apple", "banana", "cherry")
# Access the first element 	
print(my_tuple[0])
	Output
	apple

my_tuple = ("apple", "banana", "cherry")
# Access the last element using a negative index 	
print(my_tuple[-1])
	Output
	cherry

Table 2.64: Access of tuple element in Python

- **Slicing tuples**: You can access a range of elements in a tuple using slicing. The syntax for slicing is **[start:end]**, where start is the index to begin the slice, and end is the index where slicing stops (exclusive).

my_tuple = (1, 2, 3, 4, 5)
# Slice from index 1 to 3 (excludes index 3) 	
print(my_tuple[1:3])
	Output
	(2, 3)

# Slice from the beginning to index 2 (excludes index 2) 	
print(my_tuple[:2])
	Output
	(1, 2)

# Slice from index 2 to the end 	
print(my_tuple[2:])
	Output
	(3, 4, 5)

Table 2.65: Tuple slicing in Python

- **Accessing nested tuples**: When a tuple contains other tuples as elements (nested tuples), you can access elements within these nested structures by chaining indexes.

nested_tuple = (("a", "b", "c"), (1, 2, 3), ("x", "y", "z"))
# It access first element of second tuple 	
print(nested_tuple[1][0])
	Output
	1

nested_tuple = (("a", "b", "c"), (1, 2, 3), ("x", "y", "z"))
# Access the last element of the last tuple 	
print(nested_tuple[2][-1])
	Output
	z

Table 2.66: Nested tuple in Python

Tuple operations

Tuples support various operations, including concatenation, repetition, membership checks, and finding properties like length, maximum, and minimum values. Let us look at them in detail:

- **Concatenation and repetition**: Concatenation allows you to combine two or more tuples into a single tuple using the **+** operator. Since tuples are immutable, this operation produces a new tuple rather than modifying existing ones.

```tuple1 = (1, 2, 3)```
```tuple2 = (4, 5, 6)```
```# Concatenate tuples```
```combined_tuple = tuple1 + tuple2```
```print(combined_tuple)```
	Output
	
	(1, 2, 3, 4, 5, 6)

Table 2.67: Tuple operations in Python

Repetition allows you to repeat the elements of a tuple multiple times by using the ***** operator.

```my_tuple = ("apple", "banana")```
 	
```# Repeat elements in the tuple```
```repeated_tuple = my_tuple * 3```
```print(repeated_tuple)```
	Output
	('apple', 'banana', 'apple', 'banana', 'apple', 'banana')

Table 2.68: Tuple operations in Python

- **Membership check using in and not in**: The in and not in operators allow you to check if an element exists in a tuple.

```fruits = ("apple", "banana", "cherry")```
```# Check if 'apple' is in the tuple```
```print("apple" in fruits)```
	Output
	True

```fruits = ("apple", "banana", "cherry")```
```# Check if 'orange' is not in the tuple```
```print("orange" not in fruits)```
	Output
	True

Table 2.69: Membership check in Python

- **Finding length, maximum, and minimum elements**: You can use built-in functions to find the length, maximum, and minimum values in a tuple (provided the elements are of comparable types):
  - **Length**: The **len()** function returns the number of elements in the tuple.
  - **Maximum/Minimum**: The **max()** and **min()** functions return the largest and smallest elements, respectively.

```numbers = (10, 20, 30, 40, 50)```
```# Find length of the tuple```
```print(len(numbers))```
	Output
	5

```# Find the maximum value``` ```print(max(numbers))```	**Output** **50**
```# Find the minimum value``` ```print(min(numbers))```	**Output** **10**

Table 2.70: Tuple basic operations in Python

Tuple methods and built-in functions

Tuples have limited built-in methods due to their immutability, but they include some useful methods and functions. Here is a quick guide on commonly used tuple methods and relevant built-in functions:

- **Tuple methods count()**: The **count()** method returns the number of times a specified value appears in the tuple.

  Syntax: **tuple.count(value)**

`my_tuple = (1, 2, 2, 3, 4, 2)`	**Output**
`# Count occurrences of 2`	**3**
`print(my_tuple.count(2))`	

  Table 2.71: Tuple built-in function in Python

- **index()**: The **index()** method returns the index of the first occurrence of a specified value. If the value is not found, it raises a **ValueError**.

  Syntax: **tuple.index(value)**

`my_tuple = ("apple", "banana", "cherry")`	**Output**
`# Find index of 'banana'`	**1**
`print(my_tuple.index("banana"))`	

  Table 2.72: Tuple indexing in Python

- **Built-in functions len()**: The **len()** function returns the number of elements in a tuple.

`my_tuple = (10, 20, 30)`	**Output**
`# Length of the tuple`	**3**
`print(len(my_tuple))`	

  Table 2.73: Built-in function len() in Python

- **min()**: The **min()** function returns the smallest element in the tuple (if the elements are comparable).

`numbers = (10, 20, 5, 30)`	**Output**
`# Minimum value`	**5**
`print(min(numbers))`	

  Table 2.74: Tuple smallest element in Python

- **max()**: The **max()** function returns the largest element in the tuple (if the elements are comparable).

`numbers = (10, 20, 5, 30)`	**Output**
`# Maximum value`	**30**
`print(max(numbers))`	

  Table 2.75: Tuple maximum element in Python

- **sum()**: The **sum()** function returns the total of all numeric elements in the tuple.

numbers = (1, 2, 3, 4)
# Sum of all elements 	
print(sum(numbers))
	Output
	10

Table 2.76: Tuple sum() in Python

2.2.10 Dictionaries

A dictionary in programming, particularly in Python, is a data structure that stores data as key-value pairs. It is a built-in data type in Python that allows you to store and retrieve data by associating a unique key with each value. Dictionaries are incredibly versatile and widely used for situations where you need to look up information quickly.

In Python, a dictionary is defined using curly braces **{}** with a series of key-value pairs, where each key is separated from its value by a colon and each pair is separated by a comma. For example:

```
my_dictionary = {
    "name": "Alice",
    "age": 25,
    "city": "New York"
}
```

Table 2.77: Dictionary in Python

The characteristics of dictionaries are:

- **Unordered**: Dictionaries in Python are unordered, meaning that the items do not have a defined order. From Python 3.7+, dictionaries maintain the insertion order, but it is not considered ordered in the traditional sense, like a list.

- **Mutable**: Dictionaries are mutable, which means you can change the contents (add, remove, or update key-value pairs) after they are created.

- **Unique keys**: Each key in a dictionary must be unique. If you try to use the same key more than once, the latest value will overwrite the previous one.

- **Key-value pairs**: Each entry in a dictionary is a pair of a key and its corresponding value. The key acts as a unique identifier, and the value is the associated data.

- **Efficient lookups**: Dictionaries allow for fast retrieval of data through keys, which makes them suitable for situations where you need to perform frequent lookups.

- **Heterogeneous values**: Dictionary values can be of any data type (integers, strings, lists, or even other dictionaries), and there is no restriction on the types that values can hold.

Creating dictionaries

Basic dictionary creation: You can create a dictionary by directly defining key-value pairs within curly braces **{}**.

	Output
```# Creating a dictionary directly my_dictionary = { "name": "Alice", "age": 25, "city": "New York" } print(my_dictionary)```	`{'name': 'Alice', 'age': 25, 'city': 'New York'}`

Table 2.78: Dictionary creation in Python

A dictionary can be updated through the following:

	Output
```# Creating an empty dictionary and then updating elements in it my_dictionary = {} my_dictionary["name"] = "Alice" my_dictionary["age"] = 25 my_dictionary["city"] = "New York" print(my_dictionary)```	`{'name': 'Alice', 'age': 25, 'city': 'New York'}`

Table 2.79: Dictionary updation in Python

Using dictionary comprehension: Dictionary comprehension is a concise way to create dictionaries. It allows you to generate key-value pairs using a single line of code, usually based on some expression or condition.

```
{key_expression: value_expression for item in iterable}
```

Table 2.80: Basic syntax

Syntax:

- Creating a dictionary with squares of numbers as values:

	Output
```squares = {x: x**2 for x in range(1, 6)} print(squares)```	`{1: 1, 2: 4, 3: 9, 4: 16, 5: 25}`

Table 2.81: Dictionary with square of numbers

- **Creating dictionaries from lists:**

  o **Using zip() to combine two lists into a dictionary:** If you have two lists, one with keys and one with corresponding values, you can use the **zip()** function to combine them into a dictionary.

	Output
```keys = ["name", "age", "city"] values = ["Alice", 25, "New York"] my_dictionary = dict(zip(keys, values)) print(my_dictionary)```	`{'name': 'Alice', 'age': 25, 'city': 'New York'}`

Table 2.82: List combing using zip()

o **Converting a list of tuples into a dictionary**: If you have a list of tuples, where each tuple contains a key-value pair, you can use the **dict()** function to create a dictionary.

list_of_tuples = [("name", "Alice"), ("age", 25), ("city", "New York")] my_dictionary = dict(list_of_tuples) print(my_dictionary)	Output {'name': 'Alice', 'age': 25, 'city': 'New York'}

Table 2.83: Conversion of list of tuples in dictionary

Accessing and modifying dictionary elements

Here, we discuss how any element can be accessed from a dictionary and how the dictionary element may be modified. Detailed aspects in this regard is provided ahead:

- **Accessing dictionary elements**:

  o **Using square brackets**: To retrieve a value, simply use the key within square brackets.

my_dictionary = {"name": "Alice", "age": 25, "city": "New York"} print(my_dictionary["name"])	Output Alice Note: If you try to access a key that does not exist, this will raise a KeyError.

Table 2.84: Access of dictionary element in Python

  o **Using the get() method**: The **get()** method is a safer way to access dictionary values as it allows you to specify a default value if the key does not exist.

my_dictionary = {"name": "Alice", "age": 25, "city": "New York"} print(my_dictionary.get("age")) print(my_dictionary.get("country", "Not Found"))	Output 25 Not Found

Table 2.85: get() method in Python

- **Modifying dictionary elements**: Dictionaries are mutable, so you can easily update values, add new key-value pairs, or delete existing ones.

  o **Updating an existing key**: To update the value of an existing key, use square brackets **[ ]** with the key and assign a new value.

my_dictionary["age"] = 26 print(my_dictionary)	Output {'name': 'Alice', 'age': 26, 'city': 'New York'}

Table 2.86: Dictionary update in Python

  o **Adding a new key-value pair**: To add a new key-value pair, use square brackets **[ ]** with the new key and assign the value.

my_dictionary["country"] = "USA" print(my_dictionary)	Output {'name': 'Alice', 'age': 26, 'city': 'New York', 'country': 'USA'}

Table 2.87: Addition of key-value pair in Python

- **Removing elements from a dictionary**: You can remove items from a dictionary using several methods:

  o **Using the pop() method**: The **pop()** method removes the item with the specified key and returns its value. If the key does not exist, you can provide a default value to avoid errors.

my_dictionary1 = {"name": "Alice", "age": 25, "city": "New York"} age = my_dictionary1.pop("age") print(age) print(my_dictionary1)	Output 25 {'name': 'Alice', 'city': 'New York'}

Table 2.88: Dictionary pop() method in Python

  o **Using the popitem() method**: The **popitem()** method removes and returns the last inserted key-value pair. This method is useful when working with recent Python versions (Python 3.7+) that maintain insertion order in dictionaries.

last_item = my_dictionary1.popitem() print(last_item) print(my_dictionary1)	Output ('city', 'New York') {'name': 'Alice'}

Table 2.89: popitem() method in Python

  o **Using the del statement**: The **del** statement deletes the item with the specified key. This will raise a **KeyError** if the key does not exist.

my_dictionary2 = {"name": "Alice", "age": 25, "city": "New York"} del my_dictionary2["city"] print(my_dictionary2)	Output {'name': 'Alice', 'age': 25}

Table 2.90: Dictionary del statement in Python

  o **Using the clear() method**: The **clear()** method removes all items from the dictionary, resulting in an empty dictionary.

my_dictionary2 = {"name": "Alice", "age": 25, "city": "New York"} my_dictionary2.clear() print(my_dictionary2)	Output {}

Table 2.91: Dictionary clear() method in Python

Dictionary methods and functions

There exists several dictionary methods such as **keys()**, **values()**, **items()**, **update()**, **pop()**, **clear()**, **len()**, **sorted()** are discussed in detail as follows.

- **Dictionary methods**:

  o **keys()**: The **keys()** method returns a view object that displays a list of all the keys in the dictionary. This view is dynamic, meaning it reflects changes made to the dictionary.

my_dictionary = {"name": "Alice", "age": 25, "city": "New York"} print(my_dictionary.keys())	**Output** dict_keys(['name', 'age', 'city'])

Table 2.92: Dictionary methods in Python

o **values()**: The **values()** method returns a view object that contains all values in the dictionary. This view is also dynamic.

print(my_dictionary.values())	**Output** dict_values(['Alice', 25, 'New York'])

Table 2.93: Dictionary methods in Python

o **items()**: The **items()** method returns a view object that displays a list of the dictionary's key-value pairs as tuples. This view is useful for looping through both keys and values at the same time.

print(my_dictionary.items())	**Output** dict_items([('name', 'Alice'), ('age', 25), ('city', 'New York')])

Table 2.94: Dictionary methods in Python

o **update()**: The **update()** method updates the dictionary with key-value pairs from another dictionary or from an iterable of key-value pairs. If the key already exists, **update()** overwrites its value; if not, it adds the key-value pair to the dictionary.

my_dictionary.update({"age": 26, "country": "USA"}) print(my_dictionary)	**Output** {'name': 'Alice', 'age': 26, 'city': 'New York', 'country': 'USA'}

Table 2.95: Dictionary methods in Python

o **pop()**: The **pop()** method removes a specified key from the dictionary and returns its value. You can specify a default value to avoid **KeyError** if the key does not exist.

age = my_dictionary.pop("age", "Not Found") print(age) print(my_dictionary)	**Output** 26 {'name': 'Alice', 'city': 'New York', 'country': 'USA'}

Table 2.96: Dictionary methods in Python

o **clear()**: The **clear()** method removes all items from the dictionary, making it an empty dictionary.

my_dictionary.clear() print(my_dictionary)	**Output** {}

Table 2.97: Dictionary methods in Python

- **Built-in functions for dictionaries**:

  o **len()**: The **len()** function returns the number of items (key-value pairs) in the dictionary.

my_dictionary = {"name": "Alice", "age": 25, "city": "New York"} print(len(my_dictionary))	**Output** **3**

Table 2.98: Dictionary built-in function in Python

o **sorted()**: The **sorted()** function returns a sorted list of the dictionary's keys. You can also specify whether to sort in ascending (default) or descending order.

print(sorted(my_dictionary)) print(sorted(my_dictionary, reverse=True))	**Output** **['age', 'city', 'name']** **['name', 'city', 'age']**

Table 2.99: Dictionary built-in function in Python

Working with nested dictionaries

Working with nested dictionaries involves creating dictionaries within dictionaries. This structure is useful for representing hierarchical or structured data. Here is how you can create, access, update, and delete values within nested dictionaries:

* **Creating nested dictionaries**: A nested dictionary is simply a dictionary where some values are themselves dictionaries.

students = {
    "student1": {
        "name": "Alice",
        "age": 25,
        "courses": ["Math", "Science"]
    },
    "student2": {
        "name": "Bob",
        "age": 22,
        "courses": ["History", "English"]
    }
}
	Output
	
	{'student1': {'name': 'Alice', 'age': 25, 'courses': ['Math', 'Science']}, 'student2': {'name': 'Bob', 'age': 22, 'courses': ['History', 'English']}}

Table 2.100: Nested dictionary in Python

* **Accessing elements in nested dictionaries**: To access elements in a nested dictionary, chain the keys together using square brackets.

# Access the name of student1 	
print(students["student1"]["name"])
 	
# Access the list of courses for 	
student2
print(students["student2"]["courses"])
	Output
	
	Alice
	
	['History', 'English']

Table 2.101: Nested dictionary in Python

- **Accessing specific elements within inner data structures**: You can go further to access items within nested lists (or other structures) inside the nested dictionary.

# Access the first course of student1 print(students["student1"]["courses"][0])	Output Math

Table 2.102: Nested dictionary in Python

- **Updating values in nested dictionaries**: You can update values in a nested dictionary by specifying the full path of keys.

# Update student1's age students["student1"]["age"] = 26 print(students["student1"]["age"])	Output 26

Table 2.103: Nested dictionary in Python

- **Adding a new key-value pair in the inner dictionary:**

# Add a new field "grade" for student1 students["student1"]["grade"] = "A" print(students["student1"])	Output {'name': 'Alice', 'age': 26, 'courses': ['Math', 'Science'], 'grade': 'A'}

Table 2.104: Nested dictionary in Python

- **Deleting elements in nested dictionaries**: You can delete elements from nested dictionaries by specifying the full path to the key you want to remove.

- **Deleting a key-value pair**: To remove a specific key-value pair in an inner dictionary, use the del statement.

# Delete the "age" key for student2 del students["student2"]["age"] print(students["student2"])	Output {'name': 'Bob', 'courses': ['History', 'English']}

Table 2.105: Nested dictionary in Python

- **Deleting an entire inner dictionary**: You can also delete an entire nested dictionary by specifying its top-level key.

# Delete the entire record for student1 del students["student1"] print(students)	Output {'student2': {'name': 'Bob', 'courses': ['History', 'English']}}

Table 2.106: Nested dictionary in Python

- **Using get() to access nested keys safely**: When accessing nested dictionaries, using **get()** can prevent errors if a key does not exist.

`# Safely access a key that might not exist`
 	
`print(students.get("student1", {}).`
`get("grade", "Not Found"))`
	Output
	Not Found
	
	(if student1 is deleted)

Table 2.107: Nested dictionary in Python

2.2.11 Sets

A set is a built-in data structure in Python that represents an unordered collection of unique elements. Sets are useful when you want to store items without duplicates and perform mathematical set operations like union, intersection, and difference.

The definition of a set is that a set is defined by enclosing elements in curly braces **{}** or by using the **set()** function, particularly when creating an empty set, as **{}** by itself creates an empty dictionary.

`# Defining a set with elements`
`my_set = {1, 2, 3, 4}`
`print(my_set)`
`# Creating an empty set`
`empty_set = set()`
	Output
	
	`{1, 2, 3, 4}`

Table 2.108: Set in Python

The characteristics of sets are:

- **Unordered**: Sets do not maintain order, so elements may appear in a different order each time you access the set. This also means you cannot access elements using an index like you would in lists.

- **Unique elements**: Sets automatically remove duplicate values, ensuring each element is unique. If you add a duplicate, it will be ignored.

- **Mutable (but with immutable elements)**: You can add or remove items from a set, but each element within a set must be immutable (like numbers, strings, and tuples). Lists and dictionaries, for instance, cannot be set elements.

- **Unindexed**: Since sets are unordered, they do not support indexing, slicing, or other sequence-like behavior.

- **Highly optimized for membership testing**: Sets are efficient for checking if an element exists or not, making them ideal for scenarios where membership checking is needed frequently.

Creating sets

As per the following description, it is mentioned how set can be created in Python along with different set operations:

- **Basic set creation**: You can create a set by simply enclosing elements in curly braces **{}**, separated by commas. Each element in a set must be unique, so any duplicates will be automatically removed:

| ```
# Creating a set with unique elements
my_set = {1, 2, 3, 4, 5}
print(my_set)
# Set with duplicate values
my_set = {1, 2, 2, 3, 4, 4}
print(my_set)
``` | **Output**<br>{1, 2, 3, 4, 5}<br>{1, 2, 3, 4} |
|---|---|

Table 2.109: Set creation in Python

Note: To define an empty set, you cannot use {}, as this would create an empty dictionary instead. Instead, use the set() function.

- **Using set() function for set creation**: The **set()** function can be used to create a set, especially if you are starting with no elements or if you want to create a set from an iterable like a list, tuple, or string:

| ```
# Creating an empty set
empty_set = set()
print(empty_set)
# Creating a set using set() with an
iterable
my_set = set([1, 2, 3, 4])
print(my_set)
``` | **Output**<br>set()<br>{1, 2, 3, 4} |
|---|---|

Table 2.110: Set creation in Python

- **Creating sets from lists and strings**: You can use the **set()** function to create a set from other data types, such as lists and strings. This is useful if you want to eliminate duplicates in a list or extract unique characters from a string.

- **Creating a set from a list**: When you convert a list to a set, duplicates are automatically removed, leaving only unique elements:

| ```
# Creating a set from a list with
duplicate elements
my_list = [1, 2, 2, 3, 4, 4, 5]
my_set = set(my_list)
print(my_set)
``` | **Output**<br>{1, 2, 3, 4, 5} |
|---|---|

Table 2.111: Set creation from list in Python

- **Creating a set from a string**: When creating a set from a string, each character in the string becomes an element in the set, with duplicates removed.

| ```
# Creating a set from a string
my_string = "hello"
my_set = set(my_string)
print(my_set)
``` | Output<br>{'h', 'o', 'l', 'e'}<br>**# duplicates of 'l' are removed** |
|---|---|

Table 2.112: Set creation from string in Python

Accessing and modifying set elements

Following is the detail regarding how to access and modify the elements in a set. A full description is provided as follows:

- **Adding elements to a set**:
  - **Using add()**: The **add()** method allows you to add a single element to the set. If the element already exists in the set, it will not add it again, as sets only store unique values.

my_set = {1, 2, 3} my_set.add(4) print(my_set)	Output {1, 2, 3, 4}

# Attempting to add a duplicate element 	
my_set.add(3)
print(my_set)
	Output
	{1, 2, 3, 4}
	# 3 is not added again

Table 2.113: Addition of set element in Python

  - **Using update()**: The **update()** method allows you to add multiple elements to a set at once. You can pass any iterable (like a list, tuple, or another set) to **update()**, and it will add all unique elements from that iterable to the set.

my_set = {1, 2, 3}
my_set.update([4, 5, 6]) # Adding multiple elements
print(my_set)
	Output
	{1, 2, 3, 4, 5, 6}

# Adding elements from another set 	
my_set.update({7, 8})
print(my_set)
	Output
	{1, 2, 3, 4, 5, 6, 7, 8}

Table 2.114: Updation of set element in Python

- **Removing elements from a set**:
  - **Using remove()**: The **remove()** method removes a specified element from the set. If the element does not exist in the set, it raises a **KeyError**. This method is best used when you are sure the element is in the set.

my_set = {1, 2, 3, 4} my_set.remove(3) print(my_set)	Output {1, 2, 4}

# Attempting to remove an element that is not in the set 	
my_set.remove(5)
	Output
	KeyError: 5

Table 2.115: Removing of set element in Python

  - **Using discard()**: The **discard()** method also removes a specified element from the set, but unlike **remove()**, it does not raise an error if the element is not found. This makes it a safer option when you are not sure if the element is in the set.

my_set = {1, 2, 3, 4} my_set.discard(3) print(my_set)	Output {1, 2, 4}

# Attempting to discard an element that is not in the set 	
my_set.discard(5) # No error is raised
print(my_set)
	Output
	{1, 2, 4}

Table 2.116: Removing a specified element from the set in Python

o **Using pop():** The **pop()** method removes and returns an arbitrary element from the set. Since sets are unordered, you do not know which element will be removed. If the set is empty, **pop()** raises a **KeyError**.

my_set = {1, 2, 3, 4} removed_element = my_set.pop() print(removed_element) print(my_set)	Output 1 {2, 3, 4}
# Attempting to pop from an empty set # empty_set = set() # empty_set.pop()	Output KeyError: 'pop from an empty set'

Table 2.117: Set pop() method in Python

o **Using clear():** The **clear()** method removes all elements from the set, leaving it empty.

my_set = {1, 2, 3, 4} my_set.clear() print(my_set)	Output set()

Table 2.118: Set clear() method in Python

Set operations

Sets in Python support various operations that are based on mathematical set theory, making them ideal for tasks that involve grouping, overlapping, and finding distinct items. Here is a look at key set operations:

- **Union:** The union of two sets combines all unique elements from both sets. This can be achieved using the **|** operator or the **union()** method.

set1 = {1, 2, 3}
set2 = {3, 4, 5}
# Using | operator 	
union_set = set1 | set2
print(union_set)
	Output
	{1, 2, 3, 4, 5}

# Using union() method 	
union_set = set1.union(set2)
print(union_set)
	Output
	{1, 2, 3, 4, 5}

Table 2.119: Set operations in Python

- **Intersection**: The intersection of two sets returns only the elements that are common to both sets. This can be done using the **&** operator or the **intersection()** method.

| ```python
set1 = {1, 2, 3}
set2 = {3, 4, 5}
# Using & operator
intersection_set = set1 & set2
print(intersection_set)
``` | **Output** <br> {3} |
| ```python
# Using intersection() method
intersection_set = set1.intersection(set2)
print(intersection_set)
``` | **Output** <br> {3} |

Table 2.120: Set operations in Python

- **Difference**: The difference of two sets returns elements that are in the first set but not in the second. This can be achieved using — operator or the **difference()** method.

| ```python
set1 = {1, 2, 3}
set2 = {3, 4, 5}
# Using - operator
difference_set = set1 - set2
print(difference_set)
``` | **Output** <br> {1, 2} |
| ```python
# Using difference() method
difference_set = set1.difference(set2)
print(difference_set)
``` | **Output** <br> {1, 2} |

Table 2.121: Set operations in Python

- **Symmetric difference**: The symmetric difference of two sets returns elements that are in either of the sets but not in both. This can be done using the **^** operator or the **symmetric_difference()** method.

| ```python
set1 = {1, 2, 3}
set2 = {3, 4, 5}
# Using ^ operator
symmetric_difference_set = set1 ^ set2
print(symmetric_difference_set)
``` | **Output** <br> {1, 2, 4, 5} |
| ```python
# Using symmetric_difference() method
symmetric_difference_set = set1.symmetric_
difference(set2)
print(symmetric_difference_set)
``` | **Output** <br> {1, 2, 4, 5} |

Table 2.122: Set operations in Python

Additionally, Python provides convenient operators for membership testing:

- **Membership testing**: Sets are highly optimized for membership testing, which allows you to quickly check if an element exists within the set.

- **Using in**: The in keyword checks if an element is present in the set.

set1 = {1, 2, 3} print(2 in set1) print(4 in set1)	Output True False

Table 2.123: Set operations in Python

- **Using not in**: The not in keyword checks if an element is not present in the set.

set1 = {1, 2, 3} print(4 not in set1) print(2 not in set1)	Output True False

Table 2.124: Set operations in Python

Set methods

There exist different set methods in Python which are provided in detail as follows:

- **union()**:
  - o **Description**: Combines all unique elements from two or more sets.
  - o **Syntax**: `set1.union(set2, set3, ...)`

set_a = {1, 2, 3} set_b = {3, 4, 5} union_set = set_a.union(set_b) print(union_set)	Output {1, 2, 3, 4, 5}

Table 2.125: Set methods in Python

- **intersection()**:
  - o **Description**: Returns a set containing elements that are common in all sets.
  - o **Syntax**: `set1.intersection(set2, set3, ...)`

set_a = {1, 2, 3} set_b = {3, 4, 5} intersection_set = set_a. intersection(set_b) print(intersection_set)	Output {3}

Table 2.126: Set methods in Python

- **difference()**:
  - o **Description**: Returns a set containing elements that are in the first set but not in the other(s).
  - o **Syntax**: `set1.difference(set2, set3, ...)`

set_a = {1, 2, 3} set_b = {3, 4, 5} difference_set = set_a.difference(set_b) print(difference_set)	Output {1, 2}

Table 2.127: Set methods in Python

- **symmetric_difference()**:

    o **Description**: Returns a set containing elements that are in either of the sets but not in both (i.e., elements unique to each set).

    o **Syntax**: `set1.symmetric_difference(set2)`

`set_a = {1, 2, 3}`
`set_b = {3, 4, 5}`
`symmetric_difference_set = set_a.`
`symmetric_difference(set_b)`
`print(symmetric_difference_set)`
	Output
	`{1, 2, 4, 5}`

Table 2.128: Set methods in Python

- **issubset()**:

    o **Description**: Checks if all elements of the first set are present in the second set.

    o **Syntax**: `set1.issubset(set2)`

`set_a = {1, 2}`
`set_b = {1, 2, 3, 4}`
`is_subset = set_a.issubset(set_b)`
`print(is_subset)`
	Output
	True

Table 2.129: Set methods in Python

- **issuperset()**:

    o **Description**: Checks if all elements of the second set are present in the first set.

    o **Syntax**: `set1.issuperset(set2)`

`set_a = {1, 2, 3, 4}`
`set_b = {1, 2}`
`is_superset = set_a.issuperset(set_b)`
`print(is_superset)`
	Output
	True

Table 2.130: Set methods in Python

- **isdisjoint()**:

    o **Description**: Checks if two sets have no elements in common.

    o **Syntax**: `set1.isdisjoint(set2)`

`set_a = {1, 2}`
`set_b = {3, 4}`
`is_disjoint = set_a.isdisjoint(set_b)`
`print(is_disjoint)`
	Output
	True

Table 2.131: Set methods in Python

As per *Table 2.132,* a comparison of concepts is provided between MATLAB and Python:

Feature	List	Tuple	Dictionary	Set
Definition	Ordered, mutable collection	Ordered, immutable collection	Unordered collection of key-value pairs	Unordered collection of unique elements
Syntax	`list_name = [element1, element2]`	`tuple_name = (element1, element2)`	`dict_name = {key1: value1, key2: value2}`	`set_name = {element1, element2}`
Mutability	Mutable (can be modified)	Immutable (cannot be modified)	Mutable (keys cannot be modified, but values can)	Mutable (elements can be added or removed)
Order	Ordered	Ordered	Unordered	Unordered
Indexing	Supports indexing and slicing	Supports indexing and slicing	No indexing (access by key)	No indexing
Duplicates	Allows duplicates	Allows duplicates	Keys must be unique (values can be duplicates)	Does not allow duplicates
Use cases	Storing an ordered collection of elements	Storing fixed, unchangeable data	Storing key-value pairs for quick lookup	Storing unique values, membership testing
Performance	Slower for lookups compared to dictionaries and sets	Faster than lists due to immutability	Fast lookup based on keys	Faster for membership testing
Adding elements	`append()`, `insert()`, `extend()`	Not applicable (immutable)	`dict[key] = value`, `update()`	`add()`, `update()`
Removing elements	`remove()`, `pop()`, `clear()`	Not applicable (immutable)	`pop(key)`, `popitem()`, `clear()`	`remove()`, `discard()`, `clear()`
Definition	Ordered, mutable collection	Ordered, immutable collection	Unordered collection of key-value pairs	Unordered collection of unique elements
Syntax	`list_name = [element1, element2]`	`tuple_name = (element1, element2)`	`dict_name = {key1: value1, key2: value2}`	`set_name = {element1, element2}`
Mutability	Mutable (can be modified)	Immutable (cannot be modified)	Mutable (keys cannot be modified, but values can)	Mutable (elements can be added or removed)
Order	Ordered	Ordered	Unordered	Unordered

Feature	List	Tuple	Dictionary	Set
Indexing	Supports indexing and slicing	Supports indexing and slicing	No indexing (access by key)	No indexing
Duplicates	Allows duplicates	Allows duplicates	Keys must be unique (values can be duplicates)	Does not allow duplicates
Use cases	Storing an ordered collection of elements	Storing fixed, unchangeable data	Storing key-value pairs for quick lookup	Storing unique values, membership testing
Performance	Slower for lookups compared to dictionaries and sets	Faster than lists due to immutability	Fast lookup based on keys	Faster for membership testing
Adding elements	`append()`, `insert()`, `extend()`	Not applicable (immutable)	`dict[key] = value`, `update()`	`add()`, `update()`
Removing elements	`remove()`, `pop()`, `clear()`	Not applicable (immutable)	`pop(key)`, `popitem()`, `clear()`	`remove()`, `discard()`, `clear()`
Concatenation	`+ operator`	`+ operator`	Not directly, but can be merged with `update()`	`union()` method
Common methods	`append()`, `extend()`, `insert()`, `remove()`, `pop()`, `sort()`, `reverse()`	`count()`, `index()`	`keys()`, `values()`, `items()`, `get()`, `update()`	`add()`, `remove()`, `union()`, `intersection()`, `difference()`
Comprehension support	List comprehension supported	Tuple comprehension not supported	Dictionary comprehension supported	Set comprehension supported
Hashable	Unhashable (lists cannot be dictionary keys or set elements)	Hashable if containing immutable elements	Only keys are hashable	Only frozenset is hashable
Memory efficiency	Uses more memory than tuples	Uses less memory than lists	Memory efficiency depends on number of entries	More memory efficient for unique collections
Typical applications	Managing ordered, changeable collections of items	Storing data that should not change	Data structures for mappings and fast lookups	Filtering unique items, fast membership tests

Feature	List	Tuple	Dictionary	Set
Iteration	Can iterate using for loop	Can iterate using for loop	Can iterate over keys, values, or key-value pairs	Can iterate using for loop
Example	`my_list = [1, 2, 3, 4]`	`my_tuple = (1, 2, 3, 4)`	`my_dict = {"a": 1, "b": 2}`	`my_set = {1, 2, 3, 4}`

Table 2.132: Table of comparison between MATLAB and Python

2.3 Comparison of examples via MATLAB and Python

Let us look at the following examples for comparison:

- **Example 2.1:** Create a matrix and calculate the transpose, element-wise multiplication, and matrix multiplication:

MATLAB code	Python code

``
A = [1, 2; 3, 4];
B = [5, 6; 7, 8];
% Transpose
A_transpose = A';
% Element-wise multiplication
C_elementwise = A .* B;
% Matrix multiplication
C_matrix = A * B;
disp('Transpose:'), disp(A_transpose)
disp('Element-wise multiplication:'), disp(C_elementwise)
disp('Matrix multiplication:'), disp(C_matrix)
``
	``
	import numpy as np
	A = np.array([[1, 2], [3, 4]])
	B = np.array([[5, 6], [7, 8]])
	# Transpose
	A_transpose = A.T
	# Element-wise multiplication
	C_elementwise = A * B
	# Matrix multiplication
	C_matrix = A @ B
	print("Transpose:\n", A_transpose)
	print("Element-wise multiplication:\n", C_elementwise)
	print("Matrix multiplication:\n", C_matrix)
	``

Output ``` Transpose: 1 3 2 4 Element-wise multiplication: 5 12 21 32 Matrix multiplication: 19 22 43 50 ```	**Output** ``` Transpose: [[1 3] [2 4]] Element-wise multiplication: [[5 12] [21 32]] Matrix multiplication: [[19 22] [43 50]] ```

Table 2.133: Example 2.1 code in MATLAB and Python

- **Example 2.2:** Concatenate two strings, convert to uppercase, and find the position of a substring:

MATLAB code	Python code

``matlab
str1 = 'Hello';
str2 = 'World';
% Concatenate strings
combined_str = [str1, ' ', str2];
% Convert to uppercase
upper_str = upper(combined_str);
% Find position of substring
pos = strfind(combined_str, 'World');
disp('Concatenated string:'),
disp(combined_str)
disp('Uppercase string:'), disp(upper_str)
disp('Position of "World":'), disp(pos)
``
	``python
	str1 = 'Hello'
	str2 = 'World'
	# Concatenate strings
	combined_str = str1 + ' ' + str2
	# Convert to uppercase
	upper_str = combined_str.upper()
	# Find position of substring
	pos = combined_str.find('World')
	print("Concatenated string:", combined_str)
	print("Uppercase string:", upper_str)
	print('Position of "World":', pos)
	``

Output
`Concatenated string:`
`Hello World`
`Uppercase string:`
`HELLO WORLD`
`Position of "World":`
`    7`
	Output
	`Concatenated string: Hello World`
	`Uppercase string: HELLO WORLD`
	`Position of "World": 6`

Table 2.134: Example 2.2 code in MATLAB and Python

- **Example 2.3:** Define variables of different types and display them:

MATLAB code	Python code

``matlab
% Defining variables
intVar = 10;   % Integer
floatVar = 3.14;   % Float (double by default in MATLAB)
strVar = 'Hello';   % String (character array)
% Displaying variables
disp(intVar)
disp(floatVar)
disp(strVar)
``
	``python
	# Defining variables
	int_var = 10 # Integer
	float_var = 3.14 # Float
	str_var = "Hello" # String
	# Displaying variables
	print(int_var)
	print(float_var)
	print(str_var)
	``

Output
`10`
`3.1400`
`Hello`
	Output
	`10`
	`3.14`
	`Hello`

Table 2.135: Example 2.3 code in MATLAB and Python

- **Example 2.4:** Demonstrate different data types (integers, floats, and strings) and check their types:

MATLAB code	Python code
```% Data types in MATLAB```	```# Data types in Python```
```intVar = 5; % Integer```	```int_var = 5 # Integer```
```floatVar = 2.718; % Floating-point```	```float_var = 2.718 # Float```
```charVar = 'MATLAB'; % String```	```str_var = "Python" # String```
```(character array)```	```# Checking types```
```% Checking types```	```print(type(int_var))```
```disp(class(intVar))```	```print(type(float_var))```
```disp(class(floatVar))```	```print(type(str_var))```
```disp(class(charVar))```	
Output	**Output**
```double```	```<class 'int'>```
```double```	```<class 'float'>```
```char```	```<class 'str'>```

Table 2.136: Example 2.4 code in MATLAB and Python

- **Example 2.5:** Create an array/list, perform indexing, and modify an element:

MATLAB code	Python code
```% Define an array```	```# Define a list```
```array = [1, 2, 3, 4, 5];```	```array = [1, 2, 3, 4, 5]```
```% Indexing and modifying an element```	```# Indexing and modifying an element```
```second_element = array(2); % Access second element```	```second_element = array[1] # Access second element```
```array(3) = 10; % Modify third element```	```array[2] = 10 # Modify third element```
```disp(array)```	```print(array)```
Output	**Output**
```1 2 10 4 5```	```[1, 2, 10, 4, 5]```

Table 2.137: Example 2.5 code in MATLAB and Python

- **Example 2.6:** Concatenate strings, convert to uppercase, and find the position of a substring:

MATLAB code	Python code
```% Define and concatenate strings```	```# Define and concatenate strings```
```str1 = 'Hello, ';```	```str1 = "Hello, "```
```str2 = 'MATLAB';```	```str2 = "Python"```
```combinedStr = [str1, str2];```	```combined_str = str1 + str2```
```% Convert to uppercase and find substring position```	```# Convert to uppercase and find substring position```
```upperStr = upper(combinedStr);```	```upper_str = combined_str.upper()```
```position = strfind(combinedStr, 'MATLAB');```	```position = combined_str.find("Python")```
```disp(combinedStr)```	```print(combined_str)```
```disp(upperStr)```	```print(upper_str)```
```disp(position)```	```print(position)```

Output	Output
Hello, MATLAB	Hello, Python
HELLO, MATLAB	HELLO, PYTHON
8	7

Table 2.138: Example 2.6 code in MATLAB and Python

• **Example 2.7:** Create a heterogeneous collection and access its elements:

MATLAB code	Python code
| ```matlab
% Define a cell array with mixed types
cellArray = {42, 'Data', [1, 2, 3]};
% Access elements
first_element = cellArray{1};
second_element = cellArray{2};
disp(cellArray)
disp(first_element)
disp(second_element)
``` | ```python
# Define a list with mixed types
mixed_list = [42, "Data", [1, 2, 3]]
# Access elements
first_element = mixed_list[0]
second_element = mixed_list[1]
print(mixed_list)
print(first_element)
print(second_element)
``` |
| **Output**
`[42]    'Data'    [1x3 double]`
`42`
`Data` | **Output**
`[42, 'Data', [1, 2, 3]]`
`42`
`Data` |

Table 2.139: Example 2.7 code in MATLAB and Python

• **Example 2.8:** Create a structure or dictionary, add fields/keys, and access values:

MATLAB code	Python code
| ```matlab
% Define a structure with multiple fields
student.name = 'Alice';
student.age = 21;
student.grade = 85;
% Access and modify fields
disp(student.name)
student.age = 22;
disp(student)
``` | ```python
# Define a dictionary with multiple keys
student = {
    "name": "Alice",
    "age": 21,
    "grade": 85
}
# Access and modify values
print(student["name"])
student["age"] = 22
print(student)
``` |
| **Output**
`Alice`
`    name: 'Alice'`
`  scores: [95 88 92]`
`     age: 22`
`   grade: 85` | **Output**
`Alice`
`{'name': 'Alice', 'age': 22, 'grade': 85}` |

Table 2.140: Example 2.8 code in MATLAB and Python

- **Example 2.9:** Define variables for radius and height of a cylinder, and calculate its volume and surface area:

MATLAB code	Python code

`% Define variables for radius and height`
`radius = 5;`
`height = 10;`
`% Calculate volume and surface area`
`volume = pi * radius^2 * height;`
`surface_area = 2 * pi * radius * (radius + height);`
`disp(['Volume of the cylinder: ', num2str(volume)]);`
`disp(['Surface area of the cylinder: ', num2str(surface_area)]);`
	`import math`
	`# Define variables for radius and height`
	`radius = 5`
	`height = 10`
	`# Calculate volume and surface area`
	`volume = math.pi * radius**2 * height`
	`surface_area = 2 * math.pi * radius * (radius + height)`
	`print(f"Volume of the cylinder: {volume}")`
	`print(f"Surface area of the cylinder: {surface_area}")`

Output **Volume of the cylinder: 785.3982** **Surface area of the cylinder: 471.2389**	**Output** **Volume of the cylinder: 785.3981633974483** **Surface area of the cylinder: 471.23889803846896**

Table 2.141: Example 2.9 code in MATLAB and Python

- **Example 2.10:** Create a matrix (2D array) representing points on a plane, calculate the distance of each point from the origin, and store the results in an array:

MATLAB code	Python code

`% Define points as a matrix (rows are points)`
`points = [3, 4; 5, 12; 8, 15];`
`% Calculate distances from the origin`
`distances = sqrt(sum(points.^2, 2));`
`disp('Points:');`
`disp(points);`
`disp('Distances from origin:');`
`disp(distances);`
	`import numpy as np`
	`# Define points as a 2D array`
	`points = np.array([[3, 4], [5, 12], [8, 15]])`
	`# Calculate distances from the origin`
	`distances = np.sqrt(np.sum(points**2, axis=1))`
	`print("Points:\n", points)`
	`print("Distances from origin:\n", distances)`

Output
Points:
`    3    4`
`    5    12`
`    8    15`
Distances from origin:
`    5`
`    13`
`    17`
	Output
	Points:
	`[[ 3  4]`
	`[ 5 12]`
	`[ 8 15]]`
	Distances from origin:
	`[ 5. 13. 17.]`

Table 2.142: Example 2.10 code in MATLAB and Python

Conclusion

As per this chapter, readers will learn that how to get the knowledge of MATLAB and Python basics. The defining the variables, arrays, matrices in MATLAB were discussed. In Python, data types in Python, string, list, tuple, dictionary, set in Python were also discussed.

In the next chapter, basic operations in MATLAB and Python will be elaborated.

Exercises

1. Define an integer variable x with the value 50, a float y with the value 3.14, and a string z with the value "Programming is fun!". Display all three variables.

2. Refer to the following questions:

    a. Determine and display the data type of the variables $x = 42$, $y = 7.5$, and z = "Hello World!".

    b. Convert the integer 100 into a float and the float 9.8 into an integer. Display the results.

3. Perform the following operations on two numbers, $a = 15$ and $b = 4$:

    a. Addition

    b. Subtraction

    c. Multiplication

    d. Division

    e. Modulus (remainder)

    f. Exponentiation

4. Refer to the following:

    a. Check if $x = 25$ is greater than $y = 18$. Display the result.

    b. Check if conditions $x > 10$ and $y < 20$ are true. Display the result.

5. Refer to the following:

    a. Create a 3×33 times 3×33 matrix containing numbers from 1 to 9.

    b. Access and display the element in the second row, third column of the matrix.

    c. Replace the first row of the matrix with [10, 11, 12].

    d. Compute the sum of all elements in the matrix.

6. Define a string = "Learning MATLAB and Python". Perform the following:

    a. Extract the word "MATLAB".

    b. Convert the string to uppercase.

    c. Replace "MATLAB" with "Coding" in the string.

1. Refer to the following:

    a. Create a list/cell array containing the following elements:

        • An integer: 25

        • A string: "Data"

        • A float: 7.89

    b.   Access the second element of the list/cell array.

    c.   Add a new element "Science" to the list/cell array.

2.   Refer to the following:

    a.   Create a dictionary/structure with the following key-value pairs:

- Name: "John"

- Age: 30

- Occupation: "Engineer"

    b.   Access and display the value of the Occupation key/field.

    c.   Add a new key/field Salary with the value 75000.

3.   Do the following matrix operations.

    a.   Normalize a 3×3 matrix by dividing each element by the sum of all elements in the matrix.

    b.   Compute the mean of each column in the matrix.

    c.   Transpose the matrix and display the result.

4.   Perform the following:

   Create a 3×3 matrix:

$$\begin{bmatrix} 1 & 2 & 3 \\ 4 & 5 & 6 \\ 7 & 8 & 9 \end{bmatrix}$$

   Compute:

- The determinant of the matrix.

- The transpose of the matrix.

5.   Define a variable z as $z = 1.5$; then evaluate:

- $z^4 - 20z^3 - 12.8z^2 + 9.45$

- $\dfrac{z+2}{z^3} + \dfrac{z^3 - 1.8^4}{\sqrt[3]{z^2 + 6.5}}$

6.   Define the variables $a = 2.5$, $b = 6.5$ and $c = ab^2$; $d = \dfrac{b-a}{b+a}$, then evaluate:

$$\frac{e^b}{d+1} + \frac{\frac{c}{d}}{\left(\frac{a}{b} - \sqrt[4]{cd}\right)}$$

7.   Verify the following trigonometric identities for $x = 75°$

- $\tan(2x) = \dfrac{2\tan(x)}{(1 - \tan^2(x))}$

- $\dfrac{1 - 2\cos x - 3\cos^2 x}{\sin^2 x} = \dfrac{1 - 3\cos x}{1 - \cos x}$

8.   Create a program that takes the width = 18 foot and length = 20 foot of a room. Calculate and display the room's area in foot and meter as well.

9.   Write a program that calculate the perimeter of the given shape field, where the radius of the circle is 10 cm and the rectangle is 10 cm by 25 cm. Ignore the lines inside the figure.

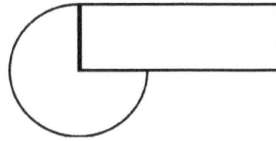

10. Write a program should that calculate and display the sum of all integers from 1 to n. You can compute the sum of the first n positive integers using the formula:

$$Sum = n \times \frac{(n+1)}{2}$$

Implement this formula in your program to find and display the result for $n = 100$.

The sum must be 5050.

11. Imagine you just opened a new savings account with a 4 percent interest rate per year. The interest you earn is added to your account at the end of each year. Write a program that starts by taking money deposited in the account. Then, calculate and show how much money will be in the savings account after 1, 2, and 3 years. Make sure to round each amount to 2 decimal places. Use the formula for

$$A = P \times (1+r)^t$$

Where:

- A = the amount in the account after t years
- P = the initial amount deposited (principal)
- r = annual interest rate (as a decimal, so 4% becomes 0.04)
- t = number of years

For this scenario, you will calculate A for $t = 1$, 2 and 3 using the same initial deposit P.

12. Calculate $a = cos(x)$, $b = sin(x)$ and $c = tan(x)$ for different x:

$$x = 0;\ x = \frac{\pi}{2};\ x = \frac{\pi}{4};\ x = \frac{\pi}{6};\ x = \pi;\ x = 2\pi.$$

The values can be created for each given value of x. Another way is to combine the values in a vector define as: $x = \begin{bmatrix} 0 & \frac{\pi}{2} & \frac{\pi}{4} & \frac{\pi}{6} & \pi & 2\pi \end{bmatrix}$

13. Create the following matrix by typing one command. Do not type individual elements explicitly.

$A =$

0. 0. 0. 0.   0.

0. 0. 1. 10. 20.

0. 0. 2. 8.   26.

0. 0. 3. 6.   32.

14. Create a program that reads a measurement in feet from the user. Then, display the equivalent distance in inches, yards, and miles. Use the following conversion factors:

- 1 foot = 12 inches
- 1 yard = 3 feet
- 1 mile = 5280 feet

Join our Discord space

Join our Discord workspace for latest updates, offers, tech happenings around the world, new releases, and sessions with the authors:

https://discord.bpbonline.com

CHAPTER 3

Basic Operations in MATLAB and Python Languages

Introduction

This chapter mentions a comparative approach to basic operations in MATLAB and Python. MATLAB has its own strengths in matrix operations and mathematical calculations, which is why it is useful in engineering and scientific fields. Python is considered for its easy-to-implement approach and readability, which is why it is widely used across various domains. This chapter will provide the basic knowledge in these languages, which will give readers the techniques to handle common programming tasks efficiently.

In this chapter, we will explore the fundamental operations and functionalities of two powerful programming languages: MATLAB and Python. MATLAB is widely recognized for its strength in numerical computations, particularly in arithmetic and matrix operations, making it a preferred tool for engineers and scientists. We will delve into its capabilities in performing basic arithmetic operations, advanced matrix manipulations, and logical operations that are essential for data analysis and algorithm development. On the other hand, Python, known for its versatility and ease of use, offers a broad range of functionalities, including arithmetic operations, string manipulation, list operations, and a variety of built-in functions that make it suitable for general-purpose programming and data handling. By understanding these core concepts in both MATLAB and Python, you will gain a solid foundation to tackle a wide array of computational problems and enhance your programming skills across different domains.

Structure

The structure of this chapter is as follows:

- 3.1 MATLAB
- 3.2 Python
- 3.3 Comparison of examples via MATLAB and Python

Objectives

In this chapter, readers will be introduced to the foundational skills necessary for performing arithmetic operations in MATLAB and Python. These skills include understanding how to execute basic mathematical calculations such as addition, subtraction, multiplication, and division, as well as more complex operations. This chapter will also explore matrix operations, a critical component of MATLAB. Readers will learn how to create, manipulate, and perform operations on matrices, including matrix addition, subtraction, and multiplication. They will also explore specialized matrix functions such as determinant calculation and inverse finding. This section aims to equip readers with the ability to handle matrix-based data efficiently, which is essential for various scientific and engineering applications.

Logical operations form another key focus of this chapter. Readers will gain an understanding of how to use logical operators to perform comparisons and make decisions based on conditions.

In the Python-specific sections, readers will explore string manipulation techniques. This includes learning how to concatenate strings, extract substrings, replace characters, and format strings for output. Additionally, readers will become familiar with various string methods that allow for efficient text processing and manipulation.

List operations in Python will also be covered, providing readers with the knowledge to create, access, modify, and manipulate lists. They will learn about list indexing, slicing, appending, and sorting, as well as how to use list comprehensions for more concise and readable code. By the end of this section, readers will be adept at using lists to store and manage collections of data effectively.

3.1 MATLAB

MATLAB is a powerful numerical computing tool widely used in engineering, science, and mathematics for efficient mathematical operations. Section *3.1.1 Arithmetic operations* cover basic computations on scalars and arrays, while Section *3.1.2 Matrix operations* highlights matrix manipulation essential for linear algebra, signal processing, and machine learning. The section, *3.1.3 Logical operations*, explores comparisons and logical operators for condition evaluation and data filtering. These capabilities make MATLAB a versatile platform for numerical analysis and algorithm development.

3.1.1 Arithmetic operations in MATLAB

MATLAB gives knowledge regarding the fundamental arithmetic operations. These operations are useful for basic computations and form the base of complex calculations in scientific tasks.

MATLAB provides comprehensive support for fundamental arithmetic operations, which serve as the foundation for complex mathematical computations. These operations are essential for performing calculations on both scalars and arrays, making MATLAB a powerful tool for numerical analysis and scientific computing. The basic arithmetic operations include the following:

- **Addition (+)**: Adds two numbers or corresponding elements of arrays.
- **Subtraction (-)**: Computes the difference between numbers or array elements.
- **Multiplication (*)**: Multiplies scalars or performs matrix multiplication when used with arrays.
- **Element-wise Multiplication (.*)**: Multiplies corresponding elements of arrays.
- **Division (/ and \)**: Computes division for scalars and matrices, including right division (/) and left division (\).
- **Element-wise Division (./ and .\)**: Divides corresponding elements of arrays.
- **Exponentiation (^)**: Raises a number or matrix to a power.
- **Element-wise Exponentiation (.^)**: Applies exponentiation to each element of an array individually.

The addition of two numbers in MATLAB can be defined as follows:

- **Addition (+)**: It provides the basic addition between numbers or matrices:

`a = 5;`
`b = 3;`
`c = a + b;`
`disp(c);`
	Output:
	8

Table 3.1: Addition between numbers

The addition of two matrices in MATLAB is as follows:

`A = [1, 2; 3, 4];`
`B = [5, 6; 7, 8];`
`C = A + B;`
`disp(C);`
	Output:
	  6 8
	 10 12

Table 3.2: Addition between matrices

- **Subtraction (-)**: It provides the simple subtraction between numbers or matrices.

The subtraction of two numbers in MATLAB is as follows:

`a = 10;`
`b = 4;`
`c = a - b;`
`disp(c);`
	Output:
	6

Table 3.3: Subtraction between numbers

The subtraction of two matrices in MATLAB is displayed as follows:

`A = [7, 5; 3, 9];`
`B = [2, 1; 4, 6];`
`C = A - B;`
`disp(C);`
	Output:
	  5 4
	 -1 3

Table 3.4: Subtraction between matrices

- **Multiplication (*)**: It provides matrix multiplication, requiring compatible matrix dimensions:

`A = [1, 2, 3;`
`     4, 5, 6];`
 	
`B = [7, 8;`
`     9, 10;`
`     11, 12];`
 	
`C = A * B;`
`disp(C);`
	Output:
	  58 64
	 139 154

Table 3.5: Matrix multiplication

- **Element-wise multiplication (.*)**: It provides element-by-element multiplication, useful for arrays:

```A = [1, 2, 3; 4, 5, 6]; B = [7, 8, 9; 10, 11, 12]; C = A .* B; disp(C);```	**Output:** 7 16 27 40 55 72

Table 3.6: Element-by-element multiplication

- **Division (/ and ./)**: Division and element-wise division.

  o **Matrix division (/ and \ operators)**: Matrix division operates under the following specific rules:

    ▪ **Right division (/)**: Divides the matrix on the left by the matrix or scalar on right.

    ▪ **Left division (\)**: Divides matrix on the right by matrix or scalar on the left:

```A = [10, 20; 30, 40]; B = [2, 5; 3, 4]; % Right matrix division C1 = A / B; % Equivalent to A * inv(B) disp(C1); % Left matrix division C2 = B \ A; % Equivalent to inv(B) * A disp(C2);```	**Output:** 2.8571 1.4286 0 10.0000 **Output:** 15.7143 17.1429 -4.2857 -2.8571

Table 3.7: Matrix division

  o **Element-wise division (./ operator)**: Element-wise division divides every element in one matrix by the corresponding elements in another matrix of the same size. The operator for this is ./ .

The element-wise division is mentioned as follows:

```A = [10, 20, 30; 40, 50, 60]; B = [2, 4, 5; 8, 10, 12]; C = A ./ B; disp(C);```	**Output:** 5 5 6 5 5 5

Table 3.8: Element-wise division

- **Exponentiation (^ and .^)**: Matrix and element-wise exponentiation.

  o **Matrix exponentiation (^ operator)**: Matrix exponentiation (e.g., A^2) needs a square matrix and includes raising the matrix to a specified power by implementing the matrix multiplications:

```A = [2, 3; 1, 4]; C = A ^ 2; % Equivalent to A * A disp(C);```	Output: 7 18 6 19

Table 3.9: Matrix exponentiation

  o **Element-wise exponentiation (.^ operator)**: Element-wise exponentiation is performed using the .^ operator, and it raises each individual element of the matrix to the specified power. This operation can be applied to non-square matrices as well:

```A = [2, 3; 1, 4]; % Element-wise exponentiation D = A .^ 2; disp(D);```	Output: 4 9 1 16

Table 3.10: Element-wise exponentiation

3.1.2 Matrix operations in MATLAB

MATLAB's strength lies in its matrix-oriented operations, allowing users to handle arrays and matrices efficiently.

In this subsection, various matrix operations are described in detail:

- **Matrix transpose (')**: Transposing matrices to switch rows and columns:

```A = [1, 2, 3; 4, 5, 6]; % Transpose of matrix A B = A'; disp(B);```	Output: 1 4 2 5 3 6

Table 3.11: Transpose of matrix

- **Inverse (inv)**: Calculate the inverse of a matrix:

```A = [4, 7; 2, 6]; % inverse of matrix A A_inv = inv(A); disp(A_inv);```	Output: 0.6000 -0.7000 -0.2000 0.4000

Table 3.12: Inverse of matrix

- **Determinant (det)**: Useful for solving linear systems:

```A = [4, 7; 2, 6]; % determinant of matrix A det_A = det(A); disp(det_A);```	**Output:** 10

Table 3.13: Determinant of matrix

- **Other matrix functions**: size, length, zeros, ones, diag, detailed as follows:
  - **size**: Determines the dimensions of a matrix. The size function returns the number of rows and columns in a matrix:

```A = [1, 2, 3; 4, 5, 6]; % size of matrix A [rows, cols] = size(A); disp(['Rows: ', num2str(rows), ', Columns: ', num2str(cols)]);```	**Output:** Rows: 2, Columns: 3

Table 3.14: Size of matrix

  - **length**: Returns the largest dimension of the matrix. The length function gives the maximum of the row and column dimensions, which is useful for vectors or finding the longest dimension of a matrix:

```B = [1, 2, 3, 4]; % length of matrix B len = length(B); disp(['Length: ', num2str(len)]);```	**Output:** Length: 4

Table 3.15: Length of matrix

  - **zeros**: Creates a matrix of all zeros. The zeros function is used to create a matrix filled with zeros. You specify the dimensions of the matrix as arguments:

```% 3x3 matrix of zeros Z = zeros(3, 3); disp(Z);```	**Output:** 0 0 0 0 0 0 0 0 0

Table 3.16: Matrix of zeros

o **ones**: Creates a matrix of all ones. The ones function generates a matrix filled with ones, with specified dimensions:

	Output:

```% 2x4 matrix of ones```
```O = ones(2, 4);```
```disp(O);```
	1 1 1 1
	
	1 1 1 1

Table 3.17: Matrix of ones

o **diag**: Creates a diagonal matrix or extracts the diagonal of a matrix. The diag function has two main uses:

- Creating a diagonal matrix from a vector:

	Output:

```v = [1, 2, 3];```
 	
```% 3x3 diagonal matrix with elements from vector v```
```D = diag(v);```
```disp(D);```
	1 0 0
	0 2 0
	0 0 3

Table 3.18: Diagonal matrix

- Extracting the diagonal elements from a matrix:

	Output:

```A = [1, 2, 3;```
```   4, 5, 6;```
```   7, 8, 9];```
 	
```% diagonal elements of matrix A```
```diag_A = diag(A);```
```disp(diag_A);```
	1
	
	5
	
	9

Table 3.19: Extracting the diagonal elements from a matrix

- **Special types of matrices**:

  o **Random matrix (rand and randn)**: MATLAB provides functions to create random matrices, like:

  - **rand**: Generates a matrix with uniformly distributed random values between 0 and 1:

	Output:

```% 3x3 matrix with random values```
```between 0 and 1```
```R = rand(3, 3);```
```disp(R);```
	0.8147 0.9134 0.2785
	0.9058 0.6324 0.5469
	0.1270 0.0975 0.9575

Table 3.20: Random matrix

- **randn**: Generates a matrix with normally distributed random values (mean 0, standard deviation 1):

% 3x3 matrix with random values from a normal distribution R_normal = randn(3, 3); disp(R_normal);	Output: 2.7694 0.7254 -0.2050 -1.3499 -0.0631 -0.1241 3.0349 0.7147 1.4897

Table 3.21: Matrix with normally distributed random values

o **Hilbert matrix (hilb):** The Hilbert matrix is a specific type of square matrix with elements defined as $H(i,j) = \frac{1}{i+j-1}$. It is often used in numerical analysis:

% 4x4 Hilbert matrix H = hilb(4); disp(H);	Output: 1.0000 0.5000 0.3333 0.2500 0.5000 0.3333 0.2500 0.2000 0.3333 0.2500 0.2000 0.1667 0.2500 0.2000 0.1667 0.1429

Table 3.22: Hilbert matrix

o **Pascal matrix (pascal):** The Pascal matrix is a symmetric positive definite matrix. It can be created using the Pascal function:

% 4x4 Pascal matrix P = pascal(4); disp(P);	Output: 1 1 1 1 1 2 3 4 1 3 6 10 1 4 10 20

Table 3.23: Pascal matrix

o **Tridiagonal matrix:**

n = 4;
% Size of tridiagonal matrix
 	
main_diag = [3, 3, 3, 3];
% Main diagonal elements
 	
upper_diag = [1, 2, 3];
% Upper diagonal elements
 	
lower_diag = [7, 8, 9];
% Lower diagonal elements
 	
% tridiagonal matrix
 	
T_custom = diag(main_diag) + diag(upper_diag, 1) + diag(lower_diag, -1);
disp(T_custom);
	Output:
	
	3 1 0 0
	
	7 3 2 0
	
	0 8 3 3
	
	0 0 9 3

Table 3.24: Tridiagonal matrix

o **Pentadiagonal matrix**:

	Output:				
| ```
n = 5;  % Size of pentadiagonal matrix

% Define each diagonal with custom values
main_diag = [10, 10, 10, 10, 10];

% Main diagonal
upper_diag1 = [3, 3, 3, 3];

% First upper diagonal
upper_diag2 = [1, 1, 1];

% Second upper diagonal
lower_diag1 = [-3, -3, -3, -3];

% First lower diagonal
lower_diag2 = [-1, -1, -1];
% Second lower diagonal

% pentadiagonal matrix
P = diag(main_diag) + diag(upper_diag1, 1) +
diag(upper_diag2, 2) ...
    + diag(lower_diag1, -1) + diag(lower_diag2,
-2);

disp(P);
``` | | | | | |

Output:

10	3	1	0	0
-3	10	3	1	0
0	-3	10	3	1
0	0	-3	10	3
0	0	0	-3	10

Table 3.25: Pentadiagonal matrix

3.1.3 Logical operations in MATLAB

Logical operations help control program flow and perform condition checks. Logical operations in MATLAB play a crucial role in decision-making, data filtering, and control flow in programming. These operations allow users to compare values, evaluate conditions, and implement logical expressions in various computational tasks.

MATLAB supports both relational and logical operators.

Relational operators (<, >, <=, >=, ==, ~=) compare values and return logical true (1) or false (0), making them essential for conditional statements, loops, and array filtering.

Logical operators (&, |, ~, xor) are used to perform element-wise logical operations, enabling complex decision-making processes in algorithms. These operators are widely applied in data processing, image analysis, machine learning, and optimization tasks.

MATLAB also provides functions like **any()**, **all()**, and **find()** to enhance logical operations by evaluating and extracting specific conditions from arrays. Understanding logical operations is essential for efficient programming, as they allow users to manipulate large datasets, implement control structures, and automate decision-based workflows effectively.

- **Comparison operators**: <, >, <=, >=, ==, ~= for comparing values.

  In MATLAB, comparison operators are used to compare values or expressions, returning logical values (true or false) as a result. Here is a summary of MATLAB's comparison operators:
```

o **Less than (<):** Returns true if the left operand is less than the right operand:

	Output:

`a = 5;`
`b = 10;`
`result = a < b   % result will be true`
	`result =`
	
	`1`

Table 3.26: Comparison operator <

o **Greater than (>):** Returns true if the left operand is greater than the right operand:

	Output:

`a = 10;`
`b = 5;`
`result = a > b   % result will be true`
	`result =`
	
	`1`

Table 3.27: Comparison operator >

o **Less than or equal to (<=):** Returns true if the left operand is less than or equal to the right operand:

	Output:

`a = 5;`
`b = 5;`
`result = a <= b   % result will be`
`true`
	`result =`
	
	`1`

Table 3.28: Comparison operator <=

o **Greater than or equal to (>=):** Returns true if the left operand is greater than or equal to the right operand:

	Output:

`a = 10;`
`b = 5;`
`result = a >= b   % result will be true`
	`result =`
	
	`1`

Table 3.29: Comparison operator >=

o **Equal to (==):** Returns true if the left operand is equal to the right operand:

	Output:

`a = 5;`
`b = 5;`
`result = a == b   % result will be true`
	`result =`
	
	`1`

Table 3.30: Comparison operator ==

o **Not equal to (~=):** Returns true if the left operand is not equal to the right operand:

	Output:

`a = 5;`
`b = 10;`
`result = a ~= b   % result will be true`
	`result =`
	
	`1`

Table 3.31: Comparison operator ~=

- **Logical operators**: **&**, **|**, and **~** for **AND, OR**, and **NOT** operations. In MATLAB, logical operators are used to perform logical operations on Boolean values (true or false). Here is a brief overview of MATLAB's main logical operators:

  o **Logical AND (&)**: Performs an element-wise **AND** operation. It returns true if both operands are true, and false otherwise:

`a = true;`
`b = false;`
`result = a & b   % result will be false`
	Output:
	`result =`
	`    0`

Table 3.32: *Logical operator AND*

  o **Logical OR (|)**: Performs an element-wise **OR** operation. It returns true if at least one operand is true, and false otherwise:

`a = true;`
`b = false;`
`result = a
	b % result will be true`	**Output:**
		`result =`
		`    1`

Table 3.33: *Logical operator OR*

  o **Logical NOT (~)**: Negates a logical value. It returns true if the operand is false, and false if the operand is true:

`a = true;`
`result = ~a;       % result will be`
`false`
	Output:
	`result =`
	`    0`

Table 3.34: *Logical operator NOT*

- **Short-circuit AND (&&)**: The **&&** operator evaluates the second operand only if the first operand is true (since false **&& any_value** is always false). If the first operand is false, MATLAB skips evaluating the second operand because the result is already determined as false:

`x = 5;`
`if (x > 0) && (10 / x > 1)`
`    disp('Both conditions are true');`
`else`
`    disp('At least one condition is false');`
`end`
	Output:
	`Both conditions are true`

Table 3.35: *Short-circuit AND*

- **Short-circuit OR (||)**: The **||** operator evaluates the second operand only if the first operand is false (since true **|| any_value** is always true). If the first operand is true, MATLAB skips evaluating the second operand because the result is already determined as true:

`x = 0;`
`if (x == 0) || (10 / x > 1)`
`    disp('At least one condition is true');`
`else`
`    disp('Both conditions are false');`
`end`
	Output:
	`At least one condition is true`

Table 3.36: *Short-circuit OR*

- **Using logical arrays**: MATLAB supports logical indexing, allowing operations based on conditions.

  In MATLAB, **logical arrays** (or **logical indexing**) are powerful tools that allow you to manipulate or access array elements based on specified conditions. This technique enables you to perform operations on specific elements of an array by creating a logical array, where true indicates that an element meets the condition and false indicates it does not.

Let us now see how logical indexing works.

A logical array is an array of true or false values. You can create it by applying a conditional expression to an array. MATLAB then uses this logical array to index into the original array, allowing you to select, modify, or perform operations only on elements that meet a condition.

- **Creating a logical array**: Let us see how to create a logical array in MATLAB:

`A = [1, 3, 5, 7, 9];`
`logicalArray = A > 4`
	Output:
	`logicalArray =`
	`    0    0    1    1    1`

Table 3.37: Logical array

- **Using a logical array to select elements**: Using a logical array to select elements allows you to filter or extract specific values from an array or matrix based on a condition, enabling efficient data manipulation and analysis:

`selectedElements = A(A > 4)`	**Output:**
	`selectedElements =`
	`    5    7    9`

Table 3.38: Logical array to select elements

- **Modifying elements based on a condition**: Modifying elements based on a condition involves applying logical indexing to update or replace values in an array or matrix that meet specific criteria, streamlining data processing tasks:

`A(A > 4) = 0`
`% Sets elements greater than 4 to 0`
	Output:
	`A =`
	`    1    3    0    0    0`

Table 3.39: Modification of elements based on a condition

- **Counting elements that meet a condition**: Counting elements that meet a condition can be done using **`sum(logical_condition)`** to find how many values satisfy the condition:

`count = sum(A > 4)`
`% Counts the number of elements greater than 4`
	Output:
	`count =`
	`    0`

Table 3.40: Counting of elements as per condition

- **Combining conditions**: You can combine conditions using logical operators (**&, |, ~**):

`A = [1, 3, 5, 7, 9];`
`selectedElements = A((A > 4) & (A < 8))`
	Output:
	`selectedElements =`
	`    5    7`

Table 3.41: Combining conditions

3.2 Python

Python is a widely used, high-level programming language known for its simplicity, readability, and extensive libraries that support diverse computational tasks. It is popular in scientific computing, data analysis, machine learning, and software development due to its powerful built-in functions and user-friendly syntax. Unlike MATLAB, which is primarily designed for numerical computing, Python offers a more versatile programming environment, supporting arithmetic, logical, string, and list operations efficiently. Python's arithmetic operations include addition, subtraction, multiplication, division, exponentiation, and integer division, making it a reliable tool for mathematical computations. It also excels in string manipulation, providing methods for concatenation, slicing, formatting, and transformation, which are essential for handling text-based data. Additionally, Python's dynamic list structures support indexing, slicing, sorting, and various modifications, enabling efficient data handling. Python's flexibility, open-source nature, and extensive ecosystem of libraries like NumPy, pandas, and Matplotlib make it a preferred choice for engineers, data scientists, and researchers looking to develop robust and scalable computational solutions across multiple domains.

3.2.1 Arithmetic operations in Python

Python also supports basic arithmetic operations, using the following similar symbols to MATLAB:

- **Addition (+)- Addition of two numbers in Python**: In Python, the addition of two numbers is performed using the + operator, which returns the sum of the operands:

```a = 5 + 3``` ```print(a)```	**Output:** **8**

Table 3.42: Arithmetic operation addition

- **Subtraction (-)**: In Python, the subtraction of two numbers is performed using the - operator, which returns the difference between the operands:

```b = 10 - 2``` ```print(b)```	**Output:** **8**

Table 3.43: Arithmetic operation subtraction

- **Multiplication (*)**: In Python, the multiplication of two numbers is performed using the ***** operator, which returns the product of the operands:

```c = 4 * 3``` ```print(c)```	**Output:** **12**

Table 3.44: Arithmetic operation multiplication

- **Division (/)**: Python performs float division by default:

```d = 10 / 3``` ```print(d)```	**Output:** **3.3333333333333335**

Table 3.45: Arithmetic operation division

Python performs **float division** by default, so even if the numbers divide evenly, the result will be a float.

- **Integer division (//)**: Divides and rounds down to the nearest integer:

e = 10 // 3 print(e)	Output: 3

Table 3.46: Integer division

Integer division returns the quotient rounded down to the nearest integer.

- **Exponentiation (**)**:

f = 2 ** 3 print(f)	Output: 8

Table 3.47: Exponentiation

3.2.2 String manipulation in Python

Python offers versatile string handling, which is not a strong feature in MATLAB. It provides powerful and flexible string handling capabilities, making it an ideal choice for text processing and manipulation.

Unlike MATLAB, Python treats strings as immutable sequences, allowing efficient indexing, slicing, and modification using built-in methods. Common operations include concatenation (+), repetition (*), and slicing ([:]) to extract substrings.

Python also offers advanced string formatting techniques such as f-strings, **.format()**, and **%** formatting for dynamic text generation. Additionally, various string methods like **.upper()**, **.lower()**, **.replace()**, **.find()**, and **.split()** simplify text transformations, searching, and splitting tasks.

Regular expressions (re-module) further enhance string manipulation, enabling complex pattern matching and data extraction. These capabilities make Python well-suited for natural language processing, data cleaning, and software development, where text-based data is prevalent.

Let us look at them in detail:

- **Concatenation**: Combining strings using +:

first_name = "John" last_name = "Doe" full_name = first_name + " " + last_name print(full_name)	Output: John Doe

Table 3.48: Concatenation of strings

- **Slicing**: Extracting substrings with **str[start:end]**:

text = "Hello, World!"
substring = text[7:12]
# Extracts characters from index 7 up to, but not including, index 12 	
print(substring)
	Output:
	World

Table 3.49: Slicing from string

- **Formatting**: Using `f"{}"`, `.format()`, or `%` for dynamic strings.
  - o **f-strings (Python 3.6+)**: A modern and efficient string formatting method using `{}` placeholders within an f-prefixed string, allowing direct variable interpolation:

`name = "Alice"`
`age = 30`
`message = f"Hello, {name}! You are {age} years old."`
`print(message)`
	Output:
	Hello, Alice! You are 30 years old.

Table 3.50: F-string

  - o **.format() method**: A versatile string formatting approach that replaces placeholders `{}` with specified values using the `.format()` function:

`name = "Alice"`
`age = 30`
`message = "Hello, {}! You are {} years old.".format(name, age)`
`print(message)`
	Output:
	Hello, Alice! You are 30 years old.

Table 3.51: .format() method

  - o **% formatting**: An older string formatting method in Python that uses format specifiers (e.g., `%s`, `%d`) to embed values into a string:

`name = "Alice"`
`age = 30`
`message = "Hello, %s! You are %d years old." % (name, age)`
`print(message)`
	Output:
	Hello, Alice! You are 30 years old.

Table 3.52: % formatting

- **Common string methods**: `upper()`, `lower()`, `replace()`, `find()`, and `split()`:
  - o **upper()**: Converts the string to uppercase:

`text = "hello"`
`uppercase_text = text.upper()`
`print(uppercase_text)`
	Output:
	HELLO

Table 3.53: String method upper()

  - o **lower()**: Converts the string to lowercase:

`text = "HELLO"`
`lowercase_text = text.lower()`
`print(lowercase_text)`
	Output:
	hello

Table 3.54: String method lower()

o **replace()**: Replaces a substring with another string:

`text = "Hello, World!"`
 	
`new_text = text.replace("World",`
`"Python")`
 	
`print(new_text)`
	Output:
	
	`Hello, Python!`

Table 3.55: String method replace()

o **find()**: Returns the index of the first occurrence of a substring (or **-1** if not found):

`text = "Hello, World!"`
`position = text.find("World")`
`print(position)`
	Output:
	
	`7`

Table 3.56: String method find()

Explanation: In this example, **"World"** starts at index 7 in the original string.

o **split()**: Splits the string into a list of substrings based on a specified delimiter:

`text = "apple,banana,cherry"`
`fruits = text.split(",")`
`print(fruits)`
	Output:
	
	`['apple', 'banana', 'cherry']`

Table 3.57: String method split()

Explanation: Here, `split(",")` separates the text at each comma, creating a list of fruits.

3.2.3 List operations in Python

Lists in Python are dynamic, supporting indexing, slicing, and various operations. Lists in Python are flexible and dynamic data structures that allow efficient storage, modification, and retrieval of elements. They support indexing (positive and negative) for accessing specific elements and slicing to extract sublists.

Python lists can store heterogeneous data types, including numbers, strings, and even other lists (nested lists). Common operations include appending (`append()`), extending (`extend()`), inserting (`insert()`), and removing elements (`remove()`, `pop()`, `del`). Lists can be sorted (`sort()`), reversed (`reverse()`), and iterated efficiently using loops or list comprehensions. Additionally, functions like `len()`, `min()`, `max()`, and `sum()` provide quick insights into list contents. With built-in methods for searching (`index()`, `count()`), modifying, and transforming data, lists play a fundamental role in Python programming, particularly in data processing, numerical computations, and algorithm development. Let us look at the details:

- **Creating lists:**

  o **Creating an empty list**: Creating an empty list in Python is done using empty square brackets, e.g., `my_list = []`:

`empty_list = []` `print(empty_list)`	**Output:** `[]`

Table 3.58: Creation of an empty list

  o **Creating a list with initial elements**: Creating a list with initial elements in Python involves placing the elements inside square brackets separated by commas:

```
numbers = [1, 2, 3, 4, 5]        | Output:
print(numbers)                   |
fruits = ["apple", "banana", "cherry"]  | [1, 2, 3, 4, 5]
print(fruits)                    | ['apple', 'banana', 'cherry']
```

Table 3.59: Creation of a list with initial elements

o **Creating a list with mixed data types**: Creating a list with mixed data types in Python is done by including elements of different types (e.g., integers, strings, floats) within square brackets:

```
mixed_list = [1, "hello", 3.14, True]  | Output:
print(mixed_list)                       | [1, 'hello', 3.14, True]
```

Table 3.60: Creation of a list with mixed data types

o **Creating a list from a range**: Creating a list from a range in Python is achieved using the **list()** function with **range()**:

```
range_list = list(range(1, 6))  #   | Output:
Creates a list of numbers from 1 to 5  | [1, 2, 3, 4, 5]
print(range_list)                    |
```

Table 3.61: Creation a list from a range

o **Creating a list using list comprehension**: Creating a list using list comprehension in Python involves defining a concise expression inside square bracket:

```
squares = [x**2 for x in range(1, 6)]  | Output:
print(squares)                          | [1, 4, 9, 16, 25]
```

Table 3.62: Creation a list using list comprehension

o **Creating a nested list (list of lists)**: Creating a nested list (list of lists) in Python involves placing lists as elements inside another list:

```
matrix = [[1, 2, 3], [4, 5, 6], [7,  | Output:
8, 9]]                               | [[1, 2, 3], [4, 5, 6], [7, 8, 9]]
print(matrix)                        |
```

Table 3.63: Creation of a nested list

o **Converting other data types to a list**: Converting other data types to a list in Python is a common operation that allows for flexible data manipulation. For instance, a string can be converted to a list using **list(string)**, which breaks the string into individual characters. Similarly, a tuple or set can be transformed into a list using the **list()** function, preserving the order of elements. This conversion is particularly useful when you need to modify or iterate over data structures that are originally immutable or unordered. By converting to a list, you gain access to a wide range of list-specific methods and operations, enhancing your ability to manage and process data effectively.

  ▪ **String to list**: In Python, converting a string to a list can be done using **list(string)**, which splits the string into individual characters and stores them as elements in a list:

```
text = "hello"              | Output:
char_list = list(text)      | ['h', 'e', 'l', 'l', 'o']
print(char_list)            |
```

Table 3.64: String to list conversion

- **Tuple to list**: In Python, converting a tuple to a list is done using **list(tuple)**, which creates a new list with the same elements as the original tuple:

`tuple_data = (1, 2, 3)`
`list_data = list(tuple_data)`
`print(list_data)`
	Output:
	[1, 2, 3]

Table 3.65: Tuple to list conversion

o **Creating a list with duplicate elements**: In Python, you can create a list with duplicate elements by simply repeating values within square brackets:

`duplicates = ["apple"] * 3` `print(duplicates)`	**Output:** **['apple', 'apple', 'apple']**

Table 3.66: Creation of a list with duplicate elements

o **Creating a list using the append() method**: In Python, you can create and populate a list using the **append()** method, which adds elements one at a time to the end of the list:

`dynamic_list = []`
`dynamic_list.append(1)`
`dynamic_list.append(2)`
`dynamic_list.append(3)`
`print(dynamic_list)`
	Output:
	[1, 2, 3]

Table 3.67: Creation of a list using the append() method

- **Indexing and slicing**: Accessing specific elements or portions, like:

  o **Basic indexing**: The concept of basic indexing in list is mentioned as follows:

    - **Accessing a single element**: Use square brackets **[ ]** with the index of the item you want to access:

Note: Python indexing starts at 0.

`My_list = [10, 20, 30, 40, 50]`
`first_element = my_list[0]`
`print(first_element)`
	Output:
	10

Table 3.68: Accessing a single element from list

    - **Accessing the last element**: Use **-1** as the index:

`last_element = my_list[-1]` `print(last_element)`	**Output:** **50**

Table 3.69: Accessing the last element from list

o   **Slicing**: Extracting a portion of a list or string.

   ▪   **Basic slicing**: `list[start:end]` extracts elements from the start index up to, but not including, the end index:

`my_list = [10, 20, 30, 40, 50]`
`subset = my_list[1:4]`
`print(subset)`
	Output:
	`[20, 30, 40]`

Table 3.70: Basic slicing from list

   ▪   **Omitting start or end**: If you omit start, slicing starts from the beginning.

`Start_from_beginning = my_list[:3]` `print(start_from_beginning)`	**Output:** **`[10, 20, 30]`**

Table 3.71: Omitting start or end in list

If you omit the end, slicing goes to the end of the list:

`end_to_last = my_list[2:]` `print(end_to_last)`	**Output:** **`[30, 40, 50]`**

Table 3.72: End to last in list

   ▪   **Using negative indices**: You can use negative indices to slice from the end of the list:

`last_two_elements = my_list[-2:]` `print(last_two_elements)`	**Output:** **`[40, 50]`**

Table 3.73: Negative indices in list

o   **Step in slicing**: `list[start:end:step]`

   ▪   **Skipping elements**: The step parameter defines the interval between elements in the slice:

`my_list = [10, 20, 30, 40, 50]`
`every_other = my_list[::2]`
`print(every_other)`
	Output:
	`[10, 30, 50]`

Table 3.74: Skipping elements in list

   ▪   **Reversing a list**: You can reverse a list by using a negative step:

`reversed_list = my_list[::-1]` `print(reversed_list)`	**Output:** **`[50, 40, 30, 20, 10]`**

Table 3.75: Reversing a list

- **Indexing and slicing strings**: The following are the codes for indexing and slicing the strings:

text = "Python"
# Accessing a single character 	
first_char = text[0]
print(first_char)
	Output 1:
	P

Table 3.76: Indexing and slicing strings

For more information refer to the following table:

text = "Python"
# Slicing a substring 	
substring = text[1:4]
print(substring)
	Output 2:
	yth

Table 3.77: Slicing a substring

The following is the code regarding reversing the string in Python:

text = "Python"
# Reversing the string 	
reversed_text = text[::-1]
print(reversed_text)
	Output:
	nohtyP

Table 3.78: Reversing the string

- **Multidimensional indexing (for lists of lists)**: For multidimensional lists (e.g., matrices), use multiple indices to access specific elements.

Matrix = [[1, 2, 3], [4, 5, 6], [7, 8, 9]] element = matrix[1][2] print(element)	**Output:** 6

Table 3.79: Multidimensional indexing

- **Appending and extending**:
  - **Appending**: Adding a single element to the end of a list with **append()**:

my_list = [1, 2, 3] my_list.append(4) print(my_list)	**Output:** **[1, 2, 3, 4]**

Table 3.80: Appending in list

o   **String appending**:

`words = ["hello", "world"]`
`words.append("Python")`
`print(words)`
	Output:
	`['hello', 'world', 'Python']`

Table 3.81: String appending

o   **Extending**: Adding multiple elements to the end of a list with **extend()**. The **extend()** method allows you to add each element of another iterable (e.g., list, tuple) to the end of the list:

`My_list = [1, 2, 3]`
`my_list.extend([4, 5, 6])`
`print(my_list)`
	Output:
	`[1, 2, 3, 4, 5, 6]`

Table 3.82: Extending a list

▪   Extending by a tuple:

`fruits = ["apple", "banana"]`
`fruits.extend(("cherry", "date"))`
`# You can extend with a tuple`
`print(fruits)`
	Output:
	`['apple', 'banana', 'cherry', 'date']`

Table 3.83: Extending by a tuple

- **Key differences between append() and extend()**:

  o   **append()** adds its argument as a single element to the end of the list, resulting in a nested structure if you append another list:

`my_list = [1, 2, 3]`
`my_list.append([4, 5])`
`print(my_list)`
	Output:
	`[1, 2, 3, [4, 5]]`

Table 3.84: append()

  o   **extend()** iterates over its argument and adds each element individually to the list, which means it is flat and not nested:

`my_list = [1, 2, 3]`
`my_list.extend([4, 5])`
`print(my_list)`
	Output:
	`[1, 2, 3, 4, 5]`

Table 3.85: extend()

- **Removing elements**: **remove()**, **pop()**, and **del**

  o   **remove()**: Removes the first occurrence of a specified value from the list. **remove()** searches for the first matching element in the list and removes it. If the element is not found, it raises a **ValueError**:

```My_list = [10, 20, 30, 20, 40]```
```my_list.remove(20)```
```# Removes the first occurrence of 20```
```print(my_list)```
	Output:
	```[10, 30, 20, 40]```

Table 3.86: remove()

o **pop()**: Removes an element at a specific index and returns it. **pop( )** is commonly used to remove an item at a given index. If no index is specified, it removes the last element by default. It also returns the removed element, allowing you to use or store it:

```my_list = [10, 20, 30, 40, 50]```
```last_element = my_list.pop()```
```# It will remove last element```
```print(last_element)```
```print(my_list)```
	Output:
	```50```
	```[10, 20, 30, 40]```

Table 3.87: pop()

Following is the code about removal of element at index 1 in a list:

```specific_element = my_list.pop(1)```
```# It will remove element at index 1```
```print(specific_element)```
```print(my_list)```
	Output:
	```20```
	```[10, 30, 40]```

Table 3.88: Removal of element at index 1

o **del**: Removes an element or a slice of elements from a list.

The **del** statement is a more general-purpose way to delete an element at a specific index or a slice of elements. Unlike **pop( )**, it does not return the removed element.

```My_list = [10, 20, 30, 40, 50]```
```del my_list[1]```
```# It will delete element at index 1```
```print(my_list)```
	Output:
	```[10, 30, 40, 50]```

Table 3.89: del statement

Deleting a slice of elements in list is provided via the following code:

```# Deleting a slice of elements```
```del my_list[1:3]```
```# It will delete elements from index 1```
```up to, but not including, index 3```
```print(my_list)```
	Output:
	```[10, 50]```

Table 3.90: Deleting a slice of elements

- **Key points**:
  - o **remove()**: Use to remove the first occurrence of a specific value.
  - o **pop()**: Use to remove an element at a specific index and get that element.
  - o **del**: Use for deleting an element or a slice without returning anything.
- **Sorting and reversing**: **sort()**, **sorted()**, and **reverse()**:
  - o **sort()**: Sorts a list in place (modifies the original list).

    sort() sorts the elements of the list in ascending order by default. You can also specify **reverse=True** to sort in descending order. This method modifies the original list and does not return a new list.

    Sorting in ascending order is mentioned via the following code:

`my_list = [5, 2, 9, 1, 7]`
`my_list.sort()`
`# It will sort in ascending order`
`print(my_list)`
	Output:
	`[1, 2, 5, 7, 9]`

Table 3.91: Sorting in ascending order

Sorting in descending order is mentioned via the following code:

`my_list.sort(reverse=True)`
`# It will sort in descending order`
`print(my_list)`
	Output:
	`[9, 7, 5, 2, 1]`

Table 3.92: Sorting in descending order

  - o **sorted()**: Returns a new sorted list, leaving the original list unchanged. **sorted()** creates a new sorted list from the original list and does not modify the original list. It also accepts **reverse=True** to sort in descending order.

    The sorted list code in Python is as follows:

`my_list = [5, 2, 9, 1, 7]`
`sorted_list = sorted(my_list)`
`# It will sort in ascending order`
`print(sorted_list)`
`print(my_list)`
	Output:
	`[1, 2, 5, 7, 9]`
	`[5, 2, 9, 1, 7]`

Table 3.93: Sorted list

Sorting in descending order of code in Python is noted as follows:

`my_list = [5, 2, 9, 1, 7]`
`# It will sort in descending order`
`sorted_descending = sorted(my_list, reverse=True)`
`print(sorted_descending)`
	Output:
	`[9, 7, 5, 2, 1]`

Table 3.94: Sorting in descending order

o **reverse()**: Reverses the order of elements in place. **reverse()** reverses the elements of the list in place (modifies the original list) and does not sort them. It does not return a new list:

`my_list = [5, 2, 9, 1, 7]`
`my_list.reverse()`
`# Reverses the order of elements`
`print(my_list)`
	Output:
	
	`[7, 1, 9, 2, 5]`

Table 3.95: Reverses the order of elements

- Key points:

  o **sort()**: It is used to sort a list in place (modifies the original list).

  o **sorted()**: It is used to create a new sorted list without modifying original list.

  o **reverse()**: It is used to reverse the order of elements in place without sorting.

3.2.4 Basic built-in functions in Python

Python gives various built-in functions to handle data types and perform common tasks:

- **len()**: Returns the length of an object. **len()** gives number of items in an object, such as; list, string, or tuple:

`my_list = [1, 2, 3, 4, 5]`
`list_length = len(my_list)`
`print(list_length)`
	Output:
	
	`5`

Table 3.96: len() of list

The code for the length of a string in Python is as follows:

`my_string = "Hello, world!"`
`string_length = len(my_string)`
`print(string_length)`
	Output:
	
	`13`

Table 3.97: len() of string

- **type()**: It checks the type of a variable. **type()** provides the data type of a variable, which is helpful to understand or to debug code:

`number = 42`
`print(type(number))`
 	
`text = "Python"`
`print(type(text))`
 	
`items = [1, 2, 3]`
`print(type(items))`
	Output:
	
	`<class 'int'>`
	
	`<class 'str'>`
	
	`<class 'list'>`

Table 3.98: type()

- **print()**: Outputs data to the screen. **print()** is used to display data to console, which is essential to check results or to debug code:

name = "Alice" age = 30 print("Name:", name, "Age:", age)	**Output:** Name: Alice Age: 30

Table 3.99: print()

The use of **print()** is described as follows with an example:

name = "Alice"
age = 30
# Using formatted strings (f-strings) 	
print(f"{name} is {age} years old.")
	Output:
	Alice is 30 years old.

Table 3.100: print()

- **sum()**: Returns the sum of a list of numbers. **sum()** calculates the total of all numbers in an iterable, such as a list or tuple:

numbers = [10, 20, 30, 40] total = sum(numbers) print(total)	**Output:** **100**

Table 3.101: sum() in list

Sum with a starting value code is mentioned as follows:

numbers = [10, 20, 30, 40]
# Sum with a starting value 	
total_with_start = sum(numbers, 10)
print(total_with_start)
	Output:
	110

Table 3.102: Sum with a starting value

- **Key points**
  - **len()**: Determines the number of elements in an object.
  - **type()**: Checks the type of a variable.
  - **print()**: Displays data to the console.
  - **sum()**: Adds up all elements in a numeric iterable.

3.3 Comparison of examples via MATLAB and Python

In this section, some examples are discussed that explain the comparative approach in MATLAB and Python. This comparison will give readers a full insight into the languages MATLAB and Python:

- **Example 3.1**: Perform addition, subtraction, multiplication, division, exponentiation, and modulus on two numbers:

MATLAB	Python

``% Defining variables
a = 12;
b = 5;
 	
% Arithmetic operations
addition = a + b;
subtraction = a - b;
multiplication = a * b;
division = a / b;
exponentiation = a ^ b;
modulus = mod(a, b);
 	
% Display of results
disp(['Addition: ',
num2str(addition)]);
disp(['Subtraction: ',
num2str(subtraction)]);
disp(['Multiplication: ',
num2str(multiplication)]);
disp(['Division: ',
num2str(division)]);
disp(['Exponentiation: ',
num2str(exponentiation)]);
disp(['Modulus: ',
num2str(modulus)]);```
	``# Defining variables
	a = 12
	b = 5
	
	# Arithmetic operations
	addition = a + b
	subtraction = a - b
	multiplication = a * b
	division = a / b
	exponentiation = a ** b
	modulus = a % b
	
	# Display of results
	print("Addition:", addition)
	print("Subtraction:", subtraction)
	print("Multiplication:",
	multiplication)
	print("Division:", division)
	print("Exponentiation:",
	exponentiation)
	print("Modulus:", modulus)```

MATLAB output: Addition: 17 Subtraction: 7 Multiplication: 60 Division: 2.4 Exponentiation: 248832 Modulus: 2	**Python output:** Addition: 17 Subtraction: 7 Multiplication: 60 Division: 2.4 Exponentiation: 248832 Modulus: 2

Table 3.103: Example 3.1 coding

- **Example 3.2**: Define two matrices, perform addition, subtraction, element-wise multiplication, and matrix multiplication:

MATLAB	Python
``% Defining matrices
A = [1 2; 3 4];
B = [5 6; 7 8];

% Matrix operations
matrix_addition = A + B;
matrix_subtraction = A - B;
elementwise_multiplication = A .* B;
matrix_multiplication = A * B;

% Display of results
disp('Matrix Addition:');
disp(matrix_addition);
disp('Matrix Subtraction:');
disp(matrix_subtraction);
disp('Element-wise Multiplication:');
disp(elementwise_multiplication);
disp('Matrix Multiplication:');
disp(matrix_multiplication);``` | ```import numpy as np

# Defining matrices
A = np.array([[1, 2], [3, 4]])
B = np.array([[5, 6], [7, 8]])

# Matrix operations
matrix_addition = A + B
matrix_subtraction = A - B
elementwise_multiplication = A * B
matrix_multiplication = A @ B

# Display of results
print("Matrix Addition:\n", matrix_addition)
print("Matrix Subtraction:\n", matrix_subtraction)
print("Element-wise Multiplication:\n", elementwise_multiplication)
print("Matrix Multiplication:\n", matrix_multiplication)``` |
| **MATLAB output:**
```Matrix Addition:
     6   8
    10   12

Matrix Subtraction:
    -4   -4
    -4   -4

Element-wise Multiplication:
     5   12
    21   32

Matrix Multiplication:
    19   22
    43   50``` | **Python output:**
```Matrix Addition:
 [[6 8]
 [10 12]]
Matrix Subtraction:
 [[-4 -4]
 [-4 -4]]
Element-wise Multiplication:
 [[5 12]
 [21 32]]
Matrix Multiplication:
 [[19 22]
 [43 50]]``` |

Table 3.104: Example 3.2 coding

- **Example 3.3**: Check if a variable a is equal to, not equal to, greater than, or less than or equal to another variable b:

MATLAB	Python
``% Defining variables
a = 7;
b = 3;

% Logical operations
isEqual = (a == b);
isNotEqual = (a ~= b);
isGreaterThan = (a > b);
isLessThanOrEqual = (a <= b);

% Display of results
disp(['Is Equal: ',
num2str(isEqual)]);
disp(['Is Not Equal: ',
num2str(isNotEqual)]);
disp(['Is Greater Than: ',
num2str(isGreaterThan)]);
disp(['Is Less Than or Equal: ',
num2str(isLessThanOrEqual)]);``` | ```# Defining variables
a = 7
b = 3

# Logical operations
is_equal = (a == b)
is_not_equal = (a != b)
is_greater_than = (a > b)
is_less_than_or_equal = (a <= b)

# Display of results
print("Is Equal:", is_equal)
print("Is Not Equal:", is_not_equal)
print("Is Greater Than:", is_greater_than)
print("Is Less Than or Equal:", is_less_than_or_equal)``` |
| **MATLAB output:**
`Is Equal: 0`
`Is Not Equal: 1`
`Is Greater Than: 1`
`Is Less Than or Equal: 0` | **Python output:**
`Is Equal: False`
`Is Not Equal: True`
`Is Greater Than: True`
`Is Less Than or Equal: False` |

Table 3.105: Example 3.3 coding

- **Example 3.4**: Write a function in both MATLAB and Python that takes a list or array of integers and returns the sum of even numbers and the sum of odd numbers separately:

MATLAB	Python
``function [evenSum, oddSum] = sum_even_odd(numbers)
% Sum even and odd numbers
evenSum = sum(numbers(mod(numbers, 2) == 0));
oddSum = sum(numbers(mod(numbers, 2) ~= 0));
end```	```def sum_even_odd(numbers):
# Sum even and odd numbers
even_sum = sum(num for num in numbers if num % 2 == 0)
odd_sum = sum(num for num in numbers if num % 2 != 0)
return even_sum, odd_sum```

Table 3.106: Example 3.4 coding

- **Example 3.5**: Write a function that removes duplicates from a list or array and returns the unique elements. Implement this in both MATLAB and Python:

MATLAB	Python

``
function unique_elements = remove_
duplicates(array)
    % Remove duplicates
    unique_elements = unique(array);
end
``
	``
	def remove_duplicates(lst):
	    # Remove duplicates
	    return list(set(lst))
	``

Table 3.107: Example 3.5 coding

- **Example 3.6**: Write a function to find and return the maximum and minimum values in a list or array. Implement this in both MATLAB and Python:

MATLAB	Python

``
function [maxValue, minValue] =
find_max_min(array)
    % Find maximum and minimum
values
    maxValue = max(array);
    minValue = min(array);
end
``
	``
	def find_max_min(lst):
	    # Find maximum and minimum values
	    max_value = max(lst)
	    min_value = min(lst)
	    return max_value, min_value
	``

Table 3.108: Example 3.6 coding

- **Example 3.7**: Write a function that takes a list or array of numbers and returns a new list where each number is squared. Implement this in both MATLAB and Python:

MATLAB	Python

``
function squaredArray = square_
elements(array)
    % Square each element in the array
    squaredArray = array .^ 2;
end
``
	``
	def square_elements(lst):
	    # Square each element in the
	list
	    return [x ** 2 for x in lst]
	``

Table 3.109: Example 3.7 coding

- **Example 3.8**: Write a function to calculate the factorial of a given number. Implement this in both MATLAB and Python using loops rather than recursion for simplicity:

MATLAB	Python

``
function result = factorial_loop(n)
    result = 1;
    for I = 1:n
        result = result * i;
    end
end
``
	``
	def factorial_loop(n):
	    result = 1
	    for i in range(1, n + 1):
	        result *= i
	    return result
	``

Table 3.110: Example 3.8 coding

- **Example 3.9**: Write a function that takes a list or array of numbers and returns the mean and standard deviation:

MATLAB	Python
```matlab function [meanValue, stdDev] = mean_ std(numbers) % mean and standard deviation meanValue = mean(numbers); stdDev = std(numbers); end ```	```python import math def mean_std(numbers): # mean mean_value = sum(numbers) / len(numbers) # standard deviation variance = sum((x-- mean_value) ** 2 for x in numbers) / len(numbers) std_dev = math.sqrt(variance) return mean_value, std_dev ```

Table 3.111: Example 3.9 coding

- **Example 3.10**: Write a function that calculates the **greatest common divisor (GCD)** of two numbers using the Euclidean algorithm:

MATLAB	Python
```matlab function gcdResult = calculate_gcd(a, b) % Euclidean algorithm for GCD while b ~= 0 temp = b; b = mod(a, b); a = temp; end gcdResult = a; end ```	```python def calculate_gcd(a, b): # Euclidean algorithm for GCD while b != 0: a, b = b, a % b return a ```

Table 3.112: Example 3.10 coding

- **Example 3.11**: Write a function that takes the coefficients of a quadratic equation and returns its roots:

MATLAB	Python

``matlab
function rootsResult = solve_quadratic(a, b, c)
    % discriminant
    discriminant = b^2-- 4 * a * c;
 	
    if discriminant > 0
        % Two real roots
        rootsResult = [(-b + sqrt(discriminant)) / (2 * a), (-b-- sqrt(discriminant)) / (2 * a)];
    elseif discriminant == 0
        % One real root
        rootsResult = -b / (2 * a);
    else
        % Complex roots
        rootsResult = [(-b + sqrt(-discriminant) * 1i) / (2 * a), (-b-- sqrt(-discriminant) * 1i) / (2 * a)];
    end
end
``
	``python
	import cmath
	
	def solve_quadratic(a, b, c):
	    # discriminant
	    discriminant = b**2-- 4 * a * c
	
	    if discriminant > 0:
	        # Two real roots
	        root1 = (-b + discriminant**0.5) / (2 * a)
	        root2 = (-b-- discriminant**0.5) / (2 * a)
	        return root1, root2
	    elif discriminant == 0:
	        # One real root
	        root = -b / (2 * a)
	        return root,
	    else:
	        # Complex roots
	        root1 = (-b + cmath.sqrt(discriminant)) / (2 * a)
	        root2 = (-b-- cmath.sqrt(discriminant)) / (2 * a)
	        return root1, root2
	``

Table 3.113: Example 3.11 coding

- **Example 3.12**: Menu-driven calculator based on the user's operation choice in MATLAB and Python.

Note: **MATLAB uses the switch-case statement to handle multiple conditions in a structured and readable way. Python introduced a similar construct called match-case in Python 3.10, enabling pattern-matching capabilities akin to switch in other languages. Unlike traditional switch statements, Python's match-case supports structural pattern matching, allowing for more powerful and expressive conditions. When working across both languages, recognizing these syntactic and functional parallels can improve code readability and portability.**

MATLAB	Python
MATLAB Example – Using switch-case	Python Example – Using match-case (Python 3.10+)

<table>
<tr>
<td>

```matlab
operation = 'Add';
a = 10;
b = 5;

switch operation
    case 'Add'
        result = a + b;
        disp(['Result: ',
num2str(result)]);
    case 'Subtract'
        result = a - b;
        disp(['Result: ',
num2str(result)]);
    case 'Multiply'
        result = a * b;
        disp(['Result: ',
num2str(result)]);
    case 'Divide'
        if b ~= 0
            result = a / b;
            disp(['Result: ',
num2str(result)]);
        else
            disp('Error: Division by
zero');
        end
    otherwise
        disp('Invalid operation');
end
```

</td>
<td>

```python
operation = 'Add'
a = 10
b = 5

match operation:
    case 'Add':
        result = a + b
        print(f"Result: {result}")
    case 'Subtract':
        result = a - b
        print(f"Result: {result}")
    case 'Multiply':
        result = a * b
        print(f"Result: {result}")
    case 'Divide':
        if b != 0:
            result = a / b
            print(f"Result: {result}")
        else:
            print("Error: Division by zero")
    case _:
        print("Invalid operation")
```

</td>
</tr>
</table>

Table 3.114: Example 3.12 coding

- **Example 3.13:** User roles determine what access level a user has: **'admin'**, **'editor'**, **'viewer'** in MATLAB and Python:

MATLAB	Python
MATLAB Example – Using switch-case	Python Example – Using match-case (Python 3.10+)
| ```matlab
role = 'editor';

switch role
    case 'admin'
        disp('Access granted: Full control');
    case 'editor'
        disp('Access granted: Can edit
content');
    case 'viewer'
        disp('Access granted: Read-only');
    otherwise
        disp('Access denied: Unknown role');
end
``` | ```python
role = 'editor'

match role:
    case 'admin':
        print("Access granted: Full
control")
    case 'editor':
        print("Access granted: Can edit
content")
    case 'viewer':
        print("Access granted: Read-only")
    case _:
        print("Access denied: Unknown
role")
``` |

Table 3.115: Example 3.13 coding

Conclusion

This chapter provided a comprehensive exploration of the core functionalities of MATLAB and Python, two powerful programming languages widely used in computational tasks. In MATLAB, the focus was on arithmetic operations, matrix manipulations, and logical operations, highlighting its strength in numerical computing and data analysis. Python, on the other hand, demonstrated its versatility through arithmetic operations, string manipulation, list operations, and basic built-in functions, showcasing its adaptability for general-purpose programming and data handling. By understanding these fundamental concepts, readers gain a solid foundation to tackle a wide range of computational problems, from mathematical modeling to text processing and beyond. The comparison of examples in MATLAB and Python further emphasized the unique strengths of each language, enabling users to choose the right tool for their specific needs. With practice exercises included, this chapter aims to reinforce learning and equip readers with the skills to apply these concepts effectively in real-world scenarios.

In the next chapter, readers will understand the concept of control flow and structures in MATLAB and Python.

Exercises

1. Write a program that prompts the user for their name and then displays a personalized greeting message.

   Hint:

   - **Input**: Enter your name: AMPRA

   - **Output**: Dear AMPRA welcome to the word of programming!

2. Develop a program that calculates the area of a cylinder given the radius of the base and length as input from the user. The formula for the area of a cylinder is $\pi r^2 h$.

3. Create a program that calculates the sum of integers from 1 to n, where n is a positive integer provided by the user. Employ the formula sum $= \frac{n(n+1)}{2}$ for the calculation.

4. A bakery sells two types of cookies: chocolate chip (weighing 25 grams each) and oatmeal raisin (weighing 35 grams each). Write a program that takes the number of each type of cookie ordered as input and calculates the total weight of the cookie order.

5. Write a program to convert measurements from feet and inches to centimeters. The program should take the number of feet and inches as separate inputs from the user and perform the conversion (1 foot = 12 inches, 1 inch = 2.54 centimeters).

6. Create a program that takes two integers, a and b, as input and performs the following operations, displaying the result of each: the sum of a and b, the difference when b is subtracted from a, the product of a and b, the quotient when a is divided by b, the remainder when a is divided by b, and the base-10 logarithm of a.

7. Write a program that takes three integers as input from the user and displays them in sorted order from smallest to largest. Use the min and max functions to identify the smallest and largest values and calculate the middle value accordingly.

8. Create two vectors of length 10. The first vector should contain the first six multiples of three, and the second vector should contain six terms of an arithmetic progression with a first term of 2 and a common difference of 3.

   Perform and display the results of the following operations:

   Element-wise addition, element-wise subtraction (second vector from the first), element-wise multiplication, element-wise division (first vector by the second), and raising each element of the first vector to the second power.

9. Consider a vector $C = [13, 26, 28, 15, 12]$ representing marks in different subjects. Calculate and display a new vector D containing the modified marks after applying the following transformations: adding two marks to each value, doubling the second subject's marks, halving the fourth subject's marks, and then calculating the difference between the original marks (C) and the updated marks (D).

10. Given the matrix $C = [1\ 3\ 4;\ 5\ 6\ 7;\ 5\ 0\ 9]$, write code to extract and display: the element in the first row and second column, the elements of the third row in the first and second columns, the element accessed by $C(6)$ (explain the indexing), all elements of the second row, and the elements in the second and third rows of the first and second columns.

11. Using linspace, create a vector x containing the first ten multiples of three. Then, create three new vectors derived from $x: r$ (containing the first 5 elements of x), s (containing elements of with indices from 5 to 7 inclusive), and t (containing elements of x with even indices). Display the vectors r, s, and t.

12. Construct the following matrix A using a single command (avoiding explicit element-by-element entry):

    $A =$

    0 0 0 0 0

    0 0 1 10 20

    0 0 2 8 26

    0 0 3 6 32

13. Given the vector $X = [8, 10, 2, 5, 4, 6, 17, 32]$, perform and display the following:

    a. Create a vector Y containing the elements of X in reverse order.

    b. Find the indices of elements in X that are greater than 2.

    c. Create a vector Z containing elements of X that are smaller than 4.

14. Generate the following matrices using concise commands: a 4×4 matrix of ones, a 4×1 matrix of zeros, and a 3×2 matrix where all elements are equal to 0.78.

15. Write a program that takes an integer n as input and generates an $n \times n$ diagonal matrix. The diagonal elements should be the squares of the integers from 1 to n, and all other elements should be zero. Display the resulting matrix.

16. Generate two 3×3 matrices with random integers between 1 and 10 (inclusive). Calculate and display the element-wise sum of these matrices, as well as the sum of all elements within each individual matrix.

17. Write a program that takes two matrices as input (assuming they are compatible for multiplication). Perform matrix multiplication and display the resulting product matrix. Include error handling to ensure the matrices are compatible for multiplication.

18. Create a 4×4 matrix populated with random floating-point numbers between 0 and 1. Calculate and display the average of each row and the average of each column of this matrix.

19. Write a program that takes a square matrix as input. Calculate and display both the transpose of the matrix and its trace (the sum of its diagonal elements).

20. Write a program that takes a matrix (of any size) and a scalar value as input. Multiply each element of the matrix by the scalar value and display the resulting scaled matrix.

Join our Discord space

Join our Discord workspace for latest updates, offers, tech happenings around the world, new releases, and sessions with the authors:

https://discord.bpbonline.com

CHAPTER 4
Control Flow and Structures in MATLAB and Python

Introduction

In this chapter, we will explore the basic concepts of control flow and structures in MATLAB and Python, two widely used programming languages in scientific computing, data analysis, and engineering. Control flow refers to the order in which individual statements, instructions, or function calls are executed or evaluated within a program. By mastering control flow, you will be able to create more efficient programs that can make decisions and repeat tasks based on specific conditions.

The chapter is divided into three main sections, the first two focusing on MATLAB and Python languages, respectively, and the third one is related to their common examples. In the MATLAB section, you will learn about conditional statements and loops.

In the Python section, you will explore similar concepts but with some syntactic differences. Python uses conditional statements like if, elseif, and else to implement decision-making logic. Additionally, Python's loops, such as; for and while, allow you to iterate over sequences like lists, tuples, and dictionaries, or to repeat code until a condition becomes false. Python's flexibility and readability make it a powerful tool for implementing control flow in a wide range of applications.

By the end of this chapter, you will have a solid understanding of how to use conditional statements and loops in MATLAB and Python. You will be able to write programs that can make decisions, handle repetitive tasks, and process data efficiently. Whether you are analyzing data, developing algorithms, or automating workflows, these skills will be invaluable in your programming journey.

Structure

In this chapter, we will learn the following topics:

- 4.1 Control flow in MATLAB
- 4.2 Control flow in Python
- 4.3 Common examples in MATLAB and Python

Objectives

In this chapter, you will gain practical skills in implementing control flow structures in both MATLAB and Python, enabling you to write efficient and dynamic programs. For MATLAB, you will learn how to use conditional statements (if, elseif, else) to execute code based on logical conditions and how to employ loops (for, while) to iterate over arrays or repeat tasks until a condition is met. In Python, you will master conditional statements (if, elif, else) for decision-making and explore loops (for, while) to iterate over sequences like lists or perform repetitive tasks until a condition becomes false. By the end of this chapter, you will be equipped to handle data processing, automate workflows, and implement logical decision-making in these languages, enhancing your ability to solve real-world programming challenges.

4.1. Control flow in MATLAB

Control flow in MATLAB refers to the order in which statements and commands are executed within a program. It allows you to control the execution of code based on specific conditions or to repeat tasks efficiently. MATLAB provides several constructs for implementing control flow, including **conditional statements** and **loops**. Conditional statements, such as if, elseif, and else, enable you to execute different blocks of code depending on whether certain logical conditions are true or false. For example, you can use an if statement to check if a variable meets a specific criterion and then perform calculations or display results accordingly. Loops, such as for and while, allow you to repeat a block of code multiple times. A for loop is typically used to iterate over a range of values or elements in an array, while a while loop continues executing as long as a specified condition remains true. These control flow structures are essential for tasks like data analysis, algorithm implementation, and automation, making MATLAB a powerful tool for scientific and engineering applications. By mastering control flow in MATLAB, you can write more efficient and flexible programs.

4.1.1 Conditional statements in MATLAB

MATLAB provides the if, elseif, and else constructs for the execution of code based on logical conditions. Such statements allow for branching execution paths depending on the evaluation of logical expressions.

Conditional statements in MATLAB are fundamental for implementing decision-making logic in your programs. The if statement evaluates a logical expression and executes a block of code only if the condition is true. The elseif statement allows you to check additional conditions if the initial if condition is false, providing multiple branching paths. The else statement serves as a catch-all, executing a block of code when none of the preceding conditions are met. These constructs are particularly useful for handling complex logic, such as categorizing data, validating inputs, or controlling program behavior based on dynamic conditions. By combining if, elseif, and else, you can create robust and flexible programs that adapt to varying scenarios.

Syntax:

```
if condition
    % It will be executed if condition is true
elseif another_condition
    % It will be executed if second condition is true
else
    % It will be executed if none of above conditions are true
end
```

Let us look at an example:

Example 4.1: Check if a number is positive, negative, or zero:

```
number = input('Enter a number: ');
if number > 0
    fprintf('The number is positive.\n');
```

```
elseif number < 0
    fprintf('The number is negative.\n');
else
    fprintf('The number is zero.\n');
end
```

Let us look at the outputs:

- **Output 1**:
  ```
  Enter a number: 5
  The number is positive.
  ```

- **Output 2**:
  ```
  Enter a number: -1
  The number is negative.
  ```

- **Output 3**:
  ```
  Enter a number: 0
  The number is zero.
  ```

Explanation: The if block is evaluated first. If the condition is true, the corresponding block of code is executed. If the condition is false, MATLAB moves to elseif block, and finally to the else block if all other conditions are false. This structure ensures that only one block is executed.

4.1.2 Loops in MATLAB

Loops are used to execute a block of code multiple times. MATLAB supports for loops for iterating over arrays and while loops for condition-based iteration.

For loop

A **for** loop iterates over a sequence of values, often specified by a range or an array. In MATLAB, the for loop is a control flow structure used to repeatedly execute a block of code for a specified number of iterations. It is particularly useful when you need to perform operations on each element of an array, iterate over a sequence of values, or repeat a task a fixed number of times. The loop begins with the keyword for, followed by a loop variable that takes on values from a defined range or array, and ends with the **end** keyword. For example, **for i = 1:10** will execute the loop 10 times, with the variable **i** taking values from **1** to **10**. Inside the loop, you can perform calculations, manipulate data, or call functions using the loop variable. The for loop is highly efficient for tasks like matrix operations, numerical computations, and data processing, making it a cornerstone of MATLAB programming for handling repetitive tasks systematically.

Syntax:

```
for variable = start:increment:end
    % Code to execute
end
```

Example 4.2: Sum of the first 10 natural numbers:

```
sum = 0;
for i = 1:10
    sum = sum + i;
end
fprintf('The sum of the first 10 natural numbers is %d.\n', sum);
```

The output is as follows:

```
The sum of the first 10 natural numbers is 55.
```

Explanation: The loop runs from 1 to 10, incrementing the variable i by 1 in each iteration. The sum is accumulated in the variable sum.

While Loop

A while loop continues execution as long as a specified condition is true.

Syntax:

```
while condition
    % Code to execute
end
```

Example 4.3: Factorial of a number:

```
number = input('Enter a number: ');
factorial = 1;
i = 1;
while i <= number
    factorial = factorial * i;
    i = i + 1;
end
fprintf('The factorial of %d is %d.\n', number, factorial);
```

Output:

```
Enter a number: 5
The factorial of 5 is 120.
```

Explanation: The loop starts with **i = 1** and continues until **i** exceeds the input number. The factorial is calculated by multiplying the factorial by i in each iteration.

4.2. Control flow in Python

Control flow in Python refers to the order in which statements and instructions are executed within a program, allowing you to dictate how your code behaves under different conditions or how it repeats certain tasks. Python provides a variety of constructs to manage control flow, including conditional statements and loops. Conditional statements, such as **if**, **elseif**, and **else**, enable you to execute specific blocks of code based on the evaluation of logical conditions. For instance, you can use an if statement to check whether a variable meets a certain criterion and then perform actions accordingly. Loops, such as for and while, allow you to repeat a block of code multiple times. A for loop is typically used to iterate over sequences like lists, tuples, or strings, while a while loop continues executing as long as a specified condition remains true. These control flow structures are essential for tasks like data processing, algorithm implementation, and automation.

4.2.1 Conditional statements in Python

Python provides the **if**, **elif**, and **else** constructs for conditional execution. These statements allow for flexible decision-making in the code.

Syntax:

```
if condition:
    # Code to execute if condition is true
```

```
elif another_condition:
    # Code to execute if the second condition is true
else:
    # Code to execute if none of the above conditions are true
```

Example 4.4: Check if a number is positive, negative, or zero:

```
number = float(input('Enter a number: '))
if number > 0:
    print('The number is positive.')
elif number < 0:
    print('The number is negative.')
else:
    print('The number is zero.')
```

Let us look at the outputs:

- **Output 1**:
  ```
  Enter a number: 5
  The number is positive.
  ```

- **Output 2**:
  ```
  Enter a number: -1
  The number is negative.
  ```

- **Output 3**:
  ```
  Enter a number: 0
  The number is zero.
  ```

Explanation: The structure is similar to MATLAB's if-elseif-else, but Python uses elif instead of elseif and requires colons (:) after each condition.

4.2.2 Loops in Python

Loops are used to execute a block of code repeatedly. Python supports for loops for iterating over sequences and while loops for condition-based iteration.

Loops in Python are powerful tools for automating repetitive tasks and processing collections of data. The for loop is commonly used to iterate over sequences such as lists, tuples, strings, or ranges, allowing you to perform operations on each element. On the other hand, the while loop repeatedly executes a block of code as long as a specified condition remains true, making it ideal for scenarios where the number of iterations is not known in advance. Both types of loops can be controlled using statements like break to exit the loop prematurely or continue to skip the current iteration and move to the next. By leveraging loops, you can write concise and efficient code to handle tasks like data manipulation, mathematical computations, and iterative algorithms.

For loop

A for loop iterates over items in a sequence, such as a list, tuple, or range.

Syntax:

```
for variable in sequence:
    # Code to execute
```

Example 4.5: Sum of first 10 natural numbers:

	Output:
```python sum = 0 for i in range(1, 11): sum += i print(f'The sum of the first 10 natural numbers is {sum}.') ```	The sum of the first 10 natural numbers is 55.

Table 4.1: Example for loop in Python

Explanation: The range function generates a sequence of numbers from 1 to 10. The loop iterates over this range, adding each value to the sum variable.

While Loop

A while loop continues execution as long as the specified condition evaluates to true.

Syntax:

```python
while condition:
    # Code to execute
```

Example 4.6: Factorial of a number:

	Output:
```python number = int(input('Enter a number: ')) factorial = 1 while number > 0: factorial *= number number -= 1 print(f'The factorial is {factorial}.') ```	Enter a number: 5 The factorial is 120.

Table 4.2: Example while loop in Python

Explanation: The loop continues until the number becomes zero. In each iteration, the value of the number is multiplied by the factorial, and the number is decremented.

4.3. Common examples in MATLAB and Python

Example 4.7: Check if a number is even or odd:

MATLAB:	Python:
```matlab number = input('Enter a number: '); if mod(number, 2) == 0 fprintf('The number is even.\n'); else fprintf('The number is odd.\n'); end ```	```python number = int(input('Enter a number: ')) if number % 2 == 0: print('The number is even.') else: print('The number is odd.') ```
MATLAB output:	**Python output:**
Enter a number: -2 The number is even.	Enter a number: -2 The number is even.

Table 4.3: Codes for checking whether a number is even or odd

Example 4.8: Fibonacci sequence:

MATLAB:	Python:

``
n = input('Enter the number of terms: ');
fib = zeros(1, n);
fib(1) = 0;
fib(2) = 1;
for i = 3:n
    fib(i) = fib(i-1) + fib(i-2);
end
fprintf('Fibonacci sequence: ');
disp(fib);
``
	``
	n = int(input('Enter the number of terms: '))
	fib = [0, 1]
	for i in range(2, n):
	    fib.append(fib[i-1] + fib[i-2])
	print('Fibonacci sequence:', fib)
	``

MATLAB output: Enter the number of terms: 5 Fibonacci sequence: 0 1 1 2 3	**Python output:** Enter the number of terms: 5 Fibonacci sequence: [0, 1, 1, 2, 3]

Table 4.4: Codes for Fibonacci sequence

Example 4.9: Finding the Maximum Element in an array:

MATLAB	Python

``
arr = [3, 1, 4, 1, 5, 9, 2];
max_value = arr(1);
for i = 2:length(arr)
    if arr(i) > max_value
        max_value = arr(i);
    end
end
fprintf('The maximum value is %d.\n', max_value);
``
	``
	arr = [3, 1, 4, 1, 5, 9, 2]
	max_value = arr[0]
	for i in arr:
	    if i > max_value:
	        max_value = i
	print(f'The maximum value is {max_value}.')
	``

MATLAB output The maximum value is 9.	**Python output** The maximum value is 9.

Table 4.5: Codes for finding maximum element in an array

Example 4.10: Print the first 10 natural numbers using a loop:

MATLAB	Python

``
for i = 1:10
    disp(i)
end
``
	``
	for i in range(1, 11):
	    print(i)
	``

MATLAB output:	Python output:
1	1
2	2
3	3
4	4
5	5
6	6
7	7
8	8
9	9
10	10

Table 4.6: Codes for how to print the first 10 natural numbers

Example 4.11: Calculate the sum of the first 10 natural numbers:

MATLAB	Python
| ```matlab
sum = 0;
for i = 1:10
    sum = sum + i;
end
disp(sum);
``` | ```python
sum = 0
for i in range(1, 11):
    sum += i
print(sum)
``` |
| **MATLAB output:**
55 | **Python output:**
55 |

Table 4.7: Codes to calculate the sum of the first 10 natural numbers

Example 4.12: Find the factorial of a number:

MATLAB	Python
| ```matlab
number = input('Enter a number: ');
factorial = 1;
for i = 1:number
    factorial = factorial * i;
end
disp(factorial);
``` | ```python
number = int(input('Enter a number: '))
factorial = 1
for i in range(1, number + 1):
    factorial *= i
print(factorial)
``` |
| **MATLAB output:**
Enter a number: 5
   120 | **Python output:**
Enter a number: 5
120 |

Table 4.8: Codes to find the factorial of a number

Example 4.13: Check if a number is prime:

MATLAB	Python
| ```matlab
number = input('Enter a number: ');
is_prime = true;
for i = 2:sqrt(number)
    if mod(number, i) == 0
        is_prime = false;
        break;
    end
end
if is_prime
    disp('Prime');
else
    disp('Not Prime');
end
``` | ```python
number = int(input('Enter a number: '))
is_prime = True
for i in range(2, int(number**0.5) + 1):
    if number % i == 0:
        is_prime = False
        break
if is_prime:
    print('Prime')
else:
    print('Not Prime')
``` |
| **MATLAB output:**
`Enter a number: 11`
`Prime` | **Python output:**
`Enter a number: 11`
`Prime` |

Table 4.9: Codes to check if a number is prime

Example 4.14: Print a multiplication table for a given number:

MATLAB	Python
| ```matlab
number = input('Enter a number: ');
for i = 1:10
    fprintf('%d x %d = %d\n', number, i, number * i);
end
``` | ```python
number = int(input('Enter a number: '))
for i in range(1, 11):
    print(f'{number} x {i} = {number * i}')
``` |
| **MATLAB output:**
`Enter a number: 5`
`5 x 1 = 5`
`5 x 2 = 10`
`5 x 3 = 15`
`5 x 4 = 20`
`5 x 5 = 25`
`5 x 6 = 30`
`5 x 7 = 35`
`5 x 8 = 40`
`5 x 9 = 45`
`5 x 10 = 50` | **Python output:**
`Enter a number: 5`
`5 x 1 = 5`
`5 x 2 = 10`
`5 x 3 = 15`
`5 x 4 = 20`
`5 x 5 = 25`
`5 x 6 = 30`
`5 x 7 = 35`
`5 x 8 = 40`
`5 x 9 = 45`
`5 x 10 = 50` |

Table 4.10: Codes to print a multiplication table

Example 4.15: Find the minimum element in an array:

MATLAB	Python
```matlab\narr = [3, 1, 4, 1, 5, 9, 2];\nmin_value = arr(1);\nfor i = 2:length(arr)\n if arr(i) < min_value\n min_value = arr(i);\n end\nend\ndisp(min_value);\n```	```python\narr = [3, 1, 4, 1, 5, 9, 2]\nmin_value = arr[0]\nfor i in arr:\n if i < min_value:\n min_value = i\nprint(min_value)\n```
MATLAB output: 1	**Python output:** 1

Table 4.11: Codes to find the minimum element in an array

Example 4.16: Count the number of vowels in a string:

MATLAB	Python
```matlab\nstr = input('Enter a string: ', 's'); % Input\nstring from the user\nvowels = 'aeiouAEIOU'; % Define vowels\ncount = 0; % Initialize vowel count\n\n% Loop through each character in the input string\nfor i = 1:length(str)\n if ismember(str(i), vowels) % Check if the\ncharacter is a vowel\n count = count + 1; % Increment the vowel\ncount\n end\nend\n\ndisp(['Number of vowels: ', num2str(count)]); %\nDisplay the count\n```	```python\nstr = input('Enter a string: ')\nvowels = 'aeiouAEIOU'\ncount = 0\nfor char in str:\n if char in vowels:\n count += 1\nprint(count)\n```
MATLAB output: **Enter a string: coding** **Number of vowels: 2**	**Python output:** **Enter a string: coding** 2

Table 4.12: Codes to count the number of vowels in a string

Example 4.17: Check if a number is an Armstrong number:

MATLAB	Python
| ```
num = input('Enter a number: ');
sum = 0;
temp = num;
while temp > 0
    digit = mod(temp, 10);
    sum = sum + digit^3;
    temp = floor(temp / 10);
end
if sum == num
    disp('Armstrong Number');
else
    disp('Not an Armstrong Number');
end
``` | ```
num = int(input('Enter a number: '))
sum = 0
temp = num
while temp > 0:
    digit = temp % 10
    sum += digit**3
    temp //= 10
if sum == num:
    print('Armstrong Number')
else:
    print('Not an Armstrong Number')
``` |
| **MATLAB output**:
 `Enter a number: 153`

 `Armstrong Number` | **Python output**:
 `Enter a number: 153`

 `Armstrong Number` |

Table 4.13: Codes for checking if a number is an Armstrong number

Example 4.18: Find the sum of digits of a number:

MATLAB	Python
| ```
num = input('Enter a number: ');
sum = 0;
while num > 0
    sum = sum + mod(num, 10);
    num = floor(num / 10);
end
disp(sum);
``` | ```
num = int(input('Enter a number: '))
sum = 0
while num > 0:
    sum += num % 10
    num //= 10
print(sum)
``` |
| **MATLAB output**:
 `Enter a number: 5`

 `     5` | **Python output**:
 `Enter a number: 5`

 `5` |

Table 4.14: Codes to find the sum of digits of a number

Example 4.19: Find the sum of even numbers in an array:

MATLAB	Python

``matlab
arr = [3, 1, 4, 1, 5, 9, 2];
sum_even = 0;
for i = 1:length(arr)
    if mod(arr(i), 2) == 0
        sum_even = sum_even + arr(i);
    end
end
disp(sum_even);```
	``python
	arr = [3, 1, 4, 1, 5, 9, 2]
	sum_even = sum(i for i in arr if i % 2 == 0)
	print(sum_even) # output: 6```

MATLAB output: 6	**Python output:** 6

Table 4.15: Codes to find the sum of even numbers in an array

Example 4.20: Find the sum of odd numbers in an array:

MATLAB	Python

``matlab
arr = [3, 1, 4, 1, 5, 9, 2];
sum_odd = 0;
for i = 1:length(arr)
    if mod(arr(i), 2) ~= 0
        sum_odd = sum_odd + arr(i);
    end
end
disp(sum_odd);```
	``python
	arr = [3, 1, 4, 1, 5, 9, 2]
	sum_odd = sum(i for i in arr if i % 2 != 0)
	print(sum_odd)```

MATLAB output: 19	**Python output:** 19

Table 4.16: Codes to find the sum of odd numbers in an array

Example 4.21: Check if a string contains only alphabets:

MATLAB	Python

``matlab
str = input('Enter a string: ', 's');
if all(isletter(str))
    disp('Contains only alphabets');
else
    disp('Contains other characters');
end```
	``python
	str = input('Enter a string: ')
	if str.isalpha():
	    print('Contains only alphabets')
	else:
	    print('Contains other characters')```

MATLAB output: **Enter a string: code** **Contains only alphabets**	**Python output:** **Enter a string: code** **Contains only alphabets**

Table 4.17: Codes to check if a string contains only alphabets

Example 4.22: Print a pyramid pattern using *****:

MATLAB	Python
```n = 5;for i = 1:n fprintf('%s\n', repmat('*', 1, 2*i-1));end```	```n = 5for i in range(1, n + 1): print(' ' * (n - i) + '*' * (2 * i - 1))```
MATLAB output: * *** ***** ******* *********	**Python output:** 　* 　*** 　***** 　******* *********

Table 4.18: Codes to print a pyramid pattern using *

Example 4.23: Check if a number is perfect:

MATLAB	Python
```num = input('Enter a number: ');sum = 0;for i = 1:num-1 if mod(num, i) == 0 sum = sum + i; endendif sum == num disp('Perfect Number');else disp('Not a Perfect Number');end```	```num = int(input('Enter a number: '))sum = sum(i for i in range(1, num) if num % i == 0)if sum == num: print('Perfect Number')else: print('Not a Perfect Number')```
MATLAB output: Enter a number: 28 Perfect Number	**Python output:** Enter a number: 28 Perfect Number

Table 4.19: Codes for checking if a number is perfect

Example 4.24: Print all perfect numbers in a range:

MATLAB	Python
```for num = 1:1000 sum = 0; for i = 1:num-1 if mod(num, i) == 0 sum = sum + i; end end if sum == num disp(num); endend```	```for num in range(1, 1001): if sum(i for i in range(1, num) if num % i == 0) == num: print(num)```

MATLAB output:	Python output:
6	6
28	28
496	496

Table 4.20: Codes to print all perfect numbers in a range

Example 4.25: Print the first n prime numbers:

MATLAB	Python
| ```matlab
n = input('Enter n: ');
count = 0;
num = 2;
while count < n
    is_prime = true;
    for i = 2:sqrt(num)
        if mod(num, i) == 0
            is_prime = false;
            break;
        end
    end
    if is_prime
        disp(num);
        count = count + 1;
    end
    num = num + 1;
end
``` | ```python
n = int(input('Enter n: '))
count = 0
num = 2
while count < n:
    is_prime = True
    for i in range(2, int(num**0.5) + 1):
        if num % i == 0:
            is_prime = False
            break
    if is_prime:
        print(num)
        count += 1
    num += 1
``` |
| **MATLAB output:**
Enter n: 5
    2

    3

    5

    7

    11 | **Python output:**
Enter n: 5
2
3
5
7
11 |

Table 4.21: Codes to print the first n prime numbers

Example 4.26: Check if two strings are anagrams:

MATLAB	Python

str1 = input('Enter first string: ', 's');
 	
str2 = input('Enter second string: ', 's');
 	
if isequal(sort(str1), sort(str2))
 	
   disp('The strings are anagrams.');
 	
else
 	
   disp('The strings are not anagrams.');
 	
end
	str1 = input('Enter first string: ')
	
	str2 = input('Enter second string: ')
	
	if sorted(str1) == sorted(str2):
	
	   print('The strings are anagrams.')
	
	else:
	
	   print('The strings are not anagrams.')

MATLAB output: Enter first string: triangle Enter second string: integral The strings are anagrams.	**Python output:** Enter first string: triangle Enter second string: integral The strings are anagrams.

Table 4.22: Codes to check if two strings are anagrams

Example 4.27: Check if a year is a leap year:

MATLAB	Python

year = input('Enter a year: ');
 	
if mod(year, 4) == 0 && (mod(year, 100) ~= 0 || mod(year, 400) == 0)
 	
   disp('Leap year');
 	
else
 	
   disp('Not a leap year');
 	
end
	year = int(input('Enter a year: '))
	
	if (year % 4 == 0 and year % 100 != 0) or (year % 400 == 0):
	
	   print('Leap year')
	
	else:
	
	   print('Not a leap year')

MATLAB output: Enter a year: 2025 Not a leap year	**Python output:** Enter a year: 2025 Not a leap year

Table 4.23: Codes to check if a year is a leap year

Example 4.28: Find the roots of a quadratic equation:

MATLAB	Python
```a = input('Enter coefficient a: '); b = input('Enter coefficient b: '); c = input('Enter coefficient c: '); discriminant = b^2 - 4*a*c; if discriminant > 0 root1 = (-b + sqrt(discriminant)) / (2*a); root2 = (-b - sqrt(discriminant)) / (2*a); disp(['Roots are: ', num2str(root1), ' and ', num2str(root2)]); elseif discriminant == 0 root = -b / (2*a); disp(['Root is: ', num2str(root)]); else disp('No real roots'); end```	```import cmath a = float(input('Enter coefficient a: ')) b = float(input('Enter coefficient b: ')) c = float(input('Enter coefficient c: ')) discriminant = cmath.sqrt(b**2 - 4*a*c) root1 = (-b + discriminant) / (2*a) root2 = (-b - discriminant) / (2*a) print(f'Roots are: {root1} and {root2}')```
MATLAB output: Enter coefficient a: 1 Enter coefficient b: 2 Enter coefficient c: 1 Root is: -1	**Python output:** Enter coefficient a: 1 Enter coefficient b: 2 Enter coefficient c: 1 Roots are: (-1+0j) and (-1+0j)

Table 4.24: Codes to find the roots of a quadratic equation

Example 4.29: Check if a number is divisible by 3 and 5:

MATLAB	Python
```num = input('Enter a number: '); if mod(num, 3) == 0 && mod(num, 5) == 0 disp('The number is divisible by both 3 and 5.'); else disp('The number is not divisible by both 3 and 5.'); end```	```num = int(input('Enter a number: ')) if num % 3 == 0 and num % 5 == 0: print('The number is divisible by both 3 and 5.') else: print('The number is not divisible by both 3 and 5.')```
MATLAB output: Enter a number: 15 The number is divisible by both 3 and 5.	**Python output:** Enter a number: 15 The number is divisible by both 3 and 5.

Table 4.25: Codes to check if a number is divisible by 3 and 5

Example 4.30: Check the largest of three numbers:

MATLAB	Python

a = input('Enter first number: ');
b = input('Enter second number: ');
c = input('Enter third number: ');
if a > b && a > c
    disp(['The largest number is: ',
num2str(a)]);
elseif b > c
    disp(['The largest number is: ',
num2str(b)]);
else
    disp(['The largest number is: ',
num2str(c)]);
end
	a = float(input('Enter first number: '))
	b = float(input('Enter second number: '))
	c = float(input('Enter third number: '))
	if a > b and a > c:
	    print(f'The largest number is: {a}')
	elif b > c:
	    print(f'The largest number is: {b}')
	else:
	    print(f'The largest number is: {c}')

MATLAB output: Enter first number: 3 Enter second number: 5 Enter third number: 7 The largest number is: 7	**Python output**: Enter first number: 3 Enter second number: 5 Enter third number: 7 The largest number is: 7.0

Table 4.26: Codes to check the largest of three numbers

Example 4.31: Determine if a character is a vowel or a consonant:

MATLAB	Python

ch = input('Enter a character: ', 's');
if any(ch == 'aeiouAEIOU')
    disp('The character is a vowel.');
else
    disp('The character is a consonant.');
end
	ch = input('Enter a character: ')
	if ch in 'aeiouAEIOU':
	    print('The character is a vowel.')
	else:
	    print('The character is a
	consonant.')

MATLAB output: Enter a character: m The character is a consonant.	**Python output**: Enter a character: m The character is a consonant.

Table 4.27: Codes to determine if a character is a vowel or a consonant

Example 4.32: Check if a number lies in a specific range (e.g., 10 to 50):

MATLAB	Python

`num = input('Enter a number: ');`
`if num >= 10 && num <= 50`
`    disp('The number lies within the range 10 to 50.');`
`else`
`    disp('The number does not lie within the range.');`
`end`
	`num = float(input('Enter a number: '))`
	`if 10 <= num <= 50:`
	`    print('The number lies within the range 10 to 50.')`
	`else:`
	`    print('The number does not lie within the range.')`

MATLAB output:
 	
`Enter a number: 37`
`The number lies within the range 10 to 50.`
	Python output:
	
	`Enter a number: 37`
	`The number lies within the range 10 to 50.`

Table 4.28: Codes to check if a number lies in a specific range

Example 4.33: Check if a year is a century year (divisible by 100 but not 400):

MATLAB	Python

`year = input('Enter a year: ');`
`if mod(year, 100) == 0 && mod(year, 400) ~= 0`
`    disp('The year is a century year.');`
`else`
`    disp('The year is not a century year.');`
`end`
	`year = int(input('Enter a year: '))`
	`if year % 100 == 0 and year % 400 != 0:`
	`    print('The year is a century year.')`
	`else:`
	`    print('The year is not a century year.')`

MATLAB output:
 	
`Enter a year: 2025`
`The year is not a century year.`
	Python output:
	
	`Enter a year: 2025`
	`The year is not a century year.`

Table 4.29: Codes to check if a year is a century year

Example 4.34: Check if a number is a single-digit number:

MATLAB	Python

`num = input('Enter a number: ');`
`if abs(num) < 10`
`    disp('The number is a single-digit number.');`
`else`
`    disp('The number is not a single-digit number.');`
`end`
	`num = int(input('Enter a number: '))`
	`if abs(num) < 10:`
	`    print('The number is a single-digit number.')`
	`else:`
	`    print('The number is not a single-digit number.')`

MATLAB output:
 	
`Enter a number: 10`
`The number is not a single-digit number.`
	Python output:
	
	`Enter a number: 10`
	`The number is not a single-digit number.`

Table 4.30: Codes to check if a number is a single-digit number

Example 4.35: Determine if a string contains only uppercase letters:

MATLAB	Python

```str = input('Enter a string: ', 's');```
 ```if all(isstrprop(str, 'upper'))```
     ```disp('The string contains only uppercase letters.');```
 ```else```
     ```disp('The string contains characters other than uppercase letters.');```
 ```end```
	```str = input('Enter a string: ')```
	 ```if str.isupper():```
	     ```print('The string contains only uppercase letters.')```
	 ```else:```
	     ```print('The string contains characters other than uppercase letters.')```

MATLAB output: **Enter a string: study** **The string contains characters other than uppercase letters.**	**Python output:** **Enter a string: study** **The string contains characters other than uppercase letters.**

Table 4.31: Codes to determine if a string contains only uppercase letters

Example 4.36: Check if two numbers are equal or if one is greater than the other:

MATLAB	Python

```a = input('Enter first number: ');```
 ```b = input('Enter second number: ');```
 ```if a == b```
     ```disp('The numbers are equal.');```
 ```elseif a > b```
     ```disp('The first number is greater.');```
 ```else```
     ```disp('The second number is greater.');```
 ```end```
	```a = float(input('Enter first number: '))```
	 ```b = float(input('Enter second number: '))```
	 ```if a == b:```
	     ```print('The numbers are equal.')```
	 ```elif a > b:```
	     ```print('The first number is greater.')```
	 ```else:```
	     ```print('The second number is greater.')```

MATLAB output: **Enter first number: 7** **Enter second number: 8** **The second number is greater.**	**Python output:** **Enter first number: 7** **Enter second number: 8** **The second number is greater.**

Table 4.32: Codes to check if two numbers are equal or if one is greater than the other

Example 4.37: Determine if a triangle is valid based on its angles:

MATLAB	Python

```a = input('Enter first angle: ');```
 ```b = input('Enter second angle: ');```
 ```c = input('Enter third angle: ');```
 ```if a + b + c == 180 && a > 0 && b > 0 && c > 0```
     ```disp('The triangle is valid.');```
 ```else```
     ```disp('The triangle is not valid.');```
 ```end```
	```a = float(input('Enter first angle: '))```
	 ```b = float(input('Enter second angle: '))```
	 ```c = float(input('Enter third angle: '))```
	 ```if a + b + c == 180 and a > 0 and b > 0 and c > 0:```
	     ```print('The triangle is valid.')```
	 ```else:```
	     ```print('The triangle is not valid.')```

MATLAB output:	Python output:
Enter first angle: 60	Enter first angle: 60
Enter second angle: 60	Enter second angle: 60
Enter third angle: 60	Enter third angle: 60
The triangle is valid.	The triangle is valid.

Table 4.33: Codes to determine if a triangle is valid based on its angles

Example 4.38: Determine the grade based on a score:

MATLAB	Python

score = input('Enter the score: ');
if score >= 90
    disp('Grade: A');
elseif score >= 80
    disp('Grade: B');
elseif score >= 70
    disp('Grade: C');
elseif score >= 60
    disp('Grade: D');
else
    disp('Grade: F');
end
	score = float(input('Enter the score: '))
	if score >= 90:
	    print('Grade: A')
	elif score >= 80:
	    print('Grade: B')
	elif score >= 70:
	    print('Grade: C')
	elif score >= 60:
	    print('Grade: D')
	else:
	    print('Grade: F')

MATLAB output:	**Python output:**
Enter the score: 93 Grade: A	Enter the score: 93 Grade: A

Table 4.34: Codes to determine the grade based on a score

Example 4.39: Check if a point lies in the first quadrant:

MATLAB	Python

x = input('Enter x-coordinate: ');
y = input('Enter y-coordinate: ');
if x > 0 && y > 0
    disp('The point lies in the first quadrant.');
else
    disp('The point does not lie in the first quadrant.');
end
	x = float(input('Enter x-coordinate: '))
	y = float(input('Enter y-coordinate: '))
	if x > 0 and y > 0:
	    print('The point lies in the first quadrant.')
	else:
	    print('The point does not lie in the first quadrant.')

MATLAB output:	**Python output:**
Enter x-coordinate: 1 Enter y-coordinate: 2 The point lies in the first quadrant.	Enter x-coordinate: 1 Enter y-coordinate: 2 The point lies in the first quadrant.

Table 4.35: Codes to check if a point lies in the first quadrant

Example 4.40: Check if a string contains only digits:

MATLAB	Python

```str = input('Enter a string: ', 's');```
```if all(isstrprop(str, 'digit'))```
```   disp('The string contains only```
```digits.');```
```else```
```   disp('The string contains characters```
```other than digits.');```
```end```
	```str = input('Enter a string: ')```
	```if str.isdigit():```
	``` print('The string contains only```
	```digits.')```
	```else:```
	``` print('The string contains```
	```characters other than digits.')```

MATLAB output: **Enter a string: 123** **The string contains only digits.**	**Python output:** **Enter a string: 123** **The string contains only digits.**

Table 4.36: *Codes to check if a string contains only digits*

Example 4.41: Check if two numbers are co-prime (GCD = 1):

MATLAB	Python

```a = input('Enter first number: ');```
```b = input('Enter second number: ');```
```if gcd(a, b) == 1```
```   disp('The numbers are co-prime.');```
```else```
```   disp('The numbers are not co-prime.');```
```end```
	```import math```
	```a = int(input('Enter first number: '))```
	```b = int(input('Enter second number: '))```
	```if math.gcd(a, b) == 1:```
	``` print('The numbers are co-prime.')```
	```else:```
	``` print('The numbers are not co-prime.')```

MATLAB output: **Enter first number: 3** **Enter second number: 5** **The numbers are co-prime.**	**Python output:** **Enter first number: 3** **Enter second number: 5** **The numbers are co-prime.**

Table 4.37: *Codes to check if two numbers are co-prime*

Example 4.42: Check if a number is a perfect square:

MATLAB	Python

```num = input('Enter a number: ');```
```if mod(sqrt(num), 1) == 0```
```   disp('The number is a perfect```
```square.');```
```else```
```   disp('The number is not a perfect```
```square.');```
```end```
	```import math```
	```num = int(input('Enter a number: '))```
	```if math.sqrt(num).is_integer():```
	``` print('The number is a perfect```
	```square.')```
	```else:```
	``` print('The number is not a perfect```
	```square.')```

MATLAB output: **Enter a number: 121** **The number is a perfect square.**	**Python output:** **Enter a number: 121** **The number is a perfect square.**

Table 4.38: *Codes to check if a number is a perfect square*

Example 4.43: Check if a triangle is equilateral, isosceles, or scalene:

MATLAB	Python

`a = input('Enter first side: ');`
`b = input('Enter second side: ');`
`c = input('Enter third side: ');`
`if a == b && b == c`
`    disp('The triangle is equilateral.');`
`elseif a == b || b == c || a == c`
`    disp('The triangle is isosceles.');`
`else`
`    disp('The triangle is scalene.');`
`end`
	`a = float(input('Enter first side: '))`
	`b = float(input('Enter second side: '))`
	`c = float(input('Enter third side: '))`
	`if a == b == c:`
	`    print('The triangle is equilateral.')`
	`elif a == b or b == c or a == c:`
	`    print('The triangle is isosceles.')`
	`else:`
	`    print('The triangle is scalene.')`

MATLAB output: Enter first side: 60 Enter second side: 60 Enter third side: 60 The triangle is equilateral.	Python output: Enter first side: 60 Enter second side: 60 Enter third side: 60 The triangle is equilateral.

Table 4.39: Codes to check if a triangle is equilateral, isosceles, or scalene

Example 4.44: Determine the quadrant of a point in a 2D plane:

MATLAB	Python

`x = input('Enter x-coordinate: ');`
`y = input('Enter y-coordinate: ');`
`if x > 0 && y > 0`
`    disp('The point is in the first quadrant.');`
`elseif x < 0 && y > 0`
`    disp('The point is in the second quadrant.');`
`elseif x < 0 && y < 0`
`    disp('The point is in the third quadrant.');`
`elseif x > 0 && y < 0`
`    disp('The point is in the fourth quadrant.');`
`else`
`    disp('The point is on an axis or at the origin.');`
`end`
	`x = float(input('Enter x-coordinate: '))`
	`y = float(input('Enter y-coordinate: '))`
	`if x > 0 and y > 0:`
	`    print('The point is in the first quadrant.')`
	`elif x < 0 and y > 0:`
	`    print('The point is in the second quadrant.')`
	`elif x < 0 and y < 0:`
	`    print('The point is in the third quadrant.')`
	`elif x > 0 and y < 0:`
	`    print('The point is in the fourth quadrant.')`
	`else:`
	`    print('The point is on an axis or at the origin.')`

MATLAB output: Enter x-coordinate: -1 Enter y-coordinate: -2 The point is in the third quadrant.	Python output: Enter x-coordinate: -1 Enter y-coordinate: -2 The point is in the third quadrant.

Table 4.40: Codes to determine the quadrant of a point in a 2D plane

Example 4.45: Check if a number ends with 5:

MATLAB	Python
| ```matlab
num = input('Enter a number: ');
if mod(num, 10) == 5
    disp('The number ends with 5.');
else
    disp('The number does not end with 5.');
end
``` | ```python
num = int(input('Enter a number: '))
if num % 10 == 5:
    print('The number ends with 5.')
else:
    print('The number does not end with 5.')
``` |
| **MATLAB output:**
`Enter a number: 58`
`The number does not end with 5.` | **Python output:**
`Enter a number: 58`
`The number does not end with 5.` |

Table 4.41: Codes to check if a number ends with 5

Example 4.46: Check if a string starts and ends with the same character:

MATLAB	Python
| ```matlab
str = input('Enter a string: ', 's');
if str(1) == str(end)
    disp('The string starts and ends with
the same character.');
else
    disp('The string does not start and end
with the same character.');
end
``` | ```python
str = input('Enter a string: ')
if str[0] == str[-1]:
    print('The string starts and ends with
the same character.')
else:
    print('The string does not start and
end with the same character.')
``` |
| **MATLAB output:**

`Enter a string: mathematics`

`The string does not start and end with the`
`same character.` | **Python output:**

`Enter a string: mathematics`

`The string does not start and end with the`
`same character.` |

Table 4.42: Codes to check if a string starts and ends with the same character

Example 4.47: Check if the sum of the squares of two numbers equals a third number:

MATLAB	Python
| ```matlab
a = input('Enter the first number: ');
b = input('Enter the second number: ');
c = input('Enter the third number: ');
if a^2 + b^2 == c
    disp('The sum of the squares of
the first two numbers equals the third
number.');
else
    disp('The sum of the squares of the
first two numbers does not equal the third
number.');
end
``` | ```python
a = float(input('Enter the first number: '))
b = float(input('Enter the second number: '))
c = float(input('Enter the third number: '))
if a**2 + b**2 == c:
    print('The sum of the squares of the first
two numbers equals the third number.')
else:
    print('The sum of the squares of the first
two numbers does not equal the third number.')
``` |

MATLAB output:	Python output:
Enter the first number: 1 Enter the second number: 2 Enter the third number: 3 The sum of the squares of the first two numbers does not equal the third number.	Enter the first number: 1 Enter the second number: 2 Enter the third number: 3 The sum of the squares of the first two numbers does not equal the third number.

Table 4.43: Codes to check if the sum of the squares of two numbers equals a third number

Example 4.48: Check if a number satisfies Pythagoras ($a^2 + b^2 = c^2$):

MATLAB	Python

```matlab`a = input('Enter the first number: ');`
`b = input('Enter the second number: ');`
`c = input('Enter the third number: ');`
`if a^2 + b^2 == c^2`
`    disp('The numbers satisfy the`
`Pythagoras theorem.');`
`else`
`    disp('The numbers do not satisfy the`
`Pythagoras theorem.');`
`end` ```
	```python`a = int(input('Enter the first number: '))`
	`b = int(input('Enter the second number: '))`
	`c = int(input('Enter the third number: '))`
	`if a**2 + b**2 == c**2:`
	`    print('The numbers satisfy the`
	`Pythagoras theorem.')`
	`else:`
	`    print('The numbers do not satisfy the`
	`Pythagoras theorem.')` ```

MATLAB output: Enter the first number: 3 Enter the second number: 4 Enter the third number: 5 The numbers satisfy the Pythagoras theorem.	**Python output:** Enter the first number: 3 Enter the second number: 4 Enter the third number: 5 The numbers satisfy the Pythagoras theorem.

Table 4.44: Codes to check if a number satisfies Pythagoras

Example 4.49: Check if a matrix is square (rows = columns):

MATLAB	Python

```matlab`matrix = input('Enter the matrix: ');`
`[rows, cols] = size(matrix);`
`if rows == cols`
`    disp('The matrix is square.');`
`else`
`    disp('The matrix is not square.');`
`end` ```
	```python`import numpy as np`
	`matrix = np.array(eval(input('Enter the matrix: ')))  # Use input like [[1,2],[3,4]]`
	`if matrix.shape[0] == matrix.shape[1]:`
	`    print('The matrix is square.')`
	`else:`
	`    print('The matrix is not square.')` ```

MATLAB output: Enter the matrix: [1 2; 3 4] The matrix is square.	**Python output:** Enter the matrix: [[1, 2], [3, 4]] The matrix is square.

Table 4.45: Codes to check if a matrix is square

Example 4.50: Check if a matrix is symmetric (A = A^T):

MATLAB	Python
| ```matlab
matrix = input('Enter the matrix: ');
if isequal(matrix, matrix')
    disp('The matrix is symmetric.');
else
    disp('The matrix is not symmetric.');
end
``` | ```python
import numpy as np
matrix = np.array(eval(input('Enter the matrix: ')))  # Use input like [[1,2,3],[2,4,5],[3,5,6]]
if np.array_equal(matrix, matrix.T):
    print('The matrix is symmetric.')
else:
    print('The matrix is not symmetric.')
``` |
| **MATLAB output:**
Enter the matrix: [1 2; 3 4]

The matrix is not symmetric. | **Python output:**
Enter the matrix: [[1,0,2],[0,4,5],[3,5,6]]
The matrix is not symmetric. |

Table 4.46: Codes to check if a matrix is symmetric

Example 4.51: Check if a matrix is an identity matrix:

MATLAB	Python
| ```matlab
matrix = input('Enter the matrix: ');
if isequal(matrix, eye(size(matrix)))
    disp('The matrix is an identity matrix.');
else
    disp('The matrix is not an identity matrix.');
end
``` | ```python
import numpy as np
matrix = np.array(eval(input('Enter the matrix: ')))  # Use input like [[1,0],[0,1]]
if np.array_equal(matrix, np.eye(matrix.shape[0])):
    print('The matrix is an identity matrix.')
else:
    print('The matrix is not an identity matrix.')
``` |
| **MATLAB output:**
Enter the matrix: [1 0; 0 1]

The matrix is an identity matrix. | **Python output:**
Enter the matrix: [[1,2,3],[3,4,5],[4,5,6]]
The matrix is not an identity matrix. |

Table 4.47: Codes to check if a matrix is an identity matrix

Example 4.52: Check if a matrix is diagonal (non-diagonal elements are zero):

MATLAB	Python
| ```matlab
matrix = input('Enter the matrix: ');
if isequal(matrix, diag(diag(matrix)))
    disp('The matrix is diagonal.');
else
    disp('The matrix is not diagonal.');
end
``` | ```python
import numpy as np
matrix = np.array(eval(input('Enter the matrix: ')))  # Use input like [[1,0,0],[0,2,0],[0,0,3]]
if np.array_equal(matrix, np.diag(np.diag(matrix))):
    print('The matrix is diagonal.')
else:
    print('The matrix is not diagonal.')
``` |

MATLAB output:	Python output:
Enter the matrix: [1 0 0; 0 2 0; 0 0 3]	Enter the matrix: [[1,2,0],[3,0,5],[4,5,6]]
The matrix is diagonal.	The matrix is not diagonal.

Table 4.48: Codes to check if a matrix is diagonal

Example 4.53: Check if a matrix is upper triangular (all elements below the diagonal are zero):

MATLAB	Python

matrix = input('Enter the matrix: ');
if isequal(triu(matrix), matrix)
    disp('The matrix is upper triangular.');
else
    disp('The matrix is not upper triangular.');
end
	import numpy as np
	matrix = np.array(eval(input('Enter the matrix: '))) # Use input like [[1,2,3],[0,4,5],[0,0,6]]
	if np.array_equal(matrix, np.triu(matrix)):
	    print('The matrix is upper triangular.')
	else:
	    print('The matrix is not upper triangular.')

MATLAB output: Enter the matrix: [4 5 6; 0 7 8; 0 0 9] The matrix is upper triangular.	**Python output:** Enter the matrix: [[4,5,6],[0,7,8],[0,0,9]] The matrix is upper triangular.

Table 4.49: Codes to check if a matrix is upper triangular

Example 4.54: Check if a matrix is lower triangular (all elements above the diagonal are zero):

MATLAB	Python

matrix = input('Enter the matrix: ');
if isequal(tril(matrix), matrix)
    disp('The matrix is lower triangular.');
else
    disp('The matrix is not lower triangular.');
end
	import numpy as np
	matrix = np.array(eval(input('Enter the matrix: '))) # Use input like [[1,0,0],[2,3,0],[4,5,6]]
	if np.array_equal(matrix, np.tril(matrix)):
	    print('The matrix is lower triangular.')
	else:
	    print('The matrix is not lower triangular.')

MATLAB output: Enter the matrix: [4 0 0; 5 6 0; 7 8 9] The matrix is lower triangular.	**Python output:** Enter the matrix: [[4,0,0],[5,6,0],[7,8,9]] The matrix is lower triangular.

Table 4.50: Codes to check if a matrix is lower triangular

Example 4.55: Check if two matrices are equal:

MATLAB	Python
| ```matlab
matrix1 = input('Enter the first matrix: ');
matrix2 = input('Enter the second matrix: ');
if isequal(matrix1, matrix2)
    disp('The matrices are equal.');
else
    disp('The matrices are not equal.');
end
``` | ```python
import numpy as np
matrix1 = np.array(eval(input('Enter the first matrix: ')))
matrix2 = np.array(eval(input('Enter the second matrix: ')))
if np.array_equal(matrix1, matrix2):
    print('The matrices are equal.')
else:
    print('The matrices are not equal.')
``` |
| **MATLAB output:**

Enter the first matrix: [1 2; 3 4]
Enter the second matrix: [1 2; 3 4]
The matrices are equal. | **Python output:**

Enter the first matrix: [[1,0,0],[5,6,0],[7,8,9]]
Enter the second matrix: [[2,0,0],[5,6,0],[7,8,9]]
The matrices are not equal. |

Table 4.51: Codes to check if two matrices are equal

Example 4.56: Check if a matrix is invertible (determinant ≠ 0):

MATLAB	Python
| ```matlab
matrix = input('Enter the matrix: ');
if det(matrix) ~= 0
    disp('The matrix is invertible.');
else
    disp('The matrix is not invertible.');
end
``` | ```python
import numpy as np
matrix = np.array(eval(input('Enter the matrix: ')))  # Use input like [[1,2],[3,4]]
if np.linalg.det(matrix) != 0:
    print('The matrix is invertible.')
else:
    print('The matrix is not invertible.')
``` |
| **MATLAB output:**

Enter the matrix: [1 0; 0 1]
The matrix is invertible. | **Python output:**

Enter the matrix: [[1, 2], [3, 4]]
The matrix is invertible. |

Table 4.52: Codes to check if a matrix is invertible

Example 4.57: Check if a matrix is singular (determinant = 0):

MATLAB	Python
| ```matlab
matrix = input('Enter the matrix: ');
if det(matrix) == 0
    disp('The matrix is singular.');
else
    disp('The matrix is not singular.');
end
``` | ```python
import numpy as np
matrix = np.array(eval(input('Enter the matrix: ')))
if np.linalg.det(matrix) == 0:
    print('The matrix is singular.')
else:
    print('The matrix is not singular.')
``` |
| **MATLAB output:**

Enter the matrix: [1 0; 0 0]
The matrix is singular. | **Python output:**

Enter the matrix: [[1, 2], [3, 4]]
The matrix is not singular. |

Table 4.53: Codes to check if a matrix is singular

Example 4.58: Check if a matrix is positive definite (all eigenvalues > 0):

MATLAB	Python
| ```matlab
matrix = input('Enter the matrix: ');
eigenvalues = eig(matrix);
if all(eigenvalues > 0)
    disp('The matrix is positive definite.');
else
    disp('The matrix is not positive definite.');
end
``` | ```python
import numpy as np
matrix = np.array(eval(input('Enter the matrix: ')))
eigenvalues = np.linalg.eigvals(matrix)
if all(eigenvalues > 0):
    print('The matrix is positive definite.')
else:
    print('The matrix is not positive definite.')
``` |
| **MATLAB output:** | **Python output:** |
| Enter the matrix: [1 2; 7 8]
The matrix is not positive definite. | Enter the matrix: [[2,0,0],[5,6,0],[7,8,9]]
The matrix is positive definite. |

Table 4.54: Codes to check if a matrix is positive definite

Example 4.59: Check if a matrix is sparse (most elements are zero):

MATLAB	Python
| ```matlab
matrix = input('Enter the matrix: ');
non_zero_elements = nnz(matrix);
total_elements = numel(matrix);
if non_zero_elements / total_elements < 0.5
    disp('The matrix is sparse.');
else
    disp('The matrix is not sparse.');
end
``` | ```python
import numpy as np
matrix = np.array(eval(input('Enter the matrix: ')))  # Use input like [[0,0,1],[0,0,0],[2,0,0]]
non_zero_elements = np.count_nonzero(matrix)
total_elements = matrix.size
if non_zero_elements / total_elements < 0.5:
    print('The matrix is sparse.')
else:
    print('The matrix is not sparse.')
``` |
| **MATLAB output:** | **Python output:** |
| Enter the matrix: [1 0 0 0; 0 2 0 0; 0 0 3 0; 0 0 0 4]
The matrix is sparse. | Enter the matrix: [[10,0,0,0],[0,20,0,0],[0,0,30,0], [0,0,0,40]]
The matrix is sparse. |

Table 4.55: Codes to check if a matrix is sparse

Example 4.60: Check if a matrix is orthogonal ($A^T A = I$):

MATLAB	Python
| ```matlab
matrix = input('Enter the matrix: ');
if isequal(matrix' * matrix, eye(size(matrix)))
    disp('The matrix is orthogonal.');
else
    disp('The matrix is not orthogonal.');
end
``` | ```python
import numpy as np
matrix = np.array(eval(input('Enter the matrix: ')))  # Use input like [[1,0],[0,1]]
if np.allclose(np.dot(matrix.T, matrix), np.eye(matrix.shape[0])):
    print('The matrix is orthogonal.')
else:
    print('The matrix is not orthogonal.')
``` |

MATLAB output:	Python output:
`Enter the matrix: [1 0; 0 1]`	`Enter the matrix: [[1, 2], [3, 1]]`
`The matrix is orthogonal.`	`The matrix is not orthogonal.`

Table 4.56: Codes to check if a matrix is orthogonal

Example 4.61: Check if a matrix is skew-symmetric ($A^T = -A$):

MATLAB	Python
| ```matlab
matrix = input('Enter the matrix: ');
if isequal(matrix', -matrix)
    disp('The matrix is skew-symmetric.');
else
    disp('The matrix is not skew-symmetric.');
end
``` | ```python
import numpy as np
matrix = np.array(eval(input('Enter the matrix: ')))  # Use input like [[0,-2],[2,0]]
if np.array_equal(matrix.T, -matrix):
    print('The matrix is skew-symmetric.')
else:
    print('The matrix is not skew-symmetric.')
``` |
MATLAB output:	**Python output:**
`Enter the matrix: [0 2; -2 0]`	`Enter the matrix: [[0, 2], [-2, 0]]`
`The matrix is skew-symmetric.`	`The matrix is skew-symmetric.`

Table 4.57: Codes to check if a matrix is skew-symmetric

Both MATLAB and Python support nested loops, where one loop resides within another. Nested loops are useful for handling multidimensional arrays or performing operations on matrix-like structures.

Example 4.62: Multiplication table:

MATLAB:	Python:
| ```matlab
n = 5;
for i = 1:n
    for j = 1:n
        fprintf('%d \t', i * j);
    end
    fprintf('\n');
end
``` | ```python
n = 5
for i in range(1, n + 1):
    for j in range(1, n + 1):
        print(i * j, end='\t')
    print()
``` |
| **MATLAB output:** | **Python output:** |
| <table><tr><td>1</td><td>2</td><td>3</td><td>4</td><td>5</td></tr><tr><td>2</td><td>4</td><td>6</td><td>8</td><td>10</td></tr><tr><td>3</td><td>6</td><td>9</td><td>12</td><td>15</td></tr><tr><td>4</td><td>8</td><td>12</td><td>16</td><td>20</td></tr><tr><td>5</td><td>10</td><td>15</td><td>20</td><td>25</td></tr></table> | <table><tr><td>1</td><td>2</td><td>3</td><td>4</td><td>5</td></tr><tr><td>2</td><td>4</td><td>6</td><td>8</td><td>10</td></tr><tr><td>3</td><td>6</td><td>9</td><td>12</td><td>15</td></tr><tr><td>4</td><td>8</td><td>12</td><td>16</td><td>20</td></tr><tr><td>5</td><td>10</td><td>15</td><td>20</td><td>25</td></tr></table> |

Table 4.58: Codes to print multiplication table

The break statement exits a loop prematurely, while the continue statement skips the current iteration and moves to the next one.

Example 4.63: Break statement:

MATLAB:	Python:
| ```
for i = 1:10
    if i == 5
        break;
    end
  fprintf('%d\n', i);
end
``` | ```
for i in range(1, 11):
    if i == 5:
        break
    print(i)
``` |
| **MATLAB output:**

1

2

3

4 | **Python output:**

1

2

3

4 |

Table 4.59: Codes regarding break statement

Example 4.64: Continue statement:

MATLAB:	Python:
| ```
for i = 1:10
    if mod(i, 2) == 0
        continue;
    end
    fprintf('%d\n', i);
end
``` | ```
for i in range(1, 11):
    if i % 2 == 0:
        continue
    print(i)
``` |
| **MATLAB output:**

1
3
5
7
9 | **Python output:**

1
3
5
7
9 |

Table 4.60: Codes regarding continue statement

Conclusion

In this chapter, we explored the essential concepts of control flow and structures in MATLAB and Python, two powerful programming languages widely used in scientific computing, data analysis, and automation. The chapter was divided into two main sections, each focusing on one language.

In the MATLAB section, we learned about conditional statements (if, elseif, else) for executing code based on logical conditions and loops (for, while) for repeating tasks or iterating over arrays. These constructs are fundamental for implementing decision-making logic and handling repetitive tasks efficiently in MATLAB. In the Python section, we studied conditional statements (if, elif, else) for branching logic and loops (for, while) for iterating over sequences like lists or performing condition-based iterations. Python's clear syntax and flexibility make it easy to implement complex control flow structures for a wide range of applications. Moreover, we got full insights of the discussed concept via practical examples as well. In the next chapter, we will explore the aspects about functions and scripts in MATLAB and Python in detail.

Exercises

1. Use a for loop to calculate the sum of n terms for series $\sum_{k=1}^{n} \frac{(-1)^k k}{2^k}$, $n = 4$ and 20.

2. The following is a list of 10 exam scores. Write a computer program that calculates the average of the top 3 scores.

   Exam scores: 73, 91, 37, 81, 63, 66, 50, 90, 75, 43

3. A freelance writer charges a standard rate per article up to a certain word count and 50% more for each additional word. Write a program that calculates the writer's earnings. The program should prompt the user for the number of words in the article and the standard rate per article (up to the word limit). The program then displays the writer's total earnings.

4. Prompt the user to input a numerical value. Determine and display whether the input number falls within the following ranges:

   a. Less than 10

   b. Between 10 (inclusive) and 50 (exclusive)

   c. 50 or greater

5. Write a program that generates a vector containing 25 random floating-point numbers between -15 and 15. The program should then calculate and display the product of all elements in the vector that are greater than 2.5 in absolute value.

6. Prompt the user to input an integer. Determine and display whether the input integer is even or odd. Implement error handling to ensure the user provides an integer input. If a non-integer is entered, display an appropriate error message and re-prompt the user for valid input.

7. Develop a script that utilizes for loops to implement the following:

   a. Display integers from 25 down to 5 in descending order.

   b. Calculate the sum of all integers from 15 to 75 (inclusive).

   c. Calculate the sum of all even integers between 12 and 60 (inclusive).

   d. Calculate and display the squares of all integers from 8 to 20 (inclusive).

8. Write a program that ask the user to input the dimensions (rows and columns) of a matrix. Then, using nested for loops, prompt the user to enter each element of the matrix. Store the elements in the matrix and display the resulting matrix.

9. Develop a script that uses while loops to accomplish the following:

   a. Display integers from 30 down to 2 in descending order.

   b. Calculate the sum of all odd integers between 11 and 75 (inclusive).

   c. Calculate the sum of the squares of all integers from 5 to 20 (inclusive).

10. Prompt the user to input a non-negative integer. Calculate the factorial of this number using a while loop. Include error handling to ensure the user provides a valid non-negative integer input. If the input is invalid, display an appropriate error message and re-prompt the user for input until a valid number is entered. Do not use the built-in factorial() function. Discuss the rationale behind your error-handling strategy.

11. Write a program in a script file that creates a matrix with elements that have the following values.

    a. The value of each element in the first row is the number of the column.

    b. The value of each element in the first column is the number of the row.

c. The rest of the elements each have a value equal to the sum of the element above it and the element to the left.

d. When executed, the program asks the user to enter values for n and m.

12. Write a program in a script file that finds the smallest odd integer that is divisible by 11 and whose square root is greater than 132. Use a loop in the program. The loop should start from 1 and stop when the number is found.

13. The program prints the message *The required number is:* and then prints the number.

Let X is a vector with numbers from 1 to 100. Write a program for determining the sum of the cube of all the elements of a vector that are less than 20.

14. Write a program that takes a square matrix as input from the user, prompting for its dimensions (rows and columns) and then each individual element. The program should determine if it is singular or non-singular by calculating its determinant.

15. For a given vector $W = [-2, -15, -4, 11, 30, -6, 25, 22, -1, 3, -7, 10, -3, 18, 20]$. Write a script that modifies this vector as follows:

a. Doubles any positive element that is divisible by either 2 or 5.

b. Cubes (raises to the power of 3) any negative element that is greater than -5.

16. Write a script that approximates $e^x = \sum_{n=1}^{\infty} \frac{x^n}{n!}$ using the Taylor series expansion. The script should:

a. Calculate e^2 using the sum of the series by iteratively adding terms.

b. Stop adding terms when the absolute value of the last term added is less than a specified tolerance (e.g., 0.0001).

c. Implement a safeguard by limiting the maximum number of terms added to 30. If the tolerance is not achieved within 30 terms, display a message indicating that more terms are required.

d. Utilize a while loop for the iterative calculation.

17. A recent graduate, having saved $10,000, invests in a portfolio yielding a 7% annual return. They plan to supplement their income while in further education by withdrawing 8% of their initial investment ($800) in the first year. To maintain purchasing power, they will increase this withdrawal amount annually by the inflation rate, assumed to be a constant 3%. The goal is to determine how many years the investment will last under these conditions. A program should calculate the yearly withdrawals, the remaining balance after each withdrawal, and ultimately, the number of years until the account is depleted.

18. Write a program that randomly determines the performance order of five coding competition participants: Alice, Bob, Carol, Dave, and Eve, and outputs a list displaying this randomized sequence.

19. Write a program that takes a user-input vector of numbers of arbitrary length and removes all elements less than -10. Using a for loop, the program should display the original vector, the modified vector, and the count of removed elements. For testing, use randi ([-10 20],1,25) to generate a sample 25-element vector.

20. Write a program to find all Mersenne primes, a prime number given by $2^n - 1$ lying between 1 and 5,000. Do not use built-in primality testing functions. For example, 127 is a Mersenne prime given as $(2^7 - 1)$.

Some real-world applications:

1. Write a MATLAB/Python script to check whether a given year is a leap year.

2. Using if-else, determine the grade of a student based on the score input (A, B, C, D, F).

3. Create a program that checks if a number is positive, negative, or zero.

4. Develop a parking fee calculator that charges different rates based on the number of hours parked.

5. Write a logic to apply tax slabs on income using nested if-else statements.

6. Use a for loop to compute the factorial of a number in MATLAB and Python.

7. Print all prime numbers between 1 and 100 using a loop.

8. Using a while loop, calculate the sum of the digits of a given number.

9. Simulate a bank balance update with compound interest over N years.

10. Create a multiplication table generator using nested loops.

11. Write a script to search for a target element in a list/array and exit loop when found.

12. Skip printing even numbers using continue and only display odd numbers from 1 to 20.

13. Create a loop that reads input until the user enters 'exit'.

14. Implement a menu-driven calculator that keeps running until the user selects 'Quit'.

15. Find the first number in a list that is divisible by both 5 and 7 using break.

16. Write a script to search for a target element in a list/array and exit loop when found.

17. Skip printing even numbers using continue and only display odd numbers from 1 to 20.

18. Create a loop that reads input until the user enters 'exit'.

19. Implement a menu-driven calculator that keeps running until the user selects 'Quit'.

20. Find the first number in a list that is divisible by both 5 and 7 using break.

21. Simulate tossing a coin 100 times and count how many times heads or tails occur.

22. Write a loop to process student marks and print the highest, lowest, and average score.

23. Using loops, create a pattern like a triangle or pyramid of stars.

24. Iterate through a matrix and replace all negative values with zero.

25. Create a program that simulates an ATM withdrawal: limit retries to 3 if an incorrect PIN is entered.

26. Design a script that determines eligibility for a government subsidy based on age, income, and employment status.

27. Create a hospital triage system using if-else statements that prioritizes patients based on severity codes.

28. Write code to validate a password input with rules: minimum 8 characters, one digit, and one uppercase letter.

29. Develop a car insurance premium calculator based on vehicle age, driver's age, and accident history.

30. Build a program that calculates electricity bills based on slab rates (e.g., first 100 units = ₹5/unit, next 100 = ₹7/unit, etc.).

31. Simulate population growth over 10 years using a while loop and a growth rate.

32. Create a savings tracker that computes how many months are needed to reach a financial goal.

33. Write a loop to convert a list of temperatures from Celsius to Fahrenheit.

34. Develop a program to find and count palindromes in a list of strings.

35. Using nested loops, simulate a theater seating layout and mark reserved seats.

36. Implement a CAPTCHA retry system that locks the user out after three failed attempts.

37. Build a digital clock simulation that displays time from 00:00 to 23:59 using nested loops.

38. Create a loop that checks and categorizes each word in a sentence as a noun, verb, or adjective using keyword matching.

39. Process a directory of files using a loop and skip all hidden/system files.

40. Implement a retry mechanism with exponential backoff for network requests (simulation).

41. Create a traffic light controller using switch/match-case to control stop, ready, and go signals.

42. Design a travel recommendation engine that suggests destinations based on a numeric user input (budget, climate).

43. Use match-case to build a language translator for basic words (e.g., "hello", "thank you") for three languages.

44. Simulate a basic menu in a restaurant where the user selects an item number and quantity.

45. Develop an academic system that assigns degree classification (e.g., first class, second class) based on CGPA.

46. Check for Armstrong numbers between 1 and 1000 using loops.

47. Find and sum all perfect numbers below a given number .

48. Generate a pattern for a digital LED-style clock display using nested loops.

49. Create a real-time input validator that flags invalid entries (e.g., incorrect phone number format).

50. Simulate a shopping cart billing system that loops through items, applies discounts, and stops on checkout.

Join our Discord space

Join our Discord workspace for latest updates, offers, tech happenings around the world, new releases, and sessions with the authors:

https://discord.bpbonline.com

Functions and Scripts in MATLAB and Python

Introduction

In this chapter, you will explore how to write and use functions and scripts in MATLAB and Python, in MATLAB, you will learn how to define reusable functions in separate files using the function keyword, allowing for modular and organized code. The chapter also covers MATLAB scripts, which are collections of commands executed sequentially, ideal for automating repetitive tasks. Additionally, you will discover anonymous functions created using the @ symbol, which provides a quick way to define simple, single-line functions without needing a separate file.

In the Python section, the focus shifts to defining functions with the def keyword, enabling structured and reusable code blocks. You will also learn about **lambda** functions: concise, anonymous functions defined in a single line using the **lambda** keyword; useful for short operations. By the end of this chapter, you will gain a proper understanding of function and script implementation in MATLAB and Python, enhancing your ability to write efficient and maintainable code.

This chapter will explain basic concepts of functions and scripts in MATLAB and Python. To illustrate significant concepts, we will go over each language's usage and best practices via examples. By the end of this chapter, you will have a proper knowledge of writing functions and scripts in MATLAB and Python. This will help them tackle the complex computational tasks.

Structure

The structure of this chapter is as follows:

- 5.1 Functions and scripts in MATLAB
- 5.2 Functions and scripts in Python
- 5.3 Comparative study in MATLAB and Python

Objectives

This chapter aims to provide readers with a comprehensive knowledge of function and script implementation in MATLAB and Python, focusing on practical applications in scientific computing. The primary objectives include developing proficiency in MATLAB's function creation using the function keyword and enabling readers to build reusable code modules with proper input/output handling. Readers will learn to construct and execute MATLAB scripts for automating sequences of operations, along with implementing concise anonymous functions using the @ operator for efficient inline calculations. For Python, the chapter focuses on building competence in defining structured functions with the def statement, including parameter handling and return values, while also covering script development for executable program files. A key objective is understanding Python's `lambda` functions for creating compact, anonymous functions and their effective use in functional programming paradigms. By mastering these concepts, readers will acquire the skills to write clean, modular, and efficient code in these two languages with the ability to select the appropriate tool (functions, scripts, or anonymous functions) for different programming scenarios. The chapter emphasizes practical implementation, ensuring readers can apply these techniques to real-world computational problems while adhering to best practices and maintainability.

5.1 Functions and scripts in MATLAB

Programming languages are now vital tools for academics, scientists, and engineers when it comes to processing data and building complex-natured models. Two languages that are frequently utilized in these fields are MATLAB and Python. These languages' strong functionality and script-writing aspects help users create modular and reusable code that enhances productivity and effectiveness.

However, MATLAB and Python can be used to create functions and scripts. They have a wide range of libraries and syntax. MATLAB's focus on mathematical/numerical computations makes it suitable for some specific engineering applications. Python's versatility makes it appropriate for a wide range of programming elements. The advantage of each language will be appropriately applied by users.

5.1.1 Functions

Functions in programming are essential building blocks. Functions provide reusability of code with clarity. A separate code block created for a specific task is considered a function. It has the ability to process inputs and produce outputs. Logic incorporated in functions makes code easier to understand.

Let us look at some reasons why using functions is important:

- **Modularity**: Functions allow programmers to split difficult subjects into smaller and more manageable parts.

- **Reusability**: Functions can be used repeatedly inside a program or in other programs. Due to this, redundancy is minimized, and development time is saved.

- **Abstraction**: Functions allow programmers to abstract away complicated operations.

- **Maintainability**: Code can be organized into functions to allow for bug fixes and updates without compromising the overall functionality of the application.

Functions typically consist of the following components:

- **Function name**: A descriptive identifier that indicates the purpose of the function.

- **Parameters/Arguments**: Inputs that the function can accept.

- **Return value**: Output produced by the function, which can be used in other parts of the program.

- **Body**: Block of code that defines what a function does.

Let us look at the several types of functions:

- **Built-in functions**: Built-in functions are predefined functions provided by programming languages or libraries (e.g., `len()` in Python, `sum()` in MATLAB).

- **User-defined functions**: User-defined functions are functions created by programmers to perform specific tasks tailored to their needs.

- **Anonymous functions**: Anonymous functions are the functions defined without a name, often used for short, one-time operations (e.g., `lambda` functions in Python).

Function type	When to use	Advantages
Built-in functions	When the operation is standard and provided by MATLAB (e.g., sum, mean)	Fast, reliable, optimized, and well-documented
User-defined functions	When the task is specific and not covered by built-in functions	Customizable, reusable, promotes modularity and code clarity
Anonymous functions	When the operation is short, simple, and used only in a limited context	Concise, defined inline, avoids clutter with short one-liners

Table 5.1: Types of functions

5.1.2 Creating functions in MATLAB

A useful and robust environment to create novel and distinctive capabilities is offered by MATLAB. Functions are the foundation of every complicated MATLAB program. Numerous predefined functions are available, or you may design your own exclusive ones. The following is the format to create a custom function in MATLAB:

```
function [O1, O2] = myFunc(arg1, arg2)
    % Function content goes here
end
```

The explanation of the preceding is as follows:

- **function**: This required keyword indicates the start of the function definition.

- **[O1, O2]**: These are the return values of the function, which are enclosed in square brackets. The function can return none, one, or multiple values.

- **myFunc**: This is the name of a custom function. It must be unique and should not conflict with existing MATLAB built-in functions or any script file names in the same directory.

- **(arg1, arg2)**: These are input variables (function arguments), enclosed in parentheses. A function can accept none, one, or multiple arguments.

- **Function content**: This encompasses all MATLAB code that defines what the function does, often referred to as the function's body.

- **end**: This keyword indicates the conclusion of the function definition.

After defining function, save file with a `.m` extension. This extension informs MATLAB that file contains a function definition.

Some key points to consider:

- The keyword function signifies that you are defining a function.

- The output variables (e.g., O1, O2) will hold the results of the computations performed in the function.

- The function name follows immediately after the equal sign.

- Any function arguments are listed within parentheses after the function name.

It is also important to note that functions in MATLAB can either return a value or display output without specifically returning it.

Functions can be classified in the following manner:

- Functions that compute and output a single value.

- Functions that compute and return multiple values.

- Functions that perform a specific action, such as publishing, without returning any values.

The following Examples, *5.1* and *5.2* demonstrate the functions that compute and output a single value.

Example 5.1: Function to calculate fourth power:

To illustrate how a function works in MATLAB, let us create a function called forpow which takes a single input *x* and returns 4th power of that number in the output variable *y*.

Create a file named fifthpow.m with the following content:

```
function y = forpow(x)
    y = x^4;  % Calculate the fourth power of x
end
```

This function can be called from within any MATLAB script or the Command Window by providing a number as input:

```
a = forpow(2);  % Call the function with input 2
disp(a);                % Display the result
```

Alternatively, you can call the function directly from the Command Window:

```
forpow(2)
```

Output:

16

Example 5.2: Function to calculate the distance between the vectors:

Considered another function diste which calculates the distance between two vectors, $A = [1,3]$ and $B = [4,6]$. The formula for the distance *d* between the points (x,y) and (u,v) is:

$$d = \sqrt{(x - u)^2 + (y - v)^2}$$

The function can be defined as follows:

```
function d = diste(A, B)
    d = sqrt(sum((A - B).^2));  % Calculate the distance using vectorized operations
end
```

Alternatively, you can express function using element-wise squaring:

```
function d = diste(A, B)
    d = sqrt((A(1) - B(1))^2 + (A(2) - B(2))^2);  % Calculate distance element-wise
end
```

You can call this function with the following:

```
d = diste([1, 3], [4, 6]);                % Direct call with vectors
```

You can also call this function by first defining the vectors:

```
A = [1, 3];
B = [4, 6];
d = distance(A, B);              % Call the function with defined vectors
```

Output:

4.2426

5.1.3 Function with multiple outputs

MATLAB allows functions to return multiple outputs, making it easier to get several results from a single operation. To create such a function, you list the desired outputs in square brackets in the function definition. Inside the function, you calculate each output separately. For example, a function that computes both the sum and product of two numbers would be written as function:**[sum_result, product_result] = calculate(a,b)**, where **sum_result = a + b** and **product_result = a * b**.

When you call this function, you can store the outputs in separate variables like **[x,y] = calculate(3,4)**, which would assign **7** to **x** (the sum) and **12** to **y** (the product). If you only need one output, MATLAB automatically returns just the first one. This feature is especially handy for mathematical operations, data processing, and scientific computing, where multiple related values need to be returned together. By using multiple outputs, you can write more efficient and organized code, reducing the need for extra calculations and making your programs easier to read and maintain. It is a simple but powerful tool that helps streamline your MATLAB programming.

Reasons to use square brackets **[ ]**:

- **In function definition**: Square brackets group the outputs so that MATLAB understands you are returning multiple distinct values, not just one:

  ```
  function [sum_result, product_result] = calculate(a, b)
      sum_result = a + b;
      product_result = a * b;
  end
  ```

- **In function call**: When calling the function, square brackets allow you to unpack each output into its own variable:

  ```
  [x, y] = calculate(3, 4);  % x = 7, y = 12
  ```

- **If only one output is needed**: MATLAB returns just the first output by default:

  ```
  result = calculate(3, 4);  % result = 7 (sum only)
  ```

The significance of **[ ]** is as follows:

- Clearly tells MATLAB and the programmer that multiple values are involved.

- Enables structured and organized return values.

- Reduces need for separate function calls—one call can provide many results.

- Makes code more efficient and readable, especially in scientific and numerical programming.

Example 5.3: In this example, we will create a function **sup,** which takes two numbers as input and returns their sum and product as two outputs:

Define the function in a file named **sup.m**:

```
function [s, p] = sup(x, y)
    s = x + y;    % Calculate the sum
    p = x * y;    % Calculate the product
end
```

This function can also be called from within any MATLAB script or the Command Window:

```
[a, b] = sup(2, 4);  % Call the function with inputs 2 and 4
disp(a);             % Display the sum
disp(b);             % Display the product
```

Alternatively, you can call the function directly from the Command Window:

```
[a, b] = sup(2, 4);
```

Output:

```
a = 6
b = 8
```

> Note: **Here, we use two variables to capture the results of outputs. If only one variable is used, only the first output (sum) will be returned.**

Example 5.4: Generating Fibonacci number

Create a function **fib** to use the Binet formula to generate Fibonacci number taking input from user as the number. The first few Fibonacci numbers are given as 1,1,2,3,5,8,13,21,…. The formula to generate the series is as follows:

$$F_n = \frac{\phi_1^n - (-\phi_2)^n}{\sqrt{5}}$$

Here:

$$\phi_1 = \frac{\sqrt{5}+1}{2}, \phi_2 = \frac{\sqrt{5}-1}{2}$$

Use relevant rounding formula to get the correct answer that can round off the number to the nearest integer, and start with the 1, 1 as the two terms counted in between.

Here is the function with no return of output but displaying the series:

```
function fib(n)
phi1 = (sqrt(5) + 1)/2;
phi2 = (sqrt(5) - 1)/2;
F = zeros(n, 1);               % Pre-allocate for efficiency
for i = 1:n                    % MATLAB indexing starts at 1
                               % Binet's Formula: F_n = (phi1^n - (-phi2)^n) /
                                   sqrt(5)
                               % Since MATLAB uses 1-based indexing, we use (i-1)
                               % For example:
                               % i = 1 --> F(1) = F_0 = 0
                               % i = 2 --> F(2) = F_1 = 1
                               % i = 3 --> F(3) = F_2 = 1
                               % i = 4 --> F(4) = F_3 = 2, and so on
F(i) = (phi1^(i-1) - (-phi2)^(i-1))/sqrt(5);
```

```
% Adjust exponent for 1-based indexing
end
a = round(F);
disp(a)
end
```

Example 5.5: Conversion to radian:

To get the value of **y** per given angle in radians (x), write a function called **rad**, where:

  y = 1 if x > pi/2, y = sin(x) if x is in [0, pi/2] and y = 0 otherwise.

Here is the code:

```
function y=rad(x)
    if x> pi/2
        y = 1
    else
        if x>=0 && x<=pi/2
        y=sin(x)
      else
        y=0
        end
    end
    end
```

The following command displays the result of converting 3.14 degrees to radians in MATLAB:

- **Command one**: `disp(rad(3.14))`

  The following command displays the result of converting 1 degree to radians, assuming **rad()** is a user-defined function (since MATLAB's built-in function is **deg2rad()**):

  Command two: `disp(rad(1))`

  Example 5.6: Calculating geometric sum:

  For a given r and n, write a function called geosum to calculate the sum of a geometric series:

$$1 + r + r^2 + r^3 + ... + r^n$$

  Therefore, **r** and **n** must be the function's inputs, and the total of the series must be its output.

  Here is how the code can be created to find the geometric sum:

```
function s=geosum(r, n)
        s=0;
        for i=0:n
        s=s+r^i;
        end
    end
```

  The following command displays the sum of a geometric series with ratio 2 and 5 terms, considering **geosum()** is a user-defined function:

  Command: `disp(geosum(2,5))`

  Output: 63

Example 5.7: Numerical integration:

Calculate the area bounded by the curve and the x-axis from x = 1 to 6 for the give data:

x	0	1	2	3	4	5	6
y	1	0.5	0.2	0.1	0.06	0.04	0.03

Table 5.2: Numerical integration

Use the trapezoidal rule of integration by using the following formula:

$$\int_0^6 f(x)dx = \frac{h}{2}\left[y_0 + 2(y_1 + y_2 + \cdots + y_{\{n-1\}}) + y_n\right]$$

Solve the example using the concept of vectors for loop and functions. Let us now look at the solution.

In this example, the given **x** and **y** values need to be first stored in the vector form, which is common in all three forms, and then the calculation of the integral can be calculated by the following three ways that will lead to the same solution:

- **Using vector form:**

```
clc
clear all
x=[0:6];
y=[1,0.5,0.2,0.1,0.06,0.04,0.03];
n=length(y);
h=x(2)-x(1);
sol=2*sum(y(2:end-1))+y(1)+y(end);
disp((h/2)*sol);
```

- **Using loop:**

```
clc
clear all
x=[0:6];
y=[1,0.5,0.2,0.1,0.06,0.04,0.03];
n=length(y);
h=x(2)-x(1);
s=0;
for i=2:n-1
    s=s+y(i);
end
ss=2*s+y(1)+y(end);
disp((h/2)*ss);
```

- **Using functions:**

```
function r=trp(x,y)
    h=x(2)-x(1)
    r=2*sum(y(2:end-1))+y(1)+y(end)
    r=((h/2)*r)
end
```

This function needs to be stored as **trp.m**, and then, needs to be called from the Command Window or any other program by defining **x** and **y** and calling it as **trp(x,y)**.

Following is how it can be called from the Command Window:

```
x = [0:6];
y = [1,0.5,0.2,0.1,0.06,0.04,0.03];
trp(x,y)
```

In each case, the solution is appearing as **1.4150**

5.1.4 Inline functions

Inline functions in MATLAB are a way to define functions within a single line of code. They are particularly useful for simple functions that do not require a separate M-file. While they were more commonly used in older versions of MATLAB, anonymous functions (introduced later) are generally preferred now for more flexibility. However, understanding inline functions can still be helpful when encountering older code.

Some important characteristics of inline functions are as follows:

- Inline functions are created using the inline function, and the function's expression is provided as a string.

- They are designed for single-expression functions. More complex logic requires a separate function file.

- Like regular functions, inline functions can take input arguments.

- Evaluate using feval (or directly). You can evaluate an inline function using feval or, more commonly now, by directly calling the function.

Here are some examples to give the insight:

Example 5.8: Simple quadratic function:

```
f = inline('a*x^2 + b*x + c', 'x', 'a', 'b', 'c');  % Define inline function
% Evaluate the function
result = f(2, 1, 3, -2); % x=2, a=1, b=3, c=-2
disp(result); % Output: 8
```

In this example, we have defined an inline function f that represents a quadratic equation. The string **'a*x^2 + b*x + c'** is the function's expression. The arguments are listed after the expression string in the order they should be passed to the function.

Example 5.9: Area of a circle:

```
area = inline('pi * r^2', 'r');
radius = 5;
circle_area = area(radius); % Evaluate directly
disp(circle_area); % Output: 78.5398
```

Here, the area is an inline function that calculates the area of a circle given its radius.

5.1.5 Short note on scripts in MATLAB

A script in MATLAB is a file containing a sequence of MATLAB commands saved with a **.m** extension. When executed, MATLAB runs the commands in sequence as if they were typed in the Command Window.

The features of MATLAB scripts are:

- **No input/output arguments**: Unlike functions, scripts do not accept inputs or return outputs.

- **Shares workspace**: Scripts run in the base workspace, meaning variables defined in a script persist after execution.

- **Automation**: Helps automate repetitive tasks by running multiple commands at once.

- **Easy to create and edit**: Can be written in MATLAB's built-in editor or any text editor.

The following are the steps for creating and running a script in MATLAB:

1. Open MATLAB and create a new script (File | New | Script).

2. Write MATLAB commands in the script file.

3. Save the file with a `.m` extension (e.g., `myScript.m`).

4. Run the script by doing the following:

    a. Clicking the **Run** button in the editor.

    b. Typing the script name (without `.m`) in the Command Window.

Referencing a script inside another script

You can call or reference another script by simply using its name (without the `.m` extension) from within your current script. MATLAB will execute that script as part of the current sequence.

For example, suppose you have two scripts:

- **scriptA.m:**
  ```
  disp('This is Script A')
  ```

- **mainScript.m:**
  ```
  disp('This is the Main Script')
  scriptA    % This calls and runs scriptA
  disp('Back to Main Script')
  ```

Output when you run **mainScript.**m:

```
This is the Main Script
This is Script A
Back to Main Script
```

Note: **Since scripts share the same workspace, variables in one script are accessible to another. This can be useful, but also risky if not managed carefully.**

5.2 Functions and scripts in Python

In this section, functions and scripts in the Python language are discussed in detail. Python functions and scripts are fundamental building blocks for writing efficient and reusable code. Functions, defined using the def keyword, encapsulate logic into modular units that can accept parameters and return values, improving code organization and maintainability. For quick, one-line operations, **lambda** functions provide a compact alternative. Scripts are then saved as **.py** files, which allow execution of sequential Python commands and enable automation and programmatic workflows. Together, these features empower developers to create structured, scalable, and reusable programs, making Python a powerful language for tasks ranging from simple calculations to complex data processing and application development.

5.2.1 Understanding functions

A function is a block of reusable code designed to perform a specific task. Instead of writing the same code repeatedly, you can write a function once and call it whenever needed.

Let us look at some reasons to use functions:

- Code reusability

- Improved readability and organization

- Easy debugging and testing

The syntax for defining a function is as follows:

```
def function_name(parameters):
    """Optional docstring"""
    # Function body
        return value  # Optional
```

In Python, functions are reusable blocks of code that perform specific tasks, defined using the def keyword followed by the function name and parameters in parentheses. For example, **def greet(name):** creates a function called greet that takes name as input. The function body, indented under the definition, contains the code to execute, such as **print(f"Hello, {name}!")**. To call the function, you simply use its name with arguments, like **greet("Alice")**, which outputs **"Hello, Alice!"**. Functions can return values using the **return** statement, making them versatile for calculations and data processing. By organizing code into functions, Python programs become more modular, readable, and efficient, as the same functionality can be reused without repetition. Functions also support default arguments, variable-length arguments, and keyword arguments, offering flexibility in how they are called and implemented.

Example 5.10: Function without parameters:

| ```
def greet():
    print("Hello, welcome to Python!")
greet()
``` | Output<br><br>Hello, welcome to Python! |
|---|---|

Table 5.3: Function without parameters

Example 5.11: Function with parameters:

| ```
def add_numbers(a, b):
    return a + b

result = add_numbers(5, 10)
print("Sum:", result)
``` | Output<br><br>Sum: 15 |
|---|---|

Table 5.4: Function with parameters

Example 5.12: Function with default parameters:

| ```
def power(base, exponent=2):
    return base ** exponent

print(power(5))      # 5 squared
print(power(5, 3))   # 5 cubed
``` | Output<br><br>25<br><br>125 |
|---|---|

Table 5.5: Function with default parameters
```

5.2.2 Functions with return values

In Python, functions can return values using the return statement, which allows them to compute results and pass them back to the caller. When a function reaches a **return** statement, it immediately exits and sends the specified value (or multiple values as a tuple) back to where the function was called. For example, a function like **def add(a, b): return a + b**, calculates the sum of two numbers and returns the result, which can then be stored in a variable (e.g., **result = add(3, 5)**). Functions can return any data type, including lists, dictionaries, or even other functions, and they can also return **None** if no **return** statement is provided. This feature makes functions powerful for encapsulating logic and producing reusable outputs, enabling cleaner and more modular code. Multiple values can be returned as a tuple (e.g., **return x, y**), which the caller can unpack into separate variables. Return values are essential for building flexible and efficient programs, as they allow functions to communicate results without relying on global variables.

In Python, functions return values using the **return** statement, which allows them to compute results and pass them back to the caller. When a function reaches a return statement, it immediately exits and sends the specified value (or multiple values as a tuple) back to where the function was called.

For example:

```
def add(a, b):
    return a + b
result = add(3, 5)  # result will be 8
```

Functions can return any data type, such as integers, strings, lists, dictionaries, or even other functions. If no **return** statement is specified, the function returns **None** by default.

To return multiple values, Python packs them into a tuple:

```
def calculate(a, b):
    return a + b, a * b
```

You can unpack the returned values into separate variables:

```
sum_result, product_result = calculate(3, 4)
print(sum_result)     # Output: 7
print(product_result) # Output: 12
```

Note: **This makes functions more versatile and allows cleaner, modular code by avoiding global variables and making the results directly accessible.**

Example 5.13: Returning a single value:

```def square(num): return num * num print(square(4)) # 16```	**Output** **16**

Table 5.6: Returning a single value

Example 5.14: Returning multiple values:

```def arithmetic_operations(a, b): sum_result = a + b difference = a - b return sum_result, difference s, d = arithmetic_operations(10, 5) print(f"Sum: {s}, Difference: {d}")```	**Output** **Sum: 15, Difference: 5**

Table 5.7: Returning multiple values

5.2.3 Scope of variables in functions

In Python, the scope of variables determines where a variable can be accessed within a program. Variables defined inside a function are **local** to that function, meaning they can only be used within it and are not accessible outside. For example, if you declare **x = 10** inside a function, trying to print **x** outside will raise a **NameError**. Conversely, global variables, defined outside functions, can be accessed anywhere in the code, but modifying them inside a function requires the **global** keyword (e.g., **global x**). Python also supports nonlocal variables for nested functions, allowing inner functions to modify variables from an enclosing (but non-global) scope. This scoping mechanism prevents naming conflicts and promotes modular design, ensuring functions operate independently without unintended side effects. Understanding variable scope is crucial for debugging and writing maintainable code.

Understanding variable scope in Python

In Python, the **scope** of variables determines where in the code a variable can be accessed. Variables defined **inside a function** are **local**, meaning they only exist within that function. Trying to access such a variable outside the function will raise a **NameError**.

For example:

```python
def my_function():
    x = 10  # local variable

my_function()
print(x)  # NameError: name 'x' is not defined
```

Conversely, global variables are declared outside any function and can be accessed anywhere in the script. However, if you want to modify a global variable inside a function, you must use the **global** keyword:

```python
x = 5

def update():
    global x
    x = 10

update()
print(x)  # Output: 10
```

Python also supports the **nonlocal** keyword for nested functions, allowing an inner function to modify variables from its immediate enclosing scope (not global):

```python
def outer():
    x = 5
    def inner():
        nonlocal x
        x = 10
    inner()
    print(x)  # Output: 10
```

Python using scope

Python enforces scoping rules to:

- Avoid naming conflicts by isolating variables in functions.
- Promote modularity and function independence.

- Prevent accidental changes to unrelated parts of code.

- Improve readability and maintainability, especially in larger programs.

Python managing scope

Python uses a well-defined **LEGB rule** to resolve variable names:

- **Local**: Variables defined inside the current function.

- **Enclosing**: Variables in enclosing functions (used in nested functions).

- **Global**: Variables defined at the top level of the script or module.

- **Built-in:** Predefined names like **len**, **sum**, etc.

Example 5.15: Local and global scope:

| ```python
x = 10  # Global variable

def access_variable():
    x = 5  # Local variable
    print("Inside function:", x)

access_variable()
print("Outside function:", x)
``` | **Output**<br><br>**Inside function: 5**<br><br>**Outside function: 10** |

Table 5.8: Local and global scope

Example 5.16: Modifying global variable inside function:

| ```python
x = 10

def modify_global():
    global x
    x = 20

modify_global()
print(x)  # 20
``` | **Output**<br><br>**20** |

Table 5.9: Modifying global variable inside function

5.2.4 Recursive functions

In Python, a recursive function is a function that calls itself in order to solve a problem by breaking it down into smaller, more manageable sub-problems. This approach is particularly useful for tasks that can be naturally divided into similar, smaller tasks, such as computing factorials, traversing tree structures, or implementing algorithms like the Fibonacci sequence. For example, a recursive factorial function would be defined as:

```python
def factorial(n):
    return 1 if n == 0 else n * factorial(n-1),
```

Here, the function calls itself with a progressively smaller input until it reaches the base case **(n == 0)**. While recursion can lead to elegant and concise code, it is important to ensure that each recursive call moves closer to the base case to avoid infinite recursion and stack overflow errors. Python's default recursion limit (usually around 1000) prevents excessive stack usage, but for deep recursion, iterative solutions or memorization techniques may be more efficient.

Stack trace is an excellent way to visualize what happens when recursion goes wrong, especially for teaching about infinite recursion and stack overflow.

For example, infinite recursion (no base case):

```
def infinite():
    return infinite()


infinite()
```

Output: Stack trace example

```
Traceback (most recent call last):
  File "example.py", line 4, in <module>
    infinite()
  File "example.py", line 2, in infinite
    return infinite()
  File "example.py", line 2, in infinite
    return infinite()
  File "example.py", line 2, in infinite
    return infinite()
  ...
```

RecursionError: maximum recursion depth exceeded in comparison

> Note: **Python repeats the function call over and over, pushing each onto the call stack, until it exceeds the maximum recursion depth (default ≈ 1000).**

Recursion is a powerful tool in algorithm design, but requires careful implementation to balance clarity with performance.

Recursion using the call stack LIFO

When a recursive function is called, Python internally uses a call stack to keep track of each function call. Each time a function calls itself, a new frame is pushed onto the stack. When the function hits the base case, the stack begins to unwind in reverse order—following the LIFO rule.

For example, recursive factorial with stack behavior:

```
def factorial(n):
    if n == 0:
        return 1
    else:
        return n * factorial(n - 1)
```

Let us walk through factorial(3):

- **Call stack (Build-up):**
    - factorial(3)   ← pushed on top
    - factorial(2)   ← pushed on top
    - factorial(1)   ← pushed on top
    - factorial(0)   ← pushed on top → base case hit!

- **Call stack (Unwinding begins):**
  - o factorial(0) returns 1   ← popped
  - o factorial(1) returns 1 * 1 = 1 ← popped
  - o factorial(2) returns 2 * 1 = 2 ← popped
  - o factorial(3) returns 3 * 2 = 6 ← popped

The LIFO behavior in recursion is as follows:

- **Last function called**: `factorial(0)`

- **First to finish**: `returns 1`

- Then each function waiting on the stack gets popped off and evaluated using the result from the deeper call.

This mirrors how a stack works:

- Push frames as the function dives deeper.

- Pop them as it returns back up.

Example 5.17: Factorial calculation:

```def factorial(n): if n == 1: return 1 else: return n * factorial(n - 1)print(factorial(5)) # 120```	Output 120

Table 5.10: Factorial calculation

5.2.5 Lambda functions and anonymous functions

A Lambda function is a small anonymous function that can have any number of arguments but only one expression.

In Python, **lambda** functions (also called anonymous functions) are small, single-expression functions defined without a name using the **lambda** keyword. Unlike regular functions created with **def**, **lambda** functions are concise and typically used for short, one-off operations where a full function definition would be unnecessary. For example, **square = lambda x: x ** 2** creates a **lambda** that squares its input, equivalent to **def square(x): return x ** 2**. Lambda functions are commonly used with higher-order functions like **map()**, **filter()**, or **sorted()** to provide quick, inline functionality; e.g., **sorted(list, key=lambda item: item[1])** sorts by the second element of each item. While they lack statements, annotations, or multi-line logic, lambdas offer a compact way to write throwaway functions, improving readability for simple tasks. However, for complex operations, regular named functions are preferred for clarity and maintainability.

`lambda arguments: expression`

Example 5.18: Basic **lambda** function:

```square = lambda x: x * xprint(square(4)) # 16```	Output 16

Table 5.11: Basic lambda function

Example 5.19: Multiple parameters:

	Output
`add = lambda a, b: a + b` `print(add(5, 3))  # 8`	8

Table 5.12: Multiple parameters in lambda function

Let us understand where we can use the **lambda** functions.

Lambda functions in Python are best used for short, simple operations where a full function definition would be overly verbose or unnecessary. They shine in situations requiring quick, throwaway functions, such as when you need a one-time key for sorting (**sorted(users, key=lambda x: x['age'])**), filtering data (**filter(lambda x: x % 2 == 0, numbers)**), or transforming elements (**map(lambda x: x * 2, values)**). Lambdas are also handy in GUI programming for concise event handlers or in functional programming paradigms where functions are passed as arguments. However, they should be avoided for complex logic— once a **lambda** spans multiple lines or becomes hard to read, it is better to define a properly named function using **def**. Their strength lies in their brevity for simple, inline operations, not in replacing well-structured code.

Example 5.20: Using a **lambda** function with Python's **map()** to square each element in the list **numbers = [1, 2, 3, 4]**.

Use case one: In **map()**:

	Output

`numbers = [1, 2, 3, 4]`
`squared = map(lambda x: x ** 2, numbers)`
`print(list(squared))`
	`[1, 4, 9, 16]`

Table 5.13: Use case one on lambda function

Example 5.21: Given the list **numbers = [1, 2, 3, 4]**. Following is the use of a **lambda** function with Python's **filter()** to extract only the odd numbers:

Use case two: In **filter()**:

	Output

`numbers = [1, 2, 3, 4, 5]`
`evens = filter(lambda x: x % 2 == 0, numbers)`
`print(list(evens))`
	`[2, 4]`

Table 5.14: Use case two on lambda function

Example 5.22: Given the list of student tuples **students = [("John", 90), ("Jane", 80), ("Dave", 85)]**. Following is the use of the Python's **sorted()** function with a **lambda** function to sort the students by their grades in ascending order:

Use case three: In **sorted()**:

	Output

`students = [("John", 90), ("Jane", 80),`
`("Dave", 85)]`
`sorted_students = sorted(students, key=lambda`
`x: x[1])`
`print(sorted_students)`
	`[('Jane', 80), ('Dave', 85), ('John', 90)]`

Table 5.15: Use case three on lambda function

5.2.6 Writing Python scripts

A Python script is a file with Python code (usually with **.py** extension). Scripts can:

- Define functions
- Include conditionals (like **if __name__ == '__main__'**)
- Be executed directly in the terminal/command prompt

Example script (**my_script.py**):

```python
def greet(name):
    print(f"Hello, {name}!")


if __name__ == "__main__":
    greet("Alice")
```

The steps to running Python scripts are:

1. Save script.
2. Save the file as **my_script.py**.
3. Run in terminal/command prompt:
   python my_script.py

Explanation of **if __name__ == "__main__"**:

- When the script is run directly, **__name__** is set to **"__main__"**.
- If the script is imported into another file, **__name__** will be the name of the script (**my_script**).

5.3 Comparative study in MATLAB and Python

Example 5.23: Basic function definition:

MATLAB:

```matlab
function y = squareNumber(x)
    y = x^2;
end
```

Python:

```python
def square_number(x):
        return x**2
```

Example 5.24: Function call:

MATLAB:

```matlab
squareNumber(4)
```

Python:

square_number(4)	Output
	16

Table 5.16: Example 5.24 Python code and output

Example 5.25: Multiple return values:

MATLAB:
```
function [sumResult, diffResult] = arithmetic(a, b)
    sumResult = a + b;
    diffResult = a - b;
end
```

To call the function, the following commands may be used in the Command Window:
```
[a,b]=arithmetic(2,4)
a = 6
b = -2
```

Python:
```
def arithmetic(a, b):
        return a + b, a - b
```

Example 5.26: Default arguments:

MATLAB: MATLAB does not natively support default arguments in functions. You need to use nargin to check the number of inputs:
```
function y = powerFunction(base, exponent)
    if nargin < 2
        exponent = 2;
    end
    y = base^exponent;
end
```

The following code may be run in the Command Window in order to call the function:
```
powerFunction(2,5)
ans = 32
```

Python:
```
def power_function(base, exponent=2):
        return base**exponent
```

Example 5.27: Function documentation:

MATLAB:
```
function y = squareNumber(x)
    % This function squares x
    y = x^2;
end
```

The function may be called as follows:
```
squareNumber(10)
ans = 100
```

Python:
```
def square_number(x):
    """This function squares x"""
        return x**2
```

Example 5.28: Recursive function:

MATLAB:
```
function f = factorial(n)
    if n == 1
        f = 1;
    else
        f = n * factorial(n-1);
    end
end
```

The function may be called as follows:
```
factorial(5)
ans = 120
```

Python:
```
def factorial(n):
    if n == 1:
        return 1
        return n * factorial(n-1)
```

Example 5.29: Anonymous function (Lambda):

MATLAB:
```
square = @(x) x^2;
```

Python:
```
square = lambda x: x**2
```

Example 5.30: Applying anonymous function to array:

MATLAB:
```
array = [1, 2, 3, 4];
result = arrayfun(@(x) x^2, array);
```

Python:
```
array = [1, 2, 3, 4]
result = list(map(lambda x: x**2, array))
```

Example 5.31: Writing scripts:

MATLAB: Create **myscript.m** with content:
```
disp('Hello MATLAB');
```

Python: Create **myscript.py** with content:
```
print('Hello Python')
```

Example 5.32: Running scripts:

MATLAB: Run in Command Window:
```
Myscript
```

Python: Run in terminal:
```
python myscript.py
```

Example 5.33: Function files:

MATLAB: Each function should have its own **.m** file.

Python: Functions can be stored in a single **.py** file, like:

```
def square(x):
    return x**2


def cube(x):
        return x**3
```

Example 5.34: Function returning arrays:

MATLAB:

```
function y = doubleArray(x)
    y = x * 2;
end
```

The function may be called as follows via the Command Window:

doubleArray(2)
ans = 4

Python:

```
def double_array(x):
        return [i * 2 for i in x]
```

Example 5.35: Function handles:

MATLAB:

```
f = @sin;
result = f(pi/2);
```

Python:

```
import math
f = math.sin
result = f(math.pi/2)
```

Example 5.36: Conditional logic in function:

MATLAB:

```
function y = absoluteValue(x)
    if x > 0
        y = x;
    else
        y = -x;
    end
end
```

The calling of the function may be as follows:

```
absoluteValue(-10)
ans = 10
```

Python:

```python
def absolute_value(x):
        return x if x > 0 else -x
```

Example 5.37: Looping inside functions:

MATLAB:

```matlab
function y = sumNumbers(n)
    y = 0;
    for i = 1:n
        y = y + i;
    end
end
```

The function calling will be as follows.

```matlab
sumNumbers(5)
ans = 15
```

Python:

```python
def sum_numbers(n):
    y = 0
    for i in range(1, n+1):
        y += i
        return y
```

Example 5.38: Passing a function as an argument:

MATLAB:

```matlab
function y = applyFunction(f, x)
    y = f(x);
end
```

The calling of the function will be as follows.

```matlab
applyFunction(@sqrt, 16)
ans = 4
```

Python:

```python
def apply_function(f, x):
    return f(x)
apply_function(lambda x: x**0.5, 16)
```

Example 5.39: Nested functions:

MATLAB:

```matlab
function outer()
    function inner()
        disp('Inner function');
    end
    inner();
end
```

Python:
```
def outer():
    def inner():
        print('Inner function')
        inner()
```

Example 5.40: Variable scope:

MATLAB: Global variables must be declared inside functions:
```
function setGlobal()
    global x
    x = 20;
end
```

In the Command Window, the following commands will be provided:
```
global x = 10;
setGlobal(); % Call the function
disp(x); % Will print 20
```

Python:
```
x = 10
def set_global():
    global x
        x = 20
```

Example 5.41: Argument checking (number of inputs):

MATLAB:
```
function y = powerFunction(base, exponent)
    if nargin < 2
        exponent = 2;
    end
    y = base^exponent;
end
```

The function calling will be as follows:
```
powerFunction(2,4)
ans = 16
```

Python: Python handles this more naturally:
```
def power_function(base, exponent=2):
        return base**exponent
```

Example 5.42: Main block in scripts:

MATLAB: All code in a script is executed when the script runs, no special **"main"** handling.

Python:
```
def main():
    print('This is the main block')
```

```
if __name__ == '__main__':
    main()
```

Conclusion

This chapter provided a comprehensive exploration of functions and scripts in both MATLAB and Python, highlighting their significance in structured and efficient programming. In MATLAB, we examined how to define reusable functions using the function keyword, create scripts for executing command sequences, and implement anonymous functions with the @ operator for concise calculations. These features enhance modularity and automation in numerical computing.

In Python, we covered function definition using def, enabling encapsulation of logic into reusable blocks, and introduced **lambda** functions for quick, inline operations. Additionally, we discussed the role of scripts (.py files) in running Python programs, facilitating automation and workflow execution.

By mastering these concepts, programmers can write cleaner, more efficient, and scalable code in both languages. Whether working on data analysis, scientific computing, or software development, understanding functions and scripts is essential for optimizing performance and maintaining organized projects. The skills acquired in this chapter serve as a foundation for more advanced programming techniques, ensuring adaptability across various computational tasks. In the next chapter, we will learn how to handle the data in MATLAB.

Exercises

MATLAB

Writing functions:

1. Write a MATLAB function named square_num that takes an input number and returns its square.

2. Define a function sum_two_numbers that takes two numbers as input and returns their sum.

3. Create a function factorial_calc that computes the factorial of a given number using recursion.

4. Implement a function is_even that checks whether a given number is even and returns a logical value (true or false).

5. Write a function max_of_three that takes three numbers as input and returns the largest.

6. Define a function reverse_vector that takes a vector as input and returns it in reverse order.

7. Implement a function circle_area that takes the radius of a circle as input and returns its area.

8. Write a function celsius_to_fahrenheit that converts a given Celsius temperature to Fahrenheit.

9. Define a function quadratic_roots that finds the roots of a quadratic equation given coefficients a, b, and c.

10. Create a function string_length that takes a string as input and returns the number of characters.

Scripts:

11. Write a MATLAB script that generates the first 10 Fibonacci numbers and displays them.

12. Create a script that reads an array of numbers from the user, calculates the sum, and displays it.

13. Write a script that takes a user-input number and prints whether it is positive, negative, or zero.

14. Develop a script that computes the sum of squares of numbers from 1 to 50.

15. Write a script that plots the sine and cosine functions on the same graph for values from 0 to 2π.

16. Create a script that solves a system of linear equations using MATLAB's linsolve function.

17. Develop a script that takes a user-input string and prints it in reverse.

18. Write a script that creates and saves a matrix of random numbers to a .mat file.

19. Create a script that reads data from a .csv file and plots it.

20. Write a script that simulates rolling a die 100 times and plots a histogram of the results.

Anonymous functions:

21. Define an anonymous function that computes the cube of a given number.

22. Create an anonymous function that calculates the area of a rectangle given its length and width.

23. Define an anonymous function that checks if a number is prime.

24. Implement an anonymous function that computes the square root of a given number.

25. Define an anonymous function that computes the sum of the squares of two numbers.

26. Write an anonymous function that converts temperature from Fahrenheit to Celsius.

27. Create an anonymous function that returns the maximum of two given numbers.

28. Implement an anonymous function that calculates the exponential value of a given number.

29. Define an anonymous function that computes the hypotenuse of a right triangle given two sides.

30. Create an anonymous function that checks if a given number is a palindrome.

Python

Defining functions:

31. Write a Python function square_num that takes a number as input and returns its square.

32. Define a function sum_two_numbers that takes two numbers as input and returns their sum.

33. Implement a function factorial_calc that computes the factorial of a given number using recursion.

34. Write a function is_even that checks whether a given number is even and returns True or False.

35. Define a function max_of_three that takes three numbers as input and returns the largest.

36. Write a function reverse_string that takes a string as input and returns the reversed string.

37. Implement a function circle_area that takes the radius of a circle as input and returns its area.

38. Define a function celsius_to_fahrenheit that converts a given Celsius temperature to Fahrenheit.

39. Create a function quadratic_roots that finds the roots of a quadratic equation given coefficients a, b, and c.

40. Write a function string_length that takes a string as input and returns the number of characters.

Lambda functions:

41. Write a lambda function that computes the cube of a given number.

42. Create a lambda function that calculates the area of a rectangle given its length and width.

43. Define a lambda function that checks if a number is prime.

44. Implement a lambda function that computes the square root of a given number.

45. Write a lambda function that computes the sum of the squares of two numbers.

46. Create a lambda function that converts temperature from Fahrenheit to Celsius.

47. Define a lambda function that returns the maximum of two given numbers.

48. Implement a lambda function that calculates the exponential value of a given number.

49. Write a lambda function that computes the hypotenuse of a right triangle given two sides.

50. Write a lambda function that takes a list of numbers and returns a new list with only the even numbers.

Common practice questions in MATLAB and Python

1. Create the spd function, which takes three complex integers as input and outputs the sum of the numbers.

2. Create a function called maxn that accepts two inputs and outputs the maximum value.

3. Create a function called factn that takes a number as input, computes the factorial of that number, and outputs the result.

4. To create multiples of a given integer, write a function. Enter the number and the number of multiples that are required as inputs in order to produce a vector output.

5. To find the sum of squares for each component of a vector, write a function called sos. Provide an example to illustrate it, using the vector $A = [1\ 2\ 3\ 4]$.

6. Convert a point's cartesian coordinates (x, y, z) to its cylindrical coordinates (r, θ, z) by creating a function called ctocy. The following are the conversion rules: Since $\theta = tan^{-1}\left(\frac{y}{x}\right)$; $z = z$, $r = \sqrt{x^2 + y^2}$;

   A vector whose components are the specified vector's cartesian coordinates serves as the input variable for this function.

7. To create the Fibonacci series, write a function called fibbo with the initial values 0 and 1. The sum of the two preceding terms is the next term. Provide the function with the user's phrase count as input. (Make 0 and 1 the initial two terms.).

8. Develop a function named pera that computes and returns the perimeter and area of a circle with a given radius as input.

9. Examine a function that computes and returns three output values. The function accepts a single input argument denoting a total amount of seconds and returns the equivalent hours, minutes, and remaining seconds.

10. Write a function to compute the volume and surface area of a hollow cylinder. It accepts as input parameters the radius of the cylinder's base and the height of the cylinder. The volume is expressed as $\pi r^2 h$, while the surface area is represented as $2\pi rh$.

Join our Discord space

Join our Discord workspace for latest updates, offers, tech happenings around the world, new releases, and sessions with the authors:

https://discord.bpbonline.com

## CHAPTER 6

Data Handling in MATLAB

Introduction

This chapter offers a comprehensive guide to data handling functionalities in MATLAB, aimed at helping users manage data seamlessly for analysis, computation, and visualization. MATLAB provides a robust suite of tools to read and write data from a wide variety of sources, including text files, spreadsheets, and binary files. It also supports import/export operations involving formats like **.csv**, **.xls**, **.mat**, and images and audio. Understanding such techniques is needed for anyone working with experimental measurements, simulation results, or system inputs and outputs.

The chapter starts with foundational I/O functions such as **fopen**, **fprintf**, and **fread**, and builds up to high-level functions like **readtable** and **writetable** used for tabular data. It also provides insights about practical use cases, best practices, and data cleaning techniques. Whether working in academia, research, or industry, mastering these data handling tools equips readers to develop efficient, automated workflows that are critical in engineering design, scientific experimentation, financial modeling, and beyond.

Structure

The chapter contains the following topics:

- 6.1 Introduction to data handling in MATLAB
- 6.2 Reading from and writing to files
- 6.3 Importing and exporting data
- 6.4 Handling different data formats

Objectives

By the end of this chapter, you will be able to understand the role of data handling in MATLAB for engineering, scientific, and industrial applications, read data from various file formats using built-in MATLAB functions, and write and export processed data to formats compatible with external tools and systems. You will also learn to utilize low-level I/O functions (**fopen**, **fread**, **fwrite**, **fprintf**, etc.) for custom data handling operations and apply high-level functions to efficiently work with structured data.

By the end of this chapter, you will be able to handle specialized data formats, including image and audio files, for simulation or multimedia analysis and implement best practices for data cleaning and preprocessing to ensure accurate computations and visualizations.

You will understand how to develop automated workflows for recurring data processing tasks in research labs, industrial testing setups, and financial modeling, and integrate MATLAB data handling techniques into broader analytical pipelines to support decision-making and innovation.

6.1 Introduction to data handling in MATLAB

Data handling in MATLAB plays an important role in applications ranging from basic input/output operations to advanced data analytics. With its enhanced set of built-in functions and interactive tools, MATLAB allows users to read, write, import, export, and manage data across a wide variety of formats such as plain text files, CSV files, Excel spreadsheets, MAT-files, images, audio files, and structured data formats like JSON and XML.

Efficient data handling is necessary regarding tasks that include real-time data acquisition, simulation data logging, algorithm testing with benchmark datasets, and statistical analysis. MATLAB simplifies these operations with high-level functions such as `readtable`, `writetable`, `load`, `save`, and `importdata`, as well as low-level file I/O commands like `fopen`, `fread`, and `fprintf` for custom file handling workflows.

Furthermore, data handling tools in MATLAB are integrated with its visualization and computation capabilities, which allow readers to clean, analyze, and visualize data. Whether you are processing experimental lab results, performing data-driven simulations, or integrating with sensors or other software environments, mastering data handling in MATLAB enables reproducible, scalable, and efficient analysis pipelines.

6.2 Reading from and writing to files

MATLAB offers a variety of functions for file I/O operations. Such functions allow readers to read from and write to text and binary files with precision and flexibility, which makes them essential for storing results, processing raw data, or reading configuration parameters.

For text-based data, functions such as `fopen`, `fclose`, `fprintf`, `fscanf`, and `fgets` are mostly used. Such functions give the user low-level control over file handling, enabling customized formatting, line-by-line processing, and efficient management of large textual datasets.

Binary file operations, using functions like `fread` and `fwrite`, are mainly useful when working with performance-sensitive applications or large numerical arrays. Binary formats are more compact and faster to process than text files, but they require an understanding of the underlying data structure.

Moreover, MATLAB supports high-level file access functions such as `readmatrix`, `writematrix`, `readcell`, and `writetable`, which simplify the reading and writing of structured data. These are mainly useful when dealing with delimited files or tables of mixed data types.

Whether you are logging sensor data in real-time, storing simulation results, or reading data for analysis, mastering file I/O in MATLAB is foundational for building robust and scalable data processing workflows.

6.2.1 Basic file operations

Let us look at some basic file operations:

- **fopen:** Opens a file and returns a file identifier. The **fopen** function is used to open a file for reading, writing, or appending. It returns a file identifier (an integer), which is used by other file I/O functions to refer to the file.

  Syntax:
  ```
  fileID = fopen(filename, permission);
  ```

Example:

```
fileID = fopen('data.txt', 'r'); % Opens the file for reading
```

Common permission modes:

o **'r'**: read only

o **'w'**: write (overwrites existing file or creates new)

o **'a'**: append (writes at end of file)

o **'r+'**, **'w+'**, **'a+'**: read/write combinations

- **fclose:** Closes an open file. The **fclose** function is used to close a file that was opened with **fopen**. It is good practice to always close a file after operations are complete to free system resources and prevent data corruption.

Syntax:

```
status = fclose(fileID);
```

Example:

```
fclose(fileID);
```

Note: **A status of 0 means the file closed successfully; -1 indicates an error.**

- **fprintf:** Formats and writes data to a text **file.fprintf** writes data to a file with formatting options (similar to C language syntax). It is useful for writing structured text, such as CSV lines or logs.

Syntax:

```
fprintf(fileID, formatSpec, A, ...);
```

Example:

```
fileID = fopen('output.txt', 'w');
fprintf(fileID, 'The value is: %.2f\n', 3.1416);
fclose(fileID);
```

- **fscanf /fgets:** Reads formatted/unformatted data from a file.

fscanf: Reads formatted data from a file. It reads data using a specified format and returns it in array form.

Syntax:

```
A = fscanf(fileID, formatSpec);
```

Example:

```
fileID = fopen('numbers.txt', 'r');
A = fscanf(fileID, '%f'); % Reads numeric data
fclose(fileID);
```

fgets: Reads a line of text from a file. It reads one line at a time and returns a character vector (string).

Syntax:

```
line = fgets(fileID);
```

Example:

```
fileID = fopen('log.txt', 'r');
line = fgets(fileID); % Reads first line
fclose(fileID);
```

Text file operations are useful for logging, configuration files, and processing simple datasets. Files must be opened before use and closed after operations to avoid memory leaks or data corruption.

Example 6.1: Writing to a text file:

```
fileID = fopen('example.txt','w');
fprintf(fileID,'This is a sample line.\n');
fclose(fileID);
```

This example demonstrates how to write a line of text into a new or existing text file using MATLAB. The **fopen** function is used with the **'w'** (write) mode to create or overwrite the file named example.txt. It returns a file identifier **fileID**, which is a reference used in subsequent file operations. The **fprintf** function is then used to write the string "**This is a sample line.**" followed by a newline character (**\n**) into the file. This approach is especially useful when logging information, saving results, or generating structured data files. Finally, **fclose(fileID)** is called to close the file, ensuring that all data is properly saved and system resources are released.

Example 6.2: Reading from a text file:

```
fileID = fopen('example.txt','r');
line = fgets(fileID);
disp(line);
fclose(fileID);
```

In this example, the content previously written to example.txt is read and displayed. The file is opened using **fopen** with the **'r'** (read) mode, and a file identifier **fileID** is returned. The **fgets** function is used to read a single line of text from the file, including the newline character. The content is stored in the variable line, which is then displayed in the MATLAB Command Window using the **disp** function. After reading, the file is closed using **fclose(fileID)** to ensure proper file handling. This example illustrates a fundamental way to access and process textual data line by line in MATLAB.

6.2.2 Working with binary files

Let us look at how to work with binary files:

- **fwrite:** Writes binary data. The **fwrite** function is used to write numerical or character data to a file in binary format. Binary writing is faster and more compact than text writing, making it suitable for large datasets, signal processing outputs, and applications where storage efficiency or performance is critical.

  Syntax:

  ```
  fwrite(fileID, data, precision);
  ```

  Note:

  fileID: Identifier obtained from fopen.

  data: The array or variable you want to write.

  precision: (Optional) Specifies the data type, such as 'double', 'int16', 'uint8', etc. If not specified, the default is 'uint8'.

  Example:

  ```
  fileID = fopen('binaryfile.bin', 'w');
  data = [3.14, 2.71, 1.41];
  fwrite(fileID, data, 'double');
  fclose(fileID);
  ```

- **fread:** The **fread** function reads binary data from a file into an array. It is typically used in conjunction with **fwrite** to retrieve binary-stored information for further processing.

  Syntax:

  ```
  A = fread(fileID, size, precision);
  ```

  Note:

  fileID: Identifier from fopen.

  size: (Optional) Number of elements to read or a two-element vector [m, n].

  precision: (Optional) The data type to read, e.g., 'double', 'int16'.

  Example:

  ```
  fileID = fopen('binaryfile.bin', 'r');
  readData = fread(fileID, 3, 'double');
  fclose(fileID);
  ```

  Binary files are compact and faster to read/write compared to text files. They are ideal for large datasets and performance-critical applications.

Example 6.3: Writing and reading binary data:

```
fileID = fopen('data.bin','w');
data = [1 2 3 4 5];
fwrite(fileID, data, 'double');
fclose(fileID);

fileID = fopen('data.bin','r');
newData = fread(fileID, 5, 'double');
disp(newData);
fclose(fileID);
```

The preceding example illustrates how to store numerical data in a binary file and then retrieve it using MATLAB's **fwrite** and **fread** functions. Binary files are particularly useful for efficient storage and fast I/O operations, especially when working with large numerical datasets.

In the first part of the example, a file named **data.bin** is opened in **write** mode (**'w'**) using **fopen**. The array **data = [1 2 3 4 5]** contains five double-precision numbers that are written to the file using **fwrite**. The third argument **'double'** specifies that the data should be stored in double-precision floating-point format. After writing, the file is closed using **fclose(fileID)** to ensure the data is properly saved and the file is released from memory.

In the second part, the file **data.bin** is reopened in **read** mode (**'r'**). The function **fread** reads five double-precision values from the file into the variable **newData**. This retrieves the original data that was stored, which is then displayed using **disp(newData)**. Finally, the file is closed again with **fclose**.

6.3 Importing and exporting data

Efficient data analysis in MATLAB often requires importing from and exporting to files in various formats such as **.csv**, **.xls**, or **.mat**.

Efficient data analysis in MATLAB often requires importing from and exporting to files in various formats such as **.csv**, **.xls**, **.xlsx**, **.txt**, and **.mat**. MATLAB provides a rich set of high-level functions that allow users to seamlessly read data from external sources, process it within the MATLAB environment, and then export results for documentation, further analysis, or integration with other tools.

When working with structured datasets, such as spreadsheets or tabular text files, functions like **readtable**, **readmatrix**, and **readcell** are commonly used to bring data into MATLAB in the form of tables, numeric arrays, or cell arrays, respectively. These formats are particularly useful for handling large datasets, performing statistical analysis, and visualizing trends.

On the export side, MATLAB offers corresponding functions such as **writetable**, **writematrix**, and **writecell**, which allow processed data to be saved in a format that is compatible with Excel, databases, and data-sharing platforms. This makes it easy to collaborate with non-MATLAB users or to import MATLAB results into other software tools for visualization and reporting.

Additionally, MATLAB supports reading from and writing to its own proprietary format (.mat) using load and save. MAT-files are especially useful for storing variables with complete fidelity, including complex data structures such as arrays, structs, and cell arrays.

6.3.1 Using readtable and writetable

Let us look at the details:

- **readtable**: Reads data into a table format from text/CSV/Excel.

  The **readtable** function in MATLAB is used to import data from external files such as **.txt**, **.csv**, or Excel files into a table format. Tables in MATLAB are highly structured data types that allow storage of columns with different data types (e.g., numeric, text, categorical). This function automatically detects variable names from the first row of the file and assigns them as column headers in the table, making the data easy to access and analyze using column names.

  Usage:

  ```
  T = readtable('data.csv');
  ```

  Note: **This command reads the content of data.csv into the variable T as a table. You can then reference columns using dot notation, like T.Age or T.Name.**

- **writetable**: Exports a table to text/CSV/Excel.

  The **writetable** function is used to export data from a MATLAB table to an external file in formats such as **.csv**, **.txt**, or Excel (**.xlsx**). This is especially useful when you want to share processed results or save data in a structured, readable format. It preserves column headers and automatically handles formatting for numeric and text data.

  Usage:

  ```
  writetable(T, 'output.csv');
  ```

  Note: **This command writes the table T to a file named output.csv. Column names will be written as headers in the first row of the file.**

  Tables are ideal for handling mixed-type data with named variables. They make data analysis more readable and manageable.

  Note: **In MATLAB, when writetable command is used to export a table, we can ignore writing the headers (i.e., variable names) by using the 'WriteVariableNames' option and setting it to false.**

  Syntax:

  ```
  writetable(T, 'filename.csv', 'WriteVariableNames', false);
  ```

  For example:

  ```
  T = readtable('data.csv');
  writetable(T, 'new_data.csv', 'WriteVariableNames', false);
  ```

Example 6.4: Importing data:

```
tbl = readtable('sample_data.csv');
disp(tbl);
```

In this example, the **readtable** function is used to import data from a CSV file named **sample_data.csv**. The data is read into the variable **tbl**, which becomes a MATLAB table. Tables are useful for storing column-oriented data where each column can have a different type (e.g., numeric, text, categorical), and the first row of the CSV file is typically treated as the header containing variable names. After importing, the **disp(tbl)** command is used to display the contents of the table in the MATLAB Command Window. This example demonstrates a simple and efficient way to load structured data into MATLAB for further analysis or visualization.

Example 6.5: Exporting data:

```
writetable(tbl, 'output_data.csv');
```

This example shows how to export a table from MATLAB to a new CSV file using the **writetable** function. The table variable **tbl**, which might have been created or modified in MATLAB, is written to a file named **output_data.csv**. The function automatically includes the variable names as headers in the first row of the file. This allows the data to be easily shared or imported into other software tools like Excel or Python. This operation is particularly helpful when saving processed data, intermediate results, or generating reports.

6.3.2 Working with .mat files

Let us look at how to work with **.mat** files:

- **save:** Saves workspace variables to a **.mat** file.

  The save function is used to store variables from the MATLAB workspace into a **.mat** file. MAT-files are MATLAB's proprietary binary file format designed for storing variables efficiently, preserving data types, array dimensions, and even complex structures like cell arrays or structs.

  Syntax:

  ```
  save('filename.mat', 'var1', 'var2', ...);
  ```

  o **'filename.mat':** Name of the file to save the data to. If the extension is omitted, **.mat** is used by default.

  o **'var1', 'var2', ... :** Names of the variables to be saved. If no variable names are given, all variables in the current workspace are saved.

  Example:

  ```
  A = magic(3);
  B = rand(1,5);
  save('myData.mat', 'A', 'B');
  ```

  Note. **This command saves the variables A and B into a file named myData.mat.**

- **load**: It loads variables from a **.mat** file. The load function is used to retrieve data stored in a **.mat** file and bring it back into the current MATLAB workspace. It recreates the variables with the same names and contents they had when saved.

  Syntax:

  ```
  load('filename.mat');
  ```

  Note. **This will load all variables stored in the file. To load specific variables, list them as additional arguments.**

Example:
```
load('myData.mat');  % Loads all variables
```
or
```
load('myData.mat', 'A');  % Loads only variable A
```

MAT-files are the native MATLAB format. They preserve data structure, types, and attributes efficiently.

Example 6.6: Saving and loading variables
```
A = rand(5);
save('matrixData.mat', 'A');
clear A;
load('matrixData.mat');
disp(A);
```

This example demonstrates how to save a variable to a .mat file and then load it back into the MATLAB workspace.

In the first line, the variable A is created using **rand(5)**, which generates a 55 matrix of random numbers between 0 and 1. The save function is then used to store the variable A into a file named **matrixData.mat**. This file acts as a container that preserves the full content and structure of the variable, making it easy to store and retrieve data across MATLAB sessions.

After saving, the clear A command is used to remove the variable A from the workspace, simulating a fresh environment where the variable no longer exists. Then, the load function is used to retrieve the variable A from the saved .mat file. The variable is restored with its original name and data. Finally, **disp(A)** displays the content of the matrix A in the Command Window, confirming that the data has been successfully saved and reloaded.

6.3.3 Importing Excel files

Let us look at the details:

- o **readtable: readtable** is a high-level function that reads data from an Excel file (or CSV/text file) and returns it as a MATLAB table. It is especially useful when the data contains mixed types (e.g., numbers, strings, dates) and when you want to retain variable names from the first row of the spreadsheet.

  Example:
  ```
  T = readtable('data.xlsx');
  ```

- o **readmatrix: readmatrix** reads numeric and string data from an Excel file and returns it as a numeric matrix. It is useful when your data is mostly numerical and you do not need headers or variable names.

  Example:
  ```
  M = readmatrix('data.xlsx');
  ```

- o **xlsread: xlsread** is an older function that reads data from Excel spreadsheets. It can return numeric data, text data, or both.

  Example:
  ```
  [num, txt, raw] = xlsread('data.xlsx');
  ```

  Note: **xlsread is still supported but has been largely replaced by readtable and readmatrix in newer MATLAB versions.**

Note:

Syntax for reading from a specific sheet:

```
[num, txt, raw] = xlsread('data.xlsx', 'Sheet2');  % Using sheet name
[num, txt, raw] = xlsread('data.xlsx', 2);          % Using sheet index
```

For rxample:

```
[num, txt, raw] = xlsread('data.xlsx', 'Sales2024');
```

As per the preceding command, we can read the data from read data from the sheet named 'Sales2024'.

- **writetable, writematrix, or xlswrite:**

  o **writetable: `writetable`** writes a table from MATLAB to an Excel file. It includes variable names as column headers and is ideal for saving structured data for sharing or further analysis in Excel.

    Example:
    ```
    writetable(T, 'output.xlsx');
    ```

  o **writematrix: `writematrix`** writes a numeric matrix to an Excel or CSV file. It is a fast and simple way to export purely numerical data.

    Example:
    ```
    writematrix(M, 'matrix_output.xlsx');
    ```

  o **xlswrite: `xlswrite`** is the legacy function used for writing data to Excel files. It works with numeric and cell array data.

    Example:
    ```
    xlswrite('output.xlsx', M);
    ```

    Excel files are commonly used in business and research. MATLAB functions offer compatibility with both old and new Excel formats.

6.3.4 Importing text and delimited files

MATLAB provides multiple functions to import data from text files and delimited files (like **.csv**, **.tsv**, or **.txt**). Each function serves different purposes depending on the data structure and the level of control needed:

- **readmatrix, readcell, readlines, and importdata offer various levels of control:**

  o **readmatrix**: This function reads numeric and mixed-type data from a file and returns a numeric matrix. It automatically skips non-numeric data or replaces it with NaN.

    It is best for numerical data stored in spreadsheets or delimited files.

    Example:
    ```
    data = readmatrix('data.txt');
    ```

  o **readcell**: reads the entire content of a file into a cell array. This is useful when the file contains mixed data types (numbers, strings, dates, etc.).

    Best for: Mixed-type content with unknown structure.

    Example:
    ```
    C = readcell('survey.csv');
    ```

o **readlines**: Reads a text file line by line and returns a string array, where each element represents one line of the file. It is especially helpful for logs, comments, or line-wise text analysis.

It is best for line-by-line text processing.

Example:

```
lines = readlines('logfile.txt');
```

o **Importdata**: A versatile function that attempts to detect the data format automatically. It can read numeric, text, or mixed data and return a structure containing the contents.

It is best for quick imports without knowing the format in advance.

Example:

```
data = importdata('datafile.txt');
```

- **detectImportOptions** This function is used to create and customize an import options object before reading the file. It allows you to control which columns to import, data types, delimiters, missing value handling, and more.

It is best for fine-tuning the import process for complex or messy datasets.

Example:

```
opts = detectImportOptions('data.csv');
opts.SelectedVariableNames = {'Name', 'Age'};
T = readtable('data.csv', opts);
```

Some of the basics are notified as follows.

o Use **readmatrix** for numeric data

o **readcell** for mixed content

o **readlines** for plain text

o **importdata** for flexible auto-detection

o **detectImportOptions** for precision control over file reading behavior

o Use **detectImportOptions** to fine-tune how the data is read

Example 6.7: Using **readmatrix**:

```
data = readmatrix('data.txt');
```

6.4 Handling different data formats

MATLAB supports reading and writing a wide variety of file formats. Let us look at them in detail in the following sections.

6.4.1 Supported formats

MATLAB provides comprehensive support for a wide range of file formats, enabling users to work with diverse data sources across scientific, engineering, and multimedia domains. For textual and tabular data, formats such as .txt and .csv are commonly used and can be easily imported using functions like **readtable** or **readmatrix**. Spreadsheet files in **.xls** and **.xlsx** formats are widely supported, allowing seamless integration with Excel data for both reading and writing using **readtable**, **writetable**, and similar functions.

For high-performance storage and native compatibility, MATLAB's own .mat files are ideal for saving variables and complex data structures, while .bin files offer compact, binary-level data storage for efficient

I/O operations. MATLAB also supports the **Hierarchical Data Format** (**.h5**), which is commonly used in large-scale scientific data applications, especially in fields like climate modeling, machine learning, and bioinformatics.

In addition to numerical and text-based formats, MATLAB handles multimedia files with ease. Image formats such as **.jpg**, **.png**, and .tiff can be processed using **imread** and **imwrite**, and audio formats like **.wav** and **.mp3** can be accessed using **audioread** and **audiowrite**.

MATLAB supports a wide range of file formats for data import and export, which enables users to work with various types of information across disciplines. Commonly used file formats include:

- **Text files: .txt**, **.csv**
- **Spreadsheet files: .xls**, **.xlsx**
- **Binary and MATLAB files: .mat**, **.bin**
- **Hierarchical data format: .h5**
- **Image files: .jpg**, **.png**, **.tiff**
- **Audio files: .wav**, **.mp3**

6.4.2 Using the file import tool

MATLAB's GUI-based file import tool provides a visual interface to preview and import data. It can generate equivalent code for automation.

MATLAB's GUI-based file import tool provides an intuitive and user-friendly interface for importing data from various file types such as **.txt**, **.csv**, **.xls**, and **.xlsx**. This tool is particularly useful for users who prefer a visual workflow over command-line operations or for those working with unfamiliar data formats.

When you open a file using the file import tool (e.g., by double-clicking a file in the current folder window or using the **uiimport** command), MATLAB displays a preview of the data, including headers, delimiters, and sample rows. You can interactively choose the range of data to import, specify how text and numeric values should be interpreted, select which columns to include, and define missing value representations.

One of the most powerful features of the tool is its ability to automatically generate equivalent MATLAB code (such as **readtable** or **readmatrix** commands). This allows users to replicate the same import configuration programmatically in scripts, making workflows more efficient and reproducible.

6.4.3 Data cleaning after import

Let us look at the details:

- **Use fillmissing to replace NaN values**: The **fillmissing** function is used to replace missing values (represented as NaN in numeric arrays or empty cells in tables) with more meaningful values. This can be done using methods like 'linear' interpolation, 'previous' values, or constant values.

  Example:

  ```
  cleanData = fillmissing(data, 'linear');
  ```

  Note. **This replaces NaN values with linearly interpolated values, which is useful when dealing with time series or sensor data.**

  o Sample data table with missing values:
  ```
  % Sample data with missing (NaN) values
  data = table([1; 2; NaN; 4; NaN], [10; NaN; 30; NaN; 50], ...
              'VariableNames', {'Sensor1', 'Sensor2'});
  ```

```
disp('Original Data:');
disp(data);
```

o Cleaning missing data using **fillmissing**:

```
% Fill missing values using linear interpolation
cleanData = fillmissing(data, 'linear');
disp('Cleaned Data (Linear Interpolation):');
disp(cleanData);
```

Output:

```
Sensor1    Sensor2

_____    _____

   1        10
   2        NaN
 NaN        30
   4        NaN
 NaN        50


Cleaned Data (using 'linear' method):
Sensor1    Sensor2

_____    _____

   1          10
   2          20
   3          30
   4          40
   4          50
```

- **fillmissing(data, 'linear'):** Replaces NaN with values that are linearly interpolated between existing numeric data.

  This is useful for time-series data, sensor data, or datasets where smooth transitions between values are expected.

- **Identify outliers with isoutlier:** The **isoutlier** function detects data points that are significantly different from the rest of the dataset, using statistical methods like mean ± 3 standard deviations, **interquartile range (IQR)**, or moving median.

Example:

```
outliers = isoutlier(data);
```

Note:

Sample data:

```
data = [10 12 11 13 10 100 12 11 14 10]; % 100 is an outlier
```

Identify Outliers:

```
outliers = isoutlier(data);
```

Display results:

```
disp('Original Data:');
disp(data);
```

```
disp('Outlier Flags (true = outlier):');
disp(outliers);
```

% **Optional: Extract outliers**

```
detectedOutliers = data(outliers);
disp('Detected Outliers:');
disp(detectedOutliers);
```

Output:
```
Original Data:
    10   12   11   13   10  100   12   11   14   10
Outlier Flags (isoutlier output):
false false false false false  true false false false false
Detected Outliers:
   100
```

Note. **This returns a logical array where true indicates an outlier. You can then choose to remove, replace, or analyze these outliers further.**

- **Convert text to numbers with str2double, categorical:** Imported data often includes textual entries for numeric fields (e.g., "10", "12.5" as strings) or non-numeric labels (e.g., "Low", "Medium", "High").

  MATLAB provides functions to convert these appropriately:

  o **str2double:** Converts text strings representing numbers into numeric values.
  ```
  numArray = str2double(stringArray);
  ```

  o **categorical:** Converts text labels into categorical arrays, useful for statistical modeling and grouping.
  ```
  catData = categorical({'Low', 'Medium', 'High', 'Low'});
  ```

Example 6.8: Filling Mmissing data:
```
tbl.Height = fillmissing(tbl.Height, 'linear');
```

Conclusion

This chapter provided an in-depth exploration of MATLAB's data handling capabilities. We discussed basic file operations, including reading and writing text and binary files. Next, we covered importing/exporting data using functions like readtable, writetable, load, and save. We also explored the use of the file import tool and addressed working with different file formats, including text, Excel, and .mat files. In the next chapter, data handling in Python is discussed along with a comparative study in MATLAB and Python.

Exercises

Reading from and writing to files (text and binary)

1. Write a MATLAB script to create a text file and write your name into it.
2. Create a file using fopen and write the numbers 1 to 10 using fprintf.
3. Read and display the content of a text file line by line using fgets.
4. Use fscanf to read numeric values from a formatted text file.
5. Create a binary file and store an array of 10 random numbers using fwrite.

6. Write MATLAB code to read 5 double values from a binary file.

7. Use fopen to open a non-existing file in read mode. What is the result?

8. Write a script that appends a new line of text to an existing file.

9. Count the number of lines in a given text file using file I/O functions.

10. Create a log file and write timestamps of 5 random events using fprintf.

Working with .mat Files

1. Save three variables (a matrix, a vector, and a string) to a .mat file.

2. Load only one specific variable from a .mat file using the load command.

3. Write code to check if a variable exists in a .mat file before loading.

4. Use whos('-file', filename) to list contents of a .mat file.

5. Clear all variables, then reload them from a .mat file and verify.

Importing text, CSV, and Excel files

1. Use readtable to import a CSV file and display its summary.

2. Use readmatrix to read numeric data from a .csv file.

3. Use readcell to read mixed data from a .csv file.

4. Import a .txt file using importdata and plot the data.

5. Read the first five rows and selected columns of a large Excel file.

6. Use detectImportOptions to skip header rows in a CSV import.

7. Modify import options to read only numeric columns from a text file.

8. Use readtable to import data, and plot one of its columns.

9. Use xlsread (legacy) to read both numeric and text data from an Excel file.

10. Write a script that imports a dataset and filters all rows with missing data.

Exporting data to files

1. Export a MATLAB table to a CSV file using writetable.

2. Write a numeric matrix to a text file using writematrix.

3. Use writecell to save a cell array to a CSV file.

4. Append data to an existing CSV file without overwriting it.

5. Create a table with 3 columns and write it to an Excel file.

6. Write a script that saves a matrix to both .mat and .csv formats.

7. Export MATLAB variables to .txt and read them back.

Data cleaning after Import

1. Use fillmissing to fill NaN values in imported table data.

2. Use isoutlier to identify and count outliers in a numeric dataset.

3. Convert a text column in a table to numeric using str2double.

4. Convert a column of labels (e.g., 'Low', 'Medium', 'High') to categorical.

5. Remove all rows containing missing values from a table.

6. Use standardizeMissing to define custom missing value symbols (e.g., 'NA').

Practical applications and challenges

1. Import student grades from an Excel file and compute average marks.

2. Save experimental sensor readings to a binary file for five seconds.

3. Create a script that logs daily temperature to a text file.

4. Write a script that imports time-series data and plots it.

5. Build a data report generator that reads a file, performs analysis, and exports the summary.

6. Import a large CSV file and extract top five highest values in a specific column.

7. Develop a script that reads multiple files and combines their contents into one table.

8. Create a function that accepts a filename and returns the number of rows in it.

9. Automate importing all .csv files from a folder using a loop.

10. Import a CSV file, detect categorical and numeric columns, and separate them.

11. Create a .mat file containing simulation results and a script to reload and visualize them.

12. Simulate data cleaning workflow: import | detect missing | fill | export cleaned data.

Join our Discord space

Join our Discord workspace for latest updates, offers, tech happenings around the world, new releases, and sessions with the authors:

https://discord.bpbonline.com

CHAPTER 7
Data Handling in MATLAB and Python

Introduction

In this chapter, you will explore essential file handling techniques in Python, focusing on the use of built-in functions such as open, read, write, and close to perform file operations. These functions allow for efficient reading from and writing to files, enabling data persistence and manipulation. Additionally, the chapter delves into working with popular data formats, specifically CSV and JSON. You will learn how to use Python's CSV module to read from and write to CSV files, which are commonly used for tabular data storage. The json module will be introduced to handle JSON files, a widely used format for data interchange. By the end of the chapter, you will be equipped with the skills to manage files and process data in various formats, enhancing their ability to work with real-world data in Python.

Structure

This chapter will cover the following topics:

- 7.1 File handling and data formats in Python will be discussed.

- 7.2 Comparative study of MATLAB and Python via examples will be provided.

Objectives

By the end of this chapter, you will be able to perform file operations in Python using built-in functions like open, read, write, and close to manage data storage and retrieval effectively. They will also learn to read and write data to CSV files using Python's csv module, enabling them to handle tabular data for tasks like data analysis or reporting.

This chapter will enable you to parse and generate JSON data using the json module, facilitating seamless data interchange in web APIs and configuration files, and apply file handling and data format skills to real-world scenarios, such as processing log files, managing datasets, or integrating with external systems. You will learn to develop practical solutions for automating data storage, retrieval, and transformation tasks, enhancing their ability to work with diverse data sources.

7.1 File handling and data formats in Python

Any programming language must provide file handling in order for programs to effectively store, retrieve, and alter data. Python comes with built-in routines to manage files and supports a variety of file types, including text, CSV, and JSON. Python's file handling features, including reading and writing files, working with structured data formats like CSV and JSON, and real-world applications, will all be thoroughly covered in this chapter.

Python file handling, including reading from and writing to files, will be covered in this chapter. Additionally, you will learn how to interact with different data types, including CSV and JSON. These tasks are made simple and effective by Python's built-in functions and modules.

7.1.1 File handling in Python

File handling is a fundamental aspect of programming that allows you to store, retrieve, and manipulate data persistently. In Python, file handling is straightforward and efficient, thanks to built-in functions like open, read, write, and close. The open function is used to access files in different modes, such as read ('r'), write ('w'), append ('a'), or binary ('b'). Once a file is opened, you can read its content using methods like **read**, **readline**, or **readlines**, which are useful for processing text or data line by line. For writing data, the **write** and **writelines** methods allow you to add content to files, either by overwriting existing data or appending to it. Properly closing files using the close method or the with statement ensures that resources are released and data is saved correctly. File handling is essential for tasks like logging, data storage, configuration management, and working with external datasets, making it a critical skill for real-world programming:

- **Opening and closing files**: File handling in Python begins with opening a file, performing the necessary operations, and ensuring it is properly closed to avoid resource leaks or data corruption. The **open()** function is used to access a file, requiring two main arguments: the file path and the mode, such as **'r'** for reading, **'w'** for writing, **'a'** for appending, or **'b'** for binary mode. For example, **file = open('example.txt', 'r')** opens a file in read mode. Once a file is opened, you can read its content using methods like **read()**, **readline()**, or **readlines()**, which are useful for processing text or data line by line. For writing data, methods like **write()** and **writelines()** allow you to add content to the file, such as **file.write('Hello, World!')**. After performing operations, it is crucial to close the file using the **close()** method, like **file.close()**, to free up system resources. Alternatively, the with statement is recommended as it automatically handles closing the file, even if an error occurs, making the code cleaner and safer.

  Example 7.1: Python provides the **open()** function to open files in different modes:

  ```
  # Opening a file
  file = open("CHAPTER7_DATA.txt", "r")  # Read mode
  file.close()
  ```

  Using with statement (recommended for automatic closing):

  ```
  with open("CHAPTER7_DATA.txt", "r") as file:
      content = file.read()
      print(content)
  ```

- **File modes**: File modes in Python determine how a file is opened and what operations can be performed on it. The **open()** function accepts a mode parameter, which specifies whether the file is opened for reading, writing, appending, or in binary format. The most common modes include **'r'** for reading (default mode), **'w'** for writing (which overwrites the file or creates it if it does not exist), and **'a'** for appending (which adds data to the end of the file without overwriting existing content). For binary files, modes like **read binary (rb)** and **write binary (wb)** are used, which are essential for handling non-text files such as images or executables. Additionally, the **'r+'** mode allows both reading and writing, while **'a+'** enables reading and appending. Python also supports exclusive creation with the **'x'** mode, which ensures a file is created only if it does not already exist, preventing accidental overwrites. Understanding these modes is crucial for effective file handling, as they dictate how data is accessed, modified, or stored, ensuring the integrity and proper management of files in your programs:

Mode	Description
'r'	Read mode (default)
'w'	Write mode (overwrites if file exists)
'a'	Append mode (adds content to the file)
'x'	Creates a new file, returns error if it exists
'b'	Binary mode
't'	Text mode (default)

Table 7.1: Different file modes

- **Reading files**: Python's **open()** function with the **'r'** mode, combined with methods like **read()**, **readline()**, or **readlines()**, allows you to efficiently read and process content from files.

Example 7.2: Python allows reading files using various methods:

```
# Read entire file
with open("CHAPTER7_DATA.txt", "r") as file:
    content = file.read()
    print(content)
```

Example 7.3: Reading line by line:

```
with open("CHAPTER7_DATA.txt", "r") as file:
    for line in file:
        print(line.strip())
```

Example 7.4: Reading a limited number of characters:

```
with open("CHAPTER7_DATA.txt", "r") as file:
    print(file.read(10))  # Read first 10 characters
```

Example 7.5: Reading all lines into a list:

```
with open("CHAPTER7_DATA.txt", "r") as file:
    lines = file.readlines()
    print(lines)
```

- **Writing to files**: Python's **open()** function with the **'r'** mode, combined with methods like **read()**, **readline()**, or **readlines()**, allows you to efficiently read and process content from files:

Example 7.6: To write content to a file:

```
# Writing to a file
with open("CHAPTER7_DATA.txt", "w") as file:
    file.write("Hello, this is a sample text file.")
```

Example 7.7: Appending data:

```
# Appending to a file
with open("CHAPTER7_DATA.txt", "a") as file:
    file.write("\nAppending new content.")
```

Example 7.8: Writing multiple lines:

```
lines = ["First line\n", "Second line\n", "Third line\n"]
with open("CHAPTER7_DATA.txt", "w") as file:
    file.writelines(lines)
```

7.1.2 Working with CSV files

Comma-separated values (CSV) files are widely used for storing and exchanging tabular data due to their simplicity and compatibility with various applications like Excel, databases, and data analysis tools. Python's built-in csv module provides powerful tools to read from and write to CSV files efficiently. To read a CSV file, you can use the **csv.reader()** function, which processes each row as a list of values.

This allows you to iterate through rows and perform operations like filtering or calculations. For writing data, the **csv.writer()** function is used, enabling you to create or update CSV files. Methods like **writerow()** and **writerows()** make it easy to add data row by row or in bulk. Additionally, the **csv.DictReader()** and **csv.DictWriter()** classes allow you to handle CSV data as dictionaries, which is particularly useful when working with files that include headers:

- **Reading CSV files**: Python's **csv.reader()** function allows you to read and process CSV files row by row, making it easy to extract and manipulate tabular data.

Example 7.9: Reading data from a CSV file using **csv.reader()**:

```
import csv


with open("CHAPTER7_DATA.csv", "r") as file:
    reader = csv.reader(file)
    for row in reader:
        print(row)
```

Example 7.10: Using **DictReader** to read CSV as dictionaries:

```
with open("CHAPTER7_DATA.csv", "r") as file:
    reader = csv.DictReader(file)
    for row in reader:
        print(row["YearsExperience"], row["Salary"])
```

Example 7.11: Writing to CSV files:

```
with open("CHAPTER7_DATA.csv", "w", newline="") as file:
    writer = csv.writer(file)
    writer.writerow(["YearsExperience", "Salary"])
    writer.writerow(["50", 2500000])
```

Example 7.12: Using **DictWriter**:

```
import csv
with open("CHAPTER7_DATA.csv", "w", newline="") as file:
    fieldnames = ["YearsExperience", "Salary"]
    writer = csv.DictWriter(file, fieldnames=fieldnames)
    writer.writeheader()
    writer.writerow({"YearsExperience": 51, "Salary": 2800000})
```

Example 7.13: Appending rows to CSV:

```
with open("CHAPTER7_DATA.csv", "a", newline="") as file:
```

```
writer = csv.writer(file)
writer.writerow([52, 3000000])
```

Using pandas for CSV handling

Example 7.14: Reading a CSV file:

```
import pandas as pd
df = pd.read_csv('data.csv')
print(df.head())  # Shows first 5 rows
```

Example 7.15: Writing to a CSV file:

```
import pandas as pd
data = {
    'Name': ['Alice', 'Bob'],
    'Age': [30, 25],
    'City': ['New York', 'London']
}
df = pd.DataFrame(data)
df.to_csv('output.csv', index=False)
```

Example 7.16: Merging two CSV files:

```
import pandas as pd
# Read the two CSV files
employees = pd.read_csv('employees.csv')
departments = pd.read_csv('departments.csv')
# Merge on a common column (e.g., Department ID)
merged_df = pd.merge(employees, departments, on='Dept_ID')
print(merged_df.head())
```

Example 7.17: Concatenating multiple CSV files:

```
import pandas as pd
import glob
# Read all CSV files in the folder
csv_files = glob.glob('monthly_reports/*.csv')
# Concatenate all CSVs into a single DataFrame
df_list = [pd.read_csv(file) for file in csv_files]
combined_df = pd.concat(df_list, ignore_index=True)
print(combined_df.head())
```

Example 7.18: Pivot table from CSV data:

```
df = pd.read_csv('sales_data.csv')
pivot = pd.pivot_table(df, index='Region', columns='Product', values='Sales', aggfunc='sum')
print(pivot)
```

Example 7.19: Correlation matrix from CSV data:

```
df = pd.read_csv('student_scores.csv')
correlation_matrix = df.corr()
print(correlation_matrix)
```

7.1.3 Working with JSON files

JavaScript Object Notation (JSON) is a lightweight and widely used data format for storing and exchanging structured data, commonly used in web APIs, configuration files, and data storage. Python provides the JSON module, which simplifies working with JSON data by allowing easy conversion between JSON strings and Python objects like dictionaries and lists. To read JSON data from a file, you can use the **json.load()** function, which parses the file and converts it into a Python object. When writing JSON data back to a file, you can use the **json.dump()** function with the indent parameter, which makes the output human-readable by formatting the JSON with indentation (e.g., **indent=4** gives nicely indented nested structures).

Additionally, the **json.loads()** and **json.dumps()** functions allow you to work with JSON strings directly, making it convenient for tasks like parsing API responses or serializing data. By mastering the **json** module, you can efficiently handle JSON data for tasks such as web development, configuration management, and data interchange.

- **Example 7.20**: Reading JSON files

  Python's **json.load()** function allows you to read JSON data from a file and convert it into a Python object, such as a dictionary or list, for easy access and manipulation:

  ```
  import json


  with open("1mb.json", "r") as file:
      data = json.load(file)
      print(data)
  ```

- **Example 7.21**: Writing JSON files

  Python's **json.dump()** function converts a Python object, such as a dictionary or list, into a JSON-formatted string and writes it to a file for storage or data interchange:

  ```
  data = {"Name": "Alice", "Age": 25, "City": "New York"}


  with open("output.json", "w") as file:
      json.dump(data, file, indent=4)
  ```

- **Example 7.22**: Working with JSON strings

  Python's **json.loads()** and **json.dumps()** functions allow you to parse JSON strings into Python objects and serialize Python objects into JSON strings, respectively, enabling seamless data interchange:

  ```
  json_string = '{"Name": "Alice", "Age": 25, "City": "New York"}'
  data = json.loads(json_string)
  print(data["Name"])  # Output: Alice
  ```

7.1.4 Working with other data formats

While CSV and JSON are among the most commonly used data formats, Python also provides robust support for working with a variety of other data formats, making it a versatile tool for data processing and integration. For instance, the **xml.etree.ElementTree** module allows you to parse and use XML files, which are widely used in web services and document storage. Similarly, the pandas library offers extensive functionality for reading and writing data in formats like Excel (**.xlsx**), HDF5, and Parquet, which are essential for data analysis and scientific computing. For working with binary data, Python's struct module enables you to pack and unpack data into binary formats, which is useful for low-level data processing. Additionally, libraries like PyYAML and TOML allow you to handle YAML and TOML files, commonly used for configuration files.

Let us look at the data formats in detail:

- **XML: Extensible Markup Language** (**XML**) is a widely used format for storing and transporting structured data, commonly found in web services, configuration files, and document storage. Python provides the **xml.etree.ElementTree** module, which simplifies parsing, creating, and manipulating XML data.

  Example 7.23: The **xml.etree.ElementTree** module is used to parse and create XML data:

  ```python
  import xml.etree.ElementTree as ET

  # Parsing XML data
  tree = ET.parse('data.xml')
  root = tree.getroot()

  for child in root:
      print(child.tag, child.attrib)

  # Creating XML data
  root = ET.Element('root')
  child = ET.SubElement(root, 'child')
  child.set('name', 'Alice')
  tree = ET.ElementTree(root)
  tree.write('output.xml')
  ```

- **YAML: YAML Ain't Markup Language** (**YAML**) is a human-readable data serialization format commonly used for configuration files, data exchange, and storing structured data. Python's PyYAML library provides tools to easily parse and generate YAML data.

  Example 7.24: The PyYAML library is used to work with YAML files:

  ```python
  import yaml
  # Reading YAML data
  with open('data.yaml', 'r') as file:
      data = yaml.safe_load(file)
      print(data)
  # Writing YAML data
  data = {
      'Name': 'Alice',
      'Age': 30,
      'City': 'New York'
  }
  with open('output.yaml', 'w') as file:
      yaml.dump(data, file)
  ```

- **Pickle**: Pickle is a Python-specific module used for serializing and deserializing Python objects, enabling you to save complex data structures like lists, dictionaries, and custom objects to a file and retrieve them later. It is particularly useful for saving program state or transferring data between Python programs.

  Example 7.25: The **pickle** module is used for serializing and deserializing Python objects:

  ```python
  import pickle
  # Serializing Python object
  ```

```
data = {
    'Name': 'Alice',
    'Age': 30,
    'City': 'New York'
}
with open('data.pkl', 'wb') as file:
    pickle.dump(data, file)
# Deserializing Python object
with open('data.pkl', 'rb') as file:
    data = pickle.load(file)
    print(data)
```

7.1.5 Practical examples and use cases

Python's file handling and data format capabilities make it an essential tool for real-world applications across various domains. For instance, in data analysis, Python's **csv** module is frequently used to read and process large datasets stored in CSV files, enabling tasks like cleaning, filtering, and analyzing data. Similarly, **json** module is widely used in web development to parse JSON responses from APIs or store configuration settings in a readable format. For example, a weather app might use Python to fetch JSON data from a weather API and display it to users.

In automation, Python's file handling functions like open, read, and write are used to automate repetitive tasks, such as generating reports, logging data, or managing files in bulk. For example, a script could read log files, extract specific information, and write summaries to a new file. In machine learning, CSV files are often used to load training datasets, while JSON files store model configurations or results.

Python's ability to handle multiple data formats also makes it ideal for data integration tasks, such as converting data between CSV, JSON, and other formats for compatibility across systems. For example, a script might read data from a CSV file, transform it, and save it as a JSON file for use in a web application. These practical examples demonstrate Python's versatility in solving real-world problems efficiently.

Example 7.26: Reading and writing configuration files.

Python provides modules like **json**, **yaml**, and **configparser** to easily read, write, and manage configuration files in formats such as JSON, YAML, and INI, streamlining application settings management:

```
import json

# Reading configuration from a JSON file
with open('config.json', 'r') as file:
    config = json.load(file)
    print(config)
# Writing configuration to a JSON file
config = {
    'host': 'localhost',
    'port': 8080,
    'debug': True
}
with open('config.json', 'w') as file:
    json.dump(config, file, indent=4)
```

Example 7.27: Processing large CSV files.

Python's **pandas** library, combined with chunking techniques, allows efficient processing of large CSV files by reading and manipulating data in manageable portions, avoiding memory overload:

```python
import csv

# Processing large CSV files in chunks
chunk_size = 1000
with open('large_data.csv', 'r') as file:
    reader = csv.reader(file)
    chunk = []
    for i, row in enumerate(reader):
        chunk.append(row)
        if i % chunk_size == 0 and i != 0:
            print(f'Processing chunk: {chunk}')
            chunk = []
    if chunk:
        print(f'Processing final chunk: {chunk}')
```

Example 7.28: Handling nested JSON data.

Python's **json** module, combined with dictionary manipulation techniques, allows you to easily access, modify, and extract data from nested JSON structures for seamless data processing:

```python
import json

# Handling nested JSON data
data = {
    'Name': 'Alice',
    'Age': 30,
    'Address': {
        'Street': '123 Main St',
        'City': 'New York',
        'State': 'NY'
    }
}
# Accessing nested data
print(data['Address']['City'])
# Modifying nested data
data['Address']['City'] = 'Los Angeles'
print(json.dumps(data, indent=4))
```

Example 7.29: Serializing and deserializing Python objects.

Python's **pickle** module enables the conversion of complex Python objects into a byte stream for storage or transmission and restores them back into objects when needed:

```python
import pickle
# Serializing Python object
class Person:
    def __init__(self, name, age):
        self.name = name
```

```python
        self.age = age

person = Person('Alice', 30)

with open('person.pkl', 'wb') as file:
    pickle.dump(person, file)


# Deserializing Python object
with open('person.pkl', 'rb') as file:
    loaded_person = pickle.load(file)
    print(loaded_person.name, loaded_person.age)
```

7.2 Comparative study of MATLAB and Python via examples

MATLAB and Python are powerful tools for data analysis, scientific computing, and automation, but they differ in their strengths, use cases, and ecosystems. MATLAB is renowned for its simplicity in numerical computations, matrix operations, and specialized toolboxes, making it a favorite in engineering and academia. Python, on the other hand, is a general-purpose language with a vast library ecosystem, making it versatile for a wide range of applications. In this section, a wide range of examples is provided to study the MATLAB and Python codes from a comparative point of view. You may try these codes as practice work for a better understanding of the concept:

- **Example 7.30**: Reading a text file line by line:

  MATLAB:
  ```matlab
  fileID = fopen('example.txt', 'r');
  while ~feof(fileID)
      line = fgetl(fileID);
      disp(line);
  end
  fclose(fileID);
  ```

  Python:
  ```python
  with open('CHAPTER7_DATA.txt', 'r') as file:
      for line in file:
          print(line, end='')
  ```

- **Example 7.31**: Writing multiple lines to a text file:
  ```matlab
  fileID = fopen('example.txt', 'w');
  fprintf(fileID, 'Line 1\n');
  fprintf(fileID, 'Line 2\n');
  fclose(fileID);
  ```

  Python:
  ```python
  # Open the file in write mode
  fileID = open('CHAPTER7_DATA.txt', 'w')

  # Write lines to the file
  ```

```
fileID.write('Line 1\n')
fileID.write('Line 2\n')

# Close the file
fileID.close()
```

- **Example 7.32**: Appending to a text file:

  MATLAB:
  ```
  fileID = fopen('example.txt', 'a');
  fprintf(fileID, 'Line 3\n');
  fclose(fileID);
  ```

  Python:
  ```
  with open('CHAPTER7_DATA.txt', 'a') as file:
      file.write('Line 3\n')
  ```

- **Example 7.33**: Reading a binary file

  MATLAB:
  ```
  fileID = fopen('data.bin', 'r');
  data = fread(fileID, [1, inf], 'uint8');
  fclose(fileID);
  disp(data);
  ```

  Python:
  ```
  with open('fontawesome-webfont.bin', 'rb') as file:
      data = file.read()
      print(data)
  ```

- **Example 7.34**: Writing to a binary file

  MATLAB:
  ```
  fileID = fopen('output.bin', 'w');
  fwrite(fileID, [1, 2, 3, 4], 'uint8');
  fclose(fileID);
  ```

  Python:
  ```
  with open('fontawesome-webfont.bin', 'wb') as file:
      file.write(bytes([1, 2, 3, 4]))
  ```

- **Example 7.35**: Reading a CSV file with headers

  MATLAB:
  ```
  data = readtable('data.csv');
  disp(data);
  ```

  Python:
  ```
  import pandas as pd
  data = pd.read_csv('CHAPTER7_DATA.csv')
  print(data)
  ```

- **Example 7.36**: Writing a CSV file with headers

  MATLAB:
  ```
  data = table([1; 2; 3], {'A'; 'B'; 'C'}, 'VariableNames', {'ID', 'Letter'});
  writetable(data, 'output.csv');
  ```

  Python:
  ```
  import pandas as pd
  data = pd.DataFrame({'ID': [1, 2, 3], 'Letter': ['A', 'B', 'C']})
  data.to_csv('CHAPTER7_DATA.csv', index=False)
  ```

- **Example 7.37**: Reading a JSON file:

  MATLAB:
  ```
  data = jsondecode(fileread('data.json'));
  disp(data);
  ```

  Python:
  ```
  import json
  with open('1mb.json', 'r') as file:
      data = json.load(file)
      print(data)
  ```

- **Example 7.38**: Writing to a JSON file

  MATLAB:
  ```
  data = struct('Name', 'Alice', 'Age', 30);
  fid = fopen('output.json', 'w');
  fprintf(fid, '%s', jsonencode(data));
  fclose(fid);
  ```

  Python:
  ```
  import json
  data = {'Name': 'Alice', 'Age': 30}
  with open('1mb.json', 'w') as file:
      json.dump(data, file, indent=4)
  ```

- **Example 7.39**: Reading an Excel file

  MATLAB:
  ```
  data = readtable('data.xlsx');
  disp(data);
  ```

  Python:
  ```
  import pandas as pd
  data = pd.read_excel('CHAPTER7_DATA.xlsx')
  print(data)
  ```

- **Example 7.40**: Writing to an Excel file

  MATLAB:
  ```
  data = table([1; 2; 3], {'A'; 'B'; 'C'}, 'VariableNames', {'ID', 'Letter'});
  writetable(data, 'output.xlsx');
  ```

Python:
```
import pandas as pd
data = pd.DataFrame({'ID': [1, 2, 3], 'Letter': ['A', 'B', 'C']})
data.to_excel('CHAPTER7_DATA.xlsx', index=False)
```

- **Example 7.41**: Reading a specific sheet from an Excel file:

MATLAB:
```
data = readtable('data.xlsx', 'Sheet', 'Sheet1');
disp(data);
```

Python:
```
import pandas as pd
data = pd.read_excel('data.xlsx', sheet_name='Sheet1')
print(data)
```

- **Example 7.42**: Writing to a specific sheet in an Excel file:

MATLAB:
```
data = table([1; 2; 3], {'A'; 'B'; 'C'}, 'VariableNames', {'ID', 'Letter'});
writetable(data, 'output.xlsx', 'Sheet', 'Sheet1');
```

Python:
```
import pandas as pd
data = pd.DataFrame({'ID': [1, 2, 3], 'Letter': ['A', 'B', 'C']})
with pd.ExcelWriter('CHAPTER7_DATA.xlsx') as writer:
    data.to_excel(writer, sheet_name='Sheet1', index=False)
```

- **Example 7.43**: Reading a CSV file with custom delimiter:

MATLAB:
```
data = readtable('data.csv', 'Delimiter', ';');
disp(data);
```

Python:
```
import pandas as pd
data = pd.read_csv('CHAPTER7_DATA.csv', delimiter=';')
print(data)
```

- **Example 7.44**: Writing a CSV file with a custom delimiter:

MATLAB:
```
data = table([1; 2; 3], {'A'; 'B'; 'C'}, 'VariableNames', {'ID', 'Letter'});
writetable(data, 'output.csv', 'Delimiter', ';');
```

Python:
```
import pandas as pd
data = pd.DataFrame({'ID': [1, 2, 3], 'Letter': ['A', 'B', 'C']})
data.to_csv('CHAPTER7_DATA.csv', sep=';', index=False)
```

- **Example 7.45:** Reading a CSV file with missing data:

MATLAB:
```
data = readtable('data.csv', 'TreatAsMissing', 'NA');
disp(data);
```

Python:
```
import pandas as pd
data = pd.read_csv('CHAPTER7_DATA.csv', na_values=['NA'])
print(data)
```

- **Example 7.46:** Writing a CSV file with missing data:

MATLAB:
```
data = table([1; NaN; 3], {'A'; 'B'; 'C'}, 'VariableNames', {'ID', 'Letter'});
writetable(data, 'output.csv');
```

Python:
```
import pandas as pd
import numpy as np
data = pd.DataFrame({'ID': [1, np.nan, 3], 'Letter': ['A', 'B', 'C']})
data.to_csv('output.csv', index=False)
```

- **Example 7.47:** Reading a JSON file with nested data

MATLAB
```
data = jsondecode(fileread('data.json'));
disp(data.Address.City);
```

Python:
```
import json
with open('data.json', 'r') as file:
    data = json.load(file)
    print(data['Address']['City'])
```

- **Example 7.48:** Writing a JSON file with nested data:

MATLAB:
```
data = struct('Name', 'Alice', 'Age', 30, 'Address', struct('City', 'New York'));
fid = fopen('output.json', 'w');
fprintf(fid, '%s', jsonencode(data));
fclose(fid);
```

Python:
```
import json
data = {'Name': 'Alice', 'Age': 30, 'Address': {'City': 'New York'}}
with open('output.json', 'w') as file:
    json.dump(data, file, indent=4)
```

- **Example 7.49:** Reading a CSV file with headers and skipping rows:

MATLAB:
```
data = readtable('data.csv', 'HeaderLines', 1);
disp(data);
```

Python:

```
import pandas as pd
data = pd.read_csv('data.csv', skiprows=1)
print(data)
```

- **Example 7.50**: Writing a CSV file with headers and skipping rows:

MATLAB:

```
data = table([1; 2; 3], {'A'; 'B'; 'C'}, 'VariableNames', {'ID', 'Letter'});
writetable(data, 'output.csv', 'WriteVariableNames', false);
```

Python:

```
import pandas as pd
data = pd.DataFrame({'ID': [1, 2, 3], 'Letter': ['A', 'B', 'C']})
data.to_csv('output.csv', index=False, header=False)
```

- **Example 7.51**: Reading a CSV file with specific columns:

MATLAB:

```
data = readtable('data.csv', 'SelectedVariableNames', {'ID', 'Letter'});
disp(data);
```

Python:

```
import pandas as pd
data = pd.read_csv('data.csv', usecols=['ID', 'Letter'])
print(data)
```

- **Example 7.52**: Writing a CSV file with specific columns:

MATLAB:

```
data = table([1; 2; 3], {'A'; 'B'; 'C'}, 'VariableNames', {'ID', 'Letter'});
writetable(data, 'output.csv', 'WriteVariableNames', true);
```

Python:

```
import pandas as pd
data = pd.DataFrame({'ID': [1, 2, 3], 'Letter': ['A', 'B', 'C']})
data.to_csv('output.csv', columns=['ID', 'Letter'], index=False)
```

- **Example 7.53**: Reading a CSV file with custom encoding:

MATLAB:

```
data = readtable('data.csv', 'Encoding', 'UTF-8');
disp(data);
```

Python:

```
import pandas as pd
data = pd.read_csv('data.csv', encoding='utf-8')
print(data)
```

- **Example 7.54**: Writing a CSV file with custom encoding:

  MATLAB:
  ```
  data = table([1; 2; 3], {'A'; 'B'; 'C'}, 'VariableNames', {'ID', 'Letter'});
  writetable(data, 'output.csv', 'Encoding', 'UTF-8');
  ```

  Python:
  ```
  import pandas as pd
  data = pd.DataFrame({'ID': [1, 2, 3], 'Letter': ['A', 'B', 'C']})
  data.to_csv('output.csv', encoding='utf-8', index=False)
  ```

- **Example 7.55**: Reading a CSV file with date parsing:

  MATLAB:
  ```
  data = readtable('data.csv', 'ReadVariableNames', true, 'Format', '%{yyyy-MM-dd}D');
  disp(data);
  ```

  Python:
  ```
  import pandas as pd
  data = pd.read_csv('data.csv', parse_dates=['Date'])
  print(data)
  ```

- **Example 7.56**: Writing a CSV file with date formatting:

  MATLAB:
  ```
  data = table(datetime('now'), [1; 2; 3], {'A'; 'B'; 'C'}, 'VariableNames', {'Date', 'ID', 'Letter'});
  writetable(data, 'output.csv', 'WriteVariableNames', true);
  ```

  Python:
  ```
  import pandas as pd
  from datetime import datetime
  data = pd.DataFrame({'Date': [datetime.now()], 'ID': [1, 2, 3], 'Letter': ['A', 'B', 'C']})
  data.to_csv('output.csv', index=False)
  ```

- **Example 7.57**: Reading a CSV file with custom date format:

  MATLAB:
  ```
  data = readtable('data.csv', 'ReadVariableNames', true, 'Format', '%{dd/MM/yyyy}D');
  disp(data);
  ```

  Python:
  ```
  import pandas as pd
  data = pd.read_csv('data.csv', parse_dates=['Date'], date_format='%d/%m/%Y')
  print(data)
  ```

- **Example 7.58**: Writing a CSV file with custom date format:

  MATLAB:
  ```
  data = table(datetime('now'), [1; 2; 3], {'A'; 'B'; 'C'}, 'VariableNames', {'Date', 'ID', 'Letter'});
  writetable(data, 'output.csv', 'WriteVariableNames', true);
  ```

Python:
```
import pandas as pd
from datetime import datetime
data = pd.DataFrame({'Date': [datetime.now()], 'ID': [1, 2, 3], 'Letter': ['A', 'B',
'C']})
data.to_csv('output.csv', index=False, date_format='%d/%m/%Y')
```

- **Example 7.59**: Reading a CSV file with custom missing values:

  MATLAB:
  ```
  data = readtable('data.csv', 'TreatAsMissing', {'NA', 'NaN'});
  disp(data);
  ```

  Python:
  ```
  import pandas as pd
  data = pd.read_csv('data.csv', na_values=['NA', 'NaN'])
  print(data)
  ```

- **Example 7.60**: Writing a CSV file with custom missing values:

  MATLAB:
  ```
  data = table([1; NaN; 3], {'A'; 'B'; 'C'}, 'VariableNames', {'ID', 'Letter'});
  writetable(data, 'output.csv');
  ```

  Python:
  ```
  import pandas as pd
  import numpy as np
  data = pd.DataFrame({'ID': [1, np.nan, 3], 'Letter': ['A', 'B', 'C']})
  data.to_csv('output.csv', index=False, na_rep='NA')
  ```

- **Example 7.61**: Reading a CSV file with custom quote characters:

  MATLAB:
  ```
  data = readtable('data.csv', 'Quote', '"');
  disp(data);
  ```

  Python:
  ```
  import pandas as pd
  data = pd.read_csv('data.csv', quotechar='"')
  print(data)
  ```

- **Example 7.62**: Writing a CSV file with custom quote characters:

  MATLAB:
  ```
  data = table([1; 2; 3], {'A'; 'B'; 'C'}, 'VariableNames', {'ID', 'Letter'});
  writetable(data, 'output.csv', 'Quote', '"');
  ```

  Python:
  ```
  import pandas as pd
  data = pd.DataFrame({'ID': [1, 2, 3], 'Letter': ['A', 'B', 'C']})
  data.to_csv('output.csv', index=False, quotechar='"')
  ```

- **Example 7.63**: Reading a CSV file with custom comment characters:

  MATLAB:
  ```
  data = readtable('data.csv', 'Comment', '#');
  disp(data);
  ```

  Python:
  ```
  import pandas as pd
  data = pd.read_csv('data.csv', comment='#')
  print(data)
  ```

- **Example 7.64**: Writing a CSV file with custom comment characters:

  MATLAB:
  ```
  data = table([1; 2; 3], {'A'; 'B'; 'C'}, 'VariableNames', {'ID', 'Letter'});
  writetable(data, 'output.csv', 'Comment', '#');
  ```

  Python:
  ```
  import pandas as pd

  # Create the DataFrame
  data = pd.DataFrame({'ID': [1, 2, 3], 'Letter': ['A', 'B', 'C']})

  # Define the comment(s) you want to add
  comments = [
      "# This is a comment line 1",
      "# This is a comment line 2"
  ]

  # Write the comments and DataFrame to the CSV file
  with open('output.csv', 'w') as file:
      # Write the comments
      for comment in comments:
          file.write(comment + '\n')
      # Write the DataFrame to the file
      data.to_csv(file, index=False)
  ```

- **Example 7.65**: Reading a CSV file with custom thousands separator:

  MATLAB:
  ```
  data = readtable('data.csv', 'ThousandsSeparator', ',');
  disp(data);
  ```

  Python:
  ```
  import pandas as pd
  data = pd.read_csv('CHAPTER7_DATA.csv', thousands=',')
  print(data)
  ```

- **Example 7.66**: Writing a CSV file with custom thousands separator:

  MATLAB:
  ```
  data = table([1000; 2000; 3000], {'A'; 'B'; 'C'}, 'VariableNames', {'ID', 'Letter'});
  writetable(data, 'output.csv', 'ThousandsSeparator', ',');
  ```

  Python:
  ```
  import pandas as pd

  # Create the DataFrame
  data = pd.DataFrame({'YearsExperience': [10, 20, 30], 'Salary': [10000, 20000, 30000]})

  # Format the 'Salary' column with a thousands separator
  data['Salary'] = data['Salary'].apply(lambda x: f"{x:,}")

  # Write the DataFrame to a CSV file
  data.to_csv('CHAPTER7_DATA.csv', index=False)
  ```

Conclusion

The fundamentals of Python file management, including reading from and writing to files, were addressed in this chapter. Another topic we covered was working with several data types, including CSV, JSON, XML, YAML, and Pickle. These abilities are essential for Python jobs involving serialization, configuration management, and data processing. You should be able to manage a variety of file and data format operations in your Python programs with the help of the examples given.

In the next chapter, we will understand the plotting and visualization in MATLAB and Python in full detail.

Exercises

Basic file operations

1. Create a text file and write "Hello, World!" in both MATLAB and Python.
2. Read the contents of an existing text file and display it.
3. Append new data to an existing text file without overwriting the original content.
4. Write a script to count the number of lines in a text file.
5. Write a program to check whether a given file exists before opening it.
6. Copy the contents of one file to another file.
7. Delete a file if it exists using a script.
8. Read a file line by line and display each line on the screen.
9. Create a file and write the numbers from 1 to 100 in it.
10. Write a script to find the size of a file in bytes.

Working with different file modes

1. Open a file in write mode and then read its contents. Explain what happens.
2. Open a file in append mode and write some data, then verify the changes.

3. Use a script to open a file in binary mode and write some binary data.

4. Implement error handling when opening a non-existent file.

5. Write a function to open a file in different modes ('r', 'w', 'a', 'rb', 'wb') and explain their use cases.

Reading and writing CSV files

1. Write a MATLAB/Python script to create a CSV file containing student names and scores.

2. Read a CSV file into a MATLAB table and a Python Pandas DataFrame.

3. Add a new column to an existing CSV file.

4. Sort the contents of a CSV file based on a specific column.

5. Convert a CSV file into a dictionary (Python) or a structure (MATLAB).

6. Write a script to read only specific rows and columns from a CSV file.

7. Filter rows in a CSV file based on a given condition (e.g., students who scored above 90).

8. Write a program to find the average of numerical values from a specific column.

9. Save a matrix (MATLAB) or a NumPy array (Python) into a CSV file.

10. Merge two CSV files into a single file.

Reading and writing JSON files

1. Write a JSON file containing information about three employees (name, age, department).

2. Read a JSON file and extract specific fields.

3. Convert a JSON object into a dictionary (Python) or a structure (MATLAB).

4. Modify a JSON file by updating an employee's details.

5. Convert a JSON file to a CSV file.

6. Convert a CSV file to a JSON file.

7. Write a script to pretty-print JSON data.

8. Write a function to check if a given JSON file is valid.

9. Extract only specific key-value pairs from a large JSON file.

10. Merge two JSON files into a single JSON file.

Handling binary files

1. Create a binary file and write an array of floating-point numbers to it.

2. Read a binary file and display its contents.

3. Store a MATLAB/Python matrix in a binary file and retrieve it.

4. Compare the performance of reading/writing data in binary vs text format.

5. Write a script to determine the number of bytes in a binary file.

6. Read an image file in binary mode and display its size.

7. Convert a binary file to a text file and vice versa.

8. Extract specific bytes from a binary file.

9. Write a MATLAB/Python program to encrypt and decrypt data before writing to a binary file.

10. Write a script to find the checksum of a file.

Advanced file handling operations

1. Read multiple CSV files from a directory and merge them into one.

2. Read a large file line-by-line instead of loading it all at once.

3. Write a script to detect and remove duplicate records from a CSV file.

4. Create a log file that appends timestamps whenever the script runs.

5. Write a program to process and clean text data before saving it to a file.

Join our Discord space

Join our Discord workspace for latest updates, offers, tech happenings around the world, new releases, and sessions with the authors:

https://discord.bpbonline.com

CHAPTER 8
Plotting and Visualization in MATLAB

Introduction

Data visualization is an important aspect of exploring and understanding the data, whether it is simple data in time series data, comparative analysis data between diverse categories, or interconnected data between two variables. MATLAB provides a robust set of functions to create 2D plots, which are visually catching and easy to analyze, and we will be looking into them in this chapter.

This aspect gives rise to three core and basic plot functions, such as plot, bar, and scatter. Along with this, we will explore the capabilities, customized options, and practical applications.

Structure

- 8.1. plot function as foundation of MATLAB visualization
- 8.2. Bar function and visualizing categorical data
- 8.3 Exploring variable relationship through the scatter function
- 8.4 Customization of plots in MATLAB
- 8.5. Introduction to 3D plotting
- 8.6. Specialized plots in MATLAB

Objectives

The objectives of this chapter are to equip readers with the practical skills needed to create and customize various types of plots in MATLAB for real-world applications. By learning basic 2D plotting functions such as plot, bar, and scatter, you will be able to visualize data effectively. This chapter also covers customization techniques, including adding titles, labels, and legends, and adjusting line styles to enhance plot clarity and presentation. Additionally, you will explore 3D plotting using functions like **plot3**, **surf**, and **mesh**, enabling them to represent complex data in three dimensions. Finally, the chapter introduces specialized plots such as histograms, heatmaps, and polar plots, broadening your ability to analyze and present data across different domains, from engineering and science to finance and data analytics. Through these skills, you will gain the ability to generate insightful visualizations that aid in data interpretation and decision-making.

8.1 plot function as foundation of MATLAB visualization

plot function, as shown in *Figure 8.1*, is one of the most frequently used charts to visualize data in MATLAB. It is utilized in order to create 2D line plots (continuous in nature). This is very useful to make it important regarding functions, time-series data, and other related aspects.

The basic syntax **plot(x, y)** plots the values of vector y against vector x, connecting the data points with straight lines. This type of visualization is especially valuable in disciplines such as engineering, physics, economics, and signal processing, where tracking changes over time or comparing multiple datasets is crucial. The plot function supports various customizations, such as line style, color, markers, and axis labeling, making it a versatile option for both basic and advanced graphical representation of data. Furthermore, it allows for the overlay of multiple datasets in a single figure, aiding in comparative analysis and better interpretation of relationships within the data:

```
x = 0:0.1:10;
y = sin(x);
plot(x, y);
```

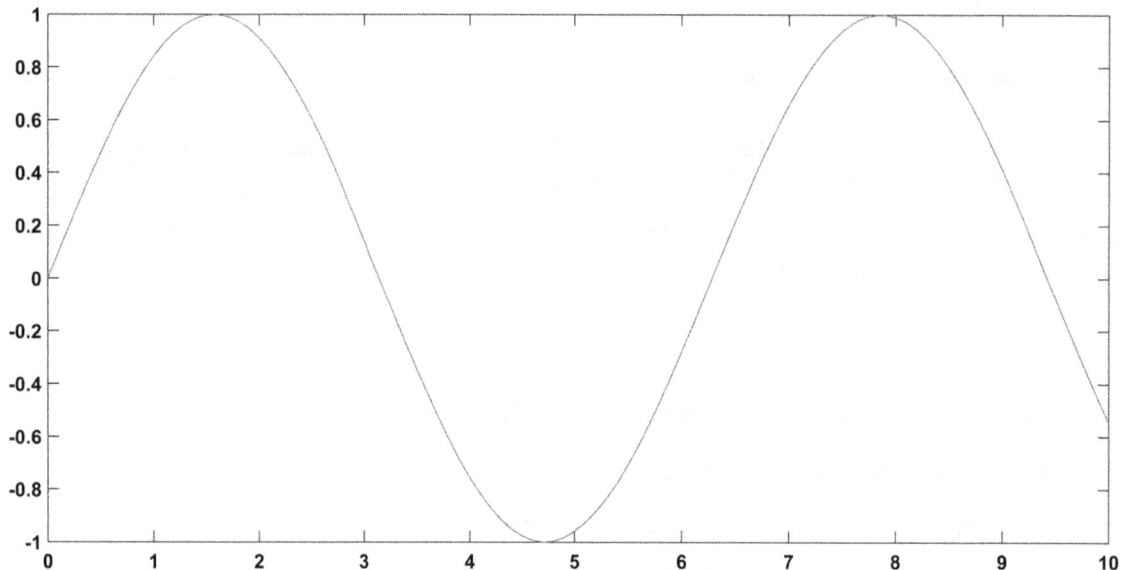

Figure 8.1: *plot() function implementation*

Let us look at the customizations in detail:

- **Addition of labels and titles**: The plot function can be customized with the help of labels and titles, as shown in *Figure 8.2*, as per the requirements of the user. The basic code in this regard is as follows:

```
x = 0:0.1:10;
y = sin(x);
plot(x, y);
xlabel('X-axis (Time in seconds)');
ylabel('Y-axis (Amplitude)');
title('Sine Wave');
grid on;
```

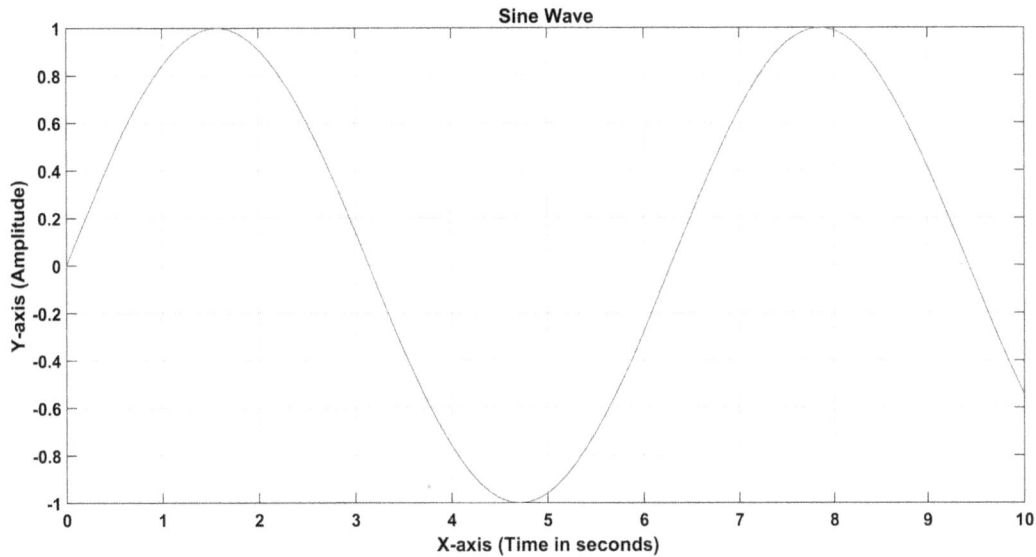

Figure 8.2: *Addition of labels and titles*

- **Customizing line styles, colors, and markers**: Customization of the MATLAB plots, as shown in *Figure 8.3,* is considered one of its strengths. It can be done in a simple and easy-to-implement way, like:

  o **Line styles**: '--' (dashed), ':' (dotted), '-.' (dash-dot)

  o **Colors**: 'r' (red), 'g' (green), 'b' (blue)

  o **Markers**: 'o' (circle), '*' (star), 'x' (cross):

  ```
  x = 0:0.1:10;
  y = sin(x);
  plot(x, y, 'r--o', 'LineWidth', 2);
  xlabel('X-axis (Time in seconds)');
  ylabel('Y-axis (Amplitude)');
  title('Sine Wave');
  grid on;
  ```

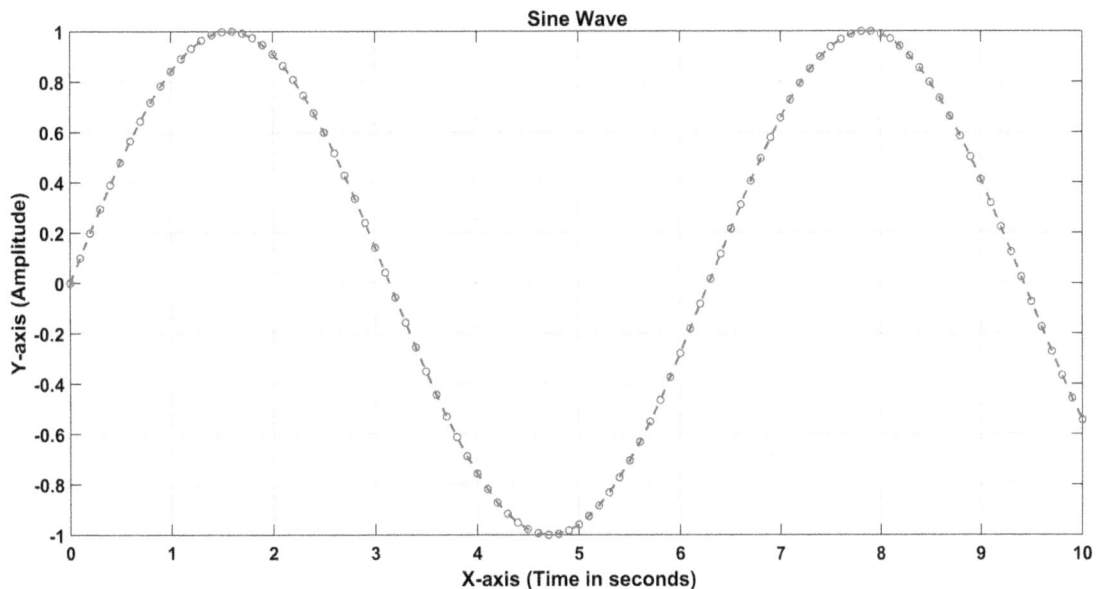

Figure 8.3: *Customization of the plots*

- **Plotting multiple lines**: To compare multiple datasets, use the plot function with additional data, as shown in *Figure 8.4*:

```
x = 0:0.1:10;
y1 = sin(x);
y2 = cos(x);
plot(x, y1, 'b', x, y2, 'g--'); % Plot sine and cosine
legend('sin(x)', 'cos(x)'); % Add a legend for clarity
```

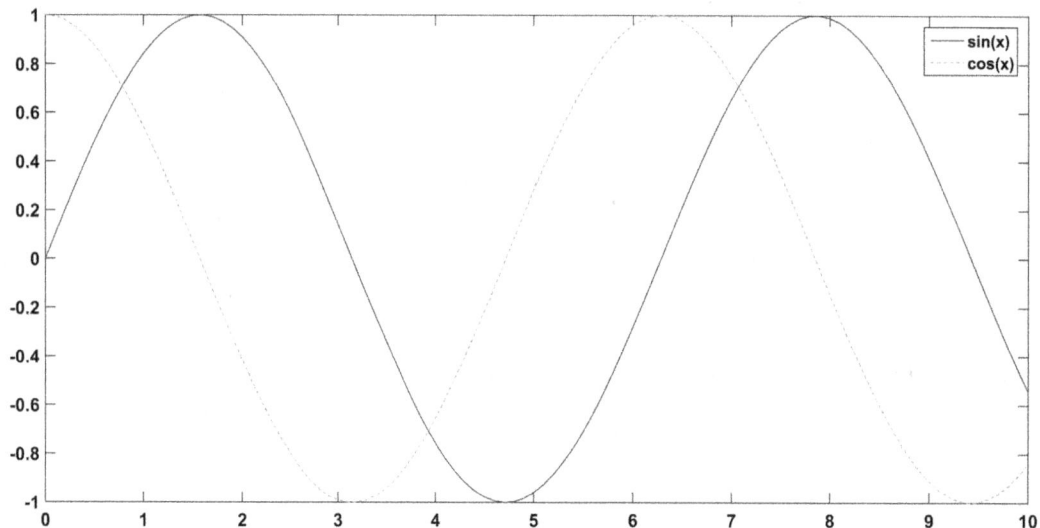

Figure 8.4: Multiple plots

- **Practical applications—trend analysis with plot**: A scientist studying population growth might use the plot function to visualize trends over decades, as shown in *Figure 8.5*:

```
years = 2000:2010;
population = [2.9, 3.1, 3.5, 3.8, 4.2, 4.5, 4.9, 5.3, 5.8, 6.2, 6.7];
plot(years, population, '-o');
title('Population Growth');
xlabel('Year');
ylabel('Population (in billions)');
```

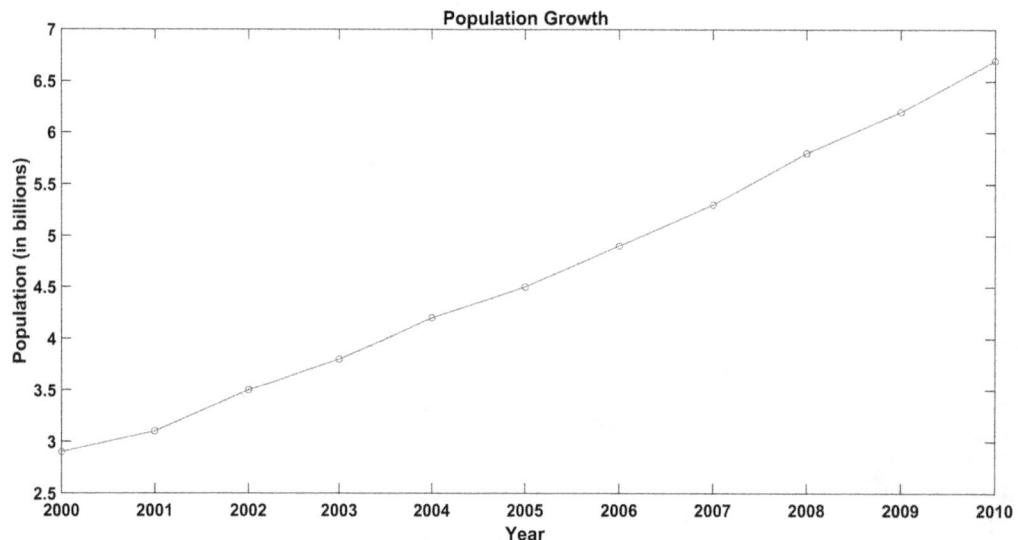

Figure 8.5: Trend Analysis with plot

8.2 Bar function and visualizing categorical data

Bar charts are essential when working with categorical data or when summarizing numerical data based on specific categories. MATLAB's bar function provides a convenient and flexible way to create bar plots that visually represent the distribution, comparison, or frequency of data across different groups. It is especially useful for highlighting differences between discrete categories and understanding the underlying structure of the data. The bar function supports both **grouped** and **stacked bar plots**, allowing users to present multi-dimensional data in a clear and organized manner. Grouped bar charts are helpful when comparing multiple sets of values side-by-side within each category, while stacked bar charts are ideal for showing how individual parts contribute to a whole. Users can customize the appearance of the bars by adjusting their color, width, edge style, and labels to enhance readability. The function also integrates well with other MATLAB features, such as annotations, legends, and data tips, making it a powerful tool for generating publication-quality graphics that convey categorical insights effectively.

Let us look at them in detail:

- **Creating a simple bar chart**: Bar charts visually compare categorical data using rectangular bars, as shown in *Figure 8.6*. MATLAB's **bar()** function creates vertical charts, while **barh()** makes horizontal ones:

```
categories = {'A', 'B', 'C', 'D'};
values = [5, 8, 3, 6];
bar(values);
set(gca, 'XTickLabel', categories);
title('Bar Chart of Categories');
ylabel('Values');
```

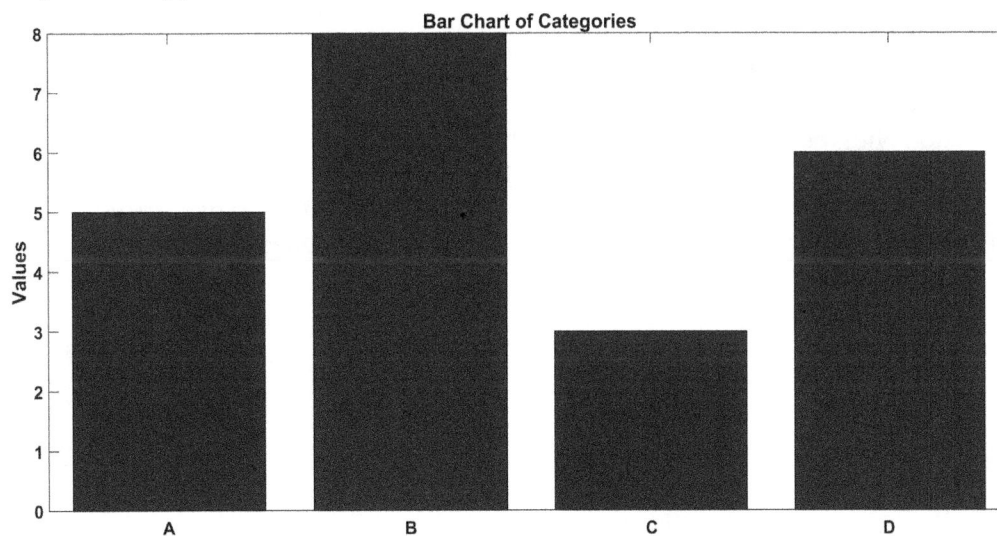

Figure 8.6: Simple bar chart

- **Grouped and stacked bar charts**: For comparing multiple groups or subcategories, MATLAB supports grouped and stacked bar charts:

  o **Grouped bars**: Grouped bars are a type of bar chart used to compare multiple datasets or variables across the same set of categories, as shown in *Figure 8.7*,. In MATLAB, grouped bar charts are created using the bar function by passing a matrix as input, where each row corresponds to a category and each column represents a different group or variable. This results in bars being placed side by side for each category, making it easy to visually compare the values across different groups. Grouped bar charts are especially useful when analyzing experimental results, survey data, or performance metrics where comparisons across multiple conditions or groups are needed. MATLAB allows customization of grouped bar charts, including changing bar colors, adding labels, and including legends to clearly differentiate each group, thereby enhancing the clarity and interpretability of the data being presented:

```
values = [5 8; 3 6; 7 4];
bar(values, 'grouped');
legend('Group 1', 'Group 2');
title('Grouped Bar Chart');
```

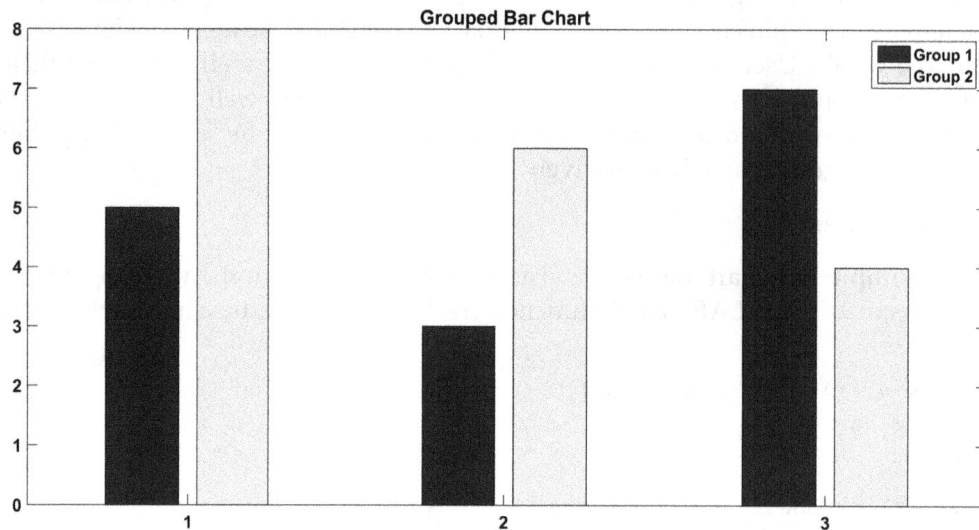

Figure 8.7: *Grouped bar chart*

o **Stacked bars**: Stacked bars are used to display the cumulative values of multiple data series for each category, with each bar divided into segments representing individual components, as shown in *Figure 8.8*. In MATLAB, stacked bar charts can be created by passing a matrix to the bar function with the `'stacked'` option. Each segment within a bar shows how much it contributes to the total value for that category. This type of visualization is useful for understanding both the total and the part-to-whole relationships within the data. Stacked bars are ideal for showing how different subgroups contribute to an overall trend across categories:

```
values = [5 8; 3 6; 7 4];
bar(values, 'stacked');
legend('Group 1', 'Group 2');
title('Stacked Bar Chart');
```

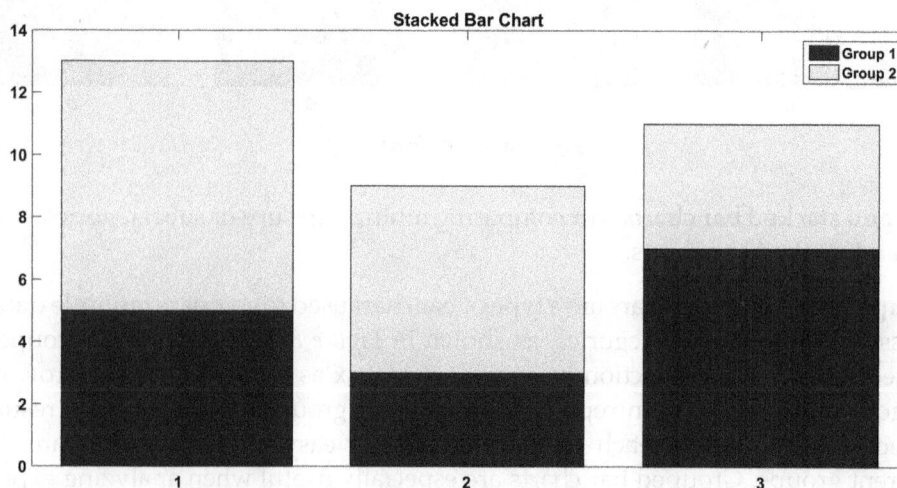

Figure 8.8: *Stacked bar chart*

- **Practical applications**: Some of the practical applications are as follows.

  o **Market share with bar**: Display and analysis of market share data can be easily done by a business analyst using a bar in an efficient way, as shown in *Figure 8.9*:

```
companies = {'Company A', 'Company B', 'Company C'};
marketShare = [40, 30, 30];
bar(marketShare);
set(gca, 'XTickLabel', companies);
title('Market Share Distribution');
ylabel('Percentage');
```

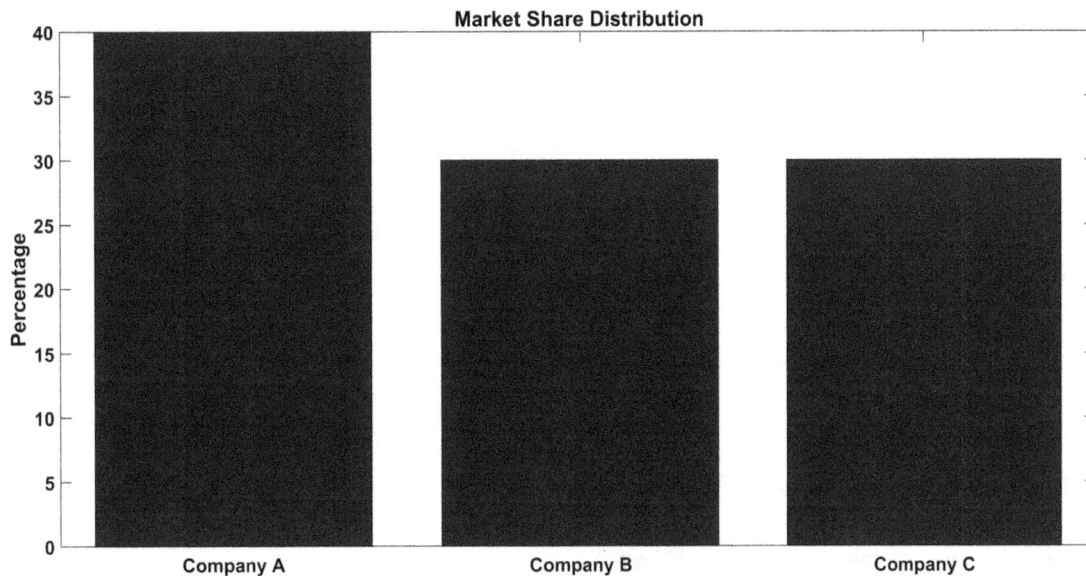

Figure 8.9: *Market share analysis with bar chart*

8.3 Exploring variable relationship through the scatter function

The scatter function is considered very useful in order to examine the relationships between two continuous variables. It plots different data points, which makes it perfect to understand and identify trends, outliers, and possible correlations in the dataset. Each point represents an observation positioned according to its values on the x and y axes, as shown in *Figure 8.10*. This visualization is particularly helpful in regression analysis, clustering, and identifying non-linear patterns. MATLAB also allows customization of marker size, color, and style, enabling users to encode additional dimensions of data for deeper analysis and better visual representation:

```
x = rand(1, 100);
y = rand(1, 100);
scatter(x, y);
xlabel('X-axis');
ylabel('Y-axis');
title('Scatter Plot');
```

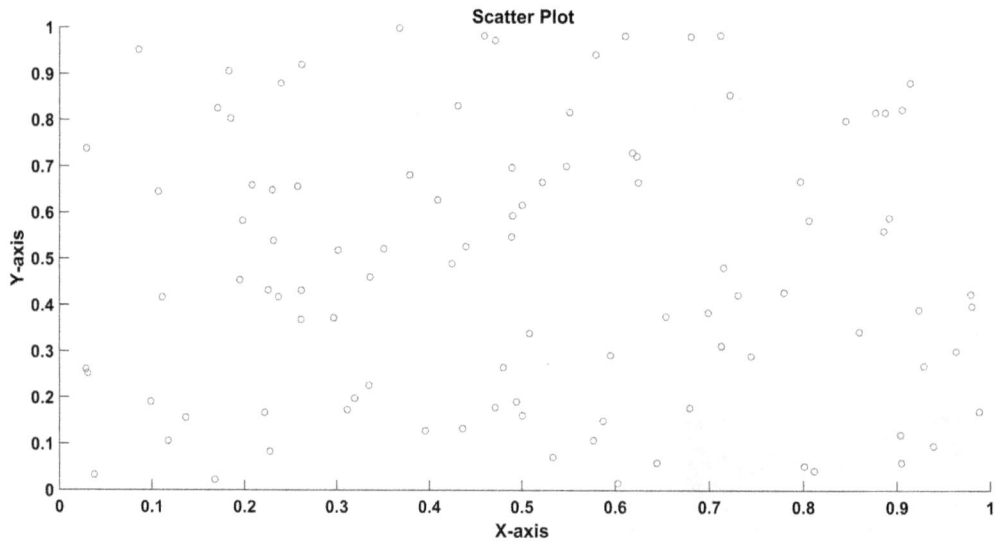

Figure 8.10: *Scatter plot*

Let us look at the option in detail:

- **Adding color and size to points**: Scatter plots can be customized by using options regarding color and size to represent additional variables, as shown in *Figure 8.11*:

```
x = rand(1, 100);
y = rand(1, 100);
sizes = 50 + 100*rand(1, 100);
colors = rand(1, 100);
scatter(x, y, sizes, colors, 'filled');
colorbar;
```

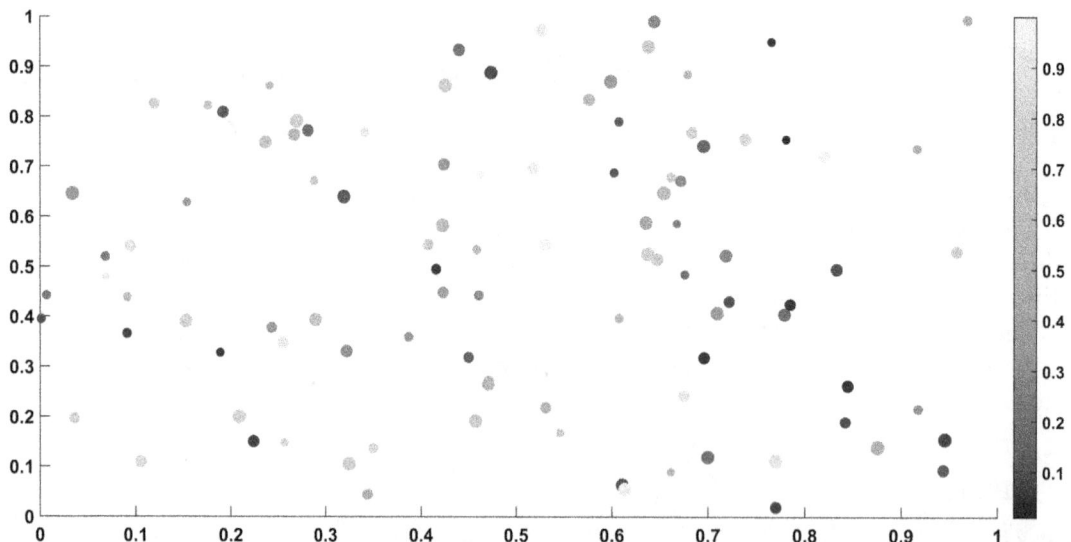

Figure 8.11: *Scatter plots customization*

- **Practical application**: Scatter diagram for correlation analysis: A researcher wants to understand the relationship between two variables considered as study hours and test scores via scatter plot, as shown in *Figure 8.12*:

```
studyHours = [1, 2, 3, 4, 5, 6, 7, 8];
testScores = [50, 55, 60, 65, 70, 75, 80, 85];
scatter(studyHours, testScores, 'filled');
xlabel('Study Hours');
ylabel('Test Scores');
title('Relationship Between Study Hours and Test Scores');
```

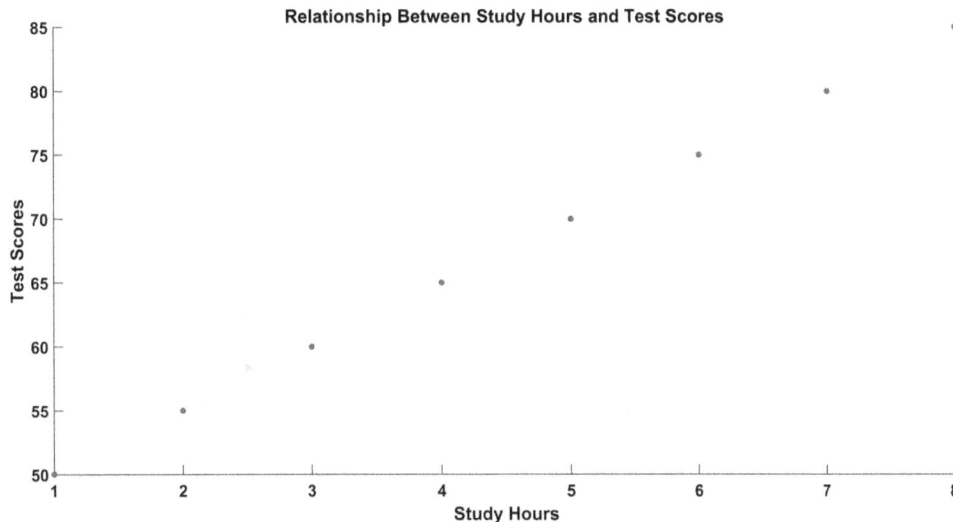

Figure 8.12: Scatter diagram for correlation analysis

8.4 Customization of plots in MATLAB

A well-presented plot is not only a piece of the data representation but also includes a story in it, which provides the communication of any complex-natured data in an efficient way. Via the customization of plots in MATLAB, clarity, readability, and the aesthetics of plots are effortlessly enhanced. Such options include the addition of titles, labels, legends, and modification of line styles. This section will provide a deep understanding on such features which will guide the readers to create professional and visually appealing plots.

8.4.1 Using titles to give context to plot

Title addition is a basic requirement from the viewer's point of view. Via the title, the main purpose and context of the plot can be shown which makes it easy to understand. Without a title, a plot may appear ambiguous or disconnected, making it harder for the reader to grasp what the data is representing. In MATLAB, the title function is used to add a descriptive heading at the top of the plot. This title can summarize the type of data being displayed, the variables involved, or the key insight the plot aims to communicate. A well-chosen title not only enhances clarity but also guides the viewer's attention and improves the overall effectiveness of the visual presentation. Additionally, titles can be formatted using different fonts, styles, and sizes, allowing readers to maintain consistency with presentation standards. Overall, including a clear and concise title is an essential aspect of professional and effective data visualization.

Let us look at titles in detail:

- **Adding a title**: The title function is mainly used to add a title of the plot as per *Figure 8.13*. The program to add the title to the chart is as follows:

```
x = 0:0.1:10;
y = sin(x);
plot(x, y);
title('Sine Wave');
```

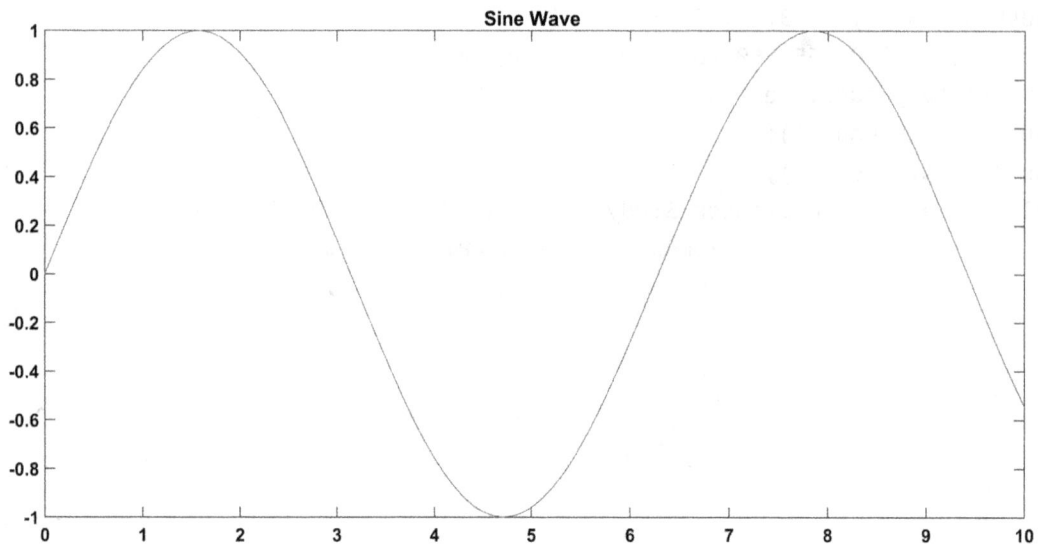

Figure 8.13: *Adding a title in plot*

- **Customizing titles**: The enhancements to the title can be done with properties such as font size, weight, and color, as shown in *Figure 8.14*:

```
x = 0:0.1:10;
y = sin(x);
plot(x, y);
title('Sine Wave');
title('Sine Wave', 'FontSize', 16, 'FontWeight', 'bold', 'Color', 'blue');
```

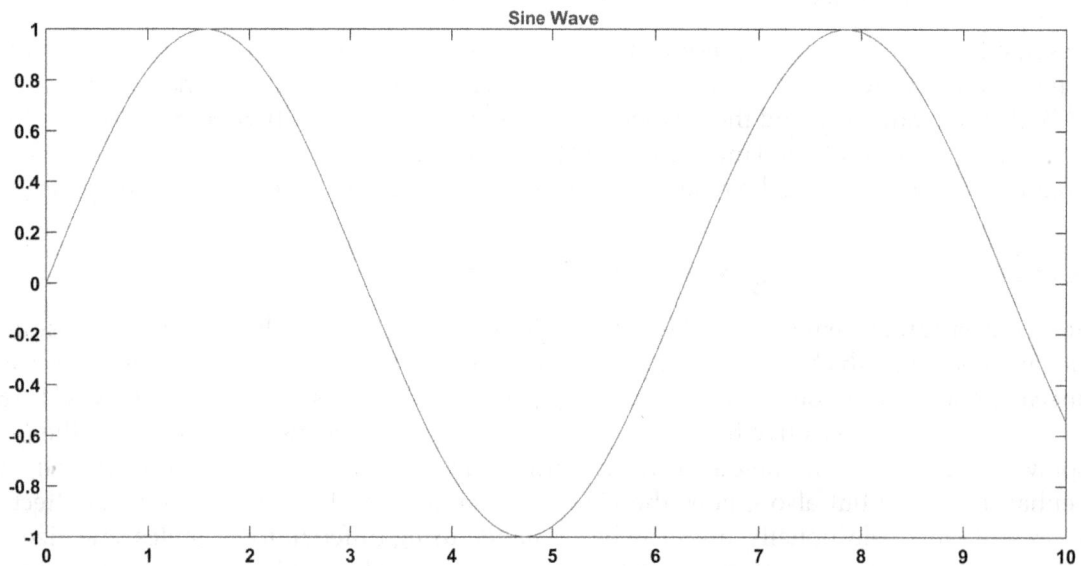

Figure 8.14: *Customization of title in plot*

- **Multiline titles**: For further elaborated plots, multiline titles can also be provided via a cell array, as shown in *Figure 8.15*:

```
x = 0:0.1:10;
y = sin(x);
plot(x, y);
title('Sine Wave');
title({'Sine Wave', 'Amplitude over Time'}, 'FontSize', 14);
```

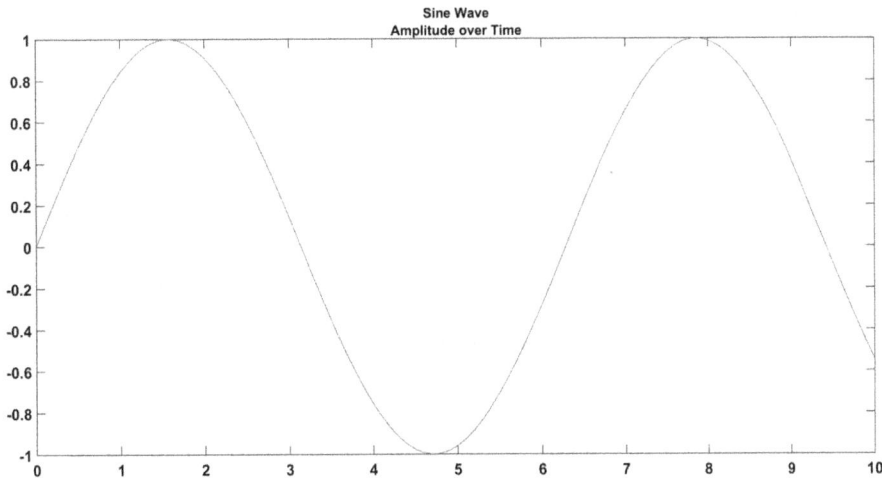

Figure 8.15: *Multiline titles*

8.4.2 Using labels to identify axes

The x-axis and y-axis labels are important to interpret the scale and meaning of the data. Labeling the axes is a critical component of any effective data visualization, as it allows the viewer to accurately interpret the information presented on the graph. The x-axis and y-axis labels provide context for the data points by describing what each axis represents; be it time, frequency, population, temperature, or any other variable. Without proper labeling, even the most accurate and well-designed plots can become confusing or misleading. In MATLAB, the **xlabel** and **ylabel** functions are used to assign text labels to the horizontal and vertical axes, respectively. These labels should be concise yet descriptive, clearly communicating the variable name and, if applicable, its units of measurement (e.g., **"Time (seconds)"**, **"Temperature (°C)"**). Proper labeling enhances the clarity of the plot and ensures that it can be understood independently, without requiring additional explanation.

Let us look at labels in detail:

- **Adding axis labels**: **xlabel** and **ylabel** functions may be used to add descriptive labels in a plot, as shown in *Figure 8.16*:

```
x = 0:0.1:10;
y = sin(x);
plot(x, y);
title('Sine Wave');
xlabel('Time (seconds)');
ylabel('Amplitude');
```

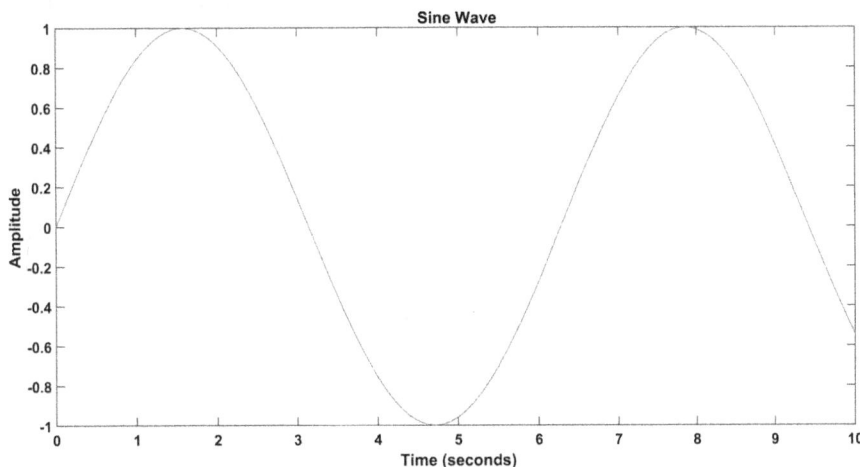

Figure 8.16: *Adding axis labels*

- **Customizing labels**: You can modify the label appearance using similar properties as the title, as shown in *Figure 8.17*:

```
x = 0:0.1:10;
y = sin(x);
plot(x, y);
title('Sine Wave');
xlabel('Time (s)', 'FontSize', 12, 'FontWeight', 'bold', 'Color', 'red');
ylabel('Amplitude', 'FontSize', 12, 'FontWeight', 'bold', 'Color', 'blue');
```

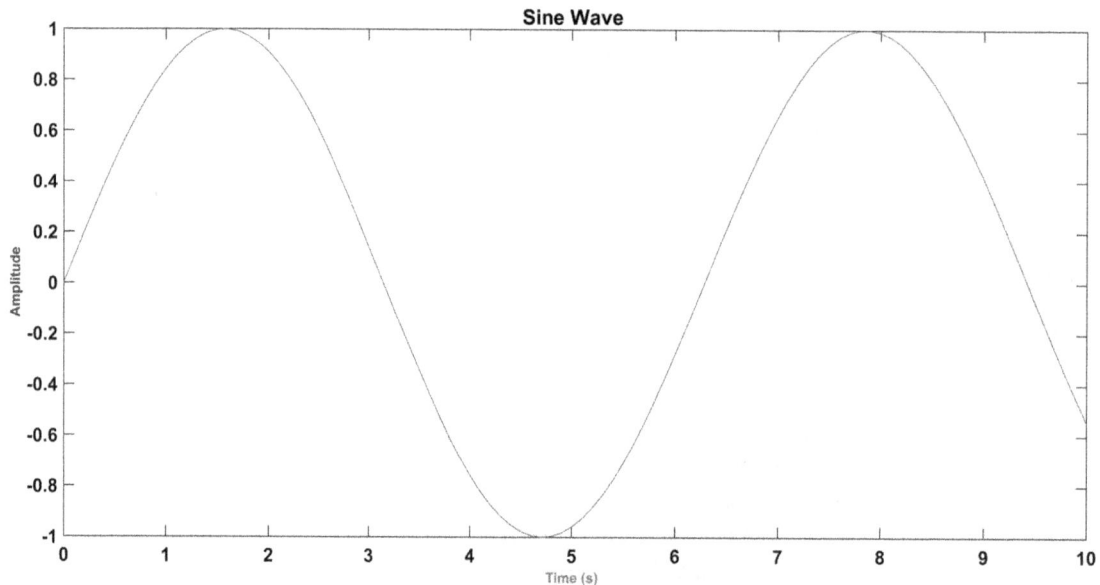

Figure 8.17: *Customizing labels*

8.4.3 Using legends for multiple data series

When multiple datasets are plotted on the same graph, it becomes essential to include a legend to clearly distinguish between them. A legend acts as a key that identifies which graphical element corresponds to which dataset, making the plot easier to interpret. Without a legend, the viewer may struggle to understand the meaning of different lines, markers, or bar groups, especially if they are visually similar. MATLAB's legend function provides a simple and effective way to add descriptive labels to each data series. Users can specify custom text for each dataset, helping to explain what each line or symbol represents. This is particularly useful in cases where the plot includes results from different experiments, models, or conditions. Legends can be placed in various locations on the plot, such as top-right, bottom-left, or outside the axes, for optimal clarity.

Let us look at legends in detail:

- **Adding a legend**: The legend function associates labels with plotted lines as shown in *Figure 8.18*:

```
x = 0:0.1:10;
y1 = sin(x);
y2 = cos(x);
plot(x, y1, x, y2);
legend('sin(x)', 'cos(x)');
```

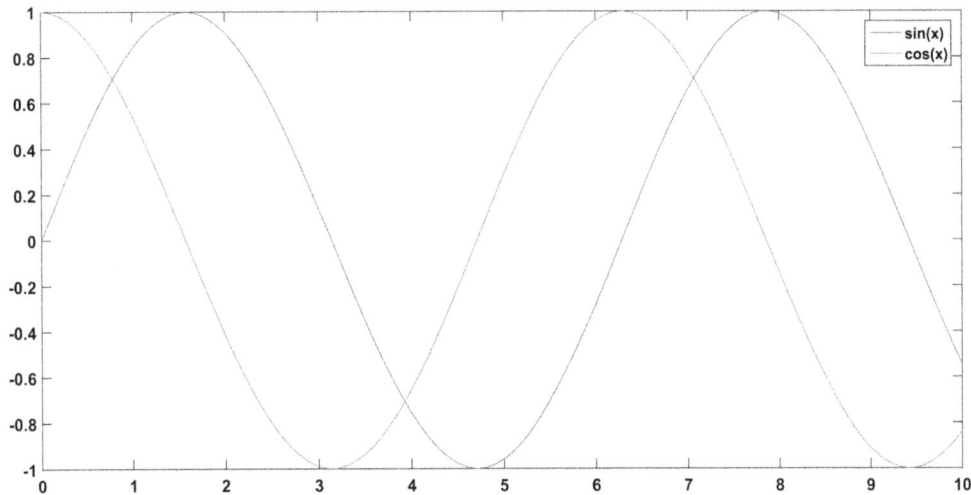

Figure 8.18: Adding a legend

- **Positioning the legend**: Legends can be moved to different locations using predefined options; `'northwest'`, `'northeast'`, `'southwest'`, `'southeast'` as provided in *Figure 8.19*:

```
x = 0:0.1:10;
y1 = sin(x);
y2 = cos(x);
plot(x, y1, x, y2);
legend('sin(x)', 'cos(x)', 'Location', 'northwest');
```

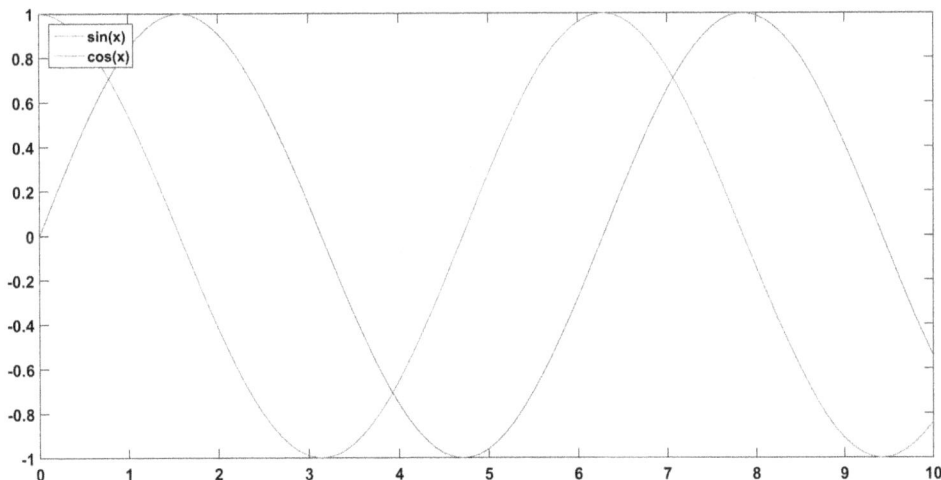

Figure 8.19: Positioning the legend

8.4.4 Using line styles to enhance plot readability

There exist diverse line styles in MATLAB. MATLAB permits customization of line types, colors, and markers to make plots more engaging and easier to interpret. By strategically combining solid ('-'), dashed ('--'), dotted (':'), or dash-dot ('-.') lines with different colors and marker symbols ('o', 's', '*'), you can create clear visual distinctions between multiple data sets on the same plot. This is particularly useful when presenting complex data or comparing multiple trends in a single figure. For example, you might use a solid red line with circle markers for experimental data, while employing a dashed blue line for theoretical predictions, making it immediately apparent which curve represents what. These styling options are specified as a combined string argument in plot commands, such as plot(x,y,'r--o') for a red dashed line with circle markers.

Let us look at them in detail:

- **Changing line styles**: MATLAB supports several predefined line styles shown in *Figure 8.20*:
  - o **Solid line**: '-'
  - o **Dashed line**: '--'
  - o **Dotted line**: ':'
  - o **Dash-dot line**: '-.'

```
x = 0:0.1:10;
y1 = sin(x);
y2 = cos(x);
plot(x, y1, '--', x, y2, '-.');
```

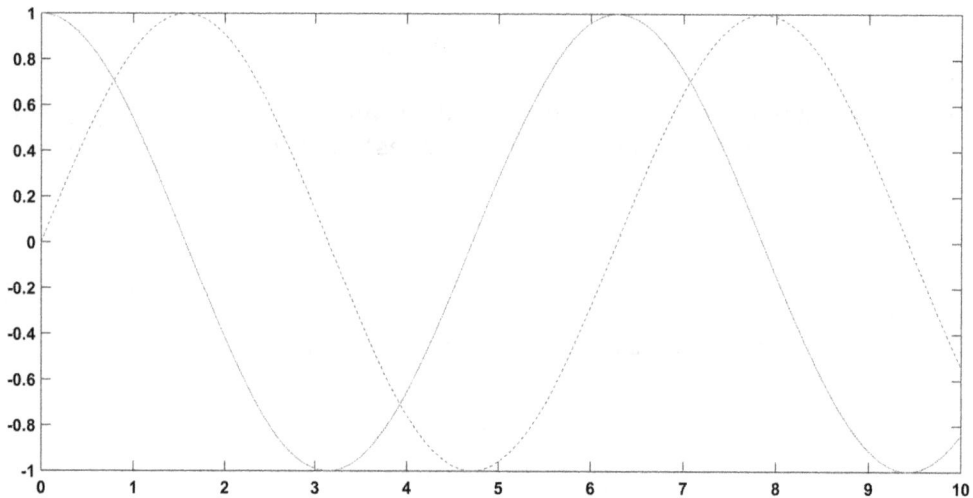

Figure 8.20: *Changing line styles*

- **Modifying line width**: Thicker or thinner lines can be used for emphasis, as shown in *Figure 8.21*:

```
x = 0:0.1:10;
y1 = sin(x);
y2 = cos(x);
plot(x, y1, '--', 'LineWidth',2);
```

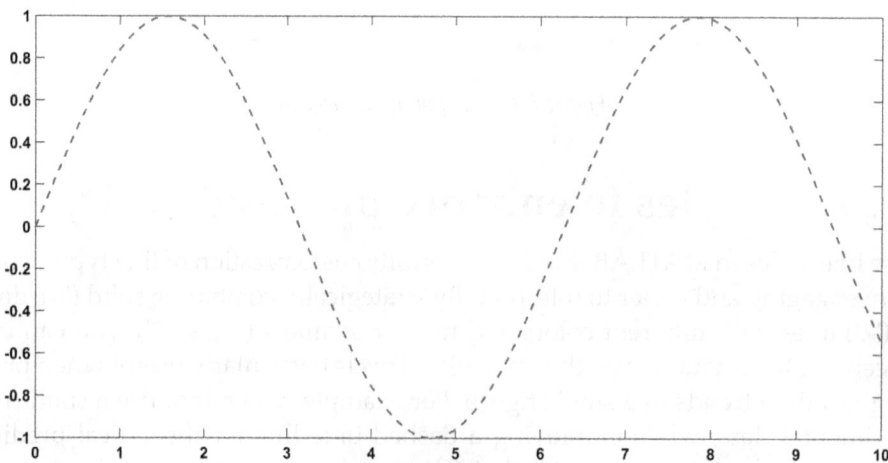

Figure 8.21: *Modifying line width*

- **Adding markers**: Through the markers, individual data points can be highlighted. Some of the common options are:

  o **Circle**: 'o'

  o **Star**: '*'

  o **Square**: 's'

  o **Diamond**: 'd'

```
x = 0:0.1:10;
y1 = sin(x);
y2 = cos(x);
plot(x, y1, '-o', 'MarkerSize', 8, 'MarkerEdgeColor', 'red', 'MarkerFaceColor',
'yellow');
```

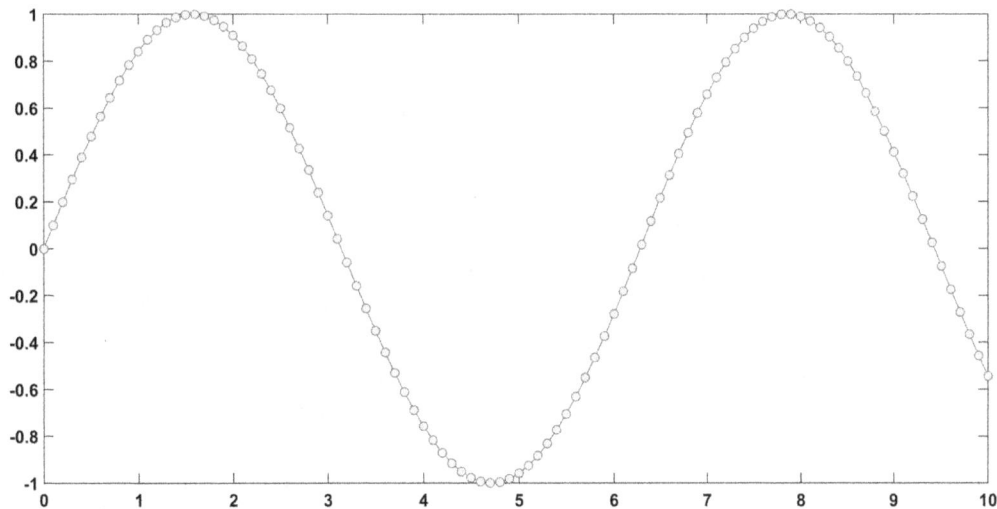

Figure 8.22: *Adding markers*

8.4.5 A customized plot

Let us combine these customization options into a comprehensive example: The sine and cosine waves plots are plotted with distinct line styles, as shown in *Figure 8.23*. **title**, **xlabel**, **ylabel**, **legend** are also included as customization:

```
% Data
x = 0:0.1:10;
y1 = sin(x);
y2 = cos(x);
plot(x, y1, '-o', 'LineWidth', 2, 'MarkerSize', 6, 'MarkerFaceColor', 'blue');
hold on;
plot(x, y2, '--', 'LineWidth', 2, 'Color', [0.8, 0.2, 0.2]);
hold off;
title('Comparison of Sine and Cosine Functions', 'FontSize', 14, 'FontWeight', 'bold');
xlabel('X-axis (Time in seconds)', 'FontSize', 12);
ylabel('Y-axis (Amplitude)', 'FontSize', 12);
legend('sin(x)', 'cos(x)', 'Location', 'southwest', 'FontSize', 12);
grid on;
axis([0 10 -1.5 1.5]);
```

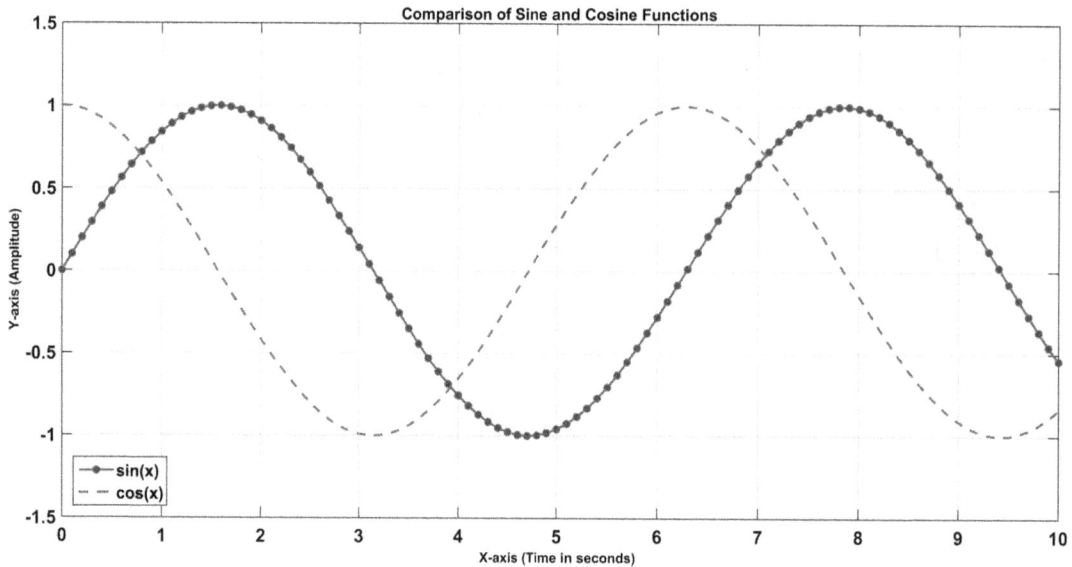

Figure 8.23: Customized plot

8.4.6 Additional customization tips

Customizing plots in MATLAB allows users to create more visually appealing and informative graphics tailored to specific needs. Beyond basic elements like titles, labels, and legends, MATLAB offers a wide range of customization options to enhance the clarity and aesthetics of a plot. Users can modify line styles, marker types, and colors using properties such as 'LineStyle', 'Marker', and 'Color' to differentiate between datasets or emphasize key points. Grid lines can be added using the grid on command, which helps better align and read data values. The axes can also be adjusted in terms of limits (**xlim**, **ylim**), tick marks, and scaling (linear or logarithmic) to suit the data distribution. Additionally, annotations such as arrows, text boxes, and shapes can be inserted using functions like annotation and text to highlight specific features or add explanatory notes:

- **Using grids**: Adding grids enhances readability. A grid is as shown in *Figure 8.24*.

```
x = 0:0.1:10;
y1 = sin(x);
y2 = cos(x);
plot(x, y1, '--', 'LineWidth',2);
grid on;
grid minor;
```

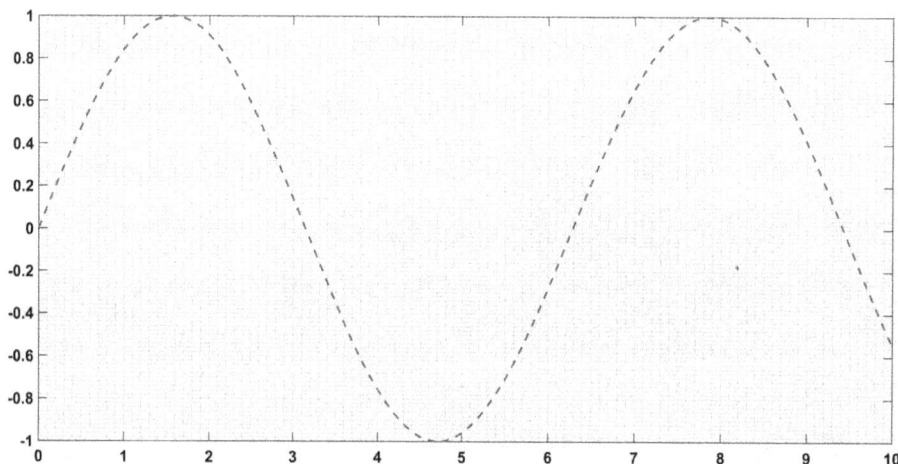

Figure 8.24: Use of grids

- **Annotations**: Annotations can highlight specific points or features:

```
x = 0:0.1:10;
y1 = sin(x);
y2 = cos(x);
plot(x, y1, '--', 'LineWidth',2);
grid on;
grid minor;
text(pi, 0, ' \leftarrow Peak', 'FontSize', 12, 'Color', 'red');
```

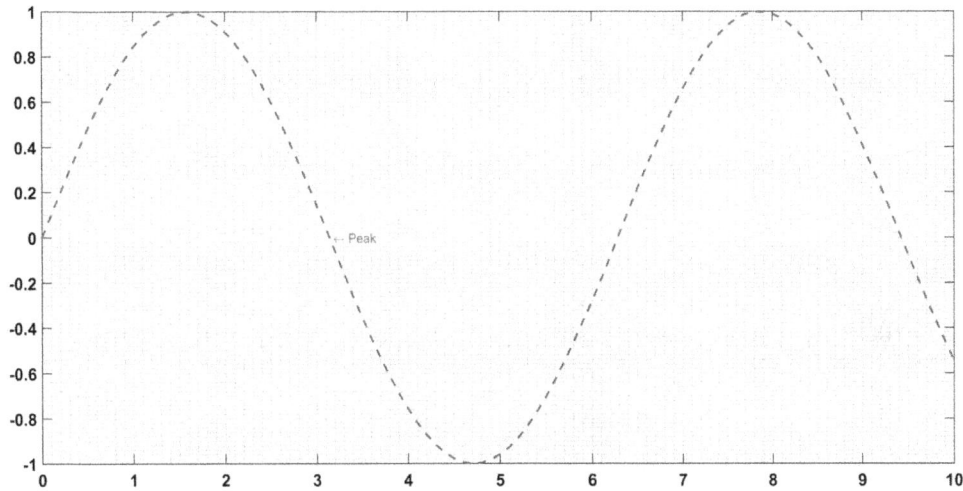

Figure 8.25: Annotations in plot

8.5 Introduction to 3D plotting

3D plots are invaluable in scenarios where data relationships are not easily discernible in two dimensions. From plotting trajectories to visualizing surfaces, MATLAB simplifies the process of creating 3D visualizations.

Some common 3D plotting functions are:

- **plot3**: Plots 3D lines or trajectories.

- **surf**: Creates 3D surface plots with filled colors.

- **mesh**: Similar to surf but creates a grid-like representation.

- **Using plot3 for 3D line plots**: The **plot3** function is ideal for plotting curves or trajectories in 3D space.

  Example: Plotting a Helix (see *Figure 8.26*):

```
t = 0:0.1:10;
x = sin(t);
y = cos(t);
z = t;
plot3(x, y, z, '-o', 'MarkerSize', 8, 'MarkerFaceColor', 'red', 'LineWidth', 1.5);
xlabel('X-axis'); ylabel('Y-axis'); zlabel('Z-axis');
title('3D Helix');
grid on;
```

3D Helix

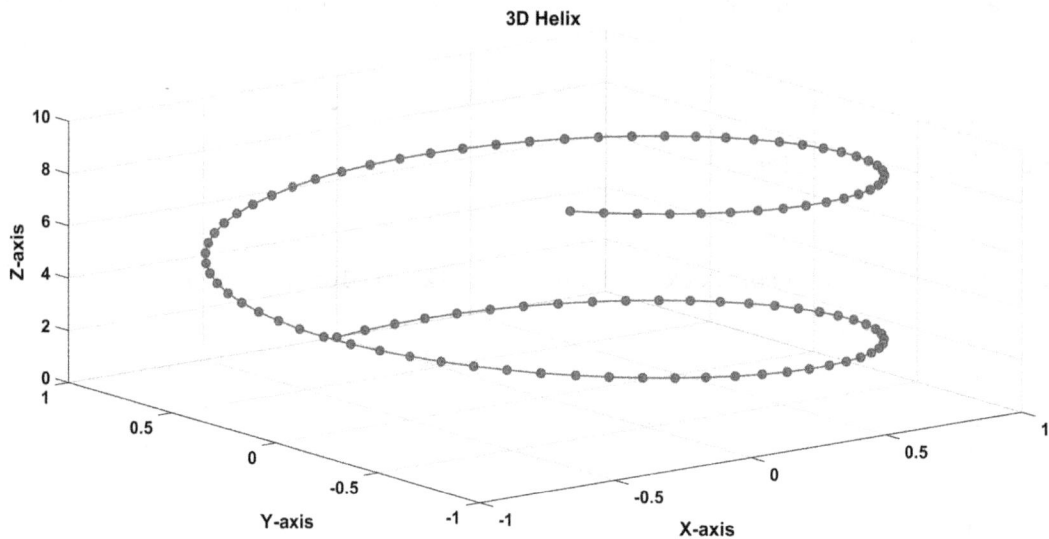

Figure 8.26: Plotting of Helix

- **Creating surface plots with surf**: The **surf** function is used to create 3D surfaces, as shown in *Figure 8.27*, where the z-values represent the height of the surface at each (x, y) point:

```
surf(X, Y, Z);
```

Example: Visualizing a mathematical function:

```
[X, Y] = meshgrid(-2:0.1:2, -2:0.1:2);
Z = X.^2 + Y.^2;
surf(X, Y, Z);
xlabel('X-axis');
ylabel('Y-axis');
zlabel('Z-axis');
title('Surface Plot of Z = X^2 + Y^2');
```

Surface Plot of Z = X^2 + Y^2

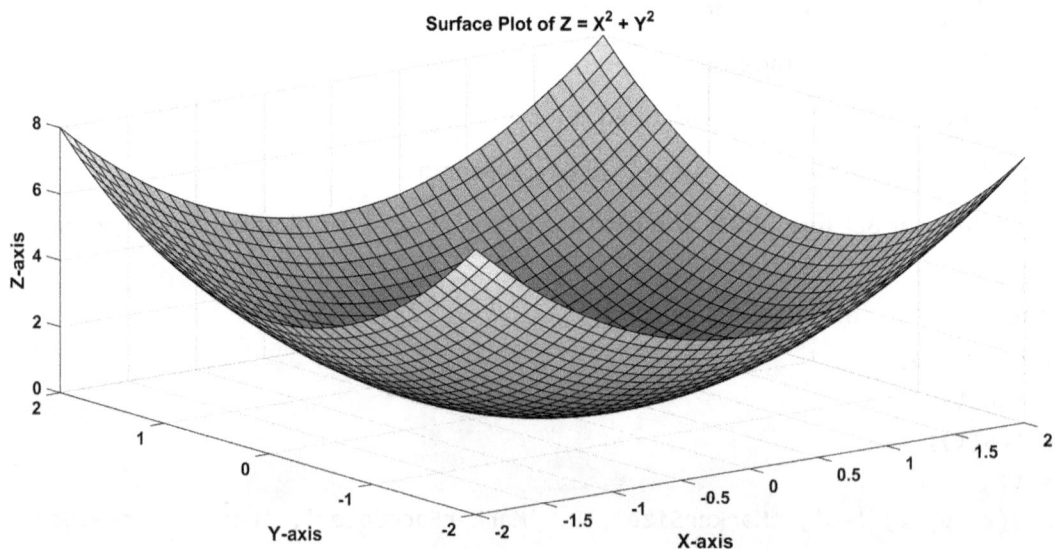

Figure 8.27: Creating surface plots

- **Customizing surface appearance**: The surface appearance can also be customized via colormap, shading, and lighting, etc.:

o **Color maps**: Change the colors using colormap (see *Figure 8.28*):

```
[X, Y] = meshgrid(-2:0.1:2, -2:0.1:2);
Z = X.^2 + Y.^2;
surf(X, Y, Z);
xlabel('X-axis');
ylabel('Y-axis');
zlabel('Z-axis');
title('Surface Plot of Z = X^2 + Y^2');
colormap jet;
```

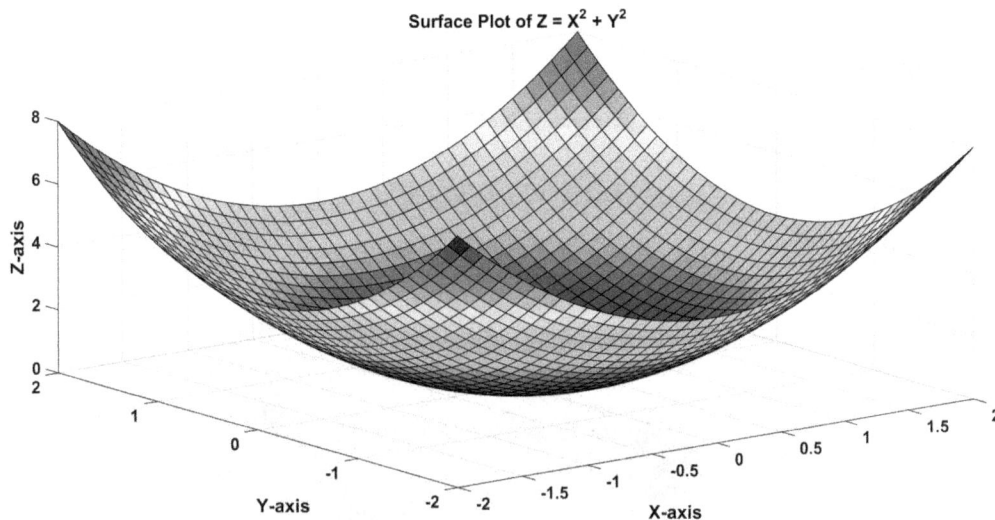

Figure 8.28: *Customizing surface appearance*

o **Shading**: Adjust shading for smoother visuals (see *Figure 8.29*):

```
[X, Y] = meshgrid(-2:0.1:2, -2:0.1:2);
Z = X.^2 + Y.^2;
surf(X, Y, Z);
xlabel('X-axis');
ylabel('Y-axis');
zlabel('Z-axis');
title('Surface Plot of Z = X^2 + Y^2');
shading interp;
```

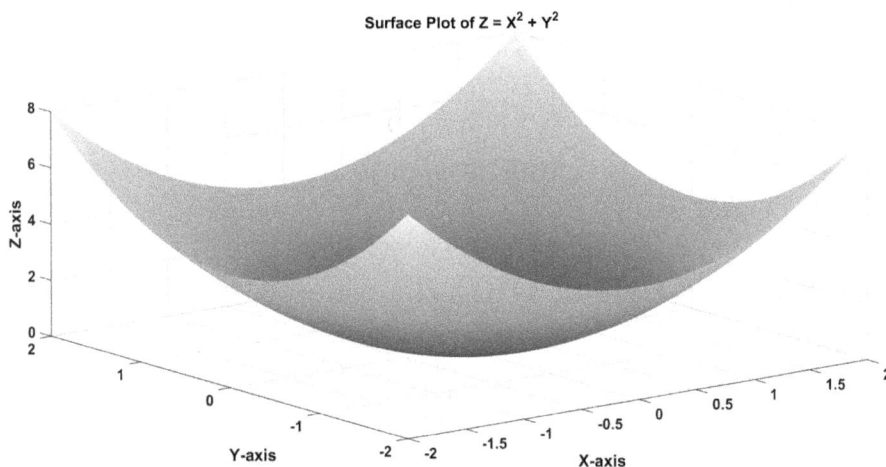

Figure 8.29: *Shading for smoother visuals*

o **Lighting**: Add lighting effects (see *Figure 8.30*):

```
[X, Y] = meshgrid(-2:0.1:2, -2:0.1:2);
Z = X.^2 + Y.^2;
surf(X, Y, Z);
xlabel('X-axis');
ylabel('Y-axis');
zlabel('Z-axis');
title('Surface Plot of  Z = X^2 + Y^2');
light;
camlight;
lighting phong;
```

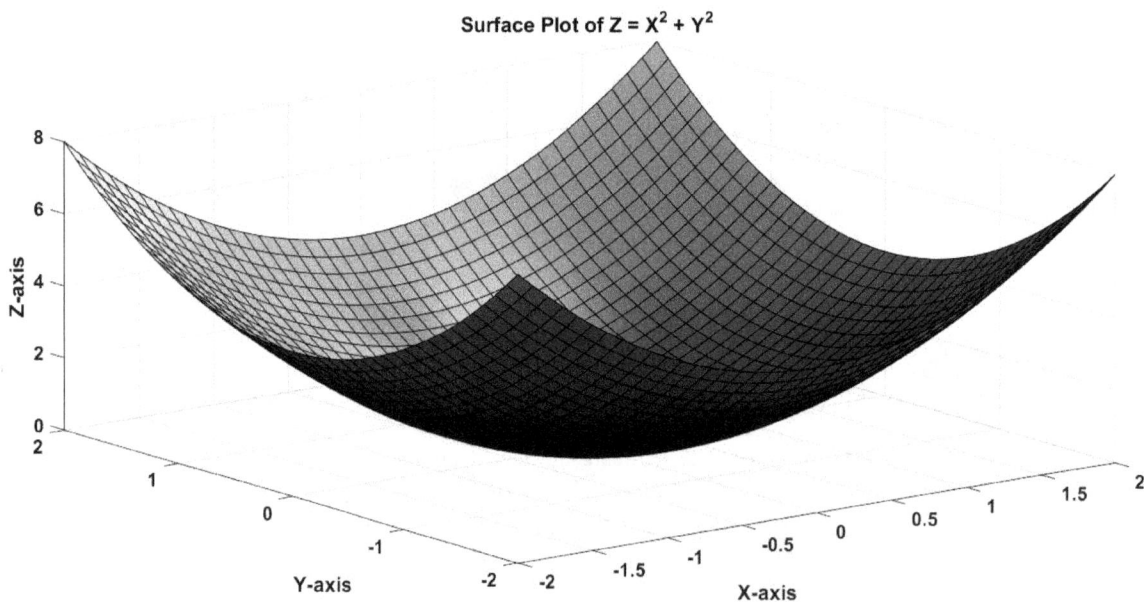

Figure 8.30: *Lighting effects*

- **Using mesh for grid-like plots**: The **mesh** function is similar to surf, but it creates a wireframe representation instead of a filled surface.

```
mesh(X, Y, Z);
```

Example: Wireframe plot (see *Figure 8.31*):

```
[X, Y] = meshgrid(-2:0.1:2, -2:0.1:2);
Z = sin(X).*cos(Y);
mesh(X, Y, Z);
xlabel('X-axis');
ylabel('Y-axis');
zlabel('Z-axis');
title('Mesh Plot of Z = sin(X) * cos(Y)');
```

Mesh Plot of Z = sin(X) * cos(Y)

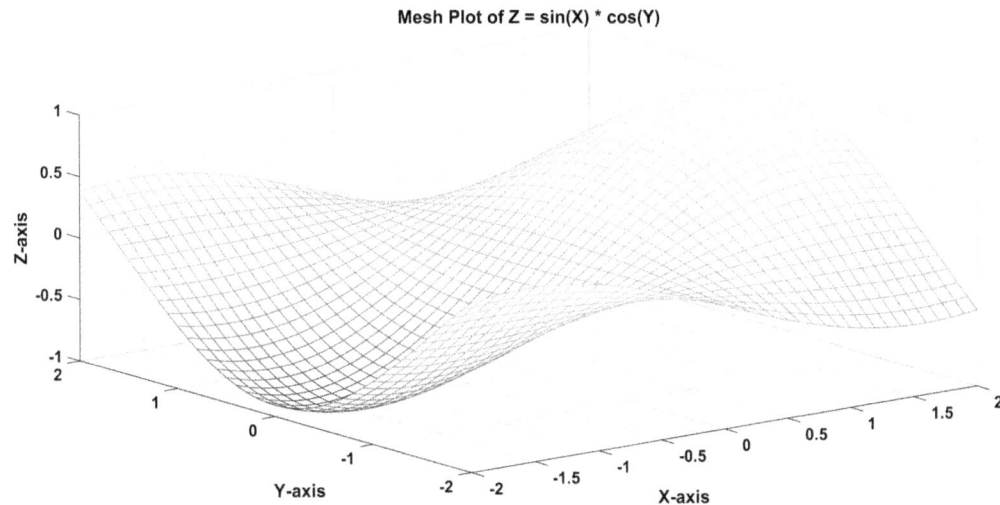

Figure 8.31: *Wireframe plot*

- **Customizing the mesh**: After the creation of mesh plots, we will now learn how this mesh plot can be customized, as shown in *Figure 8.32*. This customization is discussed in detail as follows:

  o **Grid colors**: Modify the color of the grid lines:

```
[X, Y] = meshgrid(-2:0.1:2, -2:0.1:2);
Z = sin(X).*cos(Y);
mesh(X, Y, Z, 'EdgeColor', 'blue');
xlabel('X-axis');
ylabel('Y-axis');
zlabel('Z-axis');
title('Mesh Plot of Z = sin(X) * cos(Y)');
```

Mesh Plot of Z = sin(X) * cos(Y)

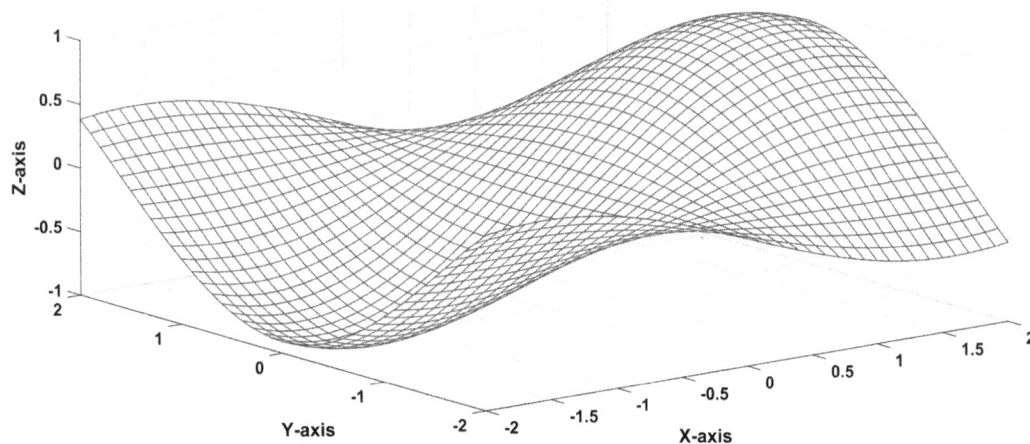

Figure 8.32: *Customizing the mesh*

  o **Transparency**: Add transparency to mesh (see *Figure 8.33*):

```
[X, Y] = meshgrid(-2:0.1:2, -2:0.1:2);
Z = sin(X).*cos(Y);
mesh(X, Y, Z);
xlabel('X-axis'); ylabel('Y-axis'); zlabel('Z-axis');
```

```
title('Mesh Plot of Z = sin(X) * cos(Y)');
alpha(0.5); % 50% transparency
```

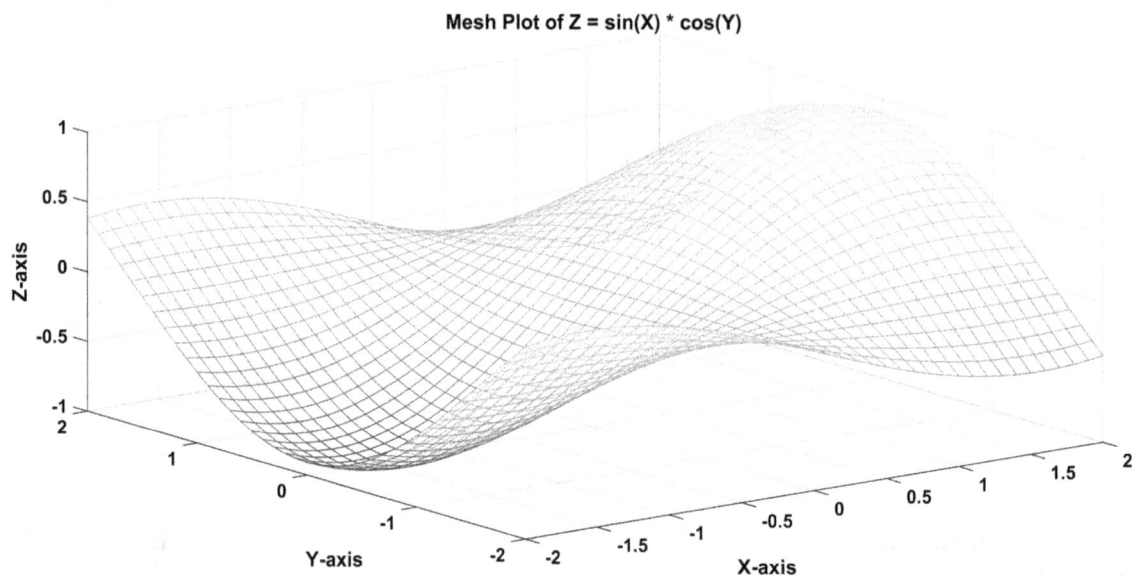

Figure 8.33: Add transparency to mesh

- **Comparison of surf and mesh**:

Feature	surf	mesh
Appearance	Filled surface	Wireframe grid
Customization	Color maps, shading	Grid color, transparency
Best For	Continuous surfaces	Structural representations

Table 8.1: Comparison table

- **Combining 3D plot types**: MATLAB allows you to overlay multiple 3D plot types to create hybrid visualizations, as shown in *Figure 8.34*.

Example: Combining **surf** and **plot3**:

```
[X, Y] = meshgrid(-2:0.1:2, -2:0.1:2);
Z = X.^2 + Y.^2;
surf(X, Y, Z, 'FaceAlpha', 0.7);
hold on;
t = 0:0.1:10;
x = sin(t); y = cos(t); z = t;
plot3(x, y, z, 'r-', 'LineWidth', 2);
hold off;
xlabel('X-axis');
ylabel('Y-axis'); zlabel('Z-axis');
title('Combined Surface and Line Plot');
```

Combined Surface and Line Plot

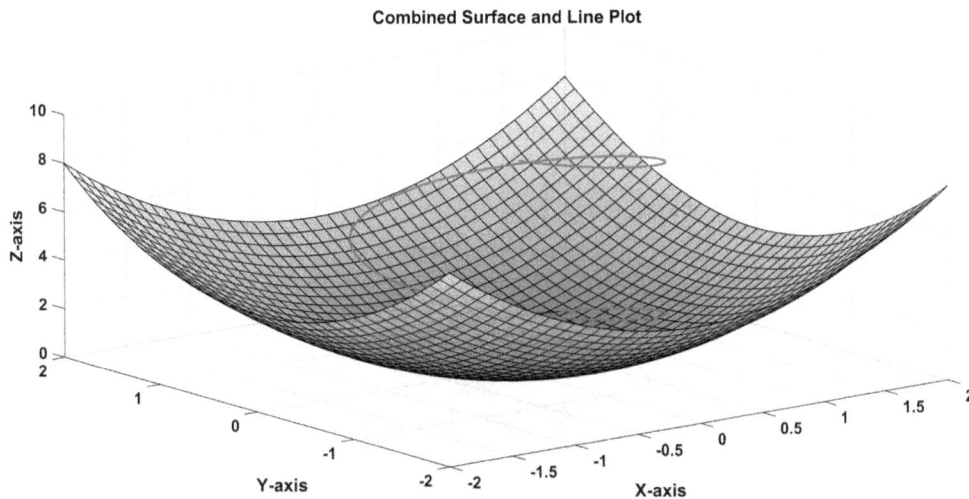

Figure 8.34: *Multiple plots*

8.6 Specialized plots in MATLAB

In MATLAB, specialized plots address particular visualization requirements, enabling you to efficiently analyze and display various data kinds. The three flexible and widely used plot types covered in this article include polar plots, heatmaps, and histograms, among others. These plots offer distinct methods for revealing trends and insights, which makes them essential resources for analysts, engineers, and academics.

8.6.1 Using histograms to visualize data distributions

By splitting a dataset into bins and counting the number of data points in each bin, histograms may be used to show the distribution of the dataset. Histograms are therefore perfect for spotting trends like outliers, skewness, and spread. Let us look at them in detail:

- **Creating a basic histogram**: Making histograms is easy with MATLAB's histogram function as follows (see *Figure 8.35*):

```
data = randn(1, 1000);
histogram(data);
title('Histogram of Random Data');
xlabel('Value');
ylabel('Frequency');
```

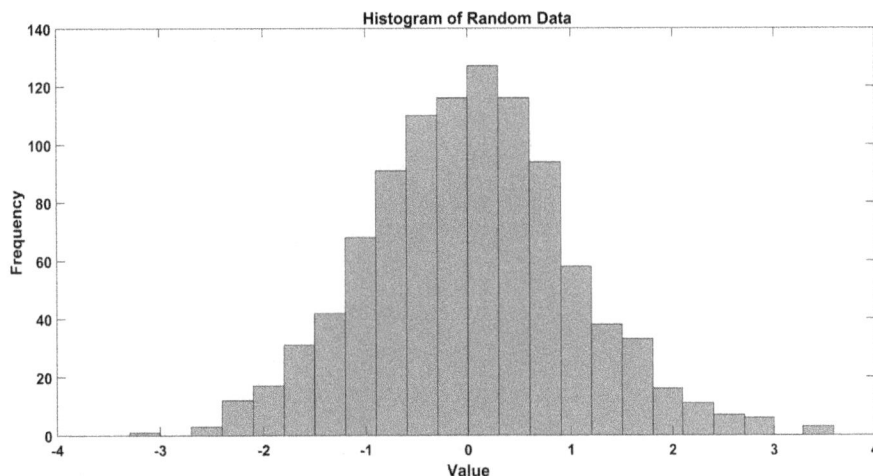

Figure 8.35: *Basic histogram*

- **Customizing histograms**: Options for customization of the histogram include changing the color, style, and quantity of bins (see *Figure 8.36*):

```
data = randn(1, 1000);
histogram(data, 'NumBins', 20, 'FaceColor', 'blue', 'EdgeColor', 'black');
title('Customized Histogram');
xlabel('Value'); ylabel('Frequency');
```

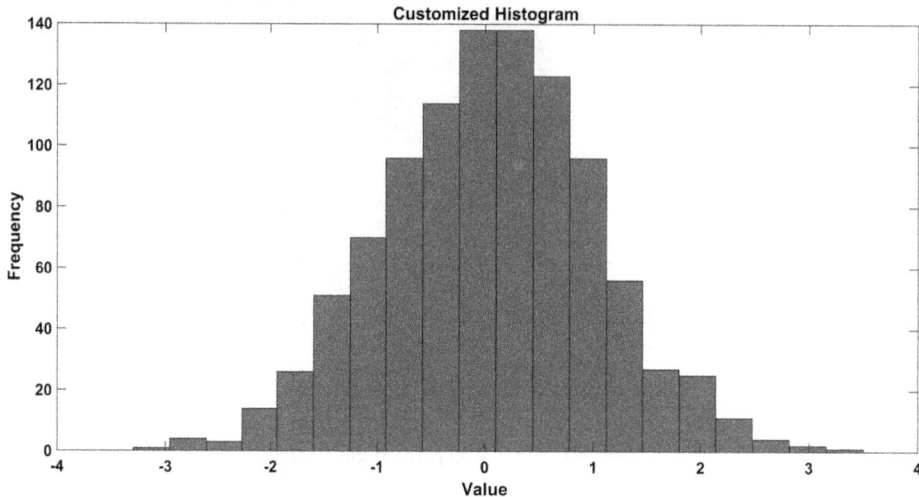

Figure 8.36: *Customizing histograms*

The explanation is as follows:

o **NumBins**: It controls number of bins.

o **FaceColor and EdgeColor**: It sets fill and edge colors of bars.

- Overlaying multiple histograms (see *Figure 8.37*):

```
data1 = randn(1, 1000);
data2 = 2 + randn(1, 1000);
hold on;
histogram(data1, 'FaceColor', 'red', 'FaceAlpha', 0.5);
histogram(data2, 'FaceColor', 'blue', 'FaceAlpha', 0.5);
hold off;
legend('Dataset 1', 'Dataset 2');
```

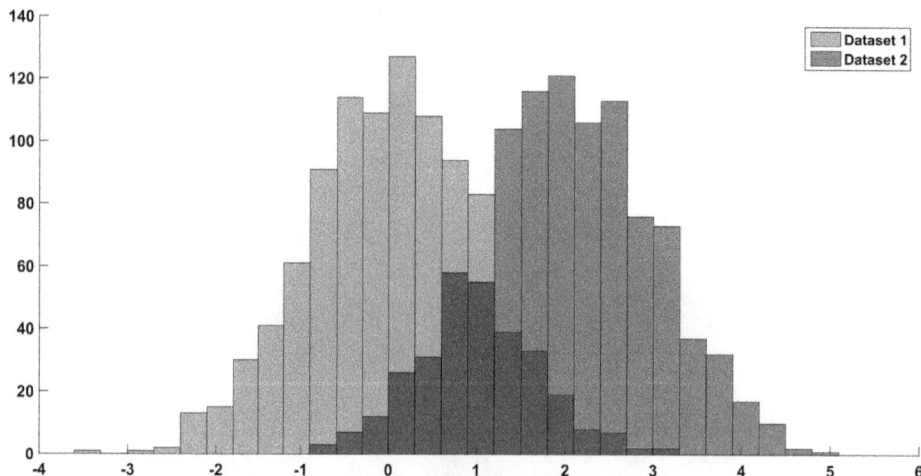

Figure 8.37: *Overlaying multiple histograms*

8.6.2 Using heatmaps to visualize matrix data

Heatmaps offer a color-coded representation of matrix data, with a color intensity assigned to each cell. They are especially helpful for finding correlations, patterns, and clusters in big datasets.

If the heatmap function is not recognized by your version of MATLAB (likely because it is an older version), you can use **imagesc** instead to create a similar visualization. However, **imagesc** is a simpler substitute and lacks some features of heatmap, such as labeled axes, automatic color scaling for categorical data, and interactivity (like tooltips). Let us see how to use headmaps:

- **Creating a basic heatmap**: Make that the heatmap function is recognized by MATLAB. If not, you might be using an outdated version of MATLAB that does not support heatmaps (see *Figure 8.38*). In that scenario, **imagesc** can be used as a substitute:

```
data = rand(10, 10);
imagesc(data);
colorbar;
title('Heatmap of Random Data');
```

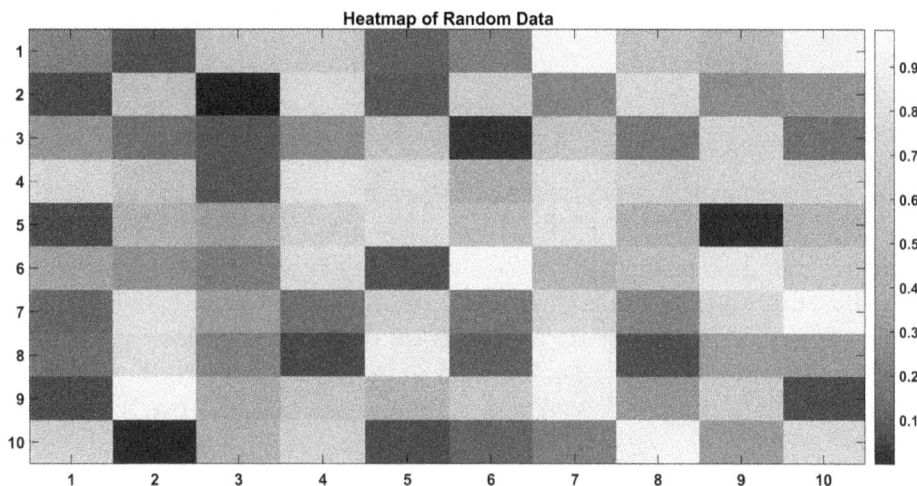

Figure 8.38: Creating a basic heatmap

- **Version check**: Check your MATLAB version using the following if the heatmap function is not recognized:

```
ver
```

It is advised to update MATLAB or use an alternative, such as **imagesc**, if your version does not support heatmaps.

8.6.3 Using polar plots to visualize angular data

Polar plots are perfect for periodic data, directional patterns, and angular relationships since they use radii and angles to describe the data. Typical domains where polar plots are commonly used include antenna radiation patterns, mechanical vibrations, wind directions, and navigation systems, where angle-based visualization is essential.

To create a basic polar plot, use the **polar** function instead, if you are using an older version of MATLAB where **polarplot** is not available (see *Figure 8.39*):

```
theta = linspace(0, 2*pi, 100);
rho = sin(2*theta);
polar(theta, rho);
title('Polar Plot of sin(2 \theta)');
```

Polar Plot of sin(2 θ)

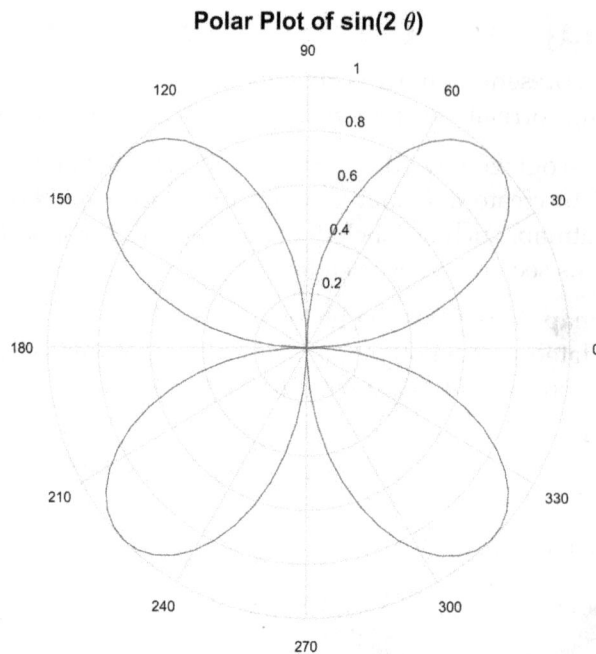

Figure 8.39: Polar plot

8.6.4 Error bar plots and representing variability

Error bar plots visualize data points along with their variability or uncertainty, often used in scientific and engineering experiments. Error bar plots visualize data points along with their variability or uncertainty, often used in scientific and engineering experiments. In MATLAB, the **errorbar()** function creates these plots by displaying vertical and/or horizontal error bars around data points. The error bars can represent different metrics of variability, including standard deviation, standard error, confidence intervals, or measurement uncertainty (see *Figure 8.40*):

```
x = 1:5;
y = [2, 4, 6, 8, 10];
errors = [0.5, 0.6, 0.7, 0.8, 0.9];
errorbar(x, y, errors, 'o-', 'LineWidth', 1.5);
xlabel('X-axis');
ylabel('Y-axis');
title('Error Bar Plot');
```

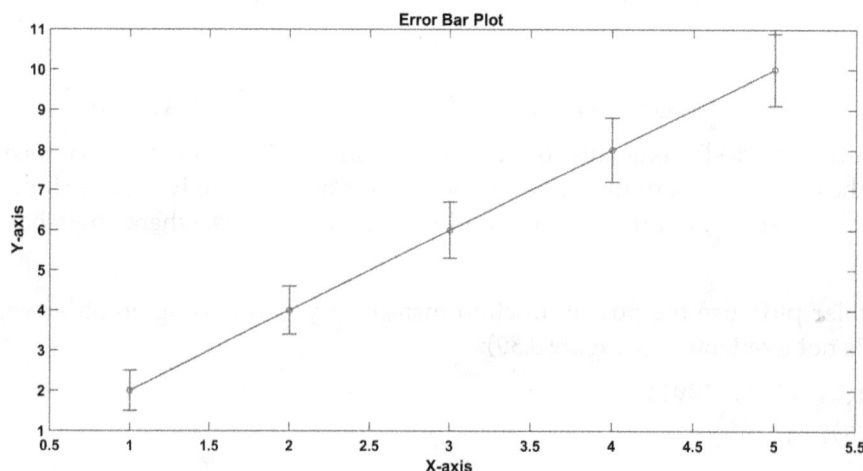

Figure 8.40: Error bar plots

Its applications are as follows:

- Displaying measurement uncertainties.
- Visualizing standard deviations or confidence intervals.

8.6.5 Stacked bar plots and comparing grouped data

Stacked bar plots represent multiple data series in one bar, showing the contribution of each series to the total, as illustrated in *Figure 8.41*:

- **Function: bar (with 'stacked')**: MATLAB's bar function with the **'stacked'** option enables powerful comparative analysis by displaying multiple data series as segmented columns. This visualization method stacks different categories on top of each other within each bar:

```
data = [3 5 2; 4 6 3; 5 8 4];
bar(data, 'stacked');
xlabel('Categories');
ylabel('Values');
title('Stacked Bar Plot');
legend('Series 1', 'Series 2', 'Series 3');
```

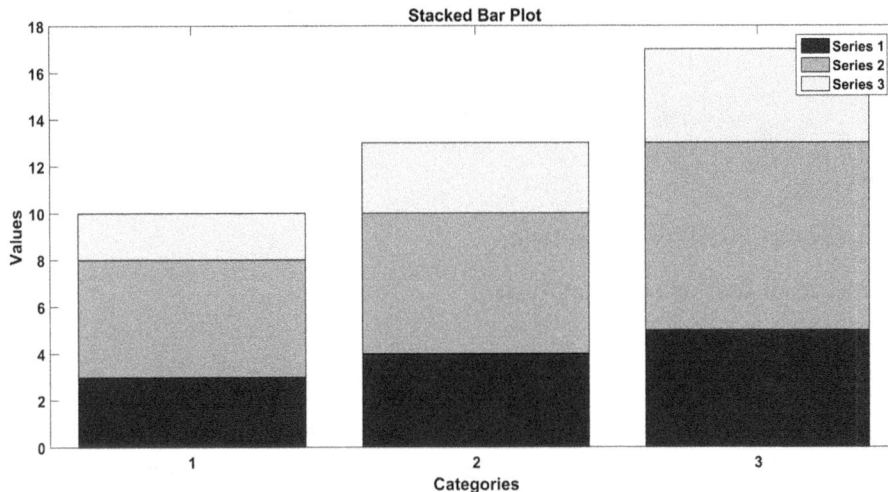

Figure 8.41: Stacked bar plot

- **Applications**:
  o Comparing grouped data, such as sales by product categories.
  o Visualizing cumulative contributions.

8.6.6 Pie charts and proportional data visualization

Pie charts, as shown in *Figure 8.42,* represent data as slices of a circle, with each slice proportional to the data value. Let us look at their function and application:

- **Function: pie**: MATLAB's pie function creates circular charts that effectively represent parts-to-whole relationships, where each slice's arc length corresponds to its percentage of the total:

```
data = [20, 30, 25, 25];
labels = {'Category A', 'Category B', 'Category C', 'Category D'};
pie(data, labels);
title('Pie Chart');
```

Pie Chart

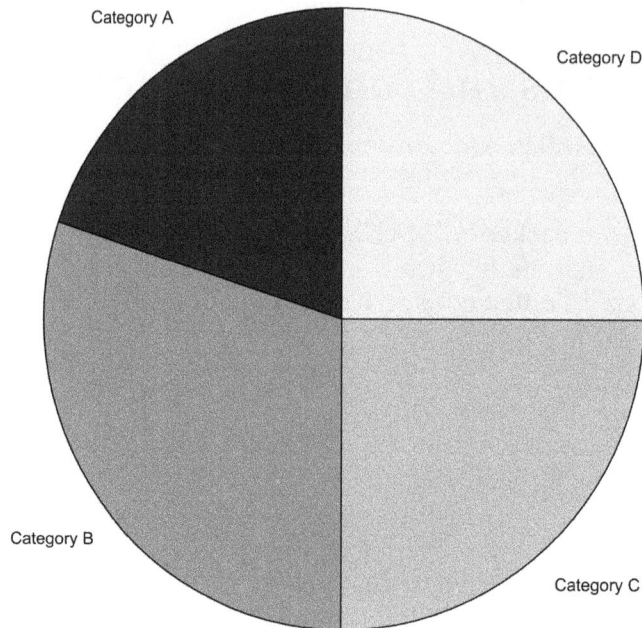

Figure 8.42: *Pie charts*

- **Applications**:
  - o   Visualizing proportions or percentages.
  - o   Survey results or market share analysis.

8.6.7 Stem plots and visualizing discrete data

Stem plots show discrete data points connected to the baseline by vertical lines, often used in signal processing. While both stem plots and bar plots display values as vertical lines, bar plots use solid, filled rectangles that represent the magnitude of a value over a categorical or continuous axis, commonly used in statistical comparisons. In contrast, stem plots use thin lines ending in a marker (usually a circle or dot) to emphasize individual, discrete data points without implying continuity or grouping, making them more suitable for time-series or indexed discrete signals.

- **Function: stem:** (see *Figure 8.43*)

```
x = 0:10;
y = sin(x);
stem(x, y, 'r', 'LineWidth', 1.5);
xlabel('X-axis');
ylabel('Y-axis');
title('Stem Plot');
```

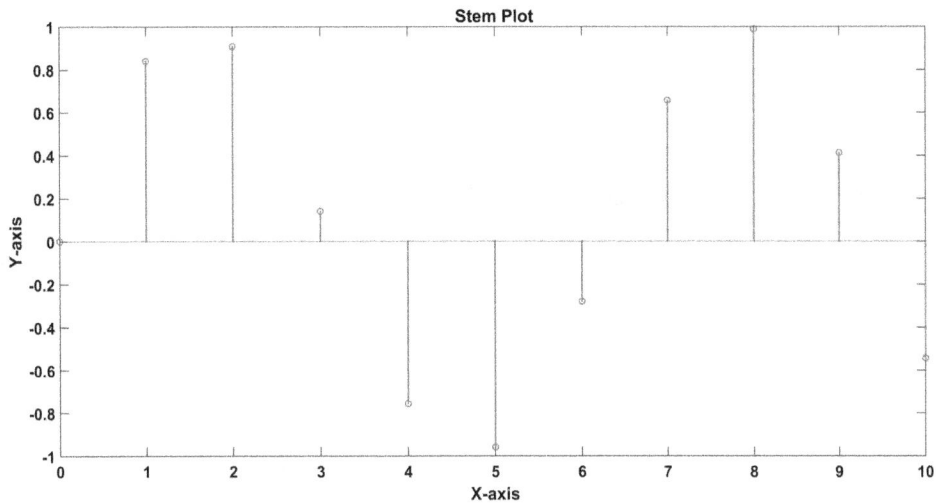

Figure 8.43: *Stem plots*

- **Applications**:
  - Representing discrete data points.
  - Analyzing sampled signals or sequences.

8.6.8 Contour plots and level curves

Contour plots display level curves of a 3D surface, making it easier to understand variations in a scalar field. Its function and application is as follows:

- **Function**: `contour`:

  MATLAB's contour function transforms 3D scalar fields into insightful 2D level curve visualizations, ideal for analyzing topographic gradients (elevation, temperature, or pressure fields), mathematical functions with complex curvature, and scientific data. (see *Figure 8.44*)

```
[X, Y] = meshgrid(-3:0.1:3, -3:0.1:3);
Z = X.^2 + Y.^2;
contour(X, Y, Z);
xlabel('X-axis');
ylabel('Y-axis');
title('Contour Plot');
```

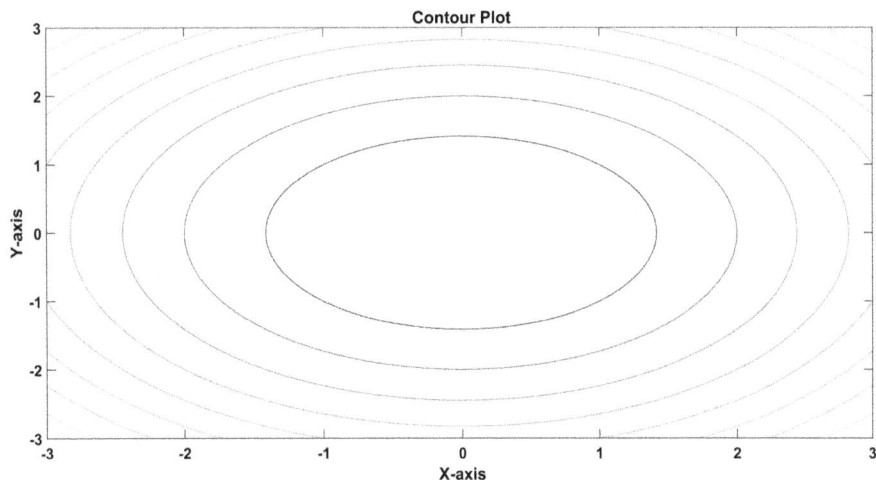

Figure 8.44: *Contour plot*

- **Applications**:
  - o Visualizing topographic data.
  - o Heat distribution or scalar fields analysis.

8.6.9 Box plots and statistical distribution

Box plots, as shown in *Figure 8.45,* summarize the distribution of data using five summary statistics: minimum, first quartile, median, third quartile, and maximum.

- **Function**: boxplot:

```
data = randn(50, 3);
% Generate random data
boxplot(data, 'Labels', {'Group 1', 'Group 2', 'Group 3'});
title('Box Plot');
```

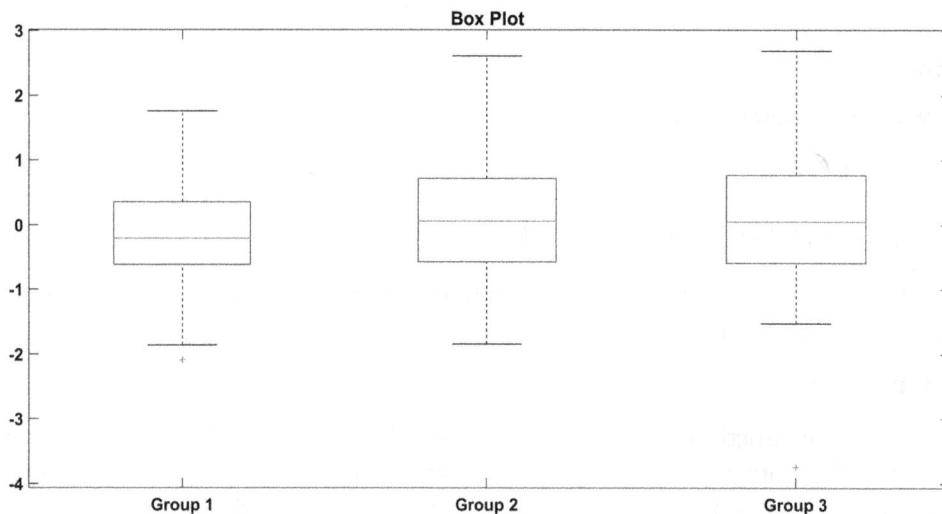

Figure 8.45: Box plot

- **Applications**:
  - o Comparing distributions of multiple datasets.
  - o Identifying outliers and variability.

8.6.10 Logarithmic plots and visualizing exponential data

Logarithmic plots help analyze data with large ranges or exponential relationships, as shown in *Figure 8.46.* MATLAB's logarithmic plotting functions (**semilogx**, **semilogy**, and **loglog**) transform axis scales to reveal hidden patterns in data that span multiple orders of magnitude:

- **Functions: semilogx**, **semilogy**, **loglog**
  - o **semilogx**: Logarithmic scale on the x-axis.
  - o **semilogy**: Logarithmic scale on the y-axis.
  - o **loglog**: Logarithmic scale on x-axis and y-axis:

    ```
    x = logspace(0.1, 2, 100);
    y = x.^2;
    loglog(x, y, 'LineWidth', 1.5);
    xlabel('Log(X)');
    ```

```
ylabel('Log(Y)');
title('Logarithmic Plot');
```

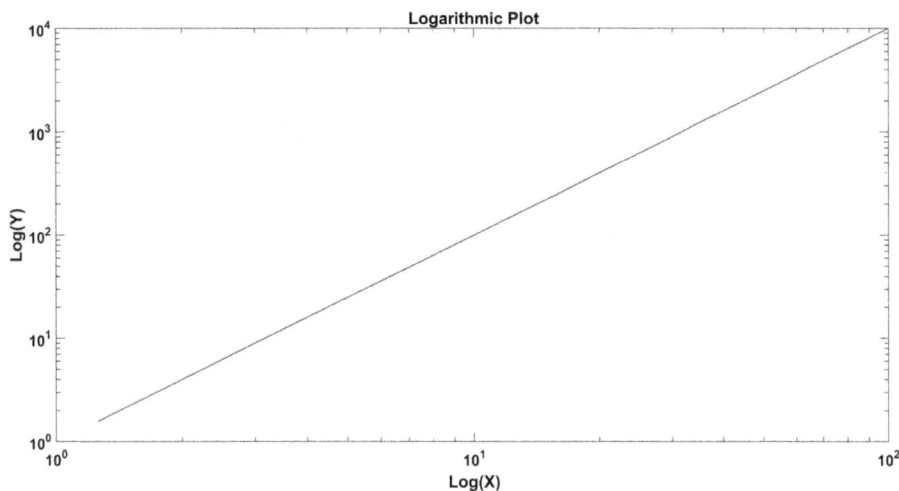

Figure 8.46: Logarithmic plot

- **Applications**:
  - o Analyzing power laws or exponential trends.
  - o Visualizing frequency responses.

8.6.11 Quiver plots and visualizing vector fields

Quiver plots, as shown in *Figure 8.47*, represent vectors at discrete points in 2D or 3D space. The following points show its function and application:

- **Function**: **quiver**: The **quiver** function creates dynamic vector field visualizations that display both magnitude and direction through arrow markers:

```
[X, Y] = meshgrid(-2:0.5:2, -2:0.5:2);
u = -Y;
v = X;
quiver(X, Y, u, v);
xlabel('X-axis');
ylabel('Y-axis');
title('Quiver Plot');
```

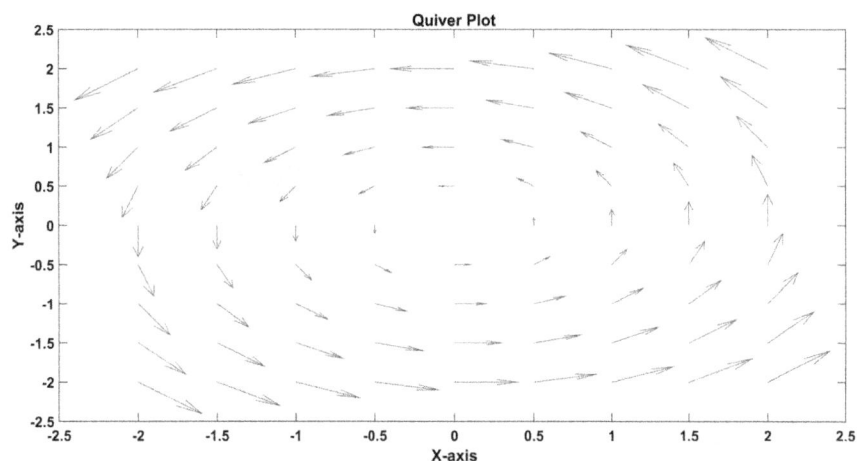

Figure 8.47: Quiver plot

- **Applications**:

  o Displaying velocity fields in fluid mechanics.

  o Analyzing vector fields in physics.

8.6.12 Waterfall plots and sequential surface representation

Waterfall plots, as shown in *Figure 8.48,* show a series of 2D slices stacked along the z-axis. Let us see their function and application:

- **Function: `waterfall`**: The **waterfall** function creates distinctive stepped 3D surface plots that maintain individual trace visibility:

```
[X, Y] = meshgrid(-2:0.1:2, -2:0.1:2);
Z = X.^2 - Y.^2;
waterfall(X, Y, Z);
xlabel('X-axis');
ylabel('Y-axis');
zlabel('Z-axis');
title('Waterfall Plot');
```

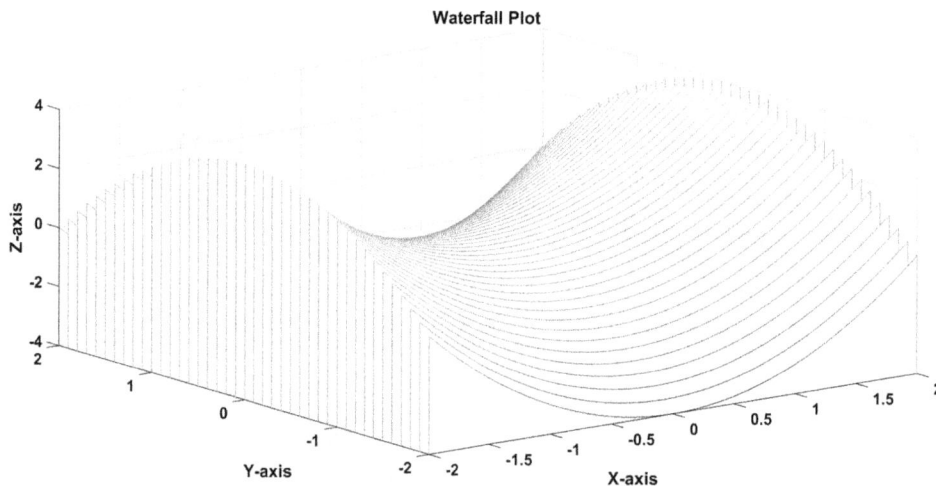

Figure 8.48: *Waterfall plot*

- **Applications**:

  o Visualizing evolving surfaces over time.

  o Analyzing time-dependent data.

8.6.13 Filled contour plots and enhanced contours

Filled contour plots, as shown in *Figure 8.49,* use color-filled areas to represent levels of a scalar field:

- **Function: `contour`**: The **contour** function generates essential level-curve visualizations that transform 3D surface data into interpretable 2D maps:

```
[X, Y] = meshgrid(-3:0.1:3, -3:0.1:3);
Z = sin(sqrt(X.^2 + Y.^2));
contourf(X, Y, Z, 20);
colormap jet;
```

```
colorbar;
xlabel('X-axis');
ylabel('Y-axis');
title('Filled Contour Plot');
```

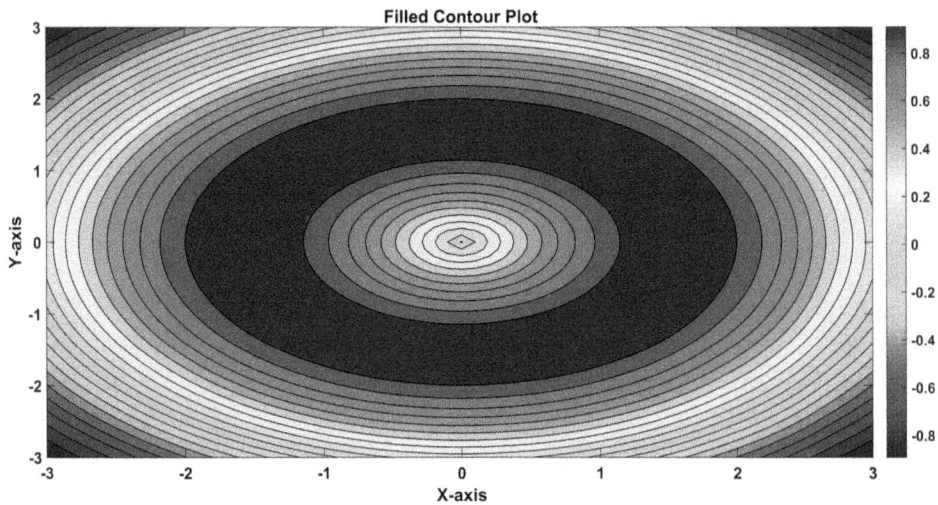

Figure 8.49: *Filled contour plot*

- **Applications**:
  - o   Visualizing heat maps with gradients.
  - o   Scalar field analysis.

8.6.14 Surface plot with contours

The **surfc** function in MATLAB combines a 3D surface plot with 2D contour lines projected onto the base of the plot, as shown in *Figure 8.50*. It is an extension of the surf function and is particularly useful for providing additional context to the surface visualization by showing how values vary in a 2D projection. This enhances 3D interpretation by clearly displaying elevation levels or gradients on the base plane, making it easier to understand the shape, slope, and variations of the surface, especially in regions where the 3D view only may be ambiguous or visually cluttered.

```
surfc(X, Y, Z);
```

The explanation is as follows:

- **X, Y, and Z**: Matrices of the same size define the grid and the surface heights.

- If X and Y are not specified, MATLAB assumes a grid based on the size of Z.
  ```
  [X, Y] = meshgrid(-3:0.1:3, -3:0.1:3);
  Z = X.^2 - Y.^2;
  surfc(X, Y, Z);
  xlabel('X-axis');
  ylabel('Y-axis');
  zlabel('Z-axis');
  title('Surface Plot with Contours (surfc)');
  ```

Surface Plot with Contours (surfc)

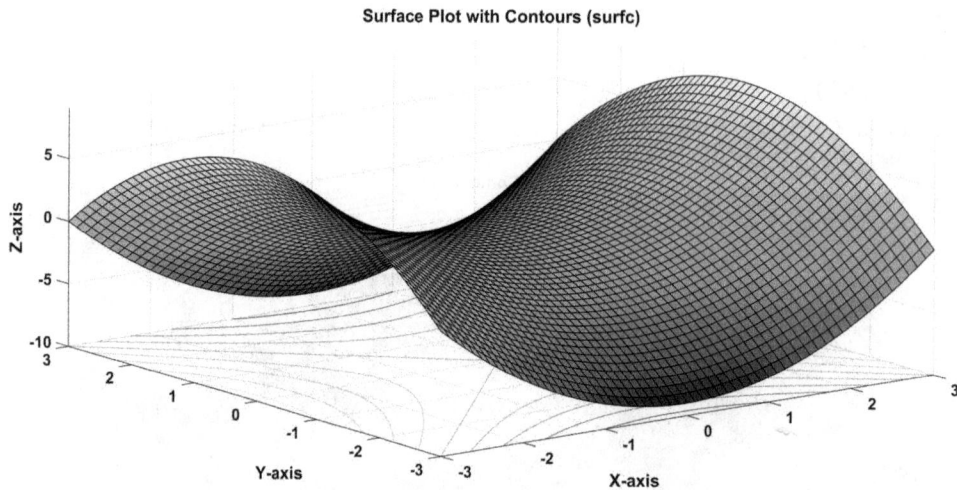

Figure 8.50: Surface Plot with contours

8.6.15 Stair plot in MATLAB

A stair plot is a specialized 2D plot in MATLAB used to visualize discrete or stepwise data, as shown in *Figure 8.51*. It connects data points with horizontal and vertical lines, resembling a staircase, making it ideal for time series data, piecewise functions, or sampled data that changes in discrete steps:

```
stairs(X, Y);
```

The explanation is as follows:

- **X**: A vector specifying the x-coordinates.

- **Y**: A vector specifying the corresponding y-coordinates.

Let us look at how to create a basic stair plot:

```
x = 0:10;
y = [0, 1, 2, 3, 5, 8, 13, 21, 34, 55, 89];
stairs(x, y);
xlabel('X-axis');
ylabel('Y-axis');
title('Basic Stair Plot');
grid on;
```

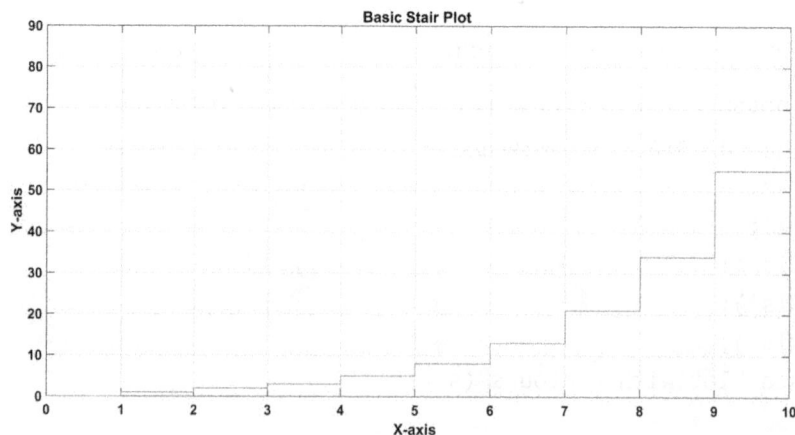

Figure 8.51: Stair plot

MATLAB's stairs function enables clear comparison of multiple stepwise data series by plotting them on shared axes, and preserving exact transition points between discrete value, while maintaining visual separation through customizable line styles and colors. It is particularly useful for analyzing time-series measurements, digital signals, or threshold-based processes where the timing and magnitude of step changes require precise comparison without interpolation artifacts.

```
x = 0:10;
y1 = [1, 2, 3, 4, 5, 6, 7, 8, 9, 10, 11];
y2 = [1, 1, 2, 3, 5, 8, 13, 21, 34, 55, 89];
stairs(x, y1, 'b-', 'LineWidth', 1.5);
hold on;
stairs(x, y2, 'r--', 'LineWidth', 1.5);
hold off;
xlabel('X-axis');
ylabel('Y-axis');
title('Comparison of Two Data Series');
legend('Data Series 1', 'Data Series 2');
grid on;
```

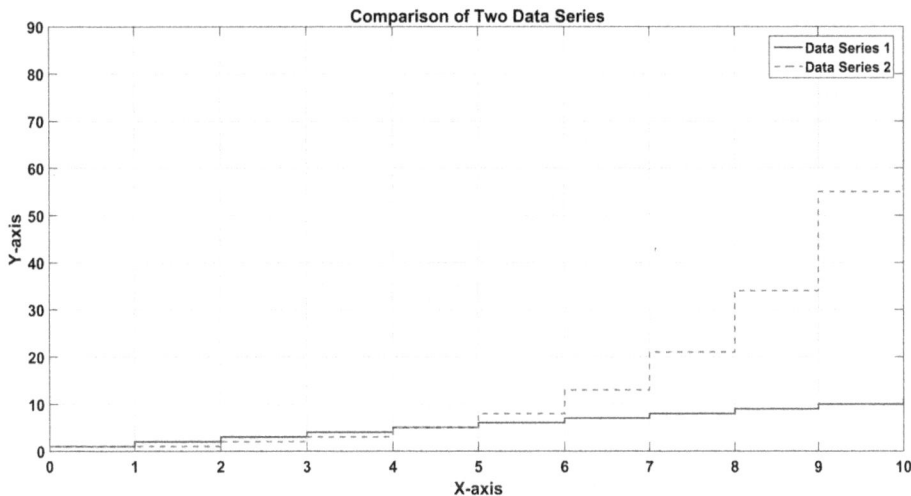

Figure 8.52: Multiple stair plots

The following table provides a summarized description of specialized plots:

Plot type	Purpose	Best for
Error bar plot	Show data variability or uncertainty	Experimental results
Stacked bar plot	Compare grouped contributions	Categorical data
Pie chart	Represent parts of a whole	Proportional data
Stem plot	Highlight discrete data points	Signal processing
Contour/Contourf	Show level curves or filled gradients	Scalar field visualization
Box plot	Summarize statistical data	Comparing data distributions
Logarithmic plots	Visualize exponential relationships	Power laws, exponential growth/decay
Streamline plot	Visualize flow in a vector field	Fluid dynamics, wind flow
Quiver plot	Display direction and magnitude of vectors	Velocity fields
Waterfall plot	Sequential surface representation	Time-dependent data visualization

Table 8.2: Description of specialized plots

Conclusion

In this chapter, we explored the powerful capabilities of MATLAB for plotting and data visualization. Starting with basic 2D plotting functions such as plot, bar, and scatter, we learned how to effectively visualize continuous and categorical data. We then covered essential customization tools, including titles, axis labels, legends, and line or marker styles, which play a key role in enhancing the readability and professionalism of plots. The chapter also introduced 3D plotting functions like plot3, surf, and mesh, which are invaluable when working with three-dimensional data or surfaces. Additionally, we looked into specialized plots such as histograms for frequency analysis, heatmaps for matrix data visualization, and polar plots for angular data representation. These tools equip users with a wide range of options to explore and present their data visually. By mastering these visualization techniques, readers can gain deeper insights into their data, communicate results more clearly, and support analytical decision-making. Overall, the chapter has provided a solid foundation for effective data plotting and graphical presentation in MATLAB. In the next chapter, we will learn the data visualization techniques in Python along with a comparative study in MATLAB and Python.

Exercises

1. Basic line plot:

   a. Plot the function $y = sin(x)$ for x ranging from 0 to 2π.

   b. Label the axes and add a title to the plot.

2. Multiple functions on the same plot:

   a. Plot $y_1 = sin(x)$ and $y_2 = cos(x)$ on the same graph for $x \in [0, 2\pi]$.

   b. Add legends to differentiate the curves and use different line styles and colors.

3. Bar plot of polynomial values:

   a. Evaluate the polynomial $y = x^3 - 2x^2 + x$ at integer values from -5 to 5.

   b. Create a bar chart to display the values.

4. Plotting derivatives:

   a. Plot the function $y = e^x$ and its derivative $y' = e^x$ on the same graph for $x \in [-2, 2]$.

   b. Use legend and grid to make the plot more readable.

5. 3D plot:

   a. Use a mesh grid to define X and Y, then plot $Z = sin(X^2 + Y^2)$ using surf.

   b. Add a title and axis labels.

6. Parametric plot:

   a. Plot the parametric equations $x = cos(t)$, $y = sin(t)$, $t \in [0, 2\pi]$ to draw a circle.

   b. Use plot and label the axes.

7. Customizing a plot:

   a. Plot $y = tan(x)$ for $x \in \left[-\frac{\pi}{2} + 0.1, \frac{\pi}{2} - 0.1\right]$.

   b. Add dashed grid lines, set axis limits, and change the font size of labels and title.

8. Generate grouped bar plots for two datasets:

   a. $A = [3,5,2,7]$

   b. $B = [4,6,1,8]$ Add labels, legends, and a title.

   c. Generate a histogram for 1000 random values from a normal distribution.

   d. Create a box plot of randomly generated data grouped into 4 categories.

CHAPTER 9

Plotting and Visualization in Python

Introduction

Data visualization serves as a critical bridge between raw data and actionable insights, transforming complex numerical information into intuitive graphical representations. This chapter provides a comprehensive exploration of Python's powerful visualization ecosystem while drawing insightful comparisons with MATLAB's established plotting capabilities.

Modern data analysis demands more than just computational tools; it requires effective communication of results. Python has emerged as a dominant force in scientific visualization, offering libraries that combine MATLAB's mathematical precision with open-source flexibility and web-ready interactivity. We begin by establishing Python's core visualization paradigm through Matplotlib, the foundational plotting library that enables MATLAB-style figures with Python's syntax. The discussion then progresses to advanced statistical visualization with Seaborn and interactive web-based plotting with Plotly.

A unique feature of this chapter is its systematic comparison between Python and MATLAB implementations. Through parallel code examples and output visualizations, we demonstrate how Python replicates, and often extends MATLAB's renowned plotting functionality.

The chapter progresses from basic line plots to advanced 3D visualizations, emphasizing customization techniques that meet publication-quality standards. Practical examples span fundamental mathematical functions, statistical distributions, and real-world datasets, with each concept illustrated through dual Python/MATLAB implementations.

Structure

In this chapter, we will learn about the following topics:

- 9.1. Data visualization and libraries in Python
- 9.2. Basic plotting in Python with Matplotlib
- 9.3. Customizing plots in Python
- 9.4. Comparison of examples via MATLAB and Python

Objectives

This chapter provides a comprehensive guide to data visualization techniques in Python while conducting a systematic comparison with MATLAB's plotting capabilities. The content is structured to take readers from basic concepts to advanced applications, beginning with an introduction to Python's visualization ecosystem and its core libraries; Matplotlib for basic plotting, Seaborn for statistical graphics, and Plotly for interactive visualizations. This chapter then progresses through essential plotting techniques, demonstrating how to create and customize various chart types, including line plots, bar charts, scatter plots, and histograms. A dedicated section focuses on advanced customization options to enhance visual appeal and clarity of plots. The comparative analysis forms a key component of this chapter, where we will examine side-by-side implementations of visualization tasks in Python and MATLAB, highlighting their respective strengths in handling different types of data representation. Through practical examples ranging from basic function plotting to complex 3D visualizations and statistical graphics, you will have proficiency in selecting and applying appropriate visualization tools. The chapter aims to equip researchers, engineers, and data scientists with the skills to effectively communicate data insights, while providing MATLAB users with a clear pathway to transition to Python's visualization ecosystem.

9.1 Data visualization and libraries in Python

An important tool to evaluate and display the data is considered as data visualization. One of the most commonly used computer languages for data analysis is Python, which contains a wide library to produce visually appealing and elaborative visualizations. Such packages contain classy frameworks for statistical and interactive visualizations and basic plotting tools. The tree most used Python libraries for the data visualization explained in this chapter are Matplotlib, Seaborn, and Plotly. These libraries fulfill almost all visualization requirements in research, engineering, and data science.

9.1.1 Importance of data visualization

Data visualization fulfills various purposes outlined as follows:

- **Exploration**: To identify the trends, patterns, and outliers in datasets.

- **Communication**: To present results in a clear and impactful approach.

- **Decision-making**: It supports informed validations via visual insights.

Via converting raw data into graphical representations, visualization fills the gap between numbers and stories.

9.1.2 Libraries for data visualization in Python

Python introduces diversified libraries to create static and interactive plots. The three most basic used libraries are mentioned as follows:

- **Matplotlib**: It is the foundation library to create 2D and basic 3D plots.

- **Seaborn**: It is formed on Matplotlib. It simplifies the formation of statistical plots.

- **Plotly**: It is ideal to create interactive and web-based visualizations.

9.1.3 Matplotlib as the foundational library

It is a flexible package to create charts. Matplotlib is considered as a base for various Python visualization tools. A wide array of static and interactive plots can be created via it.

Its features are:

- High customization possibility.

- 2D and 3D plotting support.

- Seamlessly compatibility with NumPy and Pandas.

Let us see how to create basic visualizations:

- **Line plot**: A line plot is one of the most fundamental and widely used visualization techniques in data analysis. It is particularly useful for displaying trends over time, comparing variables, and identifying patterns in sequential data, as shown in *Figure 9.1*. Python's Matplotlib library provides a simple yet powerful way to create line plots with customizable features:

```
import matplotlib.pyplot as plt
x = [1, 2, 3, 4, 5]
y = [2, 4, 6, 8, 10]
plt.plot(x, y, marker='o', color='blue', linestyle='--', linewidth=2)
plt.title('Line Plot Example')
plt.xlabel('X-axis')
plt.ylabel('Y-axis')
plt.grid(True)
plt.show()
```

Note:

x, y: Data points for the X and Y axes

Marker='o': Marks each data point with a circular marker

Color='blue': Sets the line color to blue

Linestyle='--': Dashed line style connecting the points

Linewidth=2: Sets the thickness of the plotted line to 2

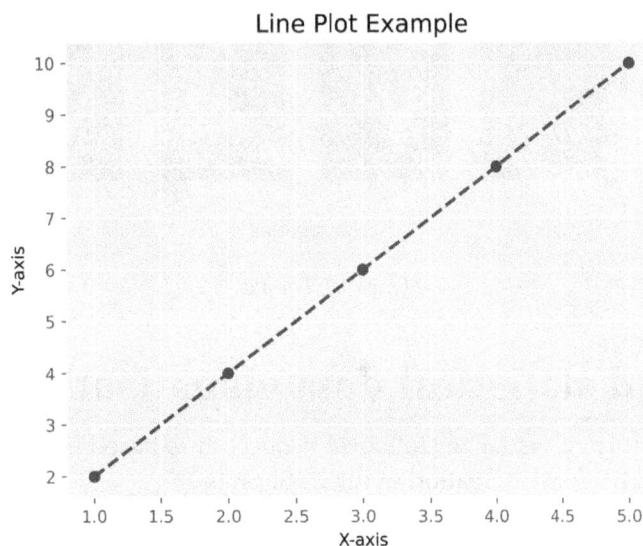

Figure 9.1: Line plot

- **Bar plot**: Bar plots, shown in *Figure 9.2,* in Python provide an essential visualization tool for comparing categorical data through rectangular bars with lengths proportional to the values they represent.

These plots are particularly valuable for business analytics, survey results, and performance metrics, allowing clear comparisons across different groups or time periods. Using Matplotlib's **plt.bar()** function, users can create basic vertical bar charts with customizable colors, widths, and borders, while **plt.barh()** generates horizontal versions ideal for longer category labels. More advanced implementations leverage Seaborn's **sns.barplot()** for statistical visualizations with built-in confidence intervals and grouping capabilities:

```
categories = ['A', 'B', 'C', 'D']
values = [5, 7, 3, 8]
plt.bar(categories, valuess, color='purple')
plt.title('Bar Chart Example')
plt.xlabel('Categories')
plt.ylabel('Values')
plt.show()
```

Note:

Categories: Labels for each bar on the X-axis ('A', 'B', etc.)

Values: Heights of each bar corresponding to the categories

Color='purple': Sets the fill color of the bars to purple

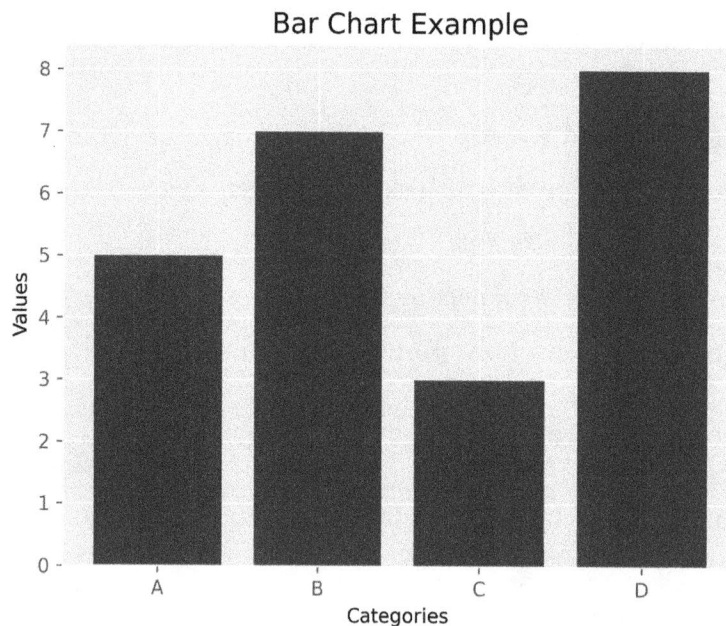

Figure 9.2: Bar plot

9.1.4 Seaborn and statistical data visualization

Seaborn was introduced mainly to visualize statistical aspects. It is based on Matplotlib. It has a high-level interface which makes it helpful for the creation of intricate plots.

Its features are as follows:

- Beautiful default styles.
- Simplified plotting syntax.
- Support for statistical data visualizations like box plots, violin plots, and pair plots.

Let us learn how to create visualizations with Seaborn:

- **Scatter plot and regression line**: Scatter plots, as shown in *Figure 9.3*, with regression lines in Python, provide a powerful way to visualize relationships between two continuous variables while quantifying their correlation. Using libraries like Matplotlib and Seaborn, analysts can create scatter plots that plot individual data points as coordinates, then overlay a linear regression line to reveal trends and predict patterns. The Seaborn library's **sns.regplot()** function is particularly useful as it automatically calculates and plots the regression line along with a confidence interval band, while also handling the scatter points visualization in a single command. This combined visualization helps identify the strength and direction of relationships, whether positive, negative, or neutral, while the regression line's slope indicates the rate of change between variables:

```
import seaborn as sns
import pandas as pd
data = pd.DataFrame({
    'X': [5, 7, 8, 7, 2, 17, 2, 9, 4, 11],
    'Y': [99, 86, 87, 88, 100, 86, 103, 87, 94, 78]
})
sns.scatterplot(data=data, x='X', y='Y', color='green', s=100)
plt.title('Scatter Plot Example')
plt.show()
```

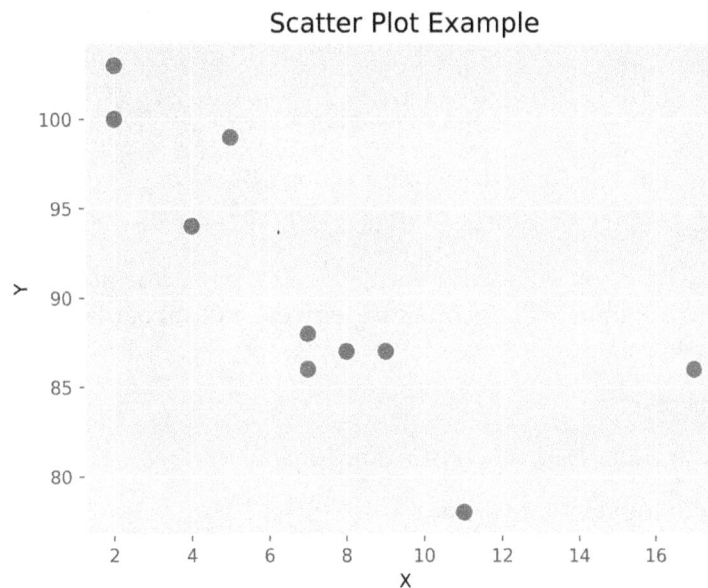

Figure 9.3: Scatter plot

- **Heatmap**: Heatmaps in Python provide an intuitive and visually compelling way to represent complex matrix data through color gradients, where each cell's color intensity corresponds to its value. These versatile visualizations, as shown in *Figure 9.4*, are particularly valuable for identifying patterns, correlations, and outliers in multidimensional datasets across various domains including finance, bioinformatics, and machine learning. Python's visualization ecosystem offers multiple approaches to creating heatmaps, with Seaborn being the most popular choice for statistical heatmaps through its **sns.heatmap()** function, which automatically handles data normalization and color mapping while supporting annotations. For more basic implementations, Matplotlib's **plt.imshow()** can generate heatmap-style displays with customizable colormaps. When interactivity is required, Plotly provides dynamic heatmaps with hover tooltips and zoom capabilities. Advanced applications leverage Seaborn's **clustermap()** for hierarchical clustering visualizations or integrate with Pandas DataFrames for seamless plotting of correlation matrices:

```
import seaborn as sns
import numpy as np
data = np.random.rand(10, 10)
sns.heatmap(data, annot=True, cmap='coolwarm', linewidths=0.5)
plt.title('Heatmap Example')
plt.show()
```

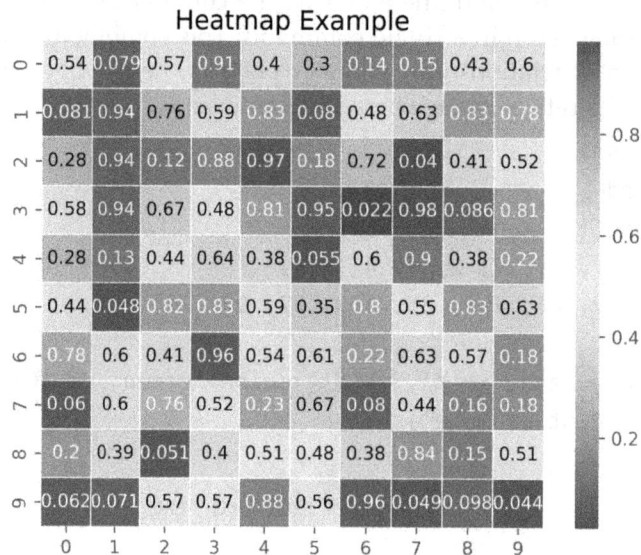

Figure 9.4: Heatmap via Seaborn

9.1.5 Plotly and interactive visualizations

A library called Plotly is used to make interactive visuals. Scatter plots, line plots, bar charts, and 3D plots are among the many chart types it supports. Plotly plots are perfect for dashboards and interactive reporting since they can be integrated into web apps.

Some key features are as follows:

- Interactive plots with zoom, pan, and hover functionalities.

- Easy integration with Jupyter Notebooks.

- Support for web-based visualization.

Let us create visualizations with Plotly:

- **Interactive line plot**: Interactive line plots, as shown in *Figure 9.5,* in Python enable data exploration through zooming, panning, and hover tooltips that reveal precise values. Plotly Express offers particularly simple syntax for generating interactive plots with just a few lines of code, while supporting animations and dropdown menus for comparing multiple trends. These features make interactive line plots invaluable for dashboards, exploratory analysis, and presentations where static images would limit insight discovery. Unlike MATLAB's static plots, Python's interactive options integrate seamlessly with web applications, providing a more immersive analytical experience:

```
import plotly.express as px
x = [1, 2, 3, 4, 5]
y = [10, 20, 30, 40, 50]
fig = px.line(x=x, y=y, title='Interactive Line Plot')
fig.show()
```

Interactive Line Plot

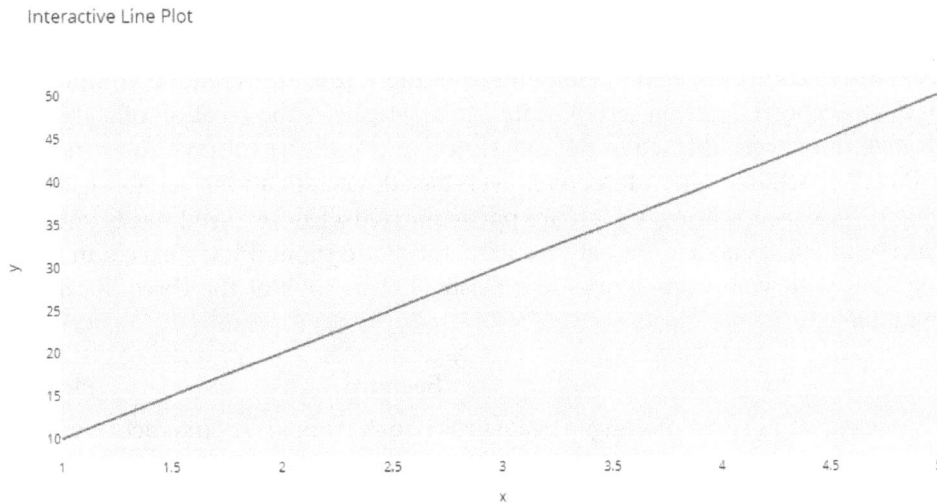

Figure 9.5: Interactive line plot

- **3D scatter plot**: 3D scatter plots in Python, as shown in *Figure 9.6,* provide powerful visualization of multivariate relationships by projecting data points in three-dimensional space. These plots are particularly useful for identifying clusters, outliers, and spatial patterns in scientific data, machine learning features, or engineering simulations. Python's 3D visualization capabilities often surpass MATLAB's in terms of customization and interactivity, especially when integrated with Jupyter Notebooks or web dashboards:

```
import plotly.express as px
import pandas as pd
data = pd.DataFrame({
    'X': [5, 7, 8, 7, 2, 17, 2, 9, 4, 11],
    'Y': [99, 86, 87, 88, 100, 86, 103, 87, 94, 78],
    'Z': [10, 20, 15, 30, 25, 35, 40, 45, 50, 60]
})
fig = px.scatter_3d(data, x='X', y='Y', z='Z', color='Z')
fig.show()
```

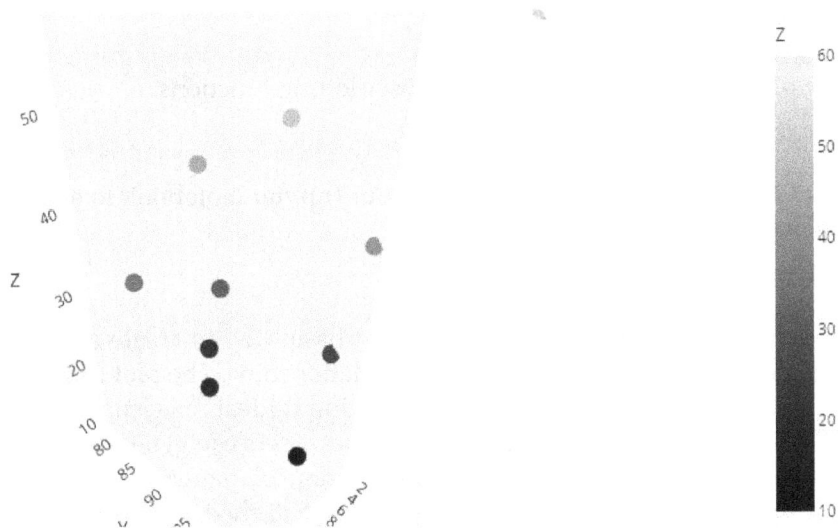

Figure 9.6: 3D scatter plot

- **Comparing libraries**: Matplotlib, Seaborn, and Plotly are three popular Python libraries for data visualization, each with distinct strengths. Matplotlib is a highly customizable, low-level library that provides extensive control over plot elements, making it ideal for creating complex and publication-quality figures. Seaborn, built on top of Matplotlib, simplifies the creation of statistical visualizations with high-level functions, attractive default styles, and built-in support for pandas DataFrames. In contrast, Plotly specializes in interactive, web-based visualizations, enabling dynamic zooming, hovering, and click interactions, which are particularly useful for dashboards and web applications. While Matplotlib and Seaborn are better suited for static plots, Plotly excels in interactivity and is often integrated with web frameworks like Dash. Let us look at the three libraries in detail in the following table:

Feature	Matplotlib	Seaborn	Plotly
Purpose	General-purpose plotting	Statistical visualizations	Interactive visualizations
Ease of use	Requires detailed coding	Simplified, high-level API	Intuitive for interactivity
Interactivity	Limited	Limited	High
Best for what	Static visualizations	Statistical data	Dashboards, web visuals

Table 9.1: Comparison of different Python libraries

9.2 Basic plotting in Python with Matplotlib

One of the most important components of Python data visualization is plotting, and Matplotlib is a powerful package that offers a variety of tools for making both simple and complex representations. Due to its ease of use and versatility, Matplotlib is a well-liked option for making 2D plots, whether you are presenting findings or exploring data.

Plot, bar, and scatter are some of the fundamental plotting tools covered in this section along with examples and best practices for producing clear, impactful visualizations.

9.2.1 Introduction to Matplotlib

A popular Python package for making static, animated, and interactive visualizations is called Matplotlib. It supports a wide variety of plot kinds and is quite customizable. Make sure Matplotlib is installed before beginning to use any particular functions:

```
pip install matplotlib
```

Import Matplotlib's **pyplot** module, which contains most plotting functions:

```
import matplotlib.pyplot as plt
```

Note: **Include %matplotlib inline at the beginning of your Jupyter Notebook to ensure that plots display correctly within the notebook.**

Let us look at different plots in detail:

- **Line plots with plot**: This plot function is the most basic way to create a 2D line plot, as shown in *Figure 9.7*. It is ideal for visualizing data trends or relationships. The plot function in Matplotlib is the fundamental method for creating 2D line plots, making it ideal for visualizing trends, relationships, or time-series data. By simply providing x and y values, users can generate a line graph that connects data points sequentially, allowing for clear observation of patterns, fluctuations, or correlations. Customization options include adjusting line styles (solid, dashed, dotted), colors, markers, and labels, enabling detailed and publication-ready visualizations. Since Matplotlib is a versatile and low-level library, plot serves as the backbone for many other plotting functions, including those in Seaborn, which builds on Matplotlib to simplify statistical visualizations.

```
import matplotlib.pyplot as plt
# Sample data
x = [0, 1, 2, 3, 4, 5]
y = [0, 1, 4, 9, 16, 25]
# Creating a line plot
plt.plot(x, y, label='y = x^2', color='blue', linestyle='--', marker='o')
# Adding title and labels
plt.title("Line Plot")
plt.xlabel("X-axis")
plt.ylabel("Y-axis")
# Display legend
plt.legend()
# Show plot
plt.show()
```

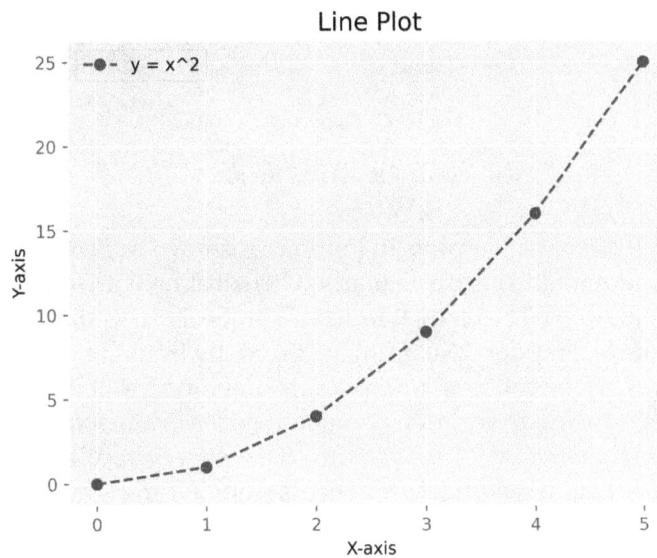

Figure 9.7: Line plot with plot

- **Bar plots with bar**: Bar plots are perfect for comparing categorical data or summarizing discrete values.

- **Vertical bar plot**: Vertical bar plots in Python, as shown in *Figure 9.8*, effectively compare categorical data using rectangular bars extending upward from the x-axis, with heights proportional to the values they represent. Created using Matplotlib's **plt.bar()** function or Seaborn's **sns.barplot()**, these plots are ideal for visualizing discrete comparisons like sales by product, survey results, or performance metrics across groups. Key customization options include bar colors, widths, edge styles, and value labels, while Seaborn adds statistical features like error bars. Vertical bars provide clearer value comparisons than horizontal versions when category names are short, making them a staple in reports and presentations. Python's implementation offers more styling flexibility than MATLAB's basic **bar()** function, particularly when integrated with Pandas DataFrames for streamlined data-to-visualization workflows:

```
categories = ['A', 'B', 'C', 'D']
values = [5, 7, 3, 8]
plt.bar(categories, values, color='teal')
plt.title("Vertical Bar Plot")
plt.xlabel("Categories")
```

```
plt.ylabel("Values")
plt.show()
```

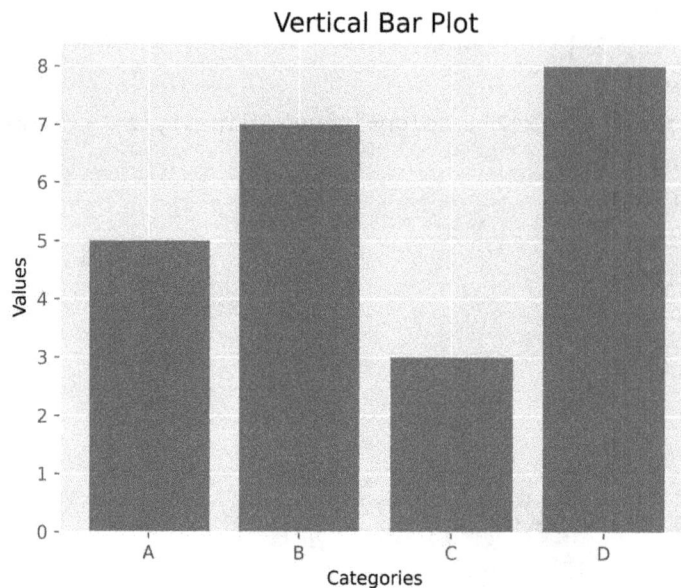

Figure 9.8: Vertical bar plot

- **Horizontal bar plot**: Horizontal bar plots in Python, as shown in *Figure 9.9*, provide an effective way to visualize categorical comparisons, particularly when dealing with long category labels or numerous groups. Using Matplotlib's **plt.barh()** function or Seaborn's **sns.barplot()** with orientation adjustment, these plots display bars extending horizontally from the y-axis, with lengths representing quantitative values. This orientation improves readability for lengthy text labels by providing ample space along the vertical axis, while maintaining clear value comparisons through bar lengths. Horizontal bars are especially useful for ranking data, survey results with many categories, or any comparison where the natural reading flow benefits from left-to-right presentation:

```
plt.barh(categories, values, color='orange')
plt.title("Horizontal Bar Plot")
plt.xlabel("Values")
plt.ylabel("Categories")
plt.show()
```

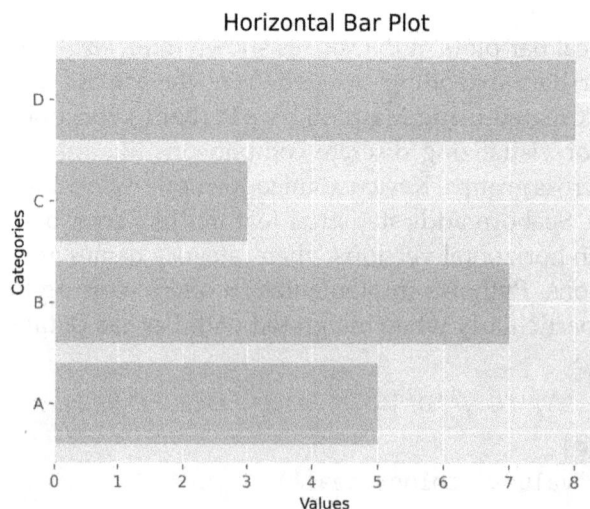

Figure 9.9: Horizontal bar plot

- **Scatter plots with scatter**: Scatter plots, as shown in *Figure 9.10,* display individual data points, making them ideal for exploring relationships between variables.

Example:

```
import numpy as np
# Generating random data
x = np.random.rand(50)
y = np.random.rand(50)
sizes = np.random.rand(50) * 100   # Bubble sizes
colors = np.random.rand(50)        # Bubble colors
plt.scatter(x, y, s=sizes, c=colors, alpha=0.7, cmap='viridis')
plt.title("Scatter Plot Example")
plt.xlabel("X-axis")
plt.ylabel("Y-axis")
plt.colorbar(label='Color Scale')  # Add a color bar
plt.show()
```

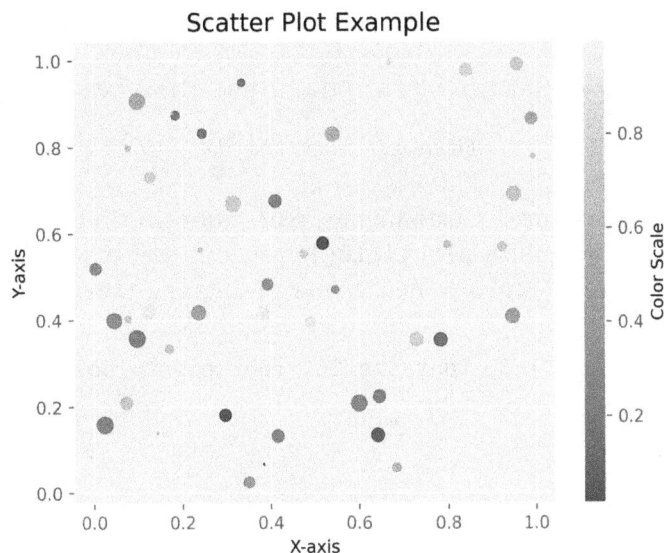

Figure 9.10: Scatter plot

9.3 Customizing plots in Python

A main aspect regarding data analysis and the story is considered data visualization. Matplotlib package of Python provides in-depth customization options in the creation of more impactful and clear plots. Aesthetic and educational aspects of the plots can also be produced with components such as titles, labels, legends, and styles. This chapter provides such important Matplotlib customization aspects and gives insightful examples to create impactful plots. Let us look at the details:

- **Adding titles to your plots**: A title summarizes the goal and background of your story and acts as its headline. It enables visitors to rapidly understand the purpose of the visualization.

- **Adding a simple title**: The **title()** function allows you to add a title to the top of your plot, as shown in, as shown in *Figure 9.11*:

```
import matplotlib.pyplot as plt
x = [0, 1, 2, 3, 4]
y = [0, 1, 4, 9, 16]
```

```
plt.plot(x, y)
plt.title("Simple Line Plot")  # Adding a title
plt.show()
```

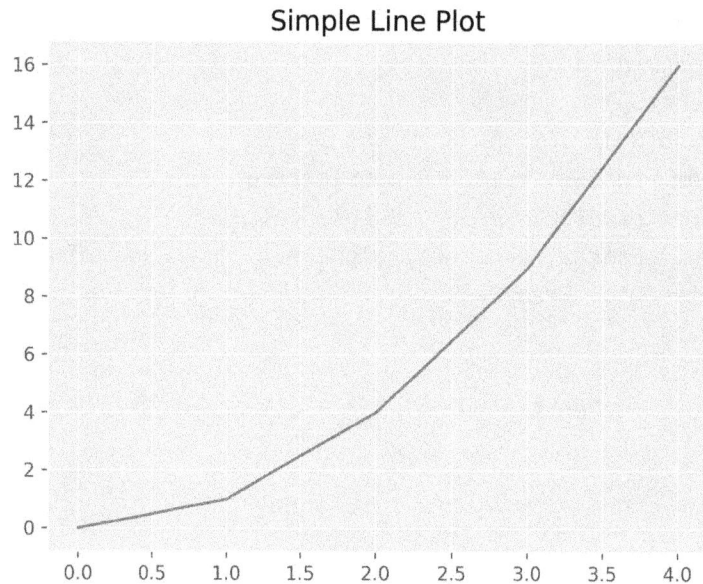

Figure 9.11: *Simple Line Plot*

- **Customizing title appearance**: Customizing plot titles in Python enhances readability and visual appeal. Using Matplotlib's **plt.title()**, you can adjust font size (**fontsize=14**), weight (**fontweight='bold'**), color (**color='red'**), and positioning (**loc='left'**) to create professional-looking visualizations:

```
plt.title("Customized Title", fontsize=16, fontweight='bold', loc='left',
color='blue')
```

The explanation is as follows

o **fontsize**: Adjusts the font size.

o **fontweight**: Options include 'light', 'normal', and 'bold'.

o **loc**: Aligns the title to 'center', 'left', or 'right'.

o **color**: Changes the color of the text.

- **Adding axis labels**: Labels for the X and Y axes provide critical information about the data being visualized. They clarify what each axis represents and the units of measurement.

- **Adding basic labels**: The **xlabel()** and **ylabel()** functions are used to add axis labels.

```
plt.plot(x, y)
plt.xlabel("X-axis: Input Values")  # Label for the X-axis
plt.ylabel("Y-axis: Squared Values")  # Label for the Y-axis
plt.show()
```

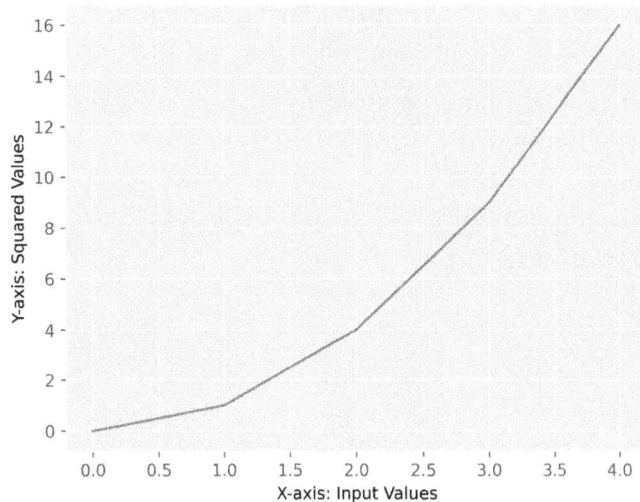

Figure 9.12: Customization of plot

- **Customizing axis labels**: To make axis labels more readable and visually appealing, you can customize their font size, color, and positioning.

```
plt.xlabel("Input (X)", fontsize=12, color='green', labelpad=10)
plt.ylabel("Output (Y)", fontsize=12, color='purple', labelpad=10)
```

The explanation is as follows:

o **fontsize**: Sets the font size of the label.

o **color**: Changes the text color.

o **labelpad**: Adjusts the distance between the label and the axis.

- **Rotating axis labels**: For plots with crowded labels, rotating the text can improve readability.

```
categories = ['January', 'February', 'March', 'April', 'May']
values = [5, 7, 8, 6, 9]
plt.bar(categories, values)
plt.xticks(rotation=45)  # Rotate X-axis labels by 45 degrees
plt.show()
```

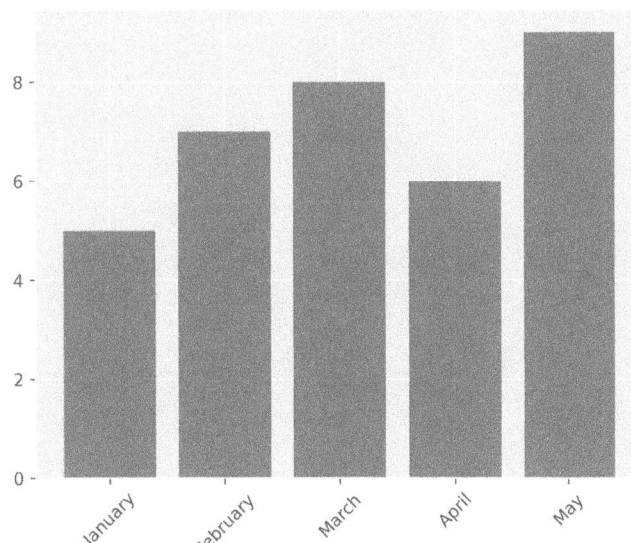

Figure 9.13: Rotation of axis labels

- **Adding and customizing legends**: When displaying several datasets on a single plot, legends are crucial. They assist viewers in determining which line, bar, or point relates to which data.

- **Adding a basic legend**: Use the label parameter within plotting functions, as shown in *Figure 9.14* to define legend labels and the **legend()** function to display them:

```
plt.plot(x, y, label='y = x^2')
plt.plot(x, [val**3 for val in x], label='y = x^3')
plt.legend()  # Display the legend
plt.show()
```

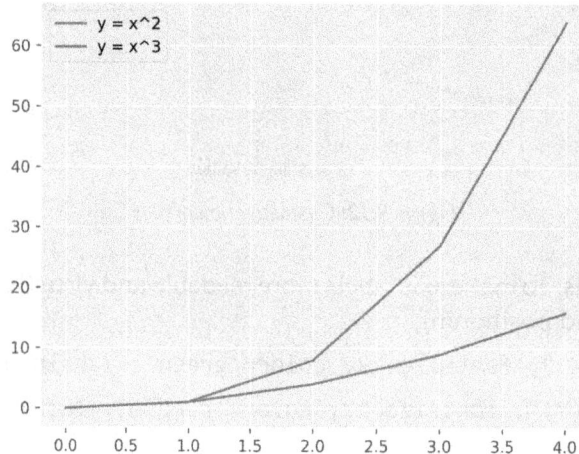

Figure 9.14: Adding legend

- **Customizing legends**: You can control the position, font size, and appearance of the legend using additional parameters.

```
plt.plot(x, y, label='y = x^2')
plt.plot(x, [val**3 for val in x], label='y = x^3')
plt.legend(
    loc='upper left',      # Legend position
    fontsize=10,           # Font size
    title="Legend Title",  # Add a title to the legend
    shadow=True,           # Add a shadow effect
    frameon=True           # Add a border around the legend
)
plt.show()
```

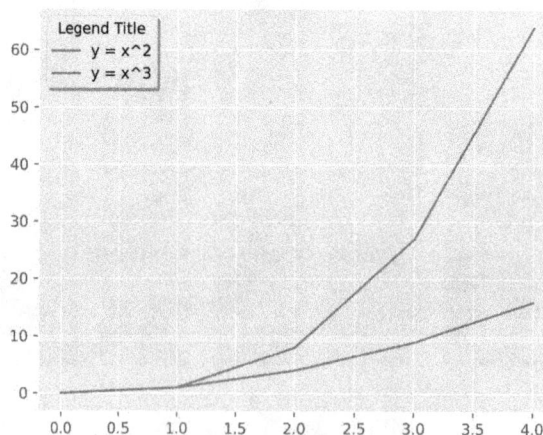

Figure 9.15: Customization of legends

- **Customizing plot styles**: Matplotlib provides a variety of styling options to ensure your plots match your desired aesthetic or branding.

- **Line styles and colors**: Modify line style, color, and width to distinguish different datasets: (see *Figure 9.16*)

```
plt.plot(x, y, linestyle='--', color='red', linewidth=2, label='Dashed Line')
plt.legend()
plt.show()
```

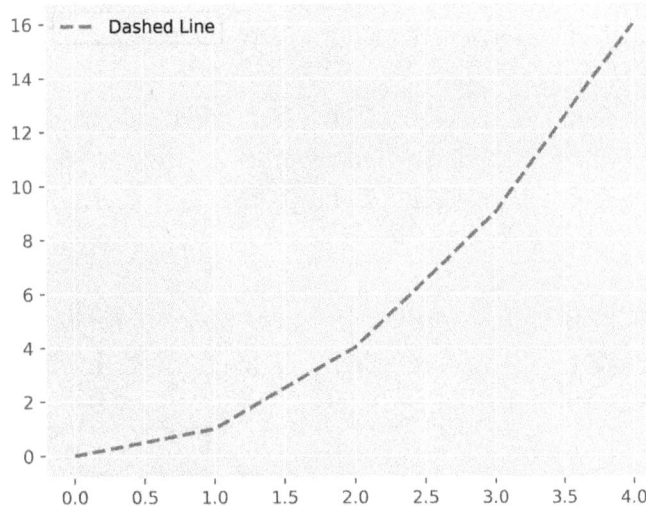

Figure 9.16: Line styles and colors

- o **linestyle**: Options include '--' (dashed), '-.' (dash-dot), ':' (dotted).

- o **color**: Use color names ('red'), HEX codes ('#1f77b4'), or **red, green, blue (RGB)** tuples ((0.1, 0.2, 0.5)).

- o **linewidth**: Adjusts line thickness

- **Grid lines and backgrounds**: Grid lines make plots easier to read by providing visual reference points.

- **Adding grid lines**: Use the **grid()** function to add grid lines to a plot. (see *Figure 9.17*)

```
plt.plot(x, y)
plt.grid(True)  # Enable grid lines
plt.show()
```

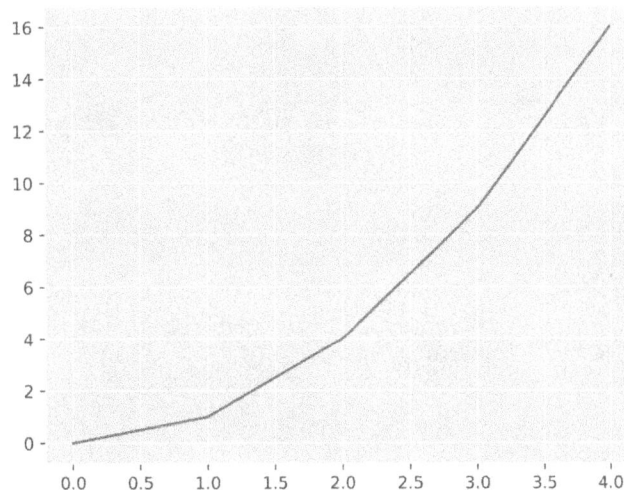

Figure 9.17: Adding grid lines

- **Customizing grid lines**: You can control the style, color, and width of grid lines: (see *Figure 9.18*)

```
plt.plot(x, y)
plt.grid(
    which='major',        # Grid for major ticks
    linestyle='--',       # Dashed grid lines
    linewidth=1,        # Line thickness
    color='red'          # Grid line color
)
plt.show()
```

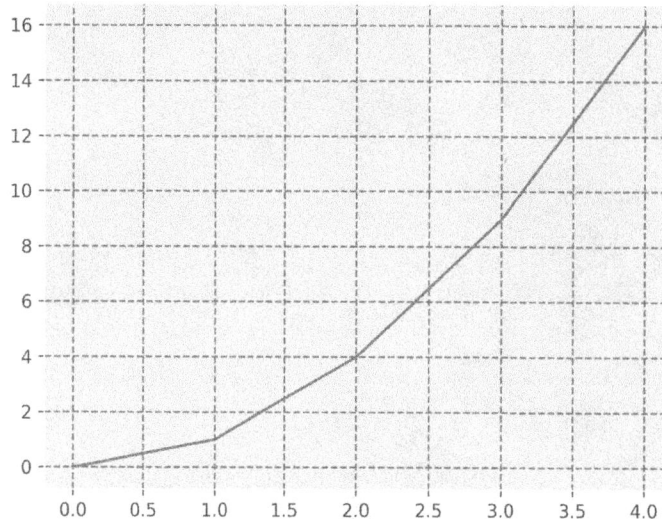

Figure 9.18: Customization of grid lines

- **Applying predefined plot styles**: Matplotlib offers several built-in styles that can be applied to give your plots a consistent, professional look.

- **Applying a style**: Use the **style.use()** function to apply a predefined style. (see *Figure 9.19*)

```
from matplotlib import style
style.use('ggplot')  # Apply the 'ggplot' style
plt.plot(x, y)
plt.show()
```

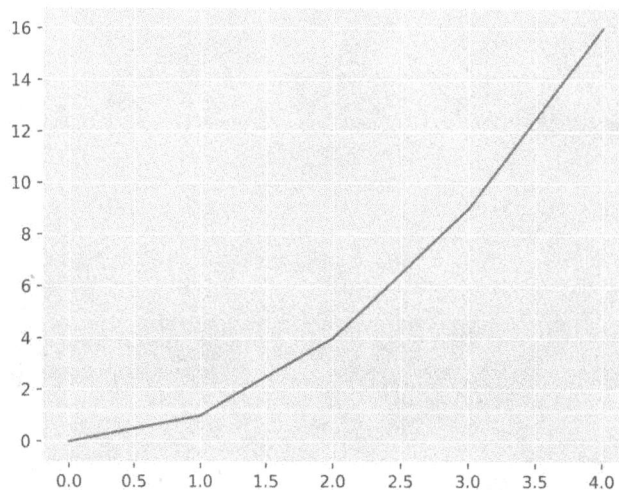

Figure 9.19: Applying a style

- **Exporting customized plots**: After customizing your plot, shown in *Figure 9.20*, save it for use in reports or presentations using the **savefig()** function:

```
plt.plot(x, y)
plt.title("Exported Plot")
plt.savefig("customized_plot.png", dpi=600, bbox_inches='tight')
```

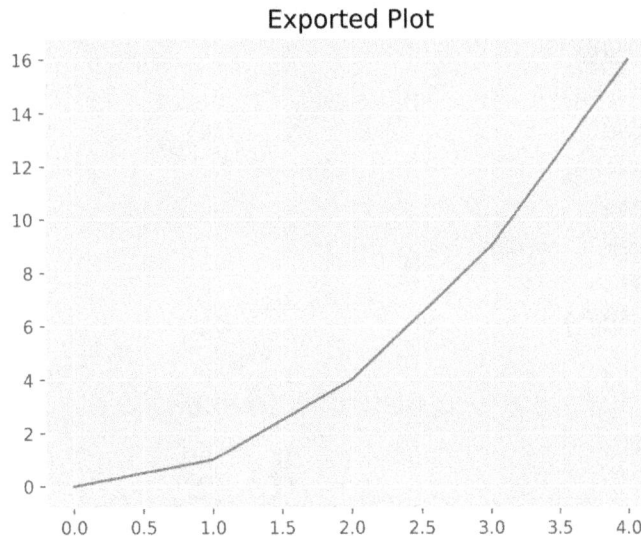

Figure 9.20: Exporting of plot

The explanation is as follows:

- **dpi**: Controls the resolution (higher values for better quality).

- **bbox_inches='tight'**: Ensures no extra white space around the plot.

9.3.1 Specialized plots in Python

With packages like Matplotlib and Seaborn, Python has emerged as a potent substitute for MATLAB, which is well-known for its strong charting capabilities. These packages let Python users make specific plots like heat maps, polar plots, and histograms that resemble MATLAB. We shall examine in this guide how Python is a flexible tool for data analysis and visualization by supporting these customized visualizations.

9.3.2 Introduction to specialized plots

Beyond simple line or bar charts, specialized plots provide tools for visualizing complex data. Inspired by MATLAB, Python offers a wide range of capabilities for making bespoke charts. Python easily mimics MATLAB's flexibility while improving accessibility with modules like Matplotlib.

To get started, perform the following steps:

1. Install the necessary libraries:

```
pip install matplotlib numpy seaborn
```

2. Import the required modules:

```
import matplotlib.pyplot as plt
import numpy as np
import seaborn as sns
```

9.3.2.1 Histograms for visualizing distributions

Histograms are essential for understanding the frequency distribution of data. They group data into bins, making it easier to identify patterns such as skewness or modality.

- **Creating a simple histogram**: A simple histogram in Python can be created using Matplotlib's **plt. hist()** function, which bins and visualizes the distribution of numerical data: (see *Figure 9.21*)

```
# Generate random data
data = np.random.normal(0, 1, 1000)
# Create a histogram
plt.hist(data, bins=30, color='blue', alpha=0.7)
# Add title and labels
plt.title("Histogram Example")
plt.xlabel("Value")
plt.ylabel("Frequency")
plt.show()
```

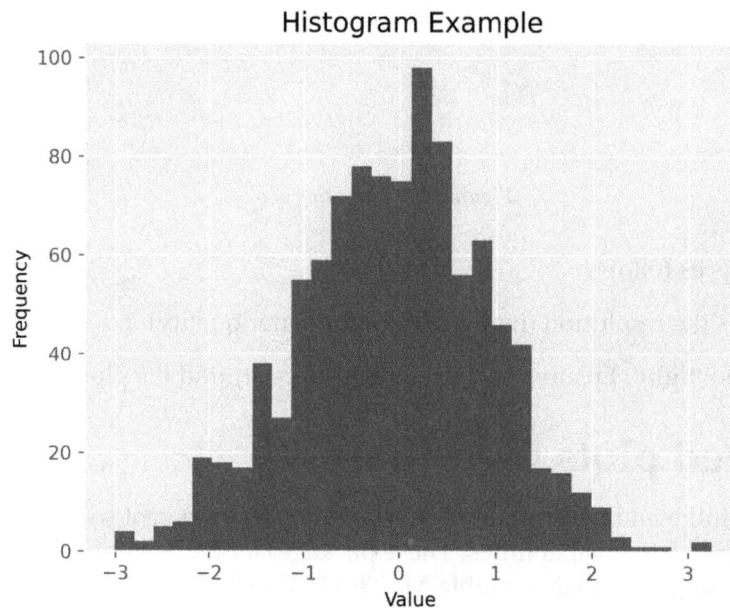

Figure 9.21: *Simple Histogram*

- o **Key parameters**:
  - **bins**: Determines the number of bins.
  - **color**: Sets the bar color.
  - **alpha**: Adjusts transparency for overlapping histograms.
- **Overlaying multiple histograms**: Compare distributions by overlaying multiple histograms: (see *Figure 9.22*)

```
data1 = np.random.normal(0, 1, 1000)
data2 = np.random.normal(2, 1.5, 1000)
plt.hist(data1, bins=30, alpha=0.5, label='Data 1', color='blue')
plt.hist(data2, bins=30, alpha=0.5, label='Data 2', color='orange')
plt.title("Overlapping Histograms")
plt.xlabel("Value")
plt.ylabel("Frequency")
```

```
plt.legend()
plt.show()
```

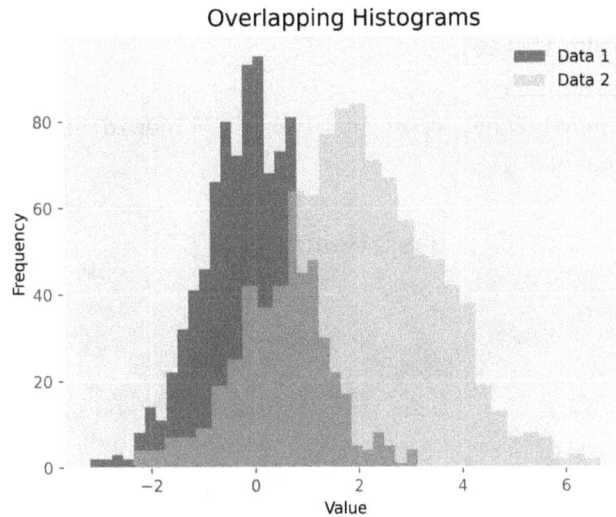

Figure 9.22: *Multiple histograms*

- **Histogram with a density curve**: Use Seaborn to overlay a density curve on the histogram: (see *Figure 9.23*)

```
sns.histplot(data, kde=True, bins=30, color='green')
plt.title("Histogram with Density Curve")
plt.xlabel("Value")
plt.ylabel("Frequency")
plt.show()
```

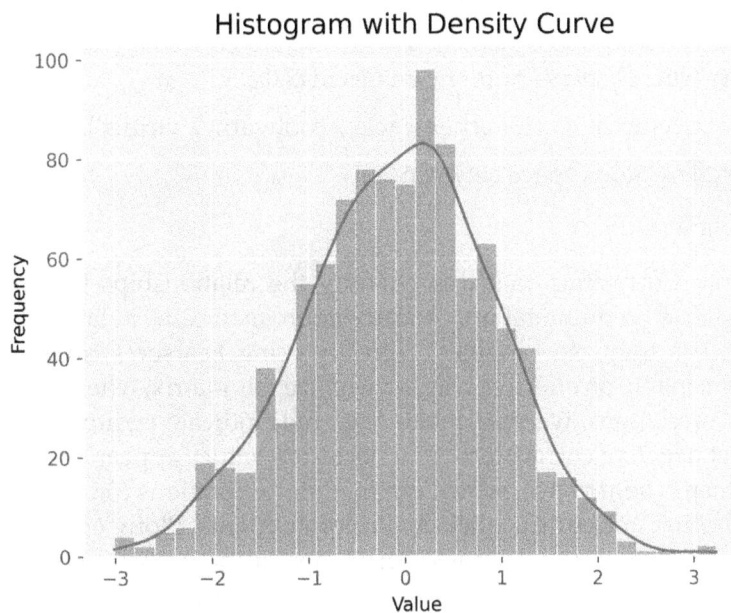

Figure 9.23: *Histogram with density curve*

9.3.2.2 Heatmaps for visualizing matrix relationships

Heatmaps use colors to represent data values in a matrix, making them ideal for analyzing correlations, confusion matrices, and tabular data. Refer to the following details:

- **Basic heatmap**: A basic heatmap in Python can be quickly created using Seaborn's **heatmap()** function, which visualizes matrix-like data through color gradients. (see *Figure 9.24*)

```
# Generate a random 10x10 matrix
data = np.random.rand(10, 10)
# Create a heatmap
sns.heatmap(data, annot=True, cmap='coolwarm', linewidths=0.5)
plt.title("Basic Heatmap")
plt.show()
```

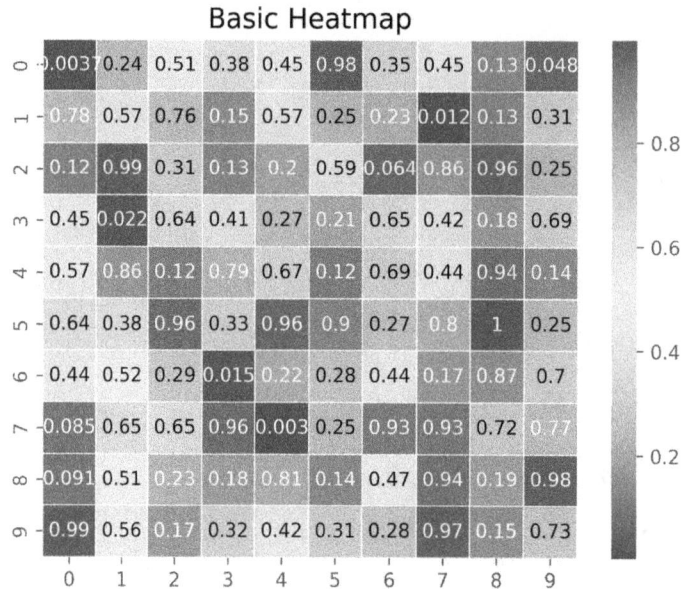

Figure 9.24: Heatmap

o   Key parameters:

  - **annot=True**: Displays numeric values in cells.

  - **cmap**: Specifies the color scheme (e.g., 'coolwarm', 'viridis').

  - **linewidths**: Adds space between cells.

The applications are as follows:

- **Correlation matrix**: Correlation matrices quantify the relationships between variables. Heatmaps provide a clear visual representation. A correlation matrix is a table that measures the linear relationships between multiple variables, typically using Pearson's correlation coefficient (ranging from -1 to 1). Heatmaps are an effective way to visualize this matrix, where colors represent the strength and direction of correlations; warmer colors (e.g., red) indicate positive relationships, cooler colors (e.g., blue) suggest negative correlations, and near-zero values appear neutral. Libraries like Seaborn simplify this with **sns.heatmap()**, which can include annotations for exact values, while Matplotlib provides customization options for labels and color gradients. Plotly enhances interactivity, allowing users to hover over cells for precise values. Correlation heatmaps are widely used in **exploratory data analysis (EDA)**, finance, and machine learning to identify multicollinearity, feature importance, and underlying patterns in datasets:

```
# Load sample data
import pandas as pd
df = sns.load_dataset('iris')
# Compute correlation matrix
corr = df.corr()
```

```
# Plot the heatmap
sns.heatmap(corr, annot=True, cmap='YlGnBu', fmt='.2f')
plt.title("Correlation Matrix Heatmap")
plt.show()
```

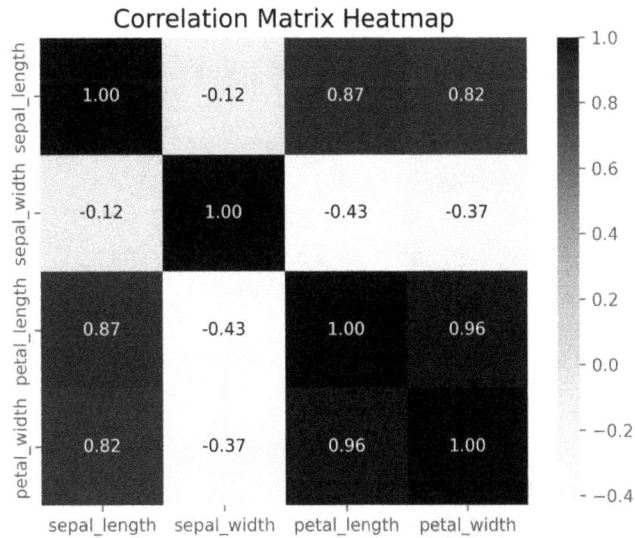

Figure 9.25: Correlation matrix heatmap

- **Confusion matrix**: Heatmaps are commonly used to visualize confusion matrices, shown in, *Figure 9.26,* in classification problems:

```
from sklearn.metrics import confusion_matrix
# Sample confusion matrix
y_true = [0, 1, 1, 0, 1, 0]
y_pred = [0, 1, 0, 0, 1, 1]
cm = confusion_matrix(y_true, y_pred)
sns.heatmap(cm, annot=True, fmt='d', cmap='Blues')
plt.title("Confusion Matrix Heatmap")
plt.xlabel("Predicted Label")
plt.ylabel("True Label")
plt.show()
```

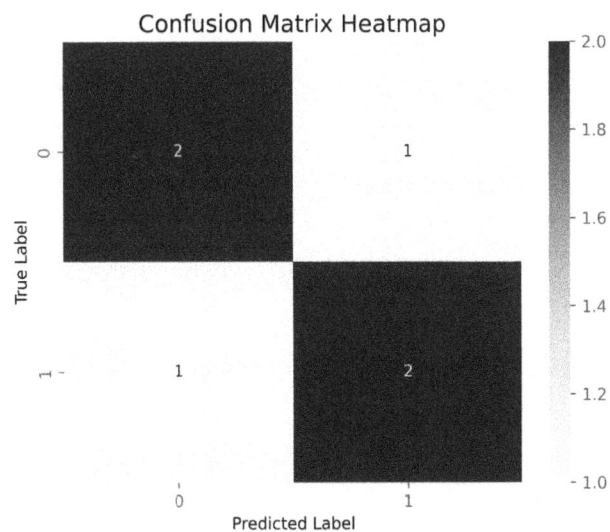

Figure 9.26: Confusion matrix

Application: Spearman rank correlation, as shown in *Figure 9.27*:

```python
import pandas as pd
import numpy as np
import seaborn as sns
import matplotlib.pyplot as plt
from scipy.stats import spearmanr  # Corrected import statement
# Data
data = {
    'Math': [78, 85, 92, 70, 88, 90, 65, 84, 76, 89],
    'Science': [80, 87, 91, 72, 85, 88, 68, 82, 78, 90],
    'English': [85, 82, 78, 88, 92, 86, 74, 80, 81, 84],
    'History': [75, 80, 85, 70, 83, 88, 66, 79, 72, 87]
}
# Convert to DataFrame
df = pd.DataFrame(data)
# Compute Spearman's rank correlation matrix
spearman_corr = df.corr(method='spearman')
# Display the rank correlation matrix
print("Spearman Rank Correlation Matrix:")
```

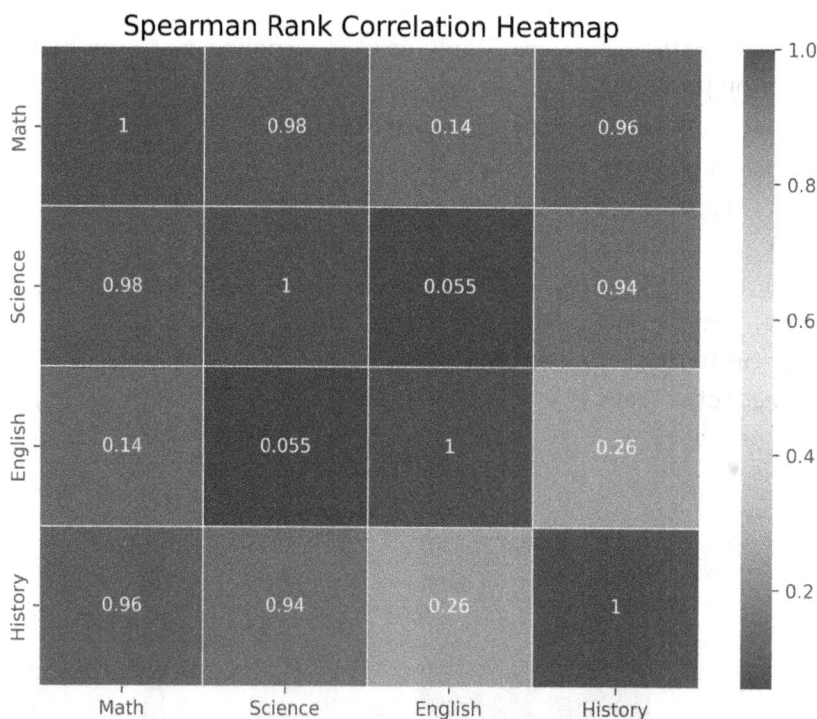

Figure 9.27: Spearman rank correlation heatmap

9.3.2.3 Polar plots using visualizing angular data

Polar plots are designed for data that is better represented in polar coordinates (e.g., angles, directions). They are particularly useful in fields like navigation, meteorology, and engineering. The following points provide more information on them:

- **Basic polar plot**: A basic polar plot in Python can be created using Matplotlib's subplot(**polar=True**), which plots data in circular coordinates (angle θ versus radius *r*). (see *Figure 9.28*)

```
theta = np.linspace(0, 2 * np.pi, 100)
r = np.abs(np.sin(2 * theta))  # Radius as a function of angle
ax = plt.subplot(111, polar=True)
ax.plot(theta, r, color='purple', linewidth=2)
plt.title("Basic Polar Plot")
plt.show()
```

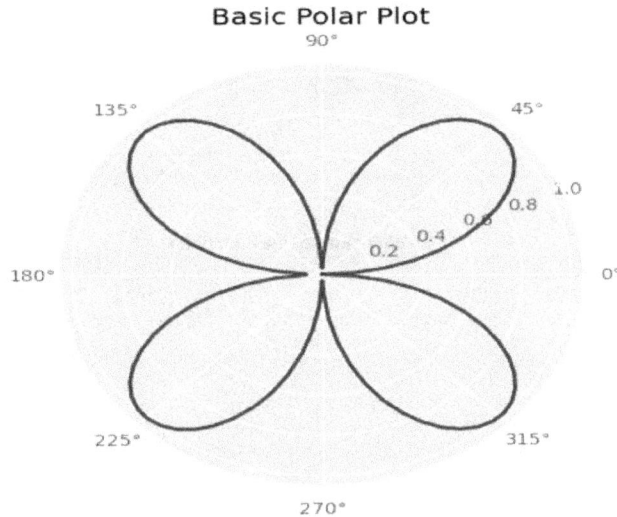

Figure 9.28: Basic Polar Plot

Key parameters:

- **polar=True**: Converts the subplot to polar coordinates.
- **theta**: Specifies angles (in radians).
- **r**: Represents radius values.

Let us compare MATLAB and Python for specialized plots through the following table:

Feature	MATLAB	Python
Histograms	`histogram()`	`plt.hist()` or `sns.histplot()`
Heatmaps	`imagesc()`	`sns.heatmap()`
Polar plots	`polarplot()`	`plt.subplot(polar=True)`
Customization	Extensive, built-in	Highly customizable with libraries
Ease of use	Intuitive but proprietary	Open-source and widely supported

Table 9.2: Comparison of specialized plots of MATLAB and Python

9.4 Comparison of examples via MATLAB and Python

This section presents a comparative study of a few selected examples implemented using MATLAB and Python. By analyzing these examples side by side, we highlight the similarities and differences in syntax, functionality, and computational efficiency between the two platforms. This comparison provides valuable insights for users in choosing the appropriate tool based on their programming preferences and application requirements.

Example 9.1: Plot the sine and cosine functions on the same graph, with appropriate labels, a title, and a legend.

MATLAB code:

```
x = 0:0.1:2*pi;
y1 = sin(x);
y2 = cos(x);
plot(x, y1, '-r', 'LineWidth', 2);
hold on;
plot(x, y2, '--b', 'LineWidth', 2);
title('Sine and Cosine Functions');
xlabel('x');
ylabel('y');
legend('sin(x)', 'cos(x)');
grid on;
```

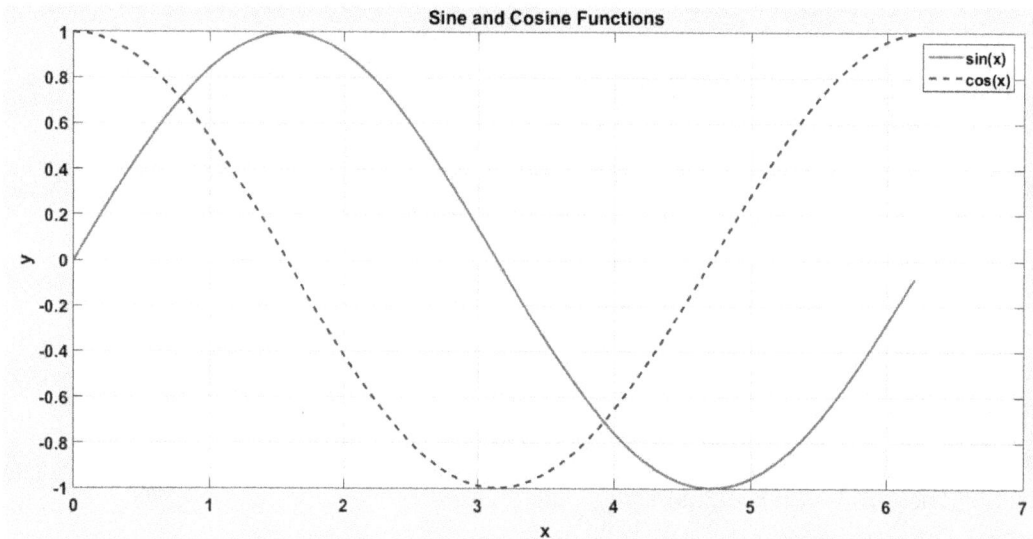

***Figure 9.29 (a)**: Sine and cosine functions plot in MATLAB*

Python code:

```
import numpy as np
import matplotlib.pyplot as plt
x = np.linspace(0, 2 * np.pi, 100)
y1 = np.sin(x)
y2 = np.cos(x)
plt.plot(x, y1, '-r', linewidth=2, label='sin(x)')
plt.plot(x, y2, '--b', linewidth=2, label='cos(x)')
plt.title('Sine and Cosine Functions')
plt.xlabel('x')
plt.ylabel('y')
plt.legend()
plt.grid(True)
plt.show()
```

Sine and Cosine Functions

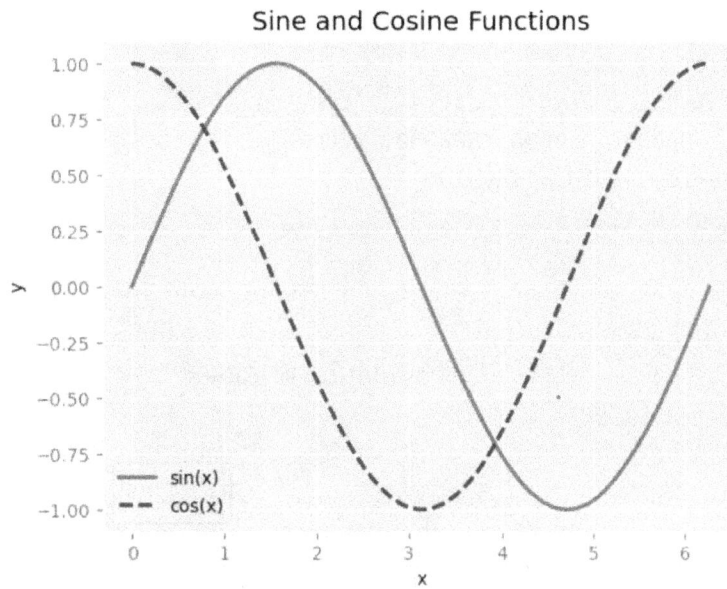

Figure 9.29 (b): Sine and cosine functions plot in Python

Example 9.2: Create a bar plot showing the population of five cities and a scatter plot comparing two datasets.

MATLAB code:

```
cities = {'City1', 'City2', 'City3', 'City4', 'City5'};
population = [500000, 700000, 650000, 800000, 900000];
bar(population);
set(gca, 'xticklabel', cities);
title('Population of Cities');
xlabel('Cities');
ylabel('Population');
```

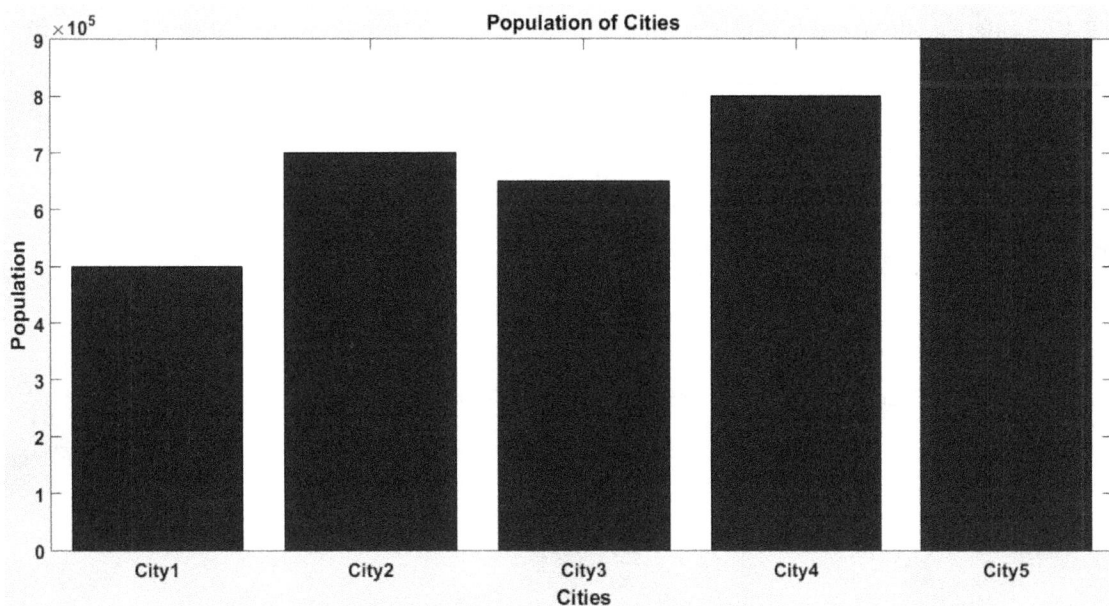

Figure 9.30 (a): Bar plot in MATLAB

Python code:
```
import matplotlib.pyplot as plt
cities = ['City1', 'City2', 'City3', 'City4', 'City5']
population = [500000, 700000, 650000, 800000, 900000]
plt.bar(cities, population, color='skyblue')
plt.title('Population of Cities')
plt.xlabel('Cities')
plt.ylabel('Population')
plt.show()
```

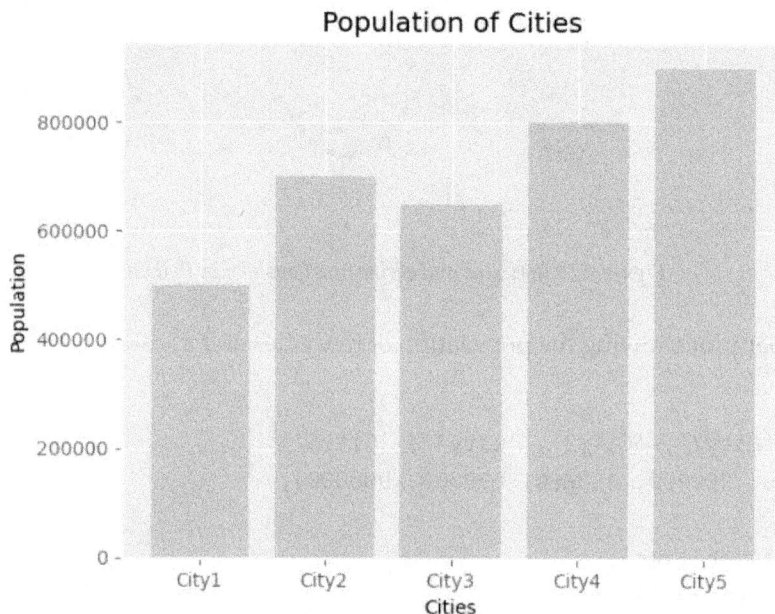

Figure 9.30 (b): Bar plot in Python

Example 9.3: Create a customized line plot with gridlines, line markers, and annotations for specific points.

MATLAB code:
```
x = 0:0.1:10;
y = x.^2;
plot(x, y, '-o', 'LineWidth', 2, 'MarkerSize', 5);
title('y = x^2');
xlabel('x');
ylabel('y');
grid on;
text(5, 25, 'Point of Interest', 'FontSize', 12, 'Color', 'r');
```

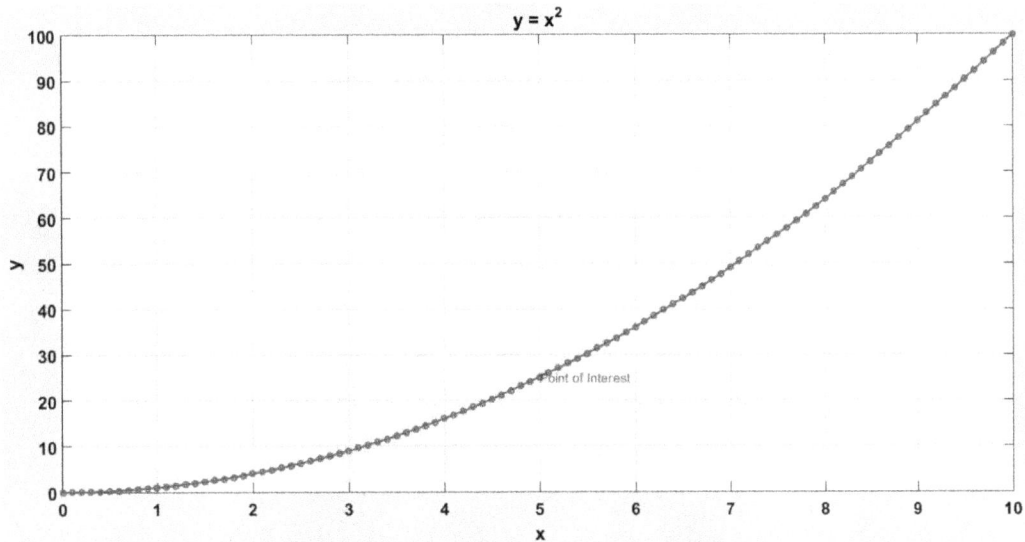

Figure 9.31 (a): Customized line plot in MATLAB

Python code:

```python
import matplotlib.pyplot as plt
import numpy as np
x = np.linspace(0, 10, 100)
y = x ** 2
plt.plot(x, y, '-o', linewidth=2, markersize=5)
plt.title('y = x^2')
plt.xlabel('x')
plt.ylabel('y')
```

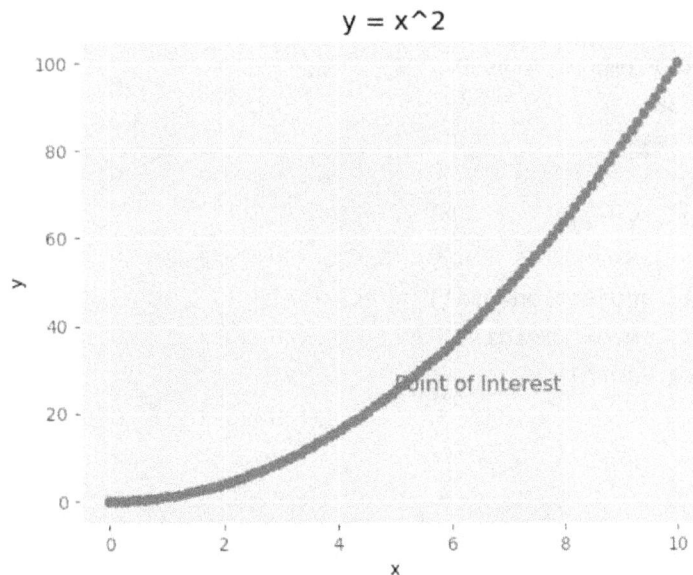

Figure 9.31 (b): Customized line plot in Python

Example 9.4: Generate a 3D surface plot of $z = sin(\sqrt{(x^2 + y^2)})$

MATLAB code:

```matlab
[X, Y] = meshgrid(-5:0.5:5, -5:0.5:5);
Z = sin(sqrt(X.^2 + Y.^2));
```

```
surf(X, Y, Z);
title('3D Surface Plot');
xlabel('X');
ylabel('Y');
zlabel('Z');
```

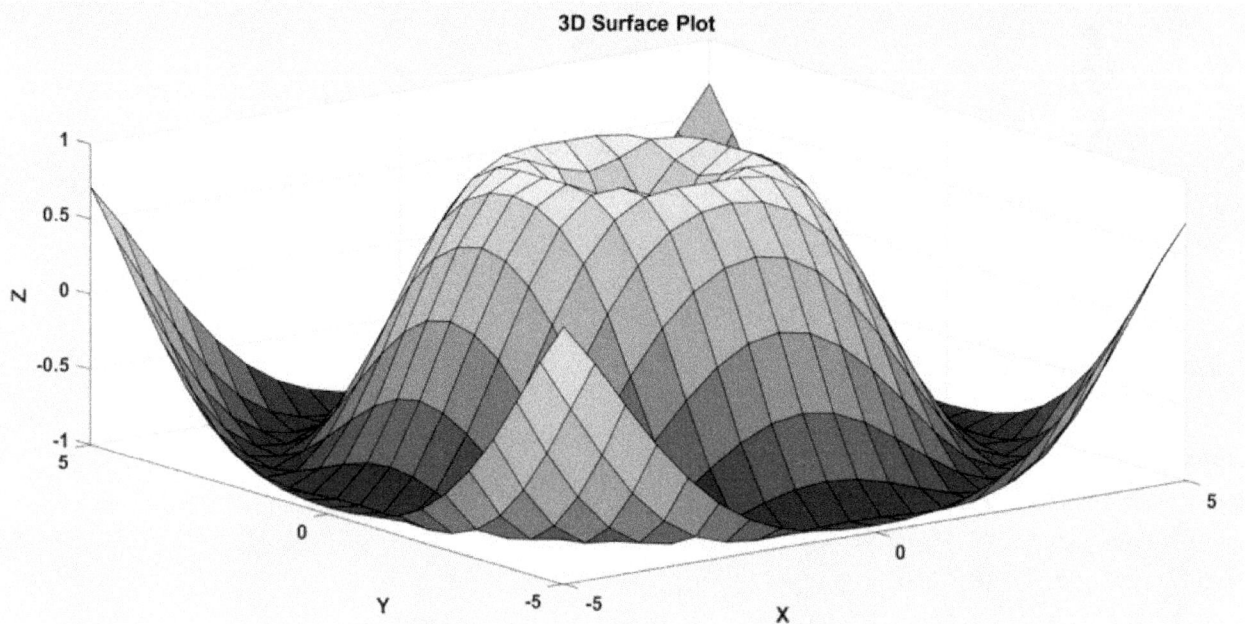

Figure 9.32 (a): 3D surface plot in MATLAB

Python code:

```
import numpy as np
import matplotlib.pyplot as plt
from mpl_toolkits.mplot3d import Axes3D
x = np.linspace(-5, 5, 50)
y = np.linspace(-5, 5, 50)
X, Y = np.meshgrid(x, y)
Z = np.sin(np.sqrt(X**2 + Y**2))
fig = plt.figure()
ax = fig.add_subplot(111, projection='3d')
ax.plot_surface(X, Y, Z, cmap='viridis')
ax.set_title('3D Surface Plot')
ax.set_xlabel('X')
ax.set_ylabel('Y')
ax.set_zlabel('Z')
plt.show()
```

3D Surface Plot

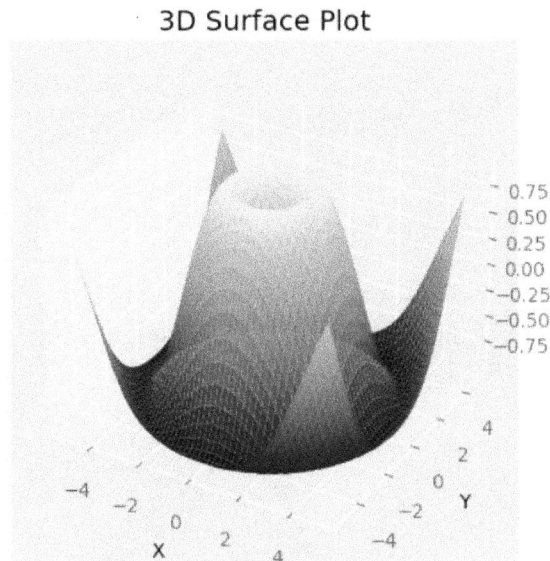

Figure 9.32 (b) : 3D surface plot in Python

Example 9.5: Plot a quadratic equation $y = ax^2 + bx + c$ for three different sets of coefficients a, b, c on the same graph with a legend.

MATLAB code:

```
x = -10:0.1:10;
y1 = 2*x.^2 + 3*x + 1;
y2 = -x.^2 + 5*x - 2;
y3 = 0.5*x.^2 - 4*x + 3;
plot(x, y1, 'r', 'LineWidth', 2);
hold on;
plot(x, y2, 'g', 'LineWidth', 2);
plot(x, y3, 'b', 'LineWidth', 2);
title('Quadratic Equations');
xlabel('x');
ylabel('y');
legend('2x^2 + 3x + 1', '-x^2 + 5x - 2', '0.5x^2 - 4x + 3');
grid on;
```

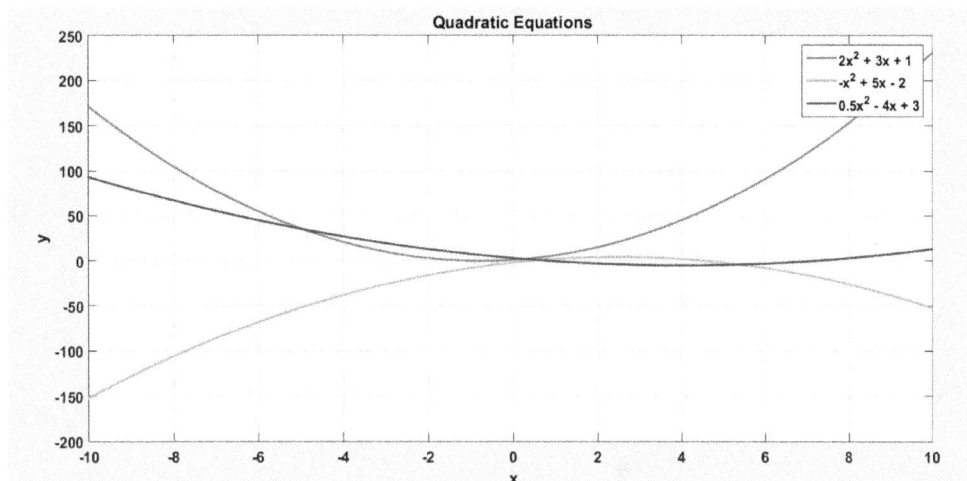

Figure 9.33 (a) : Quadratic equation plot in MATLAB

Python code:

```python
import numpy as np
import matplotlib.pyplot as plt
x = np.linspace(-10, 10, 200)
y1 = 2*x**2 + 3*x + 1
y2 = -x**2 + 5*x - 2
y3 = 0.5*x**2 - 4*x + 3
plt.plot(x, y1, 'r', label='2x^2 + 3x + 1', linewidth=2)
plt.plot(x, y2, 'g', label='-x^2 + 5x - 2', linewidth=2)
plt.plot(x, y3, 'b', label='0.5x^2 - 4x + 3', linewidth=2)
plt.title('Quadratic Equations')
plt.xlabel('x')
plt.ylabel('y')
plt.legend()
plt.grid(True)
plt.show()
```

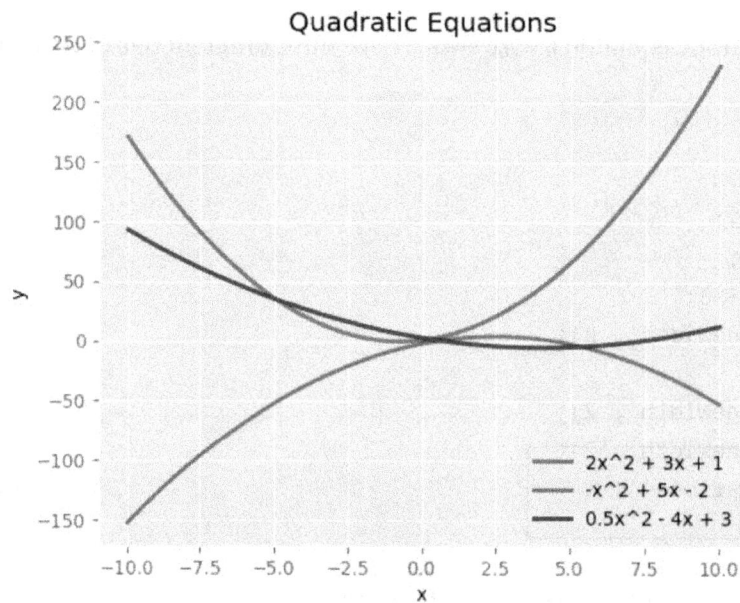

Figure 9.33 (b): *Quadratic equation plot in Python*

Example 9.6: Create a pie chart to visualize the percentage distribution of expenses in five categories (e.g., Rent, Food, Transport, Entertainment, and Savings):

MATLAB code:

```matlab
categories = {'Rent', 'Food', 'Transport', 'Entertainment', 'Savings'};
expenses = [40, 25, 15, 10, 10];
pie(expenses, categories);
title('Expense Distribution');
```

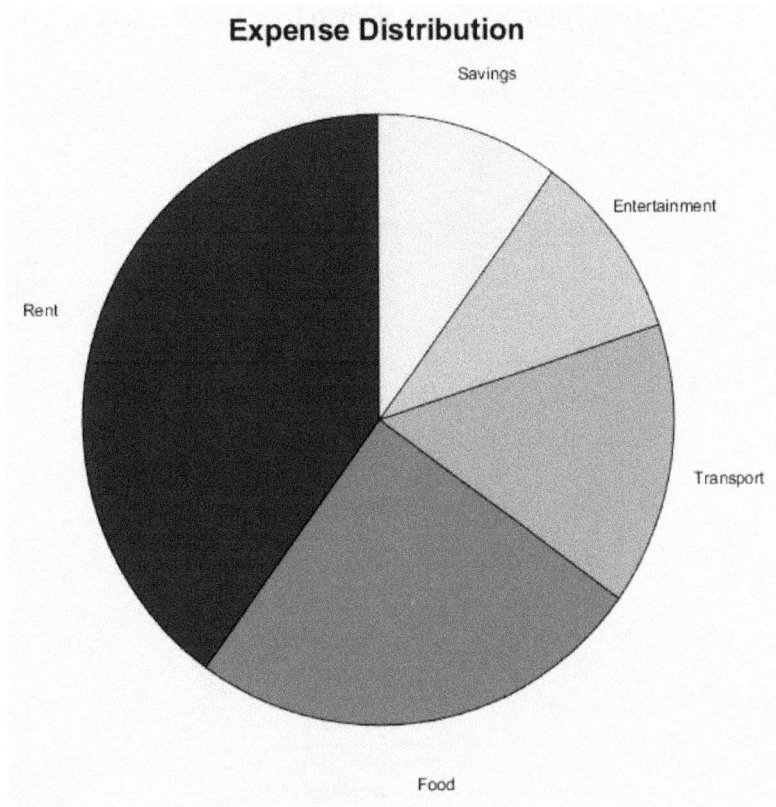

Figure 9.34 (a): Pie chart in MATLAB

Python code:

```
import matplotlib.pyplot as plt
categories = ['Rent', 'Food', 'Transport', 'Entertainment', 'Savings']
expenses = [40, 25, 15, 10, 10]
plt.pie(expenses, labels=categories, autopct='%1.1f%%', startangle=140)
plt.title('Expense Distribution')
plt.show()
```

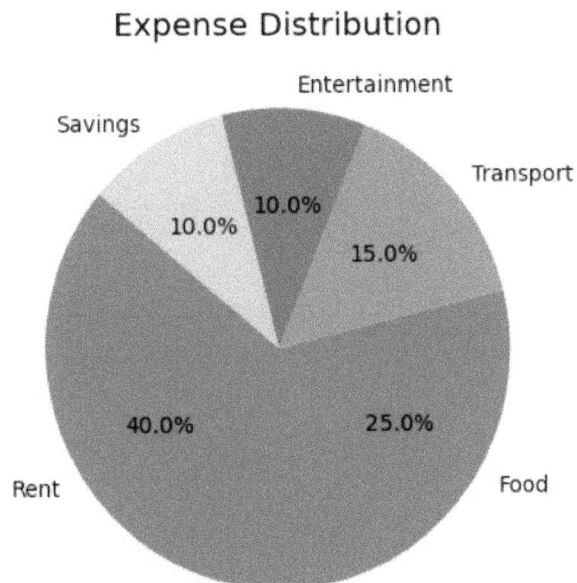

Figure 9.34 (b): Pie chart in Python

Example 9.7: Generate a 3D parametric plot of a helix defined by *x=cos(t), y=sin(t), z=t for t ∈ [0, 10π]*:

MATLAB code:

```
t = 0:0.1:10*pi;
x = cos(t);
y = sin(t);
z = t;
plot3(x, y, z, 'LineWidth', 2);
title('3D Helix');
xlabel('X');
ylabel('Y');
zlabel('Z');
grid on;
```

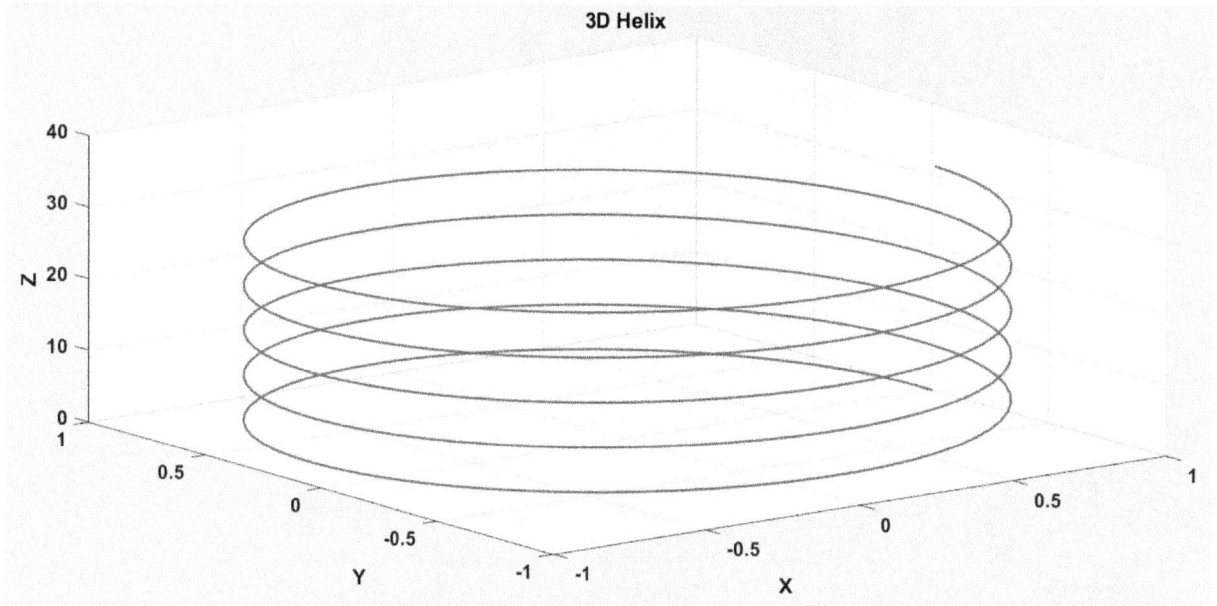

Figure 9.35 (a): 3D parametric plot in MATLAB

Python code:

```
import numpy as np
import matplotlib.pyplot as plt
t = np.linspace(0, 10 * np.pi, 500)
x = np.cos(t)
y = np.sin(t)
z = t
fig = plt.figure()
ax = fig.add_subplot(111, projection='3d')
ax.plot(x, y, z, linewidth=2)
ax.set_title('3D Helix')
ax.set_xlabel('X')
ax.set_ylabel('Y')
ax.set_zlabel('Z')
plt.show()
```

3D Helix

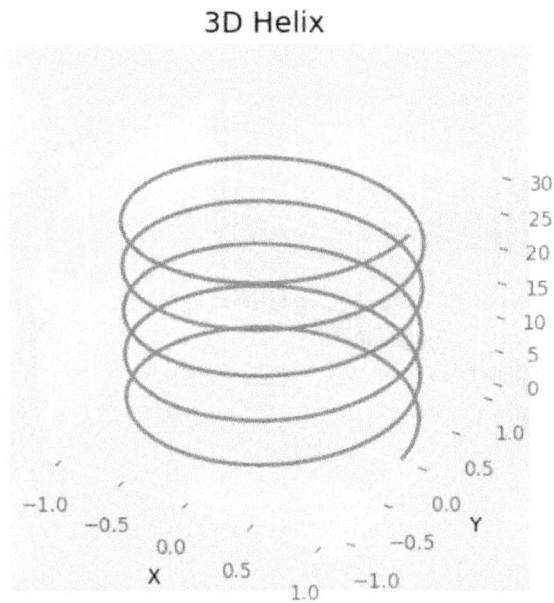

Figure 9.35 (b): 3D parametric plot in Python

Example 9.8: Correlation matrix heatmap: Generate a heatmap to visualize the Pearson correlation matrix for a dataset with multiple variables:

MATLAB code:

```
% Generate sample data
data = rand(100, 5); % 100 observations, 5 variables
% Compute Pearson correlation matrix
corrMatrix = corr(data);
% Visualize as a heatmap using imagesc
imagesc(corrMatrix);
colormap(parula); % Set colormap
colorbar; % Add color bar to indicate scale
% Add title and labels
title('Pearson Correlation Matrix');
xlabel('Variables');
ylabel('Variables');
```

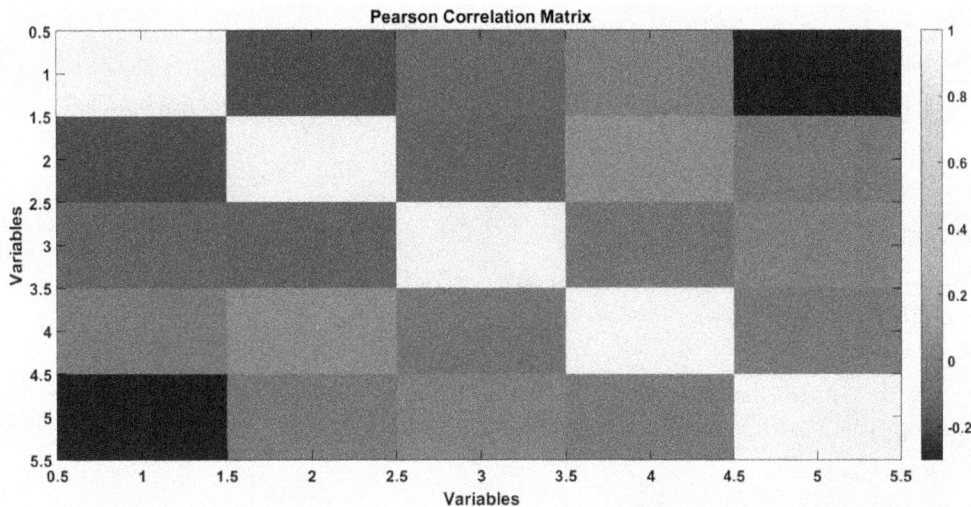

Figure 9.36 (a): Correlation Matrix Heatmap in MATLAB

Python code:

```python
import numpy as np
import pandas as pd
import seaborn as sns
import matplotlib.pyplot as plt
# Generate sample data
np.random.seed(42)
data = pd.DataFrame(np.random.rand(100, 5), columns=['Var1', 'Var2', 'Var3', 'Var4',
'Var5'])
# Compute Pearson correlation matrix
corr_matrix = data.corr(method='pearson')
# Visualize as a heatmap
plt.figure(figsize=(8, 6))
sns.heatmap(corr_matrix, annot=True, cmap='coolwarm', fmt='.2f')
plt.title('Pearson Correlation Matrix Heatmap')
plt.show()
```

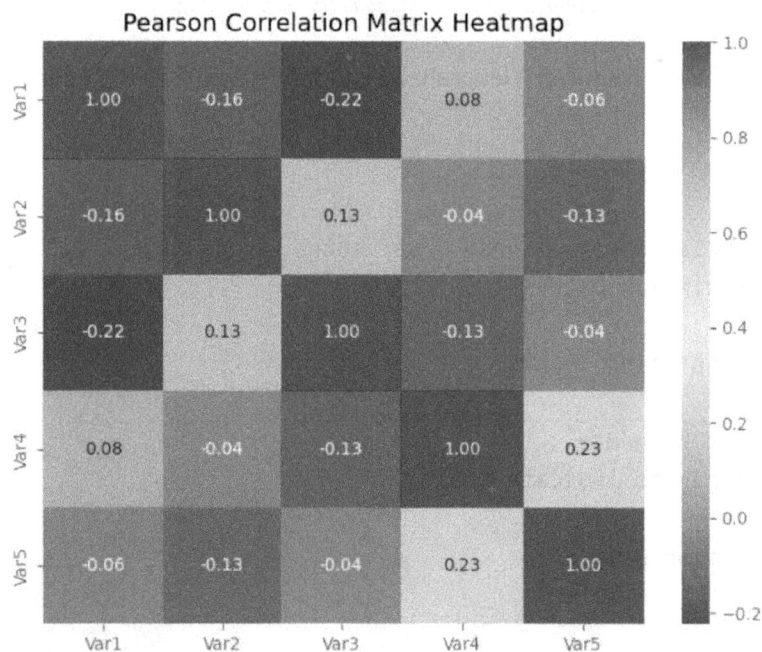

Figure 9.36 (b): Correlation matrix heatmap in Python

Example 9.9: Rank correlation matrix heatmap: Generate a heatmap to visualize the Spearman rank correlation matrix for the same dataset:

MATLAB code:

```matlab
% Compute Spearman rank correlation matrix
rankCorrMatrix = corr(data, 'Type', 'Spearman');
 % Visualize using imagesc
imagesc(rankCorrMatrix);
colormap(jet); % Set colormap to 'jet'
colorbar; % Add color bar
 % Add title and labels
title('Spearman Rank Correlation Matrix');
```

```
xlabel('Variables');
ylabel('Variables');
```

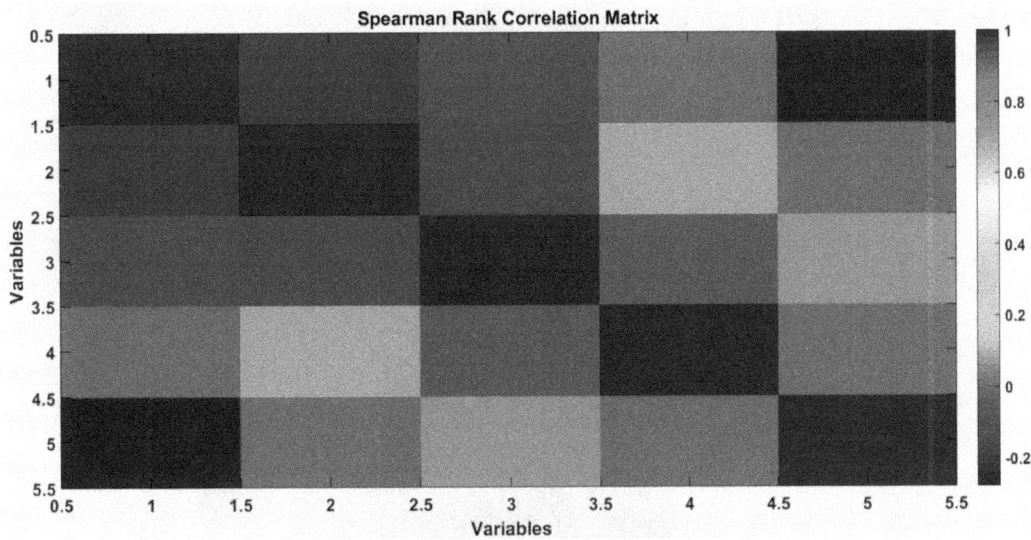

Figure 9.37 (a): Rank correlation matrix heatmap in MATLAB

Python code:

```python
# Compute Spearman rank correlation matrix
rank_corr_matrix = data.corr(method='spearman')
# Visualize as a heatmap
plt.figure(figsize=(8, 6))
sns.heatmap(rank_corr_matrix, annot=True, cmap='viridis', fmt='.2f')
plt.title('Spearman Rank Correlation Matrix Heatmap')
plt.show()
```

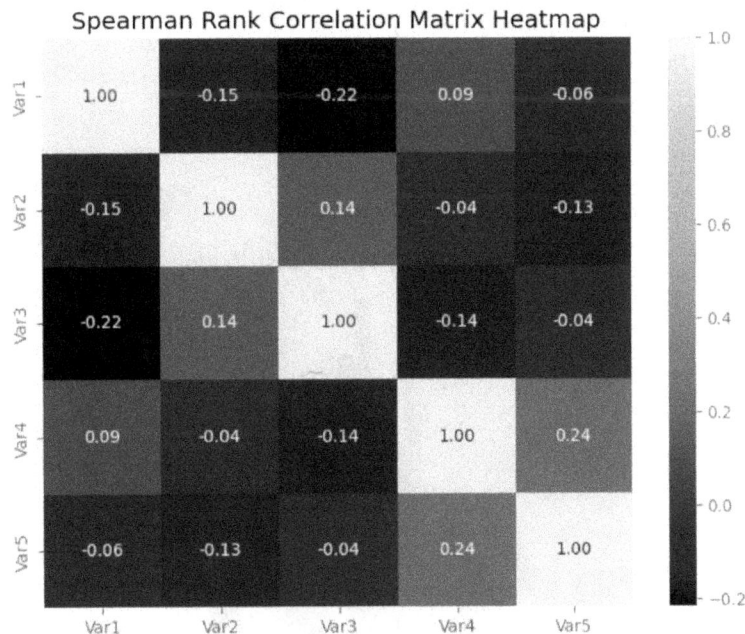

Figure 9.37 (b): Rank correlation matrix heatmap in Python

Example 9.10: Generate and visualize a histogram of random numbers sampled from a normal distribution ($\mu = 0, \sigma = 1$):

MATLAB code:

```
data = randn(1000, 1); % Normal distribution
histogram(data, 30, 'FaceColor', 'b');
title('Histogram of Normal Distribution');
xlabel('Value');
ylabel('Frequency');
grid on;
```

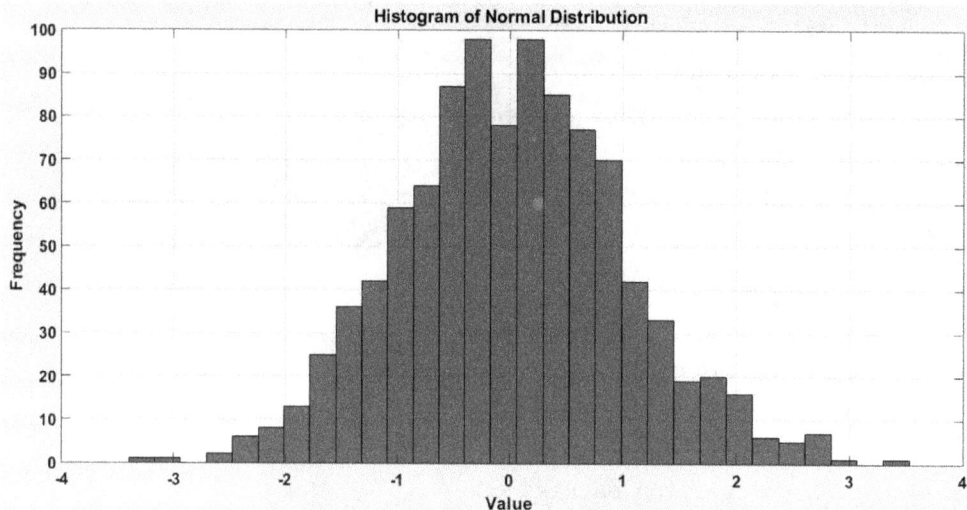

Figure 9.38 (a): Histogram in MATLAB

Python code:

```
import numpy as np
import matplotlib.pyplot as plt
data = np.random.randn(1000)  # Normal distribution
plt.hist(data, bins=30, color='b', alpha=0.7)
plt.title('Histogram of Normal Distribution')
plt.xlabel('Value')
plt.ylabel('Frequency')
plt.grid()
plt.show()
```

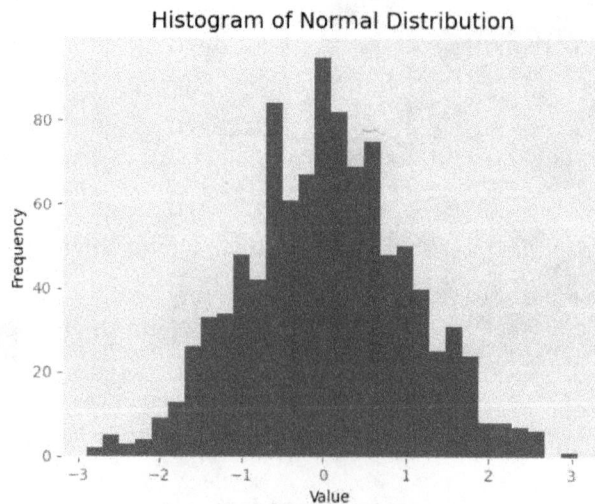

Figure 9.38 (b): Histogram in Python

Conclusion

In this chapter, we explored the fundamentals of data visualization using Python, beginning with an overview of essential libraries such as Matplotlib. We demonstrated how to create basic plots, customize visual elements like labels, legends, and colors, and present data in a visually effective and meaningful way. Through practical examples, we emphasized how visualizations can enhance data interpretation and support informed decision-making. The chapter concluded with a comparative study of MATLAB and Python, showcasing advanced-level examples to highlight the unique features, strengths, and flexibility of each platform in handling scientific and engineering visualizations. This comparative approach enables readers to appreciate the differences in syntax, plotting capabilities, and customization options between the two environments. By mastering these tools, users gain the confidence to select and apply the appropriate platform for diverse visualization tasks in academic, research, or industry-based projects.

In the next chapter, we will shift focus to signal processing and image processing using MATLAB and Python, providing foundational concepts and implementation techniques along with a comparative analysis using real-world examples to deepen understanding and application.

Exercises

1. Create a vector of 100 evenly spaced points between -5 and 5. Compute the y values for the curve $y = x^2$ and plot graph of $y = x^2$.

2. Make a plot of the function $sin(x) + x^3 - x$ using the appropriate command with x from 0 to 2π with 90 points between. Add the appropriate title and labels for the x and y axis, using the command and the toolbar of the figure window. Now save the figure as an editable file and the **.jpeg** file.

3. Write a program to generate a mesh and surface plots for $z = \frac{xy^2}{x^2+y^2}, -3 \le x \le 3, and -4 \le y \le 4$.

4. Use a plot command to get an idea about the following well-known mathematical functions and verify that this is the curve you expected:

   a. $sin(x)$ in range [-360,360]

   b. $cos^2(x)$ in range [-180,180]

   c. x^3 for x in [-10,10] with 60 points

   d. $log(x)$ for x in [-100,100]

   e. $exp(x)$ for x in [-10,10] with 40 points.

5. Write a program that generates and plots a cosine wave. The plot should clearly label the axes, include a title, and use a range of x-values from 0 to 2π.

6. Write the single command to draw the two graphs of $sin(x)$ and $cos(x)$ together. The graph of $sin(x)$ must be of green color with a dashed line and graph of $cos(x)$ must be of '+' marker and cyan color. Insert a proper legend also using the toolbar and command.

7. Create a script file and use the plot command to plot the function:

$$y = (3.5)^{-0.5x} \cos(6x), -2 \le x \le 4.$$

8. Plot the given function $8 t^2 + 5 cos(t)$ in domain [-3, 3].

9. Plot the function $3x^3 - 26x + 10$ and its first and second derivatives for x in [-2,4], all in the same figure using the plot function with the commands xlabel, ylabel and title for labels of axis and title on the axis.

10. Create a logarithmic spiral for $x = e^{k\theta} \cos(\theta)$ and $y = e^{k\theta} \sin(\theta)$ with $k = 0.05$ and θ = -10π to 10π with 2000 evenly spaced points. Use text (a, b, 'message') and gtext() command to insert a text in a graph.

11. Plot the given number of students [2, 10, 5, 1, 20, 4] with grades A, B, C, D, E, F and label them as a pie diagram. Do by defining vectors x for values and y for grades and do directly with the command without defining vectors. Also, pull the biggest and the smallest slices.

12. Let x be a vector with 10 elements from 0.1 to 20, $y = 2^{-0.2x}$. Perform the following:

    a. Draw a bar graph in vertical and horizontal direction.

    b. Draw a graph like a staircase.

    c. Draw a graph with y as stems from x axis.

13. Create a surface plot for the given function

    $z = 1.6^{-2.5\sqrt{x^2+y^2}} \sin(x) \cos(0.8y), -3 \le x \le 3, -3 \le y \le 3$ with red edges.

14. Create a 3D graph for the given function $z = \frac{x^2}{5} + 2\cos(3y), -3 \le x \le 3, -3 \le y \le 3$ using the appropriate commands, and label it appropriately.

15. Write code to draw a lemniscate in green color with asterisk markers for $x = \cos(\theta)\sqrt{2\cos(2\theta)}$ and $y = \sin(\theta)\sqrt{2\cos(2\theta)}$ for $\theta = -\frac{\pi}{4}$ to $\frac{\pi}{4}$ with 500 evenly spaced points.

16. Create a logarithmic spiral for $x = e^{k\theta}\cos(\theta)$ and $y = e^{k\theta}\sin(\theta)$ with k=0.05 and θ = -10π to 10π with 2000 evenly spaced points. Use text (a, b, 'message') and gtext() command to insert a text in a graph.

17. An object is fired at an angle θ with respect to the horizontal axis. The initial velocity of the object is 10 ms^{-1}. Trace the path of the object for different values of θ = 20° , 45° , 65°.Hint: Use the following equations of the motion for the projectile trajectory:

    a. Horizontal position (x): $x = v_0 \cos(\theta)\, t$

    b. Vertical position (y): $y = v_0 \sin(\theta)\, t - \left(\frac{1}{2}\right) g\, t^2$

    Here:

    a. v_0 is the initial velocity.

    b. θ is the launch angle.

    c. t is time to be taken from 0 to 100 sec.

    d. g is the acceleration due to gravity (approximately 9.81 m/s²).

18. Write a script file to draw the graph of $e^x + x^3 - \cos^2(3x)$ and $\frac{x^2-4}{x+5}$:

    As two subplots arranged vertically, here x has entries from 0 to 100 with total 30 points. Also insert labels, provide similar title to the graph.

19. As a single graph providing legends, create a single plot that visualizes both a given function and its derivative for $y = x^3 e^x$ with $0 \le x \le 9$. The function should be plotted with a solid line, while the derivative should be represented by a dashed line. Include a legend that distinctly identifies which line corresponds to the function and which to its derivative. Also, label both the x-axis and y-axis appropriately for proper interpretation of the graph.

20. Consider the function $f(x) = \frac{(x^2+3x-1)}{(x^2-1)}$. Determine the locations of the vertical asymptotes of this function. Divide the domain of into three distinct intervals based on the positions of these asymptotes. Subsequently, plot the function $f(x)$ within each of these intervals. Set the y-axis range of the plot to -15 to 15 and ensure proper labeling of the axes.

## CHAPTER 10

Working with Data in MATLAB and Python

Introduction

This chapter provides an inclusive approach to working with data in **Matrix Laboratory (MATLAB)** and Python. These are the two most popular programming languages for data analysis and scientific computing. This chapter is divided into three sections: MATLAB-based and Python-based concepts and a comparative study of MATLAB and Python codes. Every section contains detailed explanations and examples to understand the basics of the two languages.

In today's data-driven world, the ability to efficiently manipulate, analyze, and preprocess data is a fundamental skill across various domains, including engineering, finance, healthcare, and machine learning. This chapter introduces essential techniques for working with data in MATLAB and Python, two of the most widely used platforms for numerical computing and data analysis. MATLAB excels in matrix-based operations and provides powerful tools for statistical analysis and structured data handling through tables. Meanwhile, Python, with its rich ecosystem of libraries like Pandas and NumPy, offers flexible and scalable solutions for data manipulation, statistical computing, and preprocessing.

You will learn how to perform key operations such as indexing, reshaping, and aggregating datasets—skills that are crucial for tasks ranging from cleaning experimental data to preparing datasets for machine learning models. The chapter also covers statistical functions for computing measures like mean, variance, and correlation, enabling users to derive meaningful insights from raw data. Practical applications include processing sensor data in engineering, analyzing financial trends, and handling biomedical datasets. By the end of this chapter, you will be equipped with the foundational knowledge to tackle real-world data challenges, bridging the gap between theoretical concepts and hands-on implementation in MATLAB and Python.

Structure

In this chapter, we will learn the following topics:

- 10.1. MATLAB-based concepts
- 10.2. Python-based concepts
- 10.3. Comparative study via MATLAB and Python codes

Objectives

The objectives of this chapter are to equip readers with essential skills for handling, analyzing, and preprocessing data in MATLAB and Python, with a focus on real-world applications. By exploring data manipulation techniques, readers will learn how to efficiently index, slice, and reshape datasets; these skills are crucial for tasks like cleaning sensor data in engineering or processing financial records. The chapter also covers statistical functions, enabling users to compute measures like mean, standard deviation, and correlation, which are fundamental in fields such as biomedical research (e.g., analyzing clinical trial data) or market trend analysis.

In MATLAB, readers will gain proficiency in working with tables, a structured way to manage labeled datasets, which is particularly useful in organizing experimental results or survey data. Meanwhile, in Python, they will master Pandas and NumPy for advanced data manipulation, such as merging datasets or handling missing values, common tasks in business analytics and machine learning. The chapter emphasizes data preprocessing and teaching techniques like normalization and outlier detection, which are critical for preparing data for AI models or predictive analytics.

10.1 MATLAB-based concepts

MATLAB is a high-level programming language used to understand the basics of numerical computation, data analysis, and visualization. It is mainly useful regarding matrix operations. It is a powerful tool to manipulate data, for statistical analysis, and to work with structured data (table). In this section, we will explore MATLAB's capabilities in detail, with examples.

10.1.1 Data manipulation in MATLAB

Data manipulation is one of MATLAB's vital assets. It provides a range of functions and operators to work with matrices and other aspects. We will cover key data manipulation techniques in MATLAB ahead. Let us look at the following details:

- **Creating arrays and matrices**: MATLAB is considered to work mainly with matrices and arrays mainly. You may form arrays and matrices via square brackets [].

  Example 10.1: How to create row vector, column vector, and 3x3 matrix in MATLAB:

```
% Create a row vector
row_vector = [1, 2, 3, 4, 5]
% Create a column vector
column_vector = [1; 2; 3; 4; 5]
% Create a 3x3 matrix
matrix = [1, 2, 3; 4, 5, 6; 7, 8, 9]
```

```
Output:
row_vector =
     1     2     3     4     5
column_vector =
     1
     2
     3
     4
     5
matrix =

     1     2     3
     4     5     6
     7     8     9
```

Table 10.1: Creation of vectors in MATLAB

- **Indexing and slicing**: MATLAB has 1-based indexing, which means the first element of an array is accessed with index 1. You may use indexing to extract specific elements or slices of an array or matrix.

  Example 10.2: Indexing and slicing in MATLAB:

`% Access the 3rd element of a row vector`
`element = row_vector(3)`
 	
`% Access the element in the 2nd row, 3rd column of a matrix`
`matrix_element = matrix(2, 3)`
 	
`% Slice the first two rows and all columns of a matrix`
`sliced_matrix = matrix(1:2, :)`
 	
`% Slice the last three elements of a row vector`
`sliced_vector = row_vector(end-2:end)`
	Output:
	element =
	    3
	matrix_element =
	    6
	sliced_matrix =
	    1 2 3
	    4 5 6
	sliced_vector =
	    3 4 5

Table 10.2: Accessing and slicing the elements in MATLAB

MATLAB allows for easy data extraction and modification using indexing.

Example 10.3: Data extraction and modification in MATLAB:

`A = [1 2 3; 4 5 6; 7 8 9]`
`B = A(2, :) % Extracts second row`
`C = A(:, 3) % Extracts third column`
`D = A(1:2, 2:3) % Extracts a submatrix`
`E = A(end, :) % Extracts the last row`
`F = A(2, 2) % Extracts a single element`
`G = A(:, [1 3]); % Extract specific columns`
	Output:
	A =
	    1 2 3
	    4 5 6
	    7 8 9
	B =
	    4 5 6
	C =
	    3
	    6
	    9
	D =
	    2 3
	    5 6
	E =
	    7 8 9
	F =
	    5

Table 10.3: Extraction and modification of data in MATLAB

- **Reshaping arrays**: The reshape function allows you to change the dimensions of an array without altering its data.

Example 10.4: Reshaping arrays in MATLAB:

``matlab
matrix = [1 2 3; 2 3 4; 2 3 5];
% Reshape a 3x3 matrix into a 1x9 row vector
reshaped_vector = reshape(matrix, 1, 9)
 	
row_vector = [1, 2, 3, 4, 5, 0];
% Reshape a row vector into a 2x3 matrix
reshaped_matrix = reshape(row_vector, 2, 3)
``
	Output:
	reshaped_vector =
	
	1 2 2 2 3 3 3
	4 5
	
	reshaped_matrix =
	
	  1 3 5
	  2 4 0

Table 10.4: Reshaping arrays in MATLAB

Example 10.5: Reshaping arrays in MATLAB:

``matlab
A = [1 2 3 4 5 6];
B = reshape(A, [2,3]); % Reshape to 2x3 matrix
C = A'; % Transpose of matrix
D = permute(reshape(1:24, [4,3,2]), [2,1,3]);
% Rearrange dimensions
E = flip(A); % Reverse the order of elements
``
	Output:
	A =
	  1 2 3 4 5 6
	B =
	  1 3 5
	  2 4 6
	C =
	  1
	  2
	  3
	  4
	  5
	  6
	D(:,:,1) =
	  1 2 3 4
	  5 6 7 8
	  9 10 11 12
	D(:,:,2) =
	  13 14 15 16
	  17 18 19 20
	  21 22 23 24
	E =
	  6 5 4 3 2 1

Table 10.5: Some array operations in MATLAB

- **Concatenation**: You may concatenate arrays and matrices (horizontally or vertically) via square brackets or the cat function.

Example 10.6: Concatenation in MATLAB:

	Output:
``% Horizontal concatenation
A = [1, 2; 3, 4];
B = [5, 6; 7, 8];
C = [A, B]

% Vertical concatenation
D = [A; B]

% Concatenation using the cat function
E = cat(1, A, B) % Vertical concatenation
F = cat(2, A, B) % Horizontal concatenation``` | ```C =
     1   2   5   6
     3   4   7   8
D =
     1   2
     3   4
     5   6
     7   8
E =
     1   2
     3   4
     5   6
     7   8
F =
     1   2   5   6
     3   4   7   8``` |

Table 10.6: Concatenation of vectors in MATLAB

- **Sorting**: MATLAB offers a sort function to sort arrays and matrices.

Example 10.7: Sorting in MATLAB:

	Output:
``row_vector = [2 12 11 34 1 3 11 45];
% Sort a row vector in ascending order
sorted_vector = sort(row_vector)

matrix = [14 12 30; 40 5 61; 17 80 91];

% Sort a matrix along columns
sorted_matrix = sort(matrix, 1) % Sorts each column``` | ```sorted_vector =
     1   2   3   11   11   12   34   45
sorted_matrix =
    14   5   30
    17   12   61
    40   80   91``` |

Table 10.7: Sorting in MATLAB

Sorting and filtering support the analysis of data effectively.

Example 10.8: Sorting and filtering in MATLAB:

	Output:
``A = [3, 1, 4, 1, 5, 9, 2, 6, 5];
B = sort(A) % Sort in ascending order
C = sort(A, 'descend') % Sort in descending order
D = A(A > 4) % Filter values greater than 4
E = unique(A) % Find unique values
F = find(A > 3 & A < 7) % Find indices of elements in range```	```B =
1   1   2   3   4   5   5   6   9
C =
9   6   5   5   4   3   2   1   1
D =
5   9   6   5
E =
1   2   3   4   5   6   9
F =
3   5   8   9```

Table 10.8: Sorting and filtering in MATLAB

- **Merging and splitting data**: In MATLAB, merging combines datasets (e.g., using `horzcat`, or `vertcat`), while splitting divides them (e.g., via `indexing`, `splitvars`, or `mat2cell`), enabling flexible data manipulation for analysis.

Example 10.9: Merging and splitting data in MATLAB:

`A = [1 2; 3 4];`
`B = [5 6; 7 8];`
`C = [A, B] % Horizontal concatenation`
`D = [A; B] % Vertical concatenation`
	Output:
	C =
	  1 2 5 6
	  3 4 7 8
	D =
	  1 2
	  3 4
	  5 6
	  7 8

Table 10.9: Merging and splitting data in MATLAB

- **Handling missing data**: In MATLAB, missing data is handled using functions like `rmmissing`, `fillmissing`, and `ismissing` to clean, interpolate, or flag gaps in datasets while preserving data integrity.

Example 10.10: Handling missing data in MATLAB:

`A = [1 NaN 3; 4 5 NaN; 7 8 9]`
`B = isnan(A)`
`% Identify missing values`
`C = mean(A, 'omitnan')`
`% Compute mean ignoring NaN values`
	Output:
	A =
	  1 NaN 3
	  4 5 NaN
	  7 8 9
	B =
	  0 1 0
	  0 0 1
	  0 0 0
	C =
	  4.0000 6.5000 6.0000

Table 10.10: Handling missing data in MATLAB

10.1.2 Statistical functions in MATLAB

MATLAB offers a complete set of built-in functions regarding statistical analysis. These functions are improved for performance and are easy to implement:

- **Mean and standard deviation**: The mean and std functions compute mean and standard deviation of a dataset. In MATLAB, the mean (average) is computed using **mean()**, while the standard deviation (dispersion) is calculated with **std()**. These functions work on arrays, matrices, or table columns, with options to specify dimensions (dim) or handle missing data ('omitnan').

Example 10.11: Mean and standard deviation in MATLAB:

```% Calculate the mean of a vector data = [1, 2, 3, 4, 5]; mean_value = mean(data) % Calculate the standard deviation of a vector std_value = std(data)```	**Output:** **mean_value =** **3** **std_value =** **1.5811**

Table 10.11: Mean and standard deviation in MATLAB

- **Variance and covariance**: The **var** and **cov** functions compute variance and covariance of a dataset.

  Example 10.12: Variance and covariance in MATLAB:

```% Calculate the variance of a vector data = [1, 2, 3, 4, 5]; variance_value = var(data) % Calculate the covariance between two vectors x = [1, 2, 3]; y = [4, 5, 6]; covariance_matrix = cov(x, y) % Returns a 2x2 covariance matrix```	**Output:** **variance_value =** **2.5000** **covariance_matrix =** **1 1** **1 1**

Table 10.12: Variance and covariance in MATLAB

- **Correlation coefficient**: The coefficient of correlation between two datasets is calculated using the **corrcoef** function.

  Example 10.13: Correlation coefficient in MATLAB:

```% Calculate correlation coefficient between two vectors x = [1, 2, 3]; y = [4, 5, 6]; correlation_matrix = corrcoef(x, y) % Returns a 2x2 correlation matrix```	**Output:** **correlation_matrix =** **1 1** **1 1**

Table 10.13: Correlation coefficient calculation in MATLAB

- **Histograms**: A histogram, as seen in *Figure 10.1,* of a dataset is produced via the histogram function.

  Example 10.14: Histogram creation in MATLAB:

```
% Create a histogram of a vector
data = randn(1000, 1);  % Generate random data
histogram(data, 'BinWidth', 0.5);
xlabel('Value');
ylabel('Frequency');
title('Histogram of Random Data');
```

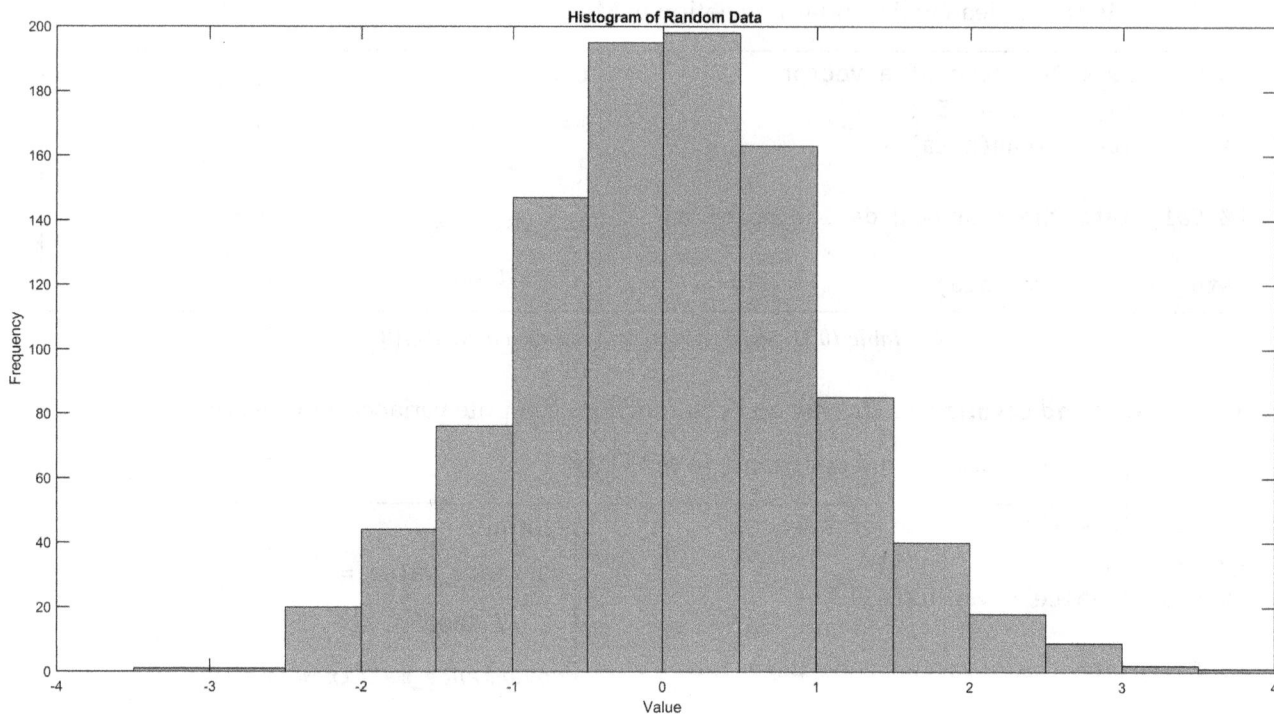

Figure 10.1: Histogram creation in MATLAB

10.1.3 Tables in MATLAB

A robust tool for storing and working with structured data is tables in MATLAB. Tables are suitable for datasets with data because they enable the use of labeled rows and columns:

- **Creating tables**: Table function may be utilized to construct a table.

Example 10.15: Creating a table in MATLAB:

| ```% Create a table with named variables
data = table([1; 2; 3], [4; 5; 6],

'VariableNames', {'Var1', 'Var2'})```	**Output:**
	data =
	
	  Var1 Var2
	
	  ____ ____
	
	   1 4
	   2 5
	   3 6

Table 10.14: Creating tables in MATLAB

- **Accessing table data**: Dot notation and indexing are two types to fetch particular columns or rows in a table.

Example 10.16: Accessing table data in MATLAB:

``matlab
data = table([1; 2; 3], [4; 5; 6],
'VariableNames', {'Var1', 'Var2'})
 	
% Access a specific column
var1_data = data.Var1
 	
% Access a specific row
row_data = data(2, :)
% Returns the second row
``
	Output:
	data =
	    Var1 Var2
	    ──── ────
	    1 4
	    2 5
	    3 6
	var1_data =
	    1
	    2
	    3
	row_data =
	    Var1 Var2
	    ──── ────
	    2 5

Table 10.15: Accessing table data in MATLAB

- **Adding and removing rows**: A table may have rows added or removed.

Example 10.17: Adding and removing rows in MATLAB:

``matlab
data = table([1; 2; 3], [4; 5; 6],
'VariableNames', {'Var1', 'Var2'})
 	
% Add a new row
new_row = {4, 7};
data = [data; new_row]
 	
% Remove the first row
data(1, :) = []
``
	Output:
	data =
	    Var1 Var2
	    ──── ────
	    1 4
	    2 5
	    3 6
	data =
	    Var1 Var2
	    ──── ────
	    1 4
	    2 5
	    3 6
	    4 7
	data =
	    Var1 Var2
	    ──── ────
	    2 5
	    3 6
	    4 7

Table 10.16: Adding and removing rows in MATLAB

- **Sorting tables**: A table may be sorted as per one or more columns.

  Example 10.18: Sorting table in MATLAB:

```data = table([21; 12; 13], [40; 5; 16], 'VariableNames', {'Var1', 'Var2'})``` ```% Sort a table by the 'Var1' column``` ```sorted_table = sortrows(data, 'Var1')```	Output: data = Var1 Var2 —— —— 21 40 12 5 13 16 sorted_table = Var1 Var2 —— —— 12 5 13 16 21 40

Table 10.17: Sorting tables in MATLAB

- **Filtering tables**: Rows in a table may be filtered as per the condition provided.

  Example 10.19: Filtering table in MATLAB:

```data = table([1; 0; 13], [40; 5; 16], 'VariableNames', {'Var1', 'Var2'})``` ```% Filter rows where 'Var1' is greater than 2``` ```filtered_table = data(data.Var1 > 2, :)```	Output: data = Var1 Var2 —— —— 1 40 0 5 13 16 filtered_table = Var1 Var2 —— —— 13 16

Table 10.18: Filtering tables in MATLAB

The statistical analysis and MATLAB data manipulation were discussed in this section. MATLAB is a useful tool for numerical calculation due to its built-in functions and matrix-based operations. Common activities, such as indexing, sorting, and filtering data, are authenticated by examples provided. Moreover, such examples explain how to compute statistical computations such as correlation coefficients, mean, and standard deviation.

In the following section, Python-based topics will be thoroughly discussed, with a focus on statistical analysis via Python tools and data manipulation using Pandas and NumPy.

10.2 Python-based concepts

Python is a useful language for programmers. Data analysis, machine learning, and scientific computing all widely use this language. Its strong library system, which consists of Pandas and NumPy, makes it a useful tool for statistical analysis and data analysis. In this section, we will methodically explore the features of Python with examples.

10.2.1 Data manipulation with Pandas and NumPy

Pandas and NumPy are two of the most popular Python packages for data manipulation. NumPy focuses on array-based numerical operations. High-level data structures like DataFrames and Series are suggested by Pandas. Let us look at them in detail:

- **Creating DataFrames and arrays:** In Python, we can create DataFrames using libraries like pandas (**pd.DataFrame()**), while arrays can be created using NumPy (**np.array()**). These are fundamental structures for data manipulation and analysis.

  o **Creating a DataFrame with Pandas**: A labeled data structure containing columns of possibly many types is called a DataFrame. It is comparable to a MATLAB table.

    Example 10.20: Creating a DataFrame with Pandas in Python:

import pandas as pd
 	
# Create a DataFrame 	
data = {'Var1': [1, 2, 3], 'Var2': [4, 5, 6]}
df = pd.DataFrame(data)
 	
print(df)
	Output:
	
	   Var1 Var2
	0 1 4
	1 2 5
	2 3 6

Table 10.19: Creating a DataFrame with Pandas in Python

  o **Creating an array with NumPy:** NumPy arrays are similar to MATLAB matrices and are optimized for numerical computations.

    Example 10.21: Creating an array with NumPy in Python:

import numpy as np
 	
# Create a 3x3 matrix 	
matrix = np.array([[1, 2, 3], [4, 5, 6], [7, 8, 9]])
 	
print(matrix)
	Output:
	[[1 2 3]
	[4 5 6]
	[7 8 9]]

Table 10.20: Creating an array with NumPy in Python

- **Indexing and slicing**: Indexing and slicing in Pandas allow us to access specific rows, columns, or subsets of data using methods like **loc[]** (label-based) and **iloc[]** (position-based). Boolean indexing further enables filtering data based on conditions for efficient data manipulation.

  o **Indexing in Pandas**: Pandas uses **0-based indexing**. You may access specific rows, columns, or elements using **.iloc** (integer-based) or **.loc** (label-based).

Example 10.22: Indexing and slicing in Python:

``python
# Access the element in the 2nd row, 1st column 	
element = df.iloc[1, 0]
print(element)
 	
# Access the 'Var1' column 	
var1_data = df['Var1']
print(var1_data)
 	
# Access rows where 'Var1' is greater than 1 	
filtered_rows = df[df['Var1'] > 1]
print(filtered_rows)
``
	Output:
	
	2
	
	0 1
	1 2
	2 3
	Name: Var1, dtype: int64
	
	    Var1 Var2
	1 2 5
	2 3 6

Table 10.21: Indexing in Pandas

Note: When transitioning between MATLAB and Python for data analysis, it is important to note the key differences in indexing and data inspection practices. MATLAB uses a 1-based indexing system, meaning arrays and matrices start from index 1, whereas Python, including libraries like NumPy and pandas, follows a 0-based indexing system. This distinction can affect how data is accessed and manipulated. Additionally, for quick data overview and statistical summaries, Python offers user-friendly functions such as `df.head()` and `df.describe()` in the pandas library.

o **Slicing in NumPy**: NumPy arrays may be sliced like MATLAB matrices.

Example 10.23: Slicing in NumPy:

``python
matrix = np.array([[1, 2, 3], [4, 5, 6], [7, 8, 9]])
# Slice the first two rows and all columns 	
sliced_matrix = matrix[0:2, :]
print(sliced_matrix)
# Slice the last two columns 	
sliced_columns = matrix[:, 1:3]
print(sliced_columns)
``
	Output:
	[[1 2 3]
	
	 [4 5 6]]
	
	[[2 3]
	
	 [5 6]
	
	 [8 9]]

Table 10.22: Slicing in NumPy

o **Reshaping arrays**: NumPy provides the reshape function to change the dimensions of an array.

Example 10.24: Reshaping arrays in Python:

``python
matrix = np.array([[1, 2, 3], [4, 5, 6], [7, 8, 9]])
# Reshape a 3x3 matrix into a 1x9 vector 	
reshaped_vector = matrix.reshape(1, 9)
print(reshaped_vector)
# Reshape a row vector into a 2x3 matrix 	
reshaped_matrix = np.array([1, 2, 3, 4, 5, 6]).
reshape(2, 3)
print(reshaped_matrix)
``
	Output:
	[[1 2 3 4 5 6 7 8 9]]
	
	[[1 2 3]
	
	 [4 5 6]]

Table 10.23: Reshaping arrays in Python

- **Concatenation**: You may concatenate arrays and DataFrames using NumPy and Pandas functions.

  o **Concatenation in NumPy**: Concatenation in NumPy (using **np.concatenate()**, **np.vstack()**, or **np.hstack()**) allows us to combine arrays along specified axes. It is useful for merging datasets or expanding arrays while maintaining numerical efficiency.

  Example 10.25: Concatenation in NumPy:

``
# Horizontal concatenation 	
A = np.array([[1, 2], [3, 4]])
B = np.array([[5, 6], [7, 8]])
C = np.hstack((A, B))
print(C)
# Vertical concatenation 	
D = np.vstack((A, B))
print(D)
``
	Output:
	`[[1 2 5 6]`
	` [3 4 7 8]]`
	`[[1 2]`
	` [3 4]`
	` [5 6]`
	` [7 8]]`

Table 10.24: Concatenation in NumPy

  o **Concatenation in Pandas**: Concatenation in Pandas (using **pd.concat()**) allows us to combine DataFrames or Series along rows (axis = 0) or columns (axis = 1). It preserves indices and can handle different shapes, making it ideal for merging datasets with similar structures.

  Example 10.26: Concatenation in Pandas:

``
# Concatenate two DataFrames vertically 	
df1 = pd.DataFrame({'Var1': [1, 2], 'Var2': [3, 4]})
df2 = pd.DataFrame({'Var1': [5, 6], 'Var2': [7, 8]})
df_concat = pd.concat([df1, df2], axis=0) # axis=0 for vertical
print(df_concat)
``
	Output:
	`   Var1  Var2`
	`0    1     3`
	`1    2     4`
	`0    5     7`
	`1    6     8`

Table 10.25: Concatenation in Pandas

- **Logical indexing**: Logical indexing helps in filtering data based on specified conditions.

  o **Logical indexing in Pandas**: Logical indexing in Pandas is useful to filter data using Boolean conditions, such as **df[df['column'] > 5]** or **df.query('column == "value"')**. This provides a flexible way to select subsets of data based on complex conditions.

  Example 10.27: Logical indexing in Pandas:

``
# Filter rows where 'Var1' is greater than 2 	
filtered_df = df[df['Var1'] > 2]
print(filtered_df)
``
	Output:
	`   Var1  Var2`
	`2    3     6`

Table 10.26: Logical indexing in Pandas

  o **Logical indexing in NumPy**: Logical indexing in NumPy is useful to filter arrays using Boolean conditions, like **arr[arr > 5]** or combining masks with **&** (and), **|** (or). This returns elements that meet the specified criteria, enabling efficient conditional selection.

Example 10.28: Logical indexing in NumPy:

``
# Find elements greater than 3 in a matrix 	
condition = matrix > 3
filtered_elements = matrix[condition]
print(filtered_elements)
``
	Output:
	[4 5 6 7 8 9]

Table 10.27: Logical indexing in NumPy

- **Sorting**: Pandas and NumPy provide functions for sorting data.

  o **Sorting in Pandas**: Sorting in Pandas is done using **df.sort_values()** for column-based sorting or **df.sort_index()** for index-based ordering. We can sort in ascending/descending order and even handle missing data placement.

  Example 10.29: Sorting in Pandas:

``
# Sort a DataFrame by the 'Var1' column 	
sorted_df=df.sort_values(by='Var1',
ascending=False)
print(sorted_df)
``
	Output:
	    Var1 Var2
	2 3 6
	1 2 5
	0 1 4

Table 10.28: Sorting in Pandas

  o **Sorting in NumPy:** Sorting in NumPy is performed using **np.sort()** for returning a sorted copy of an array, or **ndarray.sort()** for in-place sorting. We can also use **np.argsort()** to get the indices that would sort the array, enabling indirect sorting of related data.

  Example 10.30: Sorting in NumPy:

``
matrix = np.array([[11, 21, 3], [14, 15, 6], [70, 18, 91]])
# Sort a matrix along columns 	
sorted_matrix = np.sort(matrix, axis=0)
# Sorts each column 	
print(sorted_matrix)
``
	Output:
	[[11 15 3]
	 [14 18 6]
	 [70 21 91]]

Table 10.29: Sorting in NumPy

10.2.2 Statistical analysis in Python

NumPy and Pandas libraries in Python provide a wide range of functions regarding statistical analysis. Let us look at them in detail:

- **Mean and standard deviation**: In NumPy, the mean is calculated using **np.mean()** and the standard deviation with **np.std()**, which operate on arrays and support axis-based computations. Missing values (NaN) can be handled with **np.nanmean()** and **np.nanstd()** to ignore them automatically.

  o **Mean and standard deviation in NumPy**: NumPy provides efficient functions like **np.mean()** and **np.std()** to calculate the mean and standard deviation of arrays. These operations can be performed along specific axes for multi-dimensional data, making statistical analysis simple and fast.

Example 10.31: Mean and standard deviation in NumPy:

``# Calculate the mean of a vector
data = np.array([1, 2, 3, 4, 5])
mean_value = np.mean(data)
print(mean_value)
# Calculate the standard deviation of a vector
std_value = np.std(data)
print(std_value)```	**Output:** **3.0** **1.4142135623730951**

Table 10.30: Mean and standard deviation in NumPy

o **Mean and standard deviation in Pandas**: In Pandas, we can compute the mean and standard deviation using **df.mean()** and **df.std()**, which automatically exclude missing values (NaN) by default. These methods work across rows or columns (using axis parameter) for quick statistical analysis.

Example 10.32: Mean and standard deviation in Pandas:

``# Calculate the mean and standard deviation of a
DataFrame column
mean_value = df['Var1'].mean()
print(mean_value)
std_value = df['Var1'].std()
print(std_value)```	**Output:** **2.0** **1.0**

Table 10.31: Mean and standard deviation in Pandas

- **Variance and covariance**: NumPy provides **np.var()** for variance and **np.cov()** for covariance calculations, essential for analyzing data dispersion and relationships. These functions support axis-based computations and weighting options for statistical modeling.

  o **Variance and covariance in NumPy:**

     Example 10.33: Variance and covariance in NumPy:

``# Calculate the variance of a vector
variance_value = np.var(data)
print(variance_value)
# Calculate the covariance between two vectors
x = np.array([1, 2, 3])
y = np.array([4, 5, 6])
covariance_matrix = np.cov(x, y)
# Returns a 2x2 covariance matrix
print(covariance_matrix)```	**Output:** **2.0** **[[1. 1.]** **[1. 1.]]**

Table 10.32: Variance and covariance in NumPy

o **Covariance in Pandas**: In Pandas, we can compute covariance between columns using **df.cov()**, which generates a covariance matrix showing how variables vary together. For Series, **series1.cov**(series2) calculates their pairwise covariance directly.

Example 10.34: Covariance in Pandas:

# Calculate the covariance between two DataFrame columns 	
covariance_value = df['Var1'].cov(df['Var2'])
print(covariance_value)
	Output:
	
	1.0

Table 10.33: Covariance in Pandas

- **Correlation coefficient:**

  o **Correlation coefficient in NumPy**: In NumPy, we can calculate the Pearson correlation coefficient using **np.corrcoef()**, which returns a correlation matrix showing linear relationships between arrays or matrix columns.

  Example 10.35: Correlation coefficient in NumPy:

# Calculate the correlation coefficent between two vectors 	
correlation_matrix = np.corrcoef(x, y)
# Returns a 2x2 correlation matrix 	
print(correlation_matrix)
	Output:
	[[1. 1.]
	 [1. 1.]]

Table 10.34: Correlation Coefficient in NumPy

  o **Correlation coefficient in Pandas:** In Pandas, you can compute correlation coefficients using **df.corr()** (for a full correlation matrix) or **series1.corr**(series2) for pairwise correlation.

  Example 10.36: Correlation coefficient in Pandas:

# Calculate the correlation between two DataFrame columns 	
correlation_value = df['Var1'].corr(df['Var2'])
print(correlation_value)
	Output:
	1.0

Table 10.35: Correlation coefficient in Pandas

- **Histograms**: Histograms may be easily created using Matplotlib, which is a popular plotting library in Python.

Example 10.37: Histogram creation

```
import matplotlib.pyplot as plt


# Create a histogram of a vector
data = np.random.randn(1000)  # Generate random data
plt.hist(data, bins=30, edgecolor='black')
plt.xlabel('Value')
plt.ylabel('Frequency')
plt.title('Histogram of Random Data')
plt.show()
```

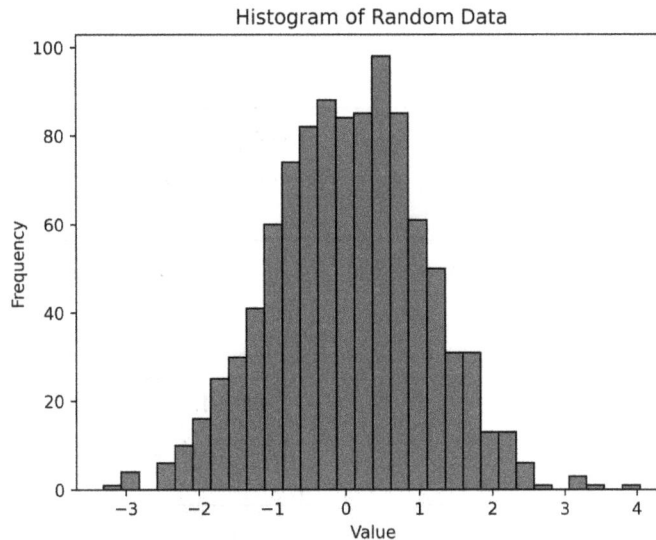

Figure 10.2*: Histogram creation in Python*

This section focused on statistical analysis and data manipulation features in Python with NumPy and Pandas. Python's tools make it useful to work with numerical and organized data. The examples demonstrated indexing, reshaping, sorting, and filtering of data. The calculation of statistical measures like mean, standard deviation, and correlation coefficients is also discussed.

In the next section, we will compare MATLAB and Python codes with an analysis of their syntax and functionality.

10.3 Comparative study via MATLAB and Python codes

Let us look at some facets of comparisons in this section.

10.3.1 Data manipulation

Data manipulation is a basic aspect of scientific computing and data analysis. MATLAB and Python offer powerful tools for this purpose, though with different approaches.

MATLAB is a high-performance numerical computing environment optimized for matrix operations. It provides built-in functions for data filtering, sorting, and transformation. MATLAB's syntax is mainly intuitive for linear algebra tasks, such as matrix multiplication (A*B) or solving systems of equations (A\b). The language also includes toolboxes for specialized tasks like signal processing and statistical analysis.

Python, on the other hand, is an open-source, general-purpose language with extensive libraries for data manipulation. Key libraries include:

- **NumPy**: It is optimized for numerical operations, offering array-based computations similar to MATLAB.

- **Pandas**: It provides DataFrame structures for tabular data, enabling SQL-like operations (filtering, grouping, merging).

- **SciPy**: It extends NumPy with advanced mathematical and statistical functions.

Python's flexibility makes it better for integrating data analysis with web scraping, machine learning (via scikit-learn), and automation tasks. While MATLAB excels in engineering and simulation, Python dominates in data science due to its ecosystem and scalability.

Example 10.38: Create a row vector in MATLAB and Python.

MATLAB:

`row_vector = [1, 2, 3, 4, 5]`	Output:
	
	`row_vector =`
	
	    `1    2    3    4    5`

Table 10.36: Creation of a row vector in MATLAB

Python (NumPy):

`import numpy as np`
`row_vector = np.array([1, 2, 3, 4, 5])`
`print(row_vector)`
	Output:
	
	`[1 2 3 4 5]`

Table 10.37: Creation of a row vector in Python

Example 10.39: Create a column vector in MATLAB and Python.

MATLAB:

`column_vector = [1; 2; 3; 4; 5]`	Output:
	
	`column_vector =`
	
	    `1`
	    `2`
	    `3`
	    `4`
	    `5`

Table 10.38: Creation of a column vector in MATLAB

Python (NumPy):

`column_vector = np.array([[1], [2], [3],`
`[4], [5]])`
`print(column_vector)`
	Output:
	
	`[[1]`
	`[2]`
	`[3]`
	`[4]`
	`[5]]`

Table 10.39: Creation of a column vector in Python

Example 10.40: Create a 3x3 matrix in MATLAB and Python.

MATLAB:

`matrix = [1, 2, 3; 4, 5, 6; 7, 8, 9]`	Output:
	
	`matrix =`
	
	    `1    2    3`
	    `4    5    6`
	    `7    8    9`

Table 10.40: Creation of a 3x3 matrix in MATLAB

Python (NumPy):

``` matrix = np.array([[1, 2, 3], [4, 5, 6], [7, 8, 9]]) print(matrix) ```	**Output:** [[1 2 3] [4 5 6] [7 8 9]]

Table 10.41: Creation of a 3x3 matrix in Python

Example 10.41: Access the element in the 2nd row, 3rd column of a matrix in MATLAB and Python.

MATLAB:

``
matrix = [1, 2, 3; 4, 5, 6; 7, 8, 9]
element = matrix(2, 3)
``
	Output:
	matrix =
	
	   1 2 3
	   4 5 6
	   7 8 9
	element =
	   6

Table 10.42: Accessing specific element in MATLAB

Python (NumPy):

``` matrix = np.array([[1, 2, 3], [4, 5, 6], [7, 8, 9]]) element = matrix[1, 2] print(element) ```	**Output:** 6

Table 10.43: Accessing specific element in Python

Example 10.42: Slice the first two rows of a matrix in MATLAB and Python.

MATLAB:

``
matrix = [1, 2, 3; 4, 5, 6; 7, 8, 9]
sliced_matrix = matrix(1:2, :)
``
	Output:
	matrix =
	
	   1 2 3
	   4 5 6
	   7 8 9
	sliced_matrix =
	   1 2 3
	   4 5 6

Table 10.44: Slicing of rows in MATLAB

Python (NumPy):

```matrix = np.array([[1, 2, 3], [4, 5, 6], [7, 8, 9]])```
 	
```sliced_matrix = matrix[0:2, :]```
```print(sliced_matrix)```
	Output:
	[[1 2 3]
	
	 [4 5 6]]

Table 10.45: Slicing of rows in Python

Example 10.43: Reshape a 3×3 matrix into a 1×9 vector in MATLAB and Python.

MATLAB:

```matrix = [1, 2, 3; 4, 5, 6; 7, 8, 9]```
```reshaped_vector = reshape(matrix, 1, 9)```
	Output:
	matrix =
	
	    1 2 3
	    4 5 6
	    7 8 9
	reshaped_vector =
	    1 4 7 2 5 8
	3 6 9

Table 10.46: Reshaping of matrix in MATLAB

Python (NumPy):

```matrix = np.array([[1, 2, 3], [4, 5, 6], [7, 8, 9]])```
```reshaped_vector = matrix.reshape(1, 9)```
```print(reshaped_vector)```
	Output:
	[[1 2 3 4 5 6 7 8 9]]

Table 10.47: Reshaping of matrix in Python

Example 10.44: Concatenate two matrices vertically in MATLAB and Python.

MATLAB:

```A = [1 2; 3 4]```
```B = [5 6; 7 8]```
```C = [A; B] % Vertical concatenation```
	Output:
	A =
	    1 2
	    3 4
	B =
	    5 6
	    7 8
	C =
	    1 2
	    3 4
	    5 6
	    7 8

Table 10.48: Concatenation of matrices vertically in MATLAB

Python (NumPy):

A = np.array([[1, 2], [3, 4]])
B = np.array([[5, 6], [7, 8]])
C = np.vstack((A, B)) # Vertical concatenation
print(C)
	Output:
	[[1 2]
	
	[3 4]
	
	[5 6]
	
	[7 8]]

Table 10.49: Concatenation of matrices vertically in Python

Example 10.45: Concatenate two matrices horizontally in MATLAB and Python.

MATLAB:

A = [1 2; 3 4]
B = [5 6; 7 8]
C = [A, B] % Horizontal concatenation
	Output:
	A =
	    1 2
	    3 4
	B =
	    5 6
	    7 8
	C =
	    1 2 5 6
	    3 4 7 8

Table 10.50: Concatenation of matrices horizontally in MATLAB

Python (NumPy):

A = np.array([[1, 2], [3, 4]])
B = np.array([[5, 6], [7, 8]])
C = np.hstack((A, B))
# Horizontal concatenation 	
print(C)
	Output:
	[[1 2 5 6]
	
	[3 4 7 8]]

Table 10.51: Concatenation of matrices horizontally in Python

Example 10.46: Filter elements greater than 3 in a matrix in MATLAB and Python.

MATLAB:

matrix = [1 2 3; 4 5 6; 5 1 2]
filtered_elements = matrix(matrix > 3)
	Output:
	matrix =
	    1 2 3
	    4 5 6
	    5 1 2
	filtered_elements =
	    4
	    5
	    5
	    6

Table 10.52: Filtering elements MATLAB code

Python (NumPy):

```matrix = np.array([[1, 2, 3], [4, 5, 6], [7, 8, 9]]) filtered_elements = matrix[matrix > 3] print(filtered_elements)```	Output: [4 5 6 7 8 9]

Table 10.53: Filtering elements Python code

Example 10.47: Sort a vector in ascending order in MATLAB and Python.

MATLAB:

```row_vector = [12 11 2 1 12 23] sorted_vector = sort(row_vector)```	Output:
	row_vector =
	   12 11 2 1 12 23
	sorted_vector =
	    1 2 11 12 12 23

Table 10.54: Sorting in MATLAB

Python (NumPy):

```row_vector = np.array([11, 2, 13, 40, 5]) sorted_vector = np.sort(row_vector) print(sorted_vector)```	**Output:** [2 5 11 13 40]

Table 10.55: Sorting in Python

10.3.2 Statistical functions

MATLAB and Python offer useful tools for statistical analysis, but with distinct advantages. MATLAB's statistics and machine learning toolbox provides concise, matrix-oriented functions for descriptive stats (**mean()**, **std()**), hypothesis testing (**ttest**, **anova1**), and regression (**fitlm**), which is ideal for engineers and interactive workflows. Python, provides open-source libraries like SciPy (**scipy.stats**), Pandas (**df.describe()**, **corr()**), and **StatsModels,** which excels in flexibility, handling real-world data (missing values, mixed types), and integrating with machine learning (scikit-learn) or visualization (Seaborn). While MATLAB simplifies matrix math and includes GUI tools, Python provides free access, scalability, and a broader ecosystem, which make it dominant in data science.

Example 10.48: Calculate the mean of a vector in MATLAB and Python.

MATLAB:

```data = [10 20 30 40 50] mean_value = mean(data)```	Output:
	data =
	   10 20 30 40 50
	mean_value =
	   30

Table 10.56: Mean of a vector in MATLAB

Python (NumPy):

``` data = np.array([11, 2, 13, 40, 5]) mean_value = np.mean(data) print(mean_value) ```	**Output:** **14.2**

Table 10.57: Mean of a vector in Python

Example 10.49: Calculate the standard deviation of a vector in MATLAB and Python.

MATLAB:

``
data = [10 20 30 40 50]
std_value = std(data)
``
	Output:
	data =
	
	    10 20 30 40 50
	
	std_value =
	
	        15.8114

Table 10.58: Standard deviation of a vector in MATLAB

Python (NumPy):

``` data = np.array([11, 2, 13, 40, 5]) std_value = np.std(data) print(std_value) ```	**Output:** **13.49666625504239**

Table 10.59: Standard deviation of a vector in Python

Example 10.50: Calculate the variance of a vector in MATLAB and Python.

MATLAB:

``
data = [10 20 30 40 50]
variance_value = var(data)
``
	Output:
	data =
	
	    10 20 30 40 50
	
	variance_value =
	
	        250

Table 10.60: Variance of a vector in MATLAB

Python (NumPy):

``` data = np.array([11, 2, 13, 40, 5]) variance_value = np.var(data) print(variance_value) ```	**Output:** **182.16**

Table 10.61: Variance of a vector in Python

Example 10.51: Calculate the correlation coefficient between two vectors in MATLAB and Python.

MATLAB:

``matlab
x = [1; 2];
y = [3; 4];
corr_coeff = corrcoef(x, y) % Returns a 2x2 matrix
``
	Output:
	corr_coeff =
	    1.0000 1.0000
	    1.0000 1.0000

Table 10.62: Correlation coefficient between two vectors in MATLAB

Python (NumPy):

``python
import numpy as np
 	
# Define column vectors 	
x = np.array([[1], [2]]) # 2x1
y = np.array([[3], [4]]) # 2x1
 	
# Convert to 1D arrays 	
corr_coeff = np.corrcoef(x.flatten(), y.flatten())
 	
# Print the result 	
print("Correlation coefficient matrix:\n", corr_coeff)
``
	Output:
	Correlation coefficient matrix:
	[[1. 1.]
	
	[1. 1.]]

Table 10.63: Correlation coefficient between two vectors in Python

Example 10.52: Calculate the covariance between two vectors in MATLAB and Python.

MATLAB:

``matlab
x = [1; 2];
y = [3; 4];
covariance_matrix = cov(x, y) % Returns a 2x2 matrix
``
	Output:
	covariance_matrix =
	    0.5000 0.5000
	    0.5000 0.5000

Table 10.64: Covariance between two vectors in MATLAB

Python (NumPy):

``python
import numpy as np
 	
# Define column vectors 	
x = np.array([[1], [2]]) # 2x1
y = np.array([[3], [4]]) # 2x1
 	
# Convert to 1D arrays before computing covariance 	
covariance_matrix = np.cov(x.flatten(), y.flatten())
 	
# Print the covariance matrix 	
print("Covariance matrix:\n", covariance_matrix)
``
	Output:
	Covariance matrix:
	[[0.5 0.5]
	
	[0.5 0.5]]

Table 10.65: Covariance between two vectors in Python

10.3.3 Working with tables/DataFrames

MATLAB's table and Python's DataFrame (from Pandas) are essential structures for handling tabular data, but differ in functionality and flexibility. MATLAB's table organizes data with named columns, supports mixed data types, and integrates well with MATLAB's statistical tools which enable operations like **summary()** or filtering with logical indexing. However, it lacks some advanced data manipulation features. Whereas Python's Pandas DataFrame is more versatile and offers operations such as **groupby()**, **pivot_table()**, and seamless handling of missing data (**dropna()**, **fillna()**). It also integrates with Python's broader ecosystem (NumPy, Scikit-learn) for machine learning and visualization.

Example 10.53: Create a table in MATLAB and a DataFrame in Python.

MATLAB:

`data = table([1; 2; 3], [4; 5; 6], 'VariableNames', {'Var1', 'Var2'})`	Output:
	data =
	    Var1 Var2
	    ____ ____
	    1 4
	    2 5
	    3 6

Table 10.66: Creation of a table in MATLAB

Python (Pandas):

`import pandas as pd`
`data = pd.DataFrame({'Var1': [1, 2, 3], 'Var2': [4, 5, 6]})`
`print(data)`
	Output:
	    Var1 Var2
	0 1 4
	1 2 5
	2 3 6

Table 10.67: Creation of DataFrame in Python

Example 10.54: Access a specific column in a table/DataFrame in MATLAB and Python.

MATLAB:

`data = table([1; 2; 3], [4; 5; 6], 'VariableNames', {'Var1', 'Var2'})`
`var1_data = data.Var1`
	Output:
	data =
	    Var1 Var2
	    ____ ____
	    1 4
	    2 5
	    3 6
	var1_data =
	    1
	    2
	    3

Table 10.68: Accessing a specific column in a table in MATLAB

Python (Pandas):

var1_data = data['Var1'] print(var1_data)	Output: 0 1 1 2 2 3 Name: Var1, dtype: int64

Table 10.69: Access a specific column in a DataFrame in Python

Example 10.55: Filter rows where a column's value is greater than 2 in MATLAB and Python.

MATLAB:

data = table([1; 2; 3], [4; 5; 6],
'VariableNames', {'Var1', 'Var2'})
filtered_table = data(data.Var1 > 2, :)
	Output:
	data =
	    Var1 Var2
	    ____ ____
	
	    1 4
	    2 5
	    3 6
	filtered_table =
	    Var1 Var2
	    ____ ____
	
	    3 6

Table 10.70: Filtering of rows with specific condition in MATLAB

Python (Pandas):

filtered_df = data[data['Var1'] > 2] print(filtered_df)	Output: Var1 Var2 2 3 6

Table 10.71: Filtering of rows with specific condition in Python

Example 10.56: Sort a table/DataFrame by a specific column in MATLAB and Python.

MATLAB:

data = table([11; 2; 13], [14; 50; 16],
'VariableNames', {'Var1', 'Var2'})
sorted_table = sortrows(data, 'Var1')
	Output:
	data =
	    Var1 Var2
	    ____ ____
	
	    11 14
	     2 50
	    13 16
	sorted_table =
	    Var1 Var2
	    ____ ____
	
	     2 50
	    11 14
	    13 16

Table 10.72: Sorting a table by a specific column in MATLAB

Python (Pandas):

sorted_df = data.sort_values(by='Var1') print(sorted_df)	Output: 　　Var1　Var2 0　　1　　4 1　　2　　5 2　　3　　6

Table 10.73: Sorting a DataFrame by a specific column in Python

Example 10.57: Add a new row to a table/DataFrame in MATLAB and Python.

MATLAB:

data = table([11; 2; 13], [14; 50; 16], 'VariableNames', {'Var1', 'Var2'}) new_row = {4, 7} data = [data; new_row]	Output: data = 　　Var1　　Var2 　　────　　──── 　　11　　14 　　2　　50 　　13　　16 new_row = 　[4]　　[7] data = 　　Var1　　Var2 　　────　　──── 　　11　　14 　　2　　50 　　13　　16 　　4　　7

Table 10.74: Addition of a new row to a table in MATLAB

Python (Pandas):

new_row = pd.DataFrame({'Var1': [4], 'Var2': [7]}) data = pd.concat([data, new_row], ignore_index=True) print(data)	Output: 　　Var1　Var2 0　　1　　4 1　　2　　5 2　　3　　6 3　　4　　7

Table 10.75: Addition of a new row to a DataFrame in Python

10.3.4 Advanced topics

In this section, some of the advanced topics are discussed regarding the languages of MATLAB and Python. Some topics discussed are cumulative sum, element-wise product, dot product, eigenvalues of a matrix, and inverse of a matrix. A comparative study of mentioned topics is provided via examples discussion. Python's strength lies in its object-oriented flexibility and integration with deep learning frameworks, while MATLAB excels in streamlined syntax for linear algebra tasks. Performance varies by operation; MATLAB often optimizes matrix math better for small-to-medium datasets, while Python scales efficiently with large data via NumPy's vectorization. These languages provide robust solutions, with the choice depending on specific use cases and ecosystem requirements.

Example 10.58: Calculate the cumulative sum of a vector in MATLAB and Python.

MATLAB:

```data = [10 20 30 40 50]```
```cumsum_vector = cumsum(data)```
	Output:
	data =
	    10 20 30 40 50
	cumsum_vector =
	    10 30 60 100 150

Table 10.76: Cumulative sum of a vector in MATLAB

Python (NumPy):

```data = np.array([10, 20, 30, 40, 50])```
```cumsum_vector = np.cumsum(data)```
```print(cumsum_vector)```
	Output:
	[10 30 60 100 150]

Table 10.77: Cumulative sum of a vector in Python

Example 10.59: Calculate the element-wise product of two vectors in MATLAB and Python.

MATLAB:

```x = [1 2];```
```y = [3 4];```
```elementwise_product = x .* y```
```% Element-wise multiplication```
	Output:
	elementwise_product =
	    3 8

Table 10.78: Element-wise product of two vectors in MATLAB

Python (NumPy):

```x = np.array([[1, 2]]) # Explicit 1x2 row vector```
```y = np.array([[3, 4]]) # Explicit 1x2 row vector```
```elementwise_product = np.multiply(x, y)```
```# Element-wise multiplication```
```print(elementwise_product)```
	Output:
	[[3 8]]

Table 10.79: Element-wise product of two vectors in Python

Example 10.60: Calculate the dot product of two vectors in MATLAB and Python.

MATLAB:

```x = [1 2];```
```y = [3 4];```
```dot_product = dot(x, y)```
	Output:
	dot_product =
	    11

Table 10.80: Dot product of two vectors in MATLAB

Python (NumPy):

```
import numpy as np

# Define row vectors
x = np.array([[1, 2]])  # 1x2
y = np.array([[3, 4]])  # 1x2

# Convert y to a column vector (2x1)
y_column = y.T  # Transpose y

# Now, perform dot product
dot_product = np.dot(x, y_column)

print("Dot product:\n", dot_product)
```

Output:
Dot product:
 [[11]]

Table 10.81: Dot product of two vectors in Python

Example 10.61: Calculate the eigenvalues of a matrix in MATLAB and Python.

MATLAB:

```
matrix = [1 2; 3 4];
eigenvalues = eig(matrix)
% Returns eigenvalues
```

Output:
eigenvalues =
    -0.3723
     5.3723

Table 10.82: Eigenvalues of a matrix in MATLAB

Python (NumPy):

```
matrix = np.array([[1, 2],
                   [3, 4]])
eigenvalues = np.linalg.eigvals(matrix)
# Returns eigenvalues
print(eigenvalues)
```

Output:
[-0.37228132 5.37228132]

Table 10.83: Eigenvalues of a matrix in Python

Example 10.62: Calculate the inverse of a matrix in MATLAB and Python.

MATLAB:

```
matrix = [1 2; 3 4];
inverse_matrix = inv(matrix)
% Returns inverse
```

Output:
inverse_matrix =
    -2.0000   1.0000
     1.5000   -0.5000

Table 10.84: Inverse of a matrix in MATLAB

Python (NumPy):

```
matrix = np.array([[1, 2],
                   [3, 4]])

inverse_matrix = np.linalg.inv(matrix)
# Returns inverse
print(inverse_matrix)
```

Output:
```
[[-2.   1. ]
 [ 1.5 -0.5]]
```

Table 10.85: Inverse of a matrix in Python

10.3.5 Visualization

This section provides some examples regarding the visualization in MATLAB and Python. A comparative study is provided via the MATLAB and Python codes, as data visualization is a critical component of data analysis. MATLAB and Python offer useful tools to create insightful plots, though with different approaches. MATLAB provides a user-friendly, integrated environment for visualization with high-level plotting functions like **plot()**, **scatter()**, and **surf()** for 2D and 3D graphics. Its syntax is concise and meant for quick visualization of numerical data, which makes it ideal for engineers and scientists. MATLAB also includes interactive tools for customizing plots and supports specialized plots like histograms (**histogram()**), boxplots (**boxplot()**), and contour plots (**contour()**).

Python leverages open-source libraries like Matplotlib, Seaborn, and Plotly to deliver a highly customizable and extensible visualization framework. Matplotlib, the foundation for many Python plotting libraries, provides MATLAB-like syntax with functions such as **plt.plot()** and **plt.scatter()**, while also enabling intricate customization for advanced users. Seaborn builds on Matplotlib to offer high-level statistical visualizations (e.g., violin plots, pair plots) with minimal code, and Plotly adds interactivity for web-based charts.

Example 10.63: Plot a line graph, shown in *Figures 10.3* and *10.4*, in MATLAB and Python.

MATLAB:

```
x = [1 2 3 4 5 6 7 8 9 10];
y = 2*x;
plot(x, y);
xlabel('X-axis');
ylabel('Y-axis');
title('Line Plot');
```

Table 10.86: Line graph code in MATLAB

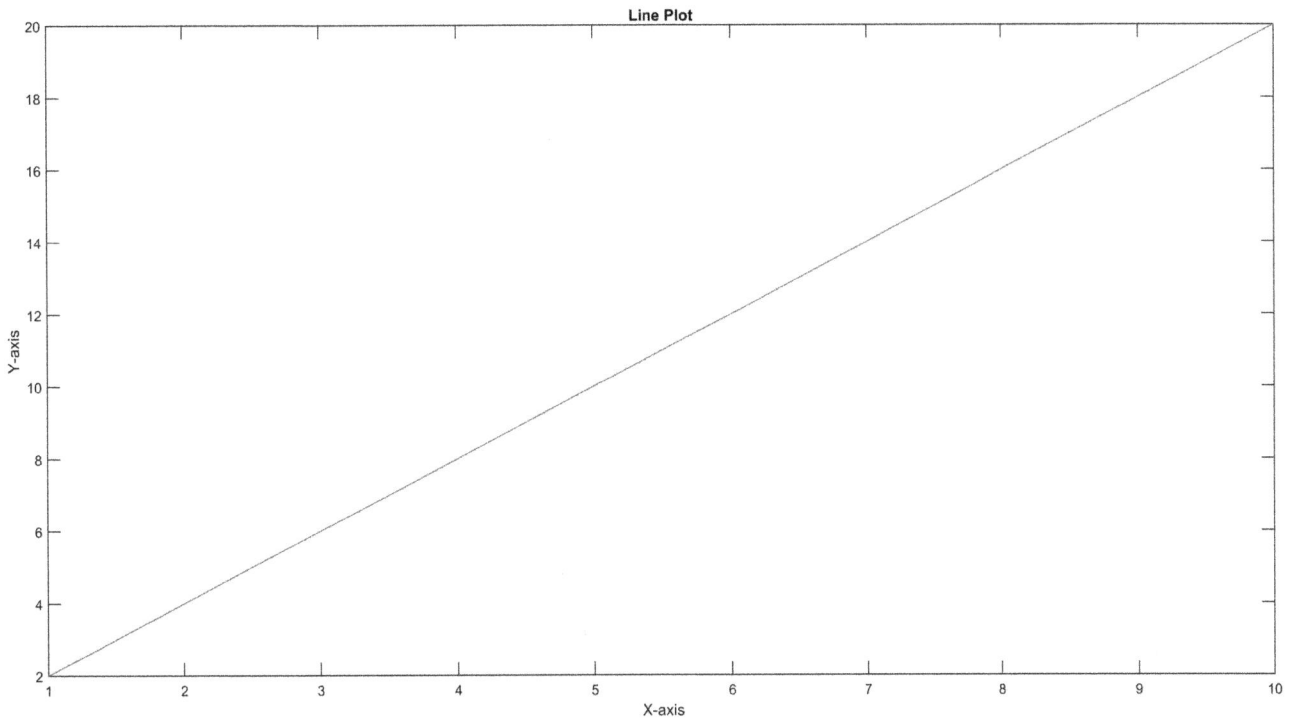

Figure 10.3: Line graph in MATLAB

Python (Matplotlib):

```
import matplotlib.pyplot as plt
x = np.array([1, 2, 3, 4, 5, 6, 7, 8, 9, 10])   # Define x as a NumPy array
y = 2 * x
plt.plot(x, y)
plt.xlabel('X-axis')
plt.ylabel('Y-axis')
plt.title('Line Plot')
plt.show()
```

Table 10.87: Line graph code in Python

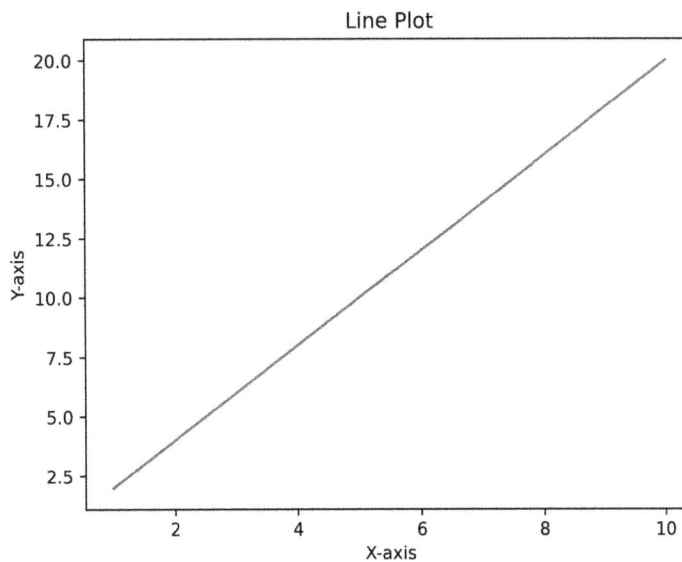

Figure 10.4: Line graph in Python

Example 10.64: Create a histogram, as shown in *Figures 10.5* and *10.6* in MATLAB and Python.

MATLAB:

```
data = [10 20 30 40 50 60 70 80]
histogram(data, 'BinWidth', 0.5);
xlabel('Value');
ylabel('Frequency');
title('Histogram');
```

Table 10.88: Histogram code in MATLAB

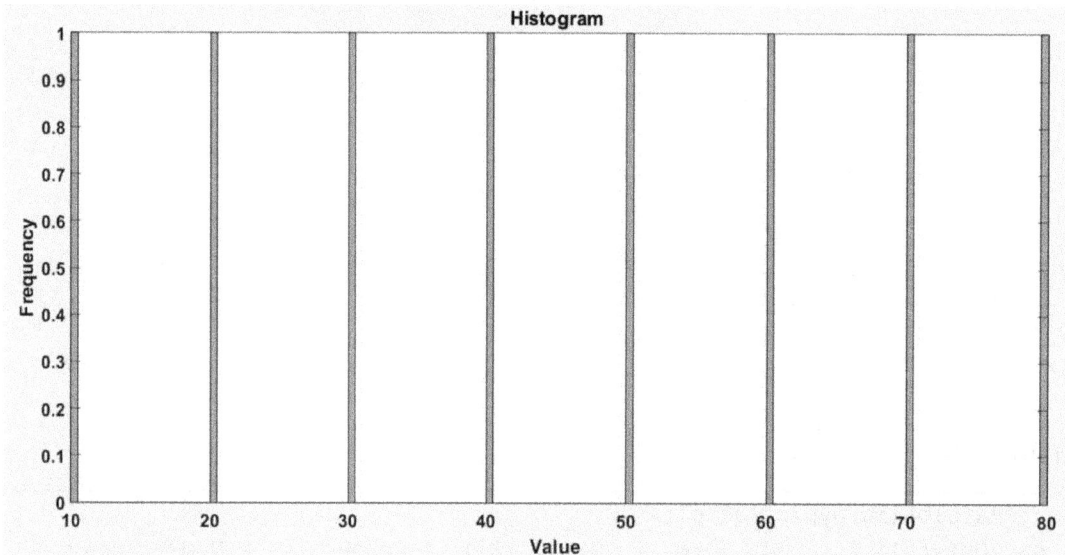

Figure 10.5: Histogram in MATLAB

Python (Matplotlib):

```
plt.hist(data, bins=30, edgecolor='black')
plt.xlabel('Value')
plt.ylabel('Frequency')
plt.title('Histogram')
plt.show()
```

Table 10.89: Histogram code in Python

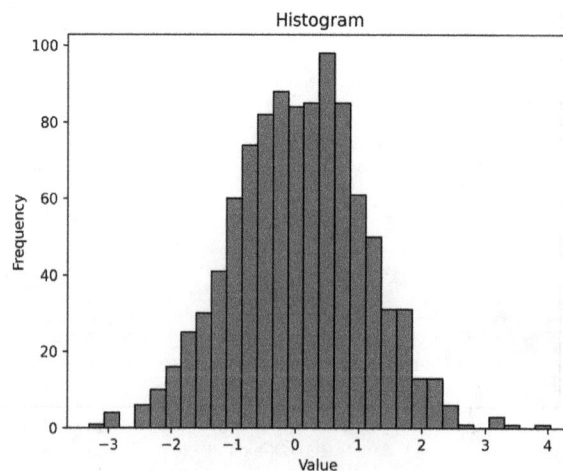

Figure 10.6: Histogram in Python

10.3.6 Miscellaneous

Several examples are discussed in this section to understand the topics in MATAB and Python. A comparative study will be useful to get full insight into MATLAB and Python implementations.

Example 10.65: Save a matrix to a file in MATLAB and Python.

MATLAB:

```
matrix = [1 2; 3 4];
save('matrix.mat', 'matrix');
```

Python (NumPy):

```
np.save('matrix.npy', matrix)
```

Example 10.66: Load a matrix from a file in MATLAB and Python.

MATLAB:

```
load('matrix.mat');
```

Python (NumPy):

```
matrix = np.load('matrix.npy')
```

Example 10.67: Generate random numbers in MATLAB and Python.

MATLAB:

`random_numbers = rand(1, 5)`
`% 5 random numbers between 0 and 1`
	Output:
	`random_numbers =`
	`0.6532    0.1084    0.0361    0.6181    0.5671`

Table 10.90: Generation of random numbers in MATLAB

Python (NumPy):

`random_numbers = np.random.rand(5)   # 5`
`random numbers between 0 and 1`
`print(random_numbers)`
	Output:
	`[0.64198129   0.10938357   0.21068257`
	`0.75185587 0.17875027]`

Table 10.91: Generation of random numbers in Python

10.3.7 Additional activities

Example 10.68: Calculate the median of a vector in MATLAB and Python.

MATLAB:

`data = [100 200 150 300 500]`
`median_value = median(data)`
	Output:
	`data =`
	`   100    200    150    300    500`
	`median_value =`
	`   200`

Table 10.92: Median of a vector in MATLAB

Python (NumPy):

``python
data = np.array([100, 200, 150, 300, 500])
median_value = np.median(data)
print(median_value)
``
	Output:
	
	200.0

Table 10.93: Median of a vector in Python

Example 10.69: Calculate the mode of a vector in MATLAB and Python.

MATLAB:

``matlab
data = [100 100 200 150 300 500]
mode_value = mode(data)
% Returns the most frequent value
``
	Output:
	data =
	  100 100 200 150 300 500
	mode_value =
	  100

Table 10.94: Mode of a vector in MATLAB

Python (SciPy):

``python
from scipy import stats
import numpy as np
 	
# Define data 	
data = np.array([100, 200, 150, 300, 500])
 	
# Compute mode 	
mode_result = stats.mode(data, keepdims=True)   #
Ensures correct shape handling
 	
# Extract mode value 	
mode_value = mode_result.mode[0]
 	
print("Mode:", mode_value)
``
	Output:
	Mode: 100

Table 10.95: Mode of a vector in Python

Example 10.70: Calculate the factorial of a number in MATLAB and Python.

MATLAB:

``matlab
factorial_value = factorial(5);
``
	Output:
	factorial_value =
	  120

Table 10.96: Factorial of a number in MATLAB

Python (Math):

import math factorial_value = math.factorial(5) print(factorial_value)	Output: **120**

Table 10.97: Factorial of a number in Python

Example 10.71: Calculate the exponential of a number in MATLAB and Python.

MATLAB:

exp_value = exp(2)	Output: **exp_value =** **7.3891**

Table 10.98: Exponential of a number in MATLAB

Python (NumPy):

exp_value = np.exp(2) print(exp_value)	Output: **7.38905609893065**

Table 10.99: Exponential of a number in Python

Example 10.72: Calculate the logarithm of a number in MATLAB and Python.

MATLAB:

log_value = log(10)	Output: **log_value =** **2.3026**

Table 10.100: Logarithm of a number in MATLAB

Python (NumPy):

log_value = np.log(10) print(log_value)	Output: **2.302585092994046**

Table 10.101: Logarithm of a number in Python

Example 10.73: Calculate the sine of an angle in MATLAB and Python.

MATLAB:

sine_value = sin(pi/2)	Output: **sine_value =** **1**

Table 10.102: Sine of an angle in MATLAB

Python (NumPy):

``` sine_value = np.sin(np.pi/2) print(sine_value) ```	**Output:** **1.0**

Table 10.103: Sine of an angle in Python

Example 10.74: Calculate the cosine of an angle in MATLAB and Python.

MATLAB:

``` cosine_value = cos(pi) ```	**Output:** **cosine_value =** **-1**

Table 10.104: Cosine of an angle in MATLAB

Python (NumPy):

``` cosine_value = np.cos(np.pi) print(cosine_value) ```	**Output:** **-1.0**

Table 10.105: Cosine of an angle in Python

Example 10.75: Calculate the tangent of an angle in MATLAB and Python.

MATLAB:

``` tangent_value = tan(pi/4) ```	**Output:** **tangent_value =** **1.0000**

Table 10.106: Tangent of an angle in MATLAB

Python (NumPy):

``` tangent_value = np.tan(np.pi/4) print(tangent_value) ```	**Output:** **0.999999999999999**

Table 10.107: Tangent of an angle in Python

Example 10.76: Calculate the square root of a number in MATLAB and Python.

MATLAB:

``` sqrt_value = sqrt(16) ```	**Output:** **sqrt_value =** **4**

Table 10.108: Square root of a number in MATLAB

Python (NumPy):

`sqrt_value = np.sqrt(16)` `print(sqrt_value)`	**Output:** **4.0**

Table 10.109: Square root of a number in Python

Example 10.77: Calculate the absolute value of a number in MATLAB and Python.

MATLAB:

`abs_value = abs(-5)`	**Output:** **abs_value =** **5**

Table 10.110: Absolute value of a number in MATLAB

Python (NumPy):

`abs_value = np.abs(-5)` `print(abs_value)`	**Output:** **5**

Table 10.111: Absolute value of a number in Python

Example 10.78: Calculate the sum of all elements in a vector in MATLAB and Python.

MATLAB:

`data = [11 12 15 16 18]`
`sum_value = sum(data)`
	Output:
	data =
	    11 12 15 16 18
	sum_value =
	    72

Table 10.112: Sum of all elements in a vector in MATLAB

Python (NumPy):

`data = np.array([11, 12, 15, 16, 18])`
`sum_value = np.sum(data)`
`print(sum_value )`
	Output:
	72

Table 10.113: Sum of all elements in a vector in Python

Example 10.79: Calculate the product of all elements in a vector in MATLAB and Python.

MATLAB:

`data = [11 12 15 16 18]`
`prod_value = prod(data)`
	Output:
	data =
	    11 12 15 16 18
	prod_value =
	       570240

Table 10.114: Product of all elements in a vector in MATLAB

Python (NumPy):

```data = np.array([11, 12, 15, 16, 18])``` ```prod_value = np.prod(data)``` ```print(prod_value)```	**Output:** **570240**

Table 10.115: Product of all elements in a vector in Python

Example 10.80: Calculate the maximum value in a vector in MATLAB and Python.

MATLAB:

```data = [11 12 15 16 18]``` ```max_value = max(data)```	**Output:** **data =** **11** **12** **15** **16** **18** **max_value =** **18**

Table 10.116: Maximum value in a vector in MATLAB

Python (NumPy):

```data = np.array([11, 12, 15, 16, 18])``` ```max_value = np.max(data)``` ```print(max_value)```	**Output:** **18**

Table 10.117: Maximum value in a vector in Python

Example 10.81: Calculate the minimum value in a vector in MATLAB and Python.

MATLAB:

```data = [11 12 15 16 18]``` ```min_value = min(data)```	**Output:** **data =** **11** **12** **15** **16** **18** **min_value =** **11**

Table 10.118: Minimum value in a vector in MATLAB

Python (NumPy):

```data = np.array([11, 12, 15, 16, 18])``` ```min_value = np.min(data)``` ```print(min_value)```	**Output:** **11**

Table 10.119: Minimum value in a vector in Python

Example 10.82: Calculate the unique elements in a vector in MATLAB and Python.

MATLAB:

data = [11 11 12 12 15 15 16 16 18] unique_values = unique(data)	Output: data = 11 11 12 12 15 15 16 16 18 unique_values = 11 12 15 16 18

Table 10.120: Unique elements in a vector in MATLAB

Python (NumPy):

data = np.array([11, 11, 12, 12, 15, 15, 16, 16, 18]) unique_values = np.unique(data) print(unique_values)	Output: [11 12 15 16 18]

Table 10.121: Unique elements in a vector in Python

Example 10.83: Calculate the cross product of two vectors in MATLAB and Python.

MATLAB:

cross_product = cross([1, 2, 3], [4, 5, 6])	Output: cross_product = -3 6 -3

Table 10.122: Cross product of two vectors in MATLAB

Python (NumPy):

cross_product = np.cross([1, 2, 3], [4, 5, 6]) print(cross_product)	Output: [-3 6 -3]

Table 10.123: Cross product of two vectors in Python

Example 10.84: Calculate the determinant of a matrix in MATLAB and Python.

MATLAB:

matrix = [1 0 0; 0 1 0; 0 0 1]
 	
det_value = det(matrix)
	Output:
	
	matrix =
	
	      1 0 0
	
	      0 1 0
	
	      0 0 1
	
	det_value =
	
	      1

Table 10.124: Determinant of a matrix in MATLAB

Python (NumPy):

```matrix = np.array([[1, 0, 0], [0, 1, 0], [0, 0, 1]]) det_value = np.linalg.det(matrix) print(det_value)```	Output: 1.0

Table 10.125: Determinant of a matrix in Python

Example 10.85: Calculate the trace of a matrix in MATLAB and Python.

MATLAB:

```matrix = [1 0 0; 0 1 0; 0 0 1]; trace_value = trace(matrix)```	Output: trace_value = 3

Table 10.126: Trace of a matrix in MATLAB

Python (NumPy):

```matrix = np.array([[1, 0, 0], [0, 1, 0], [0, 0, 1]]) trace_value = np.trace(matrix) print(trace_value)```	Output: 3

Table 10.127: Trace of a matrix in Python

Example 10.86: Calculate the rank of a matrix in MATLAB and Python.

MATLAB:

```matrix = [1 0 0; 0 1 0; 0 0 1]; rank_value = rank(matrix)```	Output: rank_value = 3

Table 10.128: Rank of a matrix in MATLAB

Python (NumPy):

```matrix = np.array([[1, 0, 0], [0, 1, 0], [0, 0, 1]]) rank_value = np.linalg.matrix_rank(matrix) print(rank_value)```	Output: 3

Table 10.129: Rank of a matrix in Python

Example 10.87: Calculate the pseudo-inverse of a matrix in MATLAB and Python.

MATLAB:

	Output:

`matrix = [1 2 3; 0 1 0; 4 5 7];`
`pinv_matrix = pinv(matrix)`
`% Returns pseudo-inverse`
	`pinv_matrix =`
	   `-1.4000   -0.2000    0.6000`
	    `0.0000    1.0000   -0.0000`
	    `0.8000   -0.6000   -0.2000`

Table 10.130: Pseudo-inverse of a matrix in MATLAB

Python (NumPy):

	Output:

`matrix = np.array([`
   `[1, 2, 3],`
   `[0, 1, 0],`
   `[4, 5, 7]`
`])`
`pinv_matrix = np.linalg.pinv(matrix)`
`# Returns pseudo-inverse`
`print(pinv_matrix)`
	`[[-1.40000000e+00 -2.00000000e-01  6.00000000e-01]`
	`[ 1.51990405e-16  1.00000000e+00 -3.95950691e-17]`
	`[ 8.00000000e-01 -6.00000000e-01 -2.00000000e-01]]`

Table 10.131: Pseudo-inverse of a matrix in Python

Conclusion

This chapter provided a comprehensive guide to handling, analyzing, and preprocessing data in MATLAB and Python, equipping readers with essential skills for real-world applications. In MATLAB, you learned key techniques for data manipulation, including merging and splitting datasets, as well as handling missing values. Statistical computations like mean (mean) and standard deviation (std) were covered. The use of tables for structured data storage and operations was also emphasized.

In Python, the focus shifted to powerful libraries like Pandas and NumPy, where you explored data manipulation with DataFrames, statistical functions (np.mean, np.std), and handled missing values. This chapter highlighted the differences in syntax and functionality between the two platforms while reinforcing their shared goals: efficient data wrangling and insightful analysis.

By mastering these tools, you can now tackle diverse challenges, from cleaning sensor data in engineering to analyzing financial trends or preparing datasets for machine learning. Whether using MATLAB's matrix-based operations or Python's flexible libraries, the skills gained here form a strong foundation for data-driven decision-making in research, industry, and beyond.

In the next chapter, you will learn about signal processing and image processing in MATLAB and Python.

Exercises

MATLAB

Data manipulation:

1. Given the following matrix, extract the second column:

$$A = \begin{bmatrix} 3 & 5 & 7 \\ 2 & 6 & 8 \\ 1 & 4 & 9 \end{bmatrix}$$

2. Create a 5×5 matrix of random integers between 1 and 100. Replace all elements greater than 50 with 50.

3. Given a row vector $v = [2,4,6,8,10]$, reshape it into a 2×3 matrix, filling the missing element with zero.

4. Generate a 10×10 identity matrix and set the diagonal elements to 5 instead of 1.

5. Given the following matrix, compute the cumulative sum along the rows:

$$B = \begin{bmatrix} 1 & 2 & 3 \\ 4 & 5 & 6 \\ 7 & 8 & 9 \end{bmatrix}$$

6. Extract all even numbers from the matrix $M = \text{randi}([1,50],4,4)$.

7. Flip a given 5×5 matrix along its main diagonal.

8. Concatenate two matrices, A and B, of size 3×3 horizontally and vertically.

Statistical functions:

1. Compute the mean and standard deviation of the elements in matrix $C = \text{randi}([1,100], 5, 5)$.

2. Find the correlation coefficient between two vectors $X = [1,2,3,4,5]$ and $Y = [2,4,6,8,10]$.

3. Compute the variance and skewness of a dataset stored in a column vector.

4. Given a time series dataset, compute the moving average of window size 5.

5. Compute the median and interquartile range (IQR) for a given dataset.

6. Create a normally distributed dataset of size 1000 and plot its histogram.

7. Determine the mode of a given dataset with repeated values.

8. Compute the z-score normalization for a dataset D in MATLAB.

Working with tables:

1. Create a MATLAB table with three columns: "Student Name", "Marks", and "Grade" with five student records.

2. Import data from a CSV file into a table and display its first five rows.

3. Sort a given table based on the "Age" column in descending order.

4. Convert a MATLAB table into a cell array and extract the first column.

5. Remove rows from a table where the "Salary" column has missing values.

6. Add a new computed column "Performance" to an existing table where performance is defined as Marks × 1.2.

7. Extract only those rows where "Marks" is greater than 80.

8. Merge two tables having common column names.

9. Convert a numeric array into a table with appropriate column names.

Python

Data manipulation with Pandas, NumPy:

1. Create a Pandas DataFrame with three columns: "ID", "Name", and "Score" with at least 5 rows.

2. Given a NumPy array arr = np.array([10, 20, 30, 40, 50]), replace all elements greater than 30 with 100.

3. Extract all odd numbers from a NumPy array of random integers between 1 and 50.

4. Reshape a 1D NumPy array into a 4×3 matrix.

5. Create a DataFrame from a dictionary containing student names and scores.

6. Read a CSV file into a Pandas DataFrame and display its column names.

7. Add a new column "Final Score" to an existing DataFrame by multiplying "Score" by 1.1.

8. Drop rows from a DataFrame where the "Age" column has NaN values.

9. Filter out students who scored more than 90 in a DataFrame.

10. Group a DataFrame by "Department" and compute the mean salary.

Statistical analysis:

1. Compute the mean, median, and standard deviation of a NumPy array containing 1000 random numbers.

2. Compute the correlation matrix of a given Pandas DataFrame containing numerical columns.

3. Generate a normally distributed dataset of 5000 points and plot its histogram.

4. Calculate the z-scores of a given dataset using scipy.stats.zscore().

5. Compute the variance and skewness of a given dataset using Pandas.

6. Given two lists, $X = [10,15,20,25,30]$ and $Y = [5,7,9,11,13]$, compute their Pearson correlation coefficient.

7. Find the mode of a dataset using Pandas.

8. Perform a t-test between two independent samples using SciPy.

9. Compute a rolling mean with a window size of 4 for a Pandas DataFrame column.

10. Generate a dataset and apply Min-Max normalization.

Advanced questions:

1. Write a MATLAB function that takes an array and returns the mean, variance, and standard deviation.

2. Write a Python function that takes a Pandas DataFrame and normalizes all numeric columns.

3. In MATLAB, generate a dataset of 1000 points following a Poisson distribution and plot the histogram.

4. In Python, generate a dataset of 2000 points following an exponential distribution and compute its mean and variance.

5. Write a MATLAB script to read a CSV file, perform basic data preprocessing (handling NaNs, normalization), and save the cleaned data.

Join our Discord space

Join our Discord workspace for latest updates, offers, tech happenings around the world, new releases, and sessions with the authors:

https://discord.bpbonline.com

CHAPTER 11

Signal and Image Processing in MATLAB and Python

Introduction

The present chapter explores techniques that are used in signal processing and image processing in MATLAB and Python environments. MATLAB and Python provide robust tools and libraries regarding the processing of signals and images, which makes them significant in fields such as telecommunications, audio analysis, and computer vision. This chapter is divided into three sections: MATLAB-based content with examples, Python-based content with examples, and a comparative study of MATLAB and Python codes with examples.

Structure

In this chapter, we will learn the following topics:

- 11.1. MATLAB-based concepts
- 11.2. Python-based concepts
- 11.3. Comparative study of MATLAB and Python codes

Objectives

This chapter equips readers with practical skills in signal and image processing using MATLAB and Python, which focus on several real-world applications. By the end of this chapter, readers will be able to process and analyze signals for applications such as audio enhancement, noise reduction, and time-series data processing. They will also learn to implement image processing techniques for tasks such as object detection, medical imaging, and automated inspection using MATLAB and Python libraries and apply Python tools (OpenCV, scikit-image, and PIL) and MATLAB functions to manipulate and enhance images for computer vision and remote sensing.

Readers will develop solutions for real-world problems, including speech processing, sensor data analysis, facial recognition, and image classification. They hands-on examples and case studies, readers will gain the expertise to tackle challenges in telecommunications, audio analysis, and computer vision using these powerful programming environments.

11.1 MATLAB-based content

MATLAB is useful in signal and image processing, offering a vast range of built-in functions and visualization tools. This section provides a detailed analysis of signal and image processing aspects in MATLAB, with practical examples and explanations. MATLAB's signal processing toolbox provides specialized functions for filtering, spectral analysis, and wavelet transforms, which enable efficient noise removal and feature extraction from signals. For image processing, the image processing toolbox supports aspects like edge detection, segmentation, and morphological operations with high precision. Moreover, MATLAB's seamless integration with Simulink facilitates the simulation and testing of signal processing algorithms in dynamic systems.

11.1.1 Signal processing in MATLAB

Signal processing includes analysis and synthesis of signals such as audio, video, and sensor data. MATLAB offers a complete set of tools to work with signals, including filtering, Fourier transforms, and noise reduction.

Key concepts regarding signal processing in MATLAB:

- **Signal representation**: Signals are represented as vectors or matrices.
- **Filtering**: Techniques for noise reduction and signal enhancement.
- **Fourier transform**: Frequency domain analysis using **Fast Fourier transform** (**FFT**).
- **Applications**: Audio signal enhancement, noise reduction, and speech processing.

Diversified examples are provided in this section to understand the different aspects of signal processing in MATLAB.

Example 11.1: Noise reduction using a moving average filter (See *Figure 11.1*)

Objective: Generate a noisy signal, apply a moving average filter to reduce noise, and visualize results.

```
% Step 1: Generate a noisy signal
t = 0:0.001:1; % Time vector (1 second duration)
x = sin(2*pi*50*t) + 0.5*randn(size(t)); % 50 Hz sine wave with noise

% Step 2: Plot the noisy signal
subplot(2,1,1);
plot(t, x);
title('Noisy Signal');
xlabel('Time (s)');
ylabel('Amplitude');

% Step 3: Apply a moving average filter
windowSize = 10; % Window size for the moving average
b = (1/windowSize)*ones(1, windowSize); % Filter coefficients
a = 1; % Denominator coefficient
y_filtered = filter(b, a, x); % Apply the filter

% Step 4: Plot the filtered signal
subplot(2,1,2);
plot(t, y_filtered);
title('Filtered Signal');
xlabel('Time (s)');
ylabel('Amplitude');
```

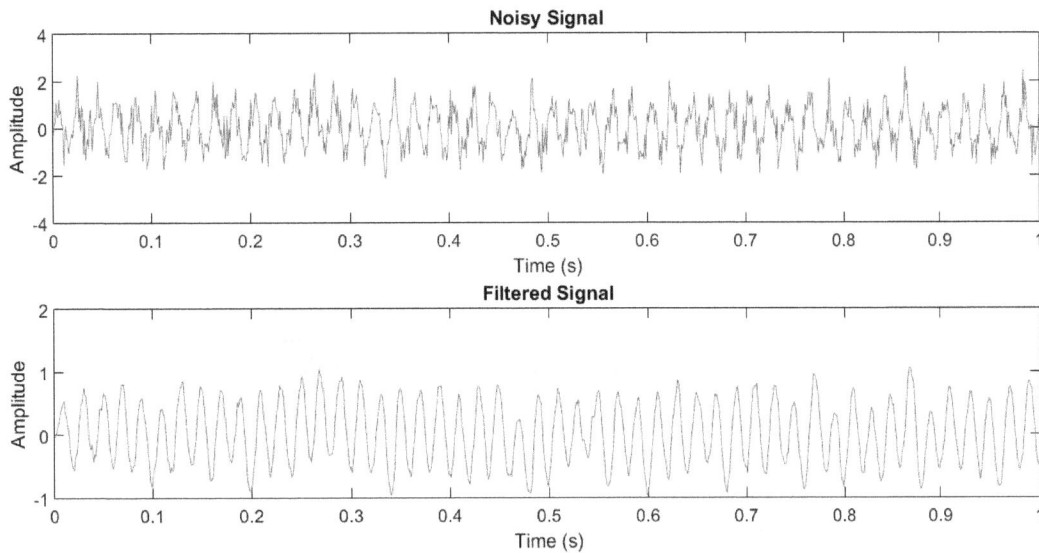

Figure 11.1: *Noise reduction using moving average filter in MATLAB*

The explanation of the preceding code is as follows:

- **Noisy signal**: A 50 Hz sine wave is generated and corrupted with Gaussian noise.

- **Moving average filter**: A simple moving average filter is designed to smooth the signal.

- **Filter application**: The filter function applies the moving average filter.

- **Visualization**: The noisy and filtered signals are plotted for comparison.

11.1.2 Image processing in MATLAB

Image processing focuses on enhancing and analyzing images to extract information or improve their quality. MATLAB provides tools for image filtering, edge detection, and feature extraction.

The key concepts regarding image processing in MATLAB:

- **Image representation**: Images are represented as matrices.

- **Color spaces**: RGB, grayscale, and other color spaces.

- **Applications**: Object detection, image restoration, and medical image analysis.

Several examples are discussed in this section to understand the different aspects of image processing in MATLAB.

Example 11.2: Image filtering using Gaussian blur (See *Figure 11.2*)

Objective: Read an image, convert it to grayscale, apply a Gaussian blur, and visualize the results.

```
% Step 1: Read an image
img = imread('imagefile.jpg'); % Load the image


% Step 2: Convert to grayscale
img_gray = rgb2gray(img); % Convert RGB image to grayscale


% Step 3: Apply a Gaussian filter
img_filtered = imgaussfilt(img_gray, 2); % Apply Gaussian blur with sigma = 2
```

```
% Step 4: Display the results
figure;
subplot(1,2,1);
imshow(img_gray);
title('Original Image');
subplot(1,2,2);
imshow(img_filtered);
title('Filtered Image');
```

Note: **The sigma parameter in `imgaussfilt(img, sigma)` controls the standard deviation of the Gaussian distribution used to blur the image. It directly influences how much the image is smoothed.**

- **Low sigma (e.g., 0.5 or 1)**: Only slight blurring occurs. Edges and fine details are mostly preserved.

- **Moderate sigma (e.g., 2)**: Noticeable blurring that smooths out small details and reduces noise.

- **High sigma (e.g., 5 or more)**: Strong blurring that can make edges and textures almost unrecognizable.

Increasing sigma makes the blur effect stronger by using a wider kernel, which averages pixel values over a larger neighborhood.

This makes sigma a tunable parameter depending on whether the goal is noise reduction, edge softening, or artistic effect.

Figure 11.2: Image filtering using Gaussian blur in MATLAB

Let us look at the explanation:

- **Image loading**: The **imread** function reads image file.

- **Grayscale conversion**: The **rgb2gray** function converts RGB image to grayscale.

- **Gaussian blur**: The **imgaussfilt** function applies a Gaussian blur to image.

- **Visualization**: Original and filtered images are displayed side by side.

Example 11.3: Edge detection using the Canny method (See *Figure 11.3*)

Objective: Detect edges in a grayscale image using the Canny edge detection algorithm.

```
% Step 1: Read and convert image to grayscale
img = imread('imagefile.jpg');
img_gray = rgb2gray(img);


% Step 2: Detect edges using Canny method
```

```
edges = edge(img_gray, 'Canny'); % Apply Canny edge detection

% Step 3: Display edges
figure;
imshow(edges);
title('Edge Detection');
```

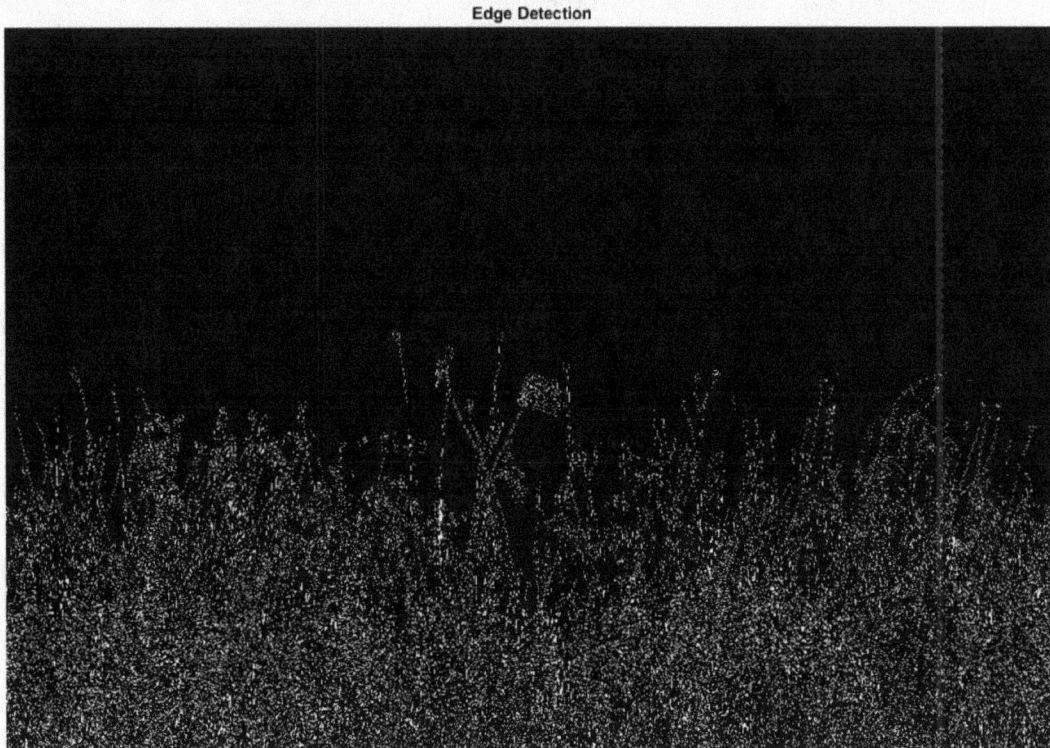

Figure 11.3: *Edge detection using the Canny method in MATLAB*

Explanation:

- **Image loading and conversion**: The image is loaded and converted to grayscale.

- **Edge detection**: Edge function with the **'Canny'** option detects edges in image.

- **Visualization**: Detected edges are displayed.

11.1.3 Advanced applications

In this section, an example is discussed to clear the aspect of object detection in an image in MATLAB. Step by step process is discussed in the provided MATLAB code to understand the concept. MATLAB provides a powerful and user-friendly platform to implement such tasks using built-in functions for color space transformation, thresholding, and image manipulation. In this section, the concept of object detection is demonstrated using color thresholding in the **hue, saturation, value (HSV)** color space. HSV is often preferred over RGB for color-based segmentation because it separates chromatic content (hue and saturation) from intensity information (value), allowing for more intuitive thresholding.

Example 11.4: Object detection in an image (See *Figure 11.4*)

Objective: Detect objects in an image via color thresholding.

```
% Step 1: Read image
img = imread('imagefile.jpg');
```

```
% Step 2: Convert to HSV color space
img_hsv = rgb2hsv(img); % Convert RGB to HSV

% Step 3: Define a color threshold for object detection
hue_threshold = [0.1, 0.5]; % Hue range for the object
saturation_threshold = [0.4, 1]; % Saturation range
value_threshold = [0.5, 1]; % Value range

% Step 4: Create a binary mask
mask = (img_hsv(:,:,1) >= hue_threshold(1) & (img_hsv(:,:,1) <= hue_threshold(2)) & ...
        (img_hsv(:,:,2) >= saturation_threshold(1)) & (img_hsv(:,:,2) <= saturation_
threshold(2)) & ...
        (img_hsv(:,:,3) >= value_threshold(1)) & (img_hsv(:,:,3) <= value_threshold(2));

% Step 5: Apply mask to original image
img_object = bsxfun(@times, img, cast(mask, 'like', img));

% Step 6: Display results
figure;
subplot(1,2,1);
imshow(img);
title('Original Image');
subplot(1,2,2);
imshow(img_object);
title('Detected Object');
```

Figure 11.4: Object detection in an image in MATLAB

Explanation:

- **Color space conversion**: The image is transformed to HSV color space for better color segmentation. Where:

  o **H**: Hue (color type, represented as an angle on a color wheel)

  o **S**: Saturation (intensity or purity of the color)

  o **V**: Value (brightness or lightness of the color)

- **Thresholding**: A binary mask is created based on stated hue, saturation, and value ranges.

- **Mask application**: Mask is applied to the original image to isolate the object.

- **Visualization**: The original image and the detected object are displayed.

This section offers a detailed introduction to signal and image processing in MATLAB, with practical examples. The next section will explore Python-based implementations.

11.2 Python-based content

Python is a multipurpose programming language with an enhanced ecosystem of libraries for signal and image processing. Libraries such as NumPy, SciPy, librosa, OpenCV, and scikit-image make Python a useful tool for analyzing signals and images. This section provides a detailed idea regarding signal and image processing techniques in Python, with practical examples.

11.2.1 Signal processing in Python

Signal processing includes analysis and modifications of signals such as audio, video, and sensor data. Python provides libraries like SciPy and librosa to work with signals, including filtering, Fourier transforms, and noise reduction.

Key concepts regarding signal processing in Python:

- **Signal representation**: Signals are signified as NumPy arrays.

- **Filtering**: Techniques regarding noise reduction and signal enhancement.

- **Fourier transform**: Frequency domain analysis using FFT.

- **Applications**: Audio signal analysis, sensor data processing, and time-series analysis.

Diversified examples are provided in this section to understand the different aspects of signal processing in Python. This will create a proper understanding of the topic.

Example 11.5: Noise reduction using a moving average filter (See *Figure 11.5*)

Objective: Generate a noisy signal, apply a moving average filter to reduce noise, and visualize the results.

```
import numpy as np
import matplotlib.pyplot as plt


# Step 1: Generate a noisy signal
t = np.linspace(0, 1, 1000)  # Time vector (1 second duration)
x = np.sin(2 * np.pi * 50 * t) + 0.5 * np.random.randn(len(t))  # 50 Hz sine wave with
noise


# Step 2: Plot the noisy signal
plt.figure(figsize=(10, 6))
plt.subplot(2, 1, 1)
plt.plot(t, x)
plt.title('Noisy Signal')
plt.xlabel('Time (s)')
plt.ylabel('Amplitude')


# Step 3: Apply a moving average filter
```

```
window_size = 10  # Window size for the moving average
b = np.ones(window_size) / window_size  # Filter coefficients
y_filtered = np.convolve(x, b, mode='same')  # Apply the filter

# Step 4: Plot the filtered signal
plt.subplot(2, 1, 2)
plt.plot(t, y_filtered)
plt.title('Filtered Signal')
plt.xlabel('Time (s)')
plt.ylabel('Amplitude')
plt.tight_layout()
plt.show()
```

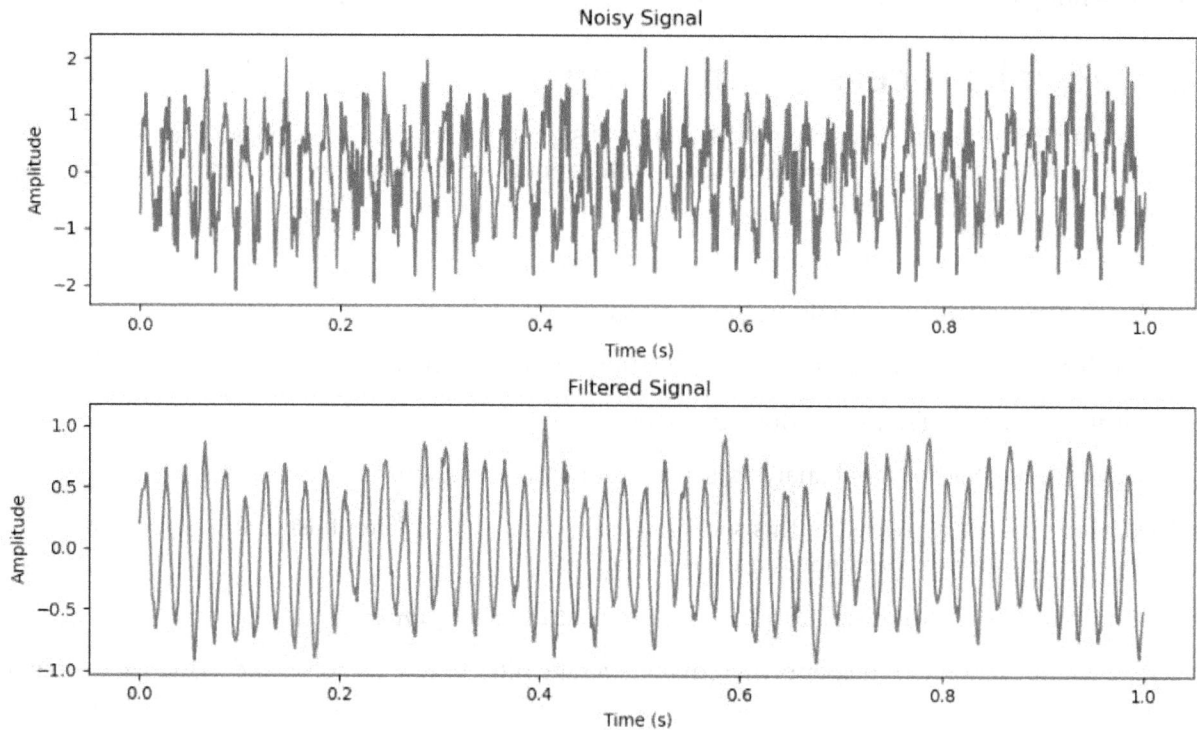

Figure 11.5: *Noise reduction using moving average filter in Python*

Explanation:

- **Noisy signal**: A 50 Hz sine wave is generated and corrupted with Gaussian noise.

- **Moving average filter**: A simple moving average filter is designed to smooth the signal.

- **Filter Application**: The **np.convolve** function applies the moving average filter.

- **Visualization**: The noisy and filtered signals are plotted for comparison.

11.2.2 Image processing in Python

Image processing focuses on enhancing and analyzing images to extract information or improve their quality. Python libraries such as OpenCV, scikit-image, and PIL (Pillow) are widely used for image processing tasks.

Key concepts regarding image processing in Python:

- **Image representation**: Images are represented as NumPy arrays.

- **Color spaces**: RGB, grayscale, and other color spaces.

- **Applications**: Facial recognition, image classification, and automated inspection systems.

Several examples are provided in this section to understand the different aspects of image processing in Python to enhance the understanding of the topics.

Example 11.6: Image filtering using Gaussian blur

Objective: Read an image, convert it to grayscale, as shown in the *Figure 11.6*, apply a Gaussian blur, and visualize the results.

```python
import cv2
import matplotlib.pyplot as plt


# Step 1: Read an image
img = cv2.imread('imagefile.jpg')  # Load the image


# Step 2: Convert to grayscale
img_gray = cv2.cvtColor(img, cv2.COLOR_BGR2GRAY)  # Convert RGB image to grayscale


# Step 3: Apply a Gaussian filter
img_filtered = cv2.GaussianBlur(img_gray, (5, 5), 0)  # Apply Gaussian blur with kernel size
5x5


# Step 4: Display the results
plt.figure(figsize=(10, 5))
plt.subplot(1, 2, 1)
plt.imshow(img_gray, cmap='gray')
plt.title('Original Image')
plt.subplot(1, 2, 2)
plt.imshow(img_filtered, cmap='gray')
plt.title('Filtered Image')
plt.show()
```

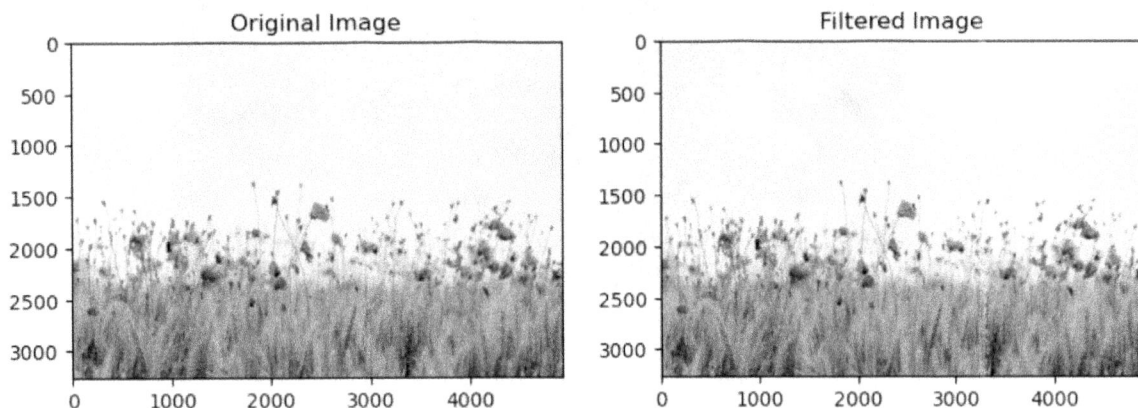

Figure 11.6: *Image filtering using Gaussian blur in Python*

Explanation:

- **Image loading**: The `cv2.imread` function reads an image file.

- **Grayscale conversion**: The `cv2.cvtColor` function converts an RGB image to grayscale.

324 ■ *Practical MATLAB and Python*

- **Gaussian blur**: The `cv2.GaussianBlur` function applies a Gaussian blur to image.
- **Visualization**: The original and filtered images are presented side by side.

Example 11.7: Edge detection using the Canny method

Objective: Detect edges in a grayscale image using the Canny edge detection algorithm, as shown in *Figure 11.7*.

```python
import cv2
import matplotlib.pyplot as plt

# Step 1: Read and convert image to grayscale
img = cv2.imread('imagefile.jpg')
img_gray = cv2.cvtColor(img, cv2.COLOR_BGR2GRAY)  # Convert to grayscale

# Step 2: Detect edges using Canny method
edges = cv2.Canny(img_gray, 100, 200)  # Apply Canny edge detection

# Step 3: Display edges
plt.imshow(edges, cmap='gray')
plt.title('Edge Detection')
plt.show()
```

Note: Edge detection helps identify boundaries and shapes within an image by detecting areas with sharp intensity changes. It is essential for image analysis tasks such as object recognition, segmentation, and feature extraction, making images easier to interpret for both humans and computer vision algorithms.

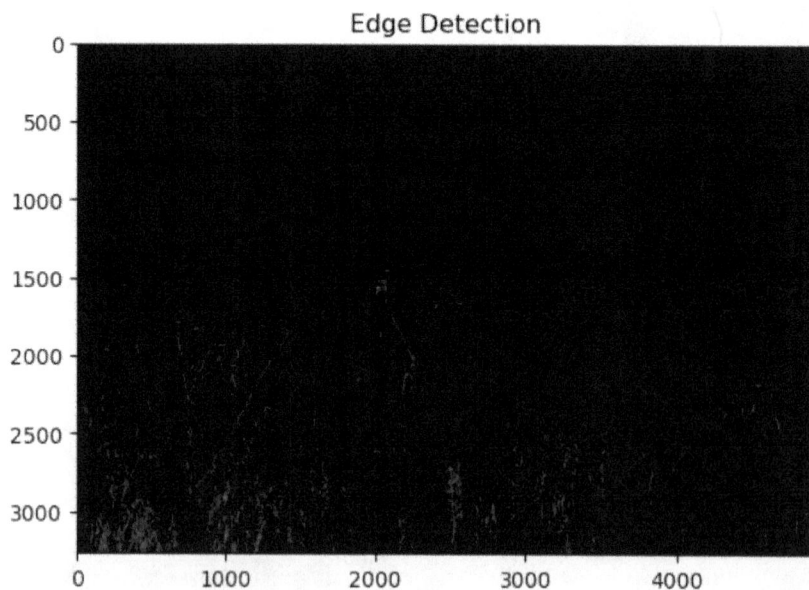

Figure 11.7: Edge detection using the Canny method in Python

Explanation:

- **Image loading and conversion**: Image is loaded and converted to grayscale.
- **Edge detection**: The `cv2.Canny` function detects edges in an image using the Canny algorithm.
- **Visualization**: Detected edges are displayed.

11.2.3 Advanced applications

Python, with its extensive libraries like OpenCV and NumPy, provides an efficient and flexible framework for performing advanced image processing tasks, such as object detection. In this section, an example is discussed to clear the aspect of object detection in an image in Python. A step-by-step process is discussed in the provided Python code to understand the concept. The process begins by reading the image and converting it from BGR (default in OpenCV) to HSV. Then, a binary mask is generated by defining upper and lower HSV bounds that correspond to the desired object's color range. The following example demonstrates how simple yet powerful color-based object detection techniques can be implemented in Python for real-world applications.

Example 11.8: Object detection in an image.

Objective: Detect objects in an image using color thresholding, as shown in *Figure 11.8*.

```python
import cv2
import numpy as np
import matplotlib.pyplot as plt


# Step 1: Read the image
img = cv2.imread('imagefile.jpg')


# Step 2: Convert to HSV color space
img_hsv = cv2.cvtColor(img, cv2.COLOR_BGR2HSV)  # Convert RGB to HSV


# Step 3: Define a color threshold for object detection
lower_bound = np.array([30, 40, 50])  # Lower bound of HSV values
upper_bound = np.array([80, 255, 255])  # Upper bound of HSV values


# Step 4: Create a binary mask
mask = cv2.inRange(img_hsv, lower_bound, upper_bound)  # Create a mask based on the
threshold


# Step 5: Apply the mask to the original image
img_object = cv2.bitwise_and(img, img, mask=mask)  # Apply the mask


# Step 6: Display the results
plt.figure(figsize=(10, 5))
plt.subplot(1, 2, 1)
plt.imshow(cv2.cvtColor(img, cv2.COLOR_BGR2RGB))
plt.title('Original Image')
plt.subplot(1, 2, 2)
plt.imshow(cv2.cvtColor(img_object, cv2.COLOR_BGR2RGB))
plt.title('Detected Object')
plt.show()
```

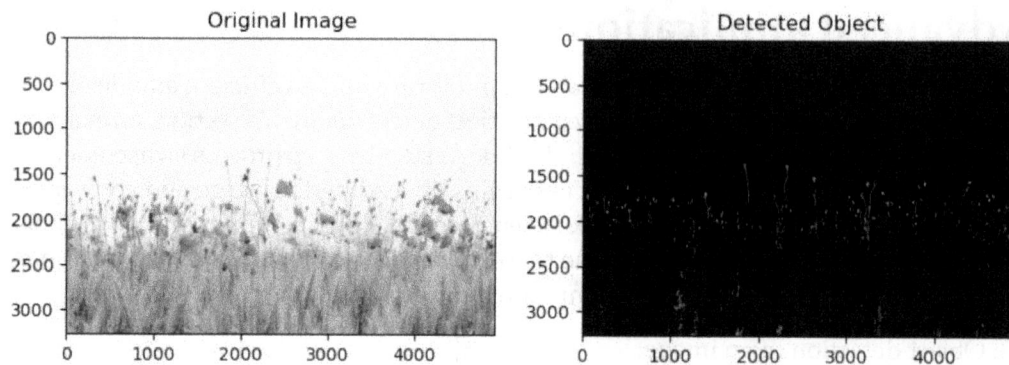

Figure 11.8: *Object detection in an image in Python*

Explanation:

- **Color space conversion**: Image is converted to HSV color space regarding better color segmentation.
- **Thresholding**: A binary mask is created based on a specified HSV range.
- **Mask application**: Mask is applied to the original image to isolate object.
- **Visualization**: The original image and detected object are displayed.

This section provides a thorough introduction to signal and image processing in Python. The next section will provide a comparative study of MATLAB and Python implementations.

11.3 Comparative study of MATLAB and Python codes

This section provides a comparative insight into MATLAB and Python implementations for various signal and image processing applications. The main goal is to highlight similarities and differences between these two environments. We will cover a few examples across signal processing, image processing, and their advanced applications.

11.3.1 Signal processing examples

In this section, several examples are discussed to study the comparative behavior of MATLAB and Python regarding signal processing. Each example in this section is discussed via MATLAB and Python codes. Examples such as signal resampling, autocorrelation computation, and chirp signal generation illustrate how both platforms approach similar problems using different syntax and libraries. In MATLAB, built-in functions like **resample**, **xcorr**, and **chirp** provide a direct and user-friendly interface for these tasks. In Python, equivalent functionality is achieved through the powerful **scipy.signal** module, often in combination with **numpy** and matplotlib for numerical operations and visualization. This comparison enables users to understand the strengths and usability of each environment, which helps them choose the right tool based on their application needs and familiarity.

Example 11.9: Generate a Sine Wave, as shown in *Figures 11.9 and 11.10*.

Objective: Generate and plot a sine wave.

MATLAB:

```
t = 0:0.01:1; % Time vector
x = sin(2*pi*5*t); % 5 Hz sine wave
plot(t, x);
title('Sine Wave');
xlabel('Time (s)');
ylabel('Amplitude');
```

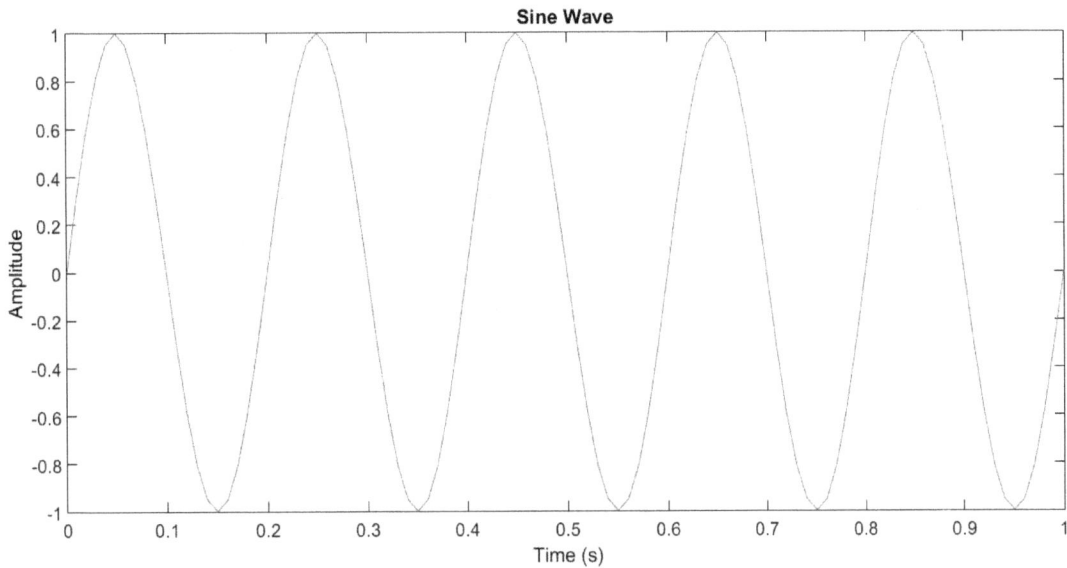

Figure 11.9: Sine wave generation in MATLAB

Python:

```
import numpy as np
import matplotlib.pyplot as plt

t = np.linspace(0, 1, 100)  # Time vector
x = np.sin(2 * np.pi * 5 * t)  # 5 Hz sine wave
plt.plot(t, x)
plt.title('Sine Wave')
plt.xlabel('Time (s)')
plt.ylabel('Amplitude')
plt.show()
```

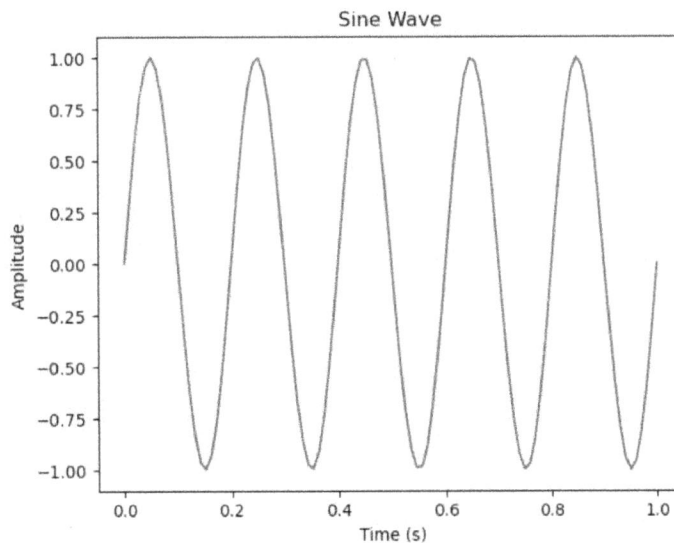

Figure 11.10: Sine wave generation in Python

Example 11.10: Add noise to a signal

Objective: Add Gaussian noise to a sine wave, as shown in *Figures 11.11 and 11.12.*

MATLAB:

```
x = sin(2*pi*5*t) + 0.1*randn(size(t)); % Add noise
plot(t, x);
title('Noisy Sine Wave');
```

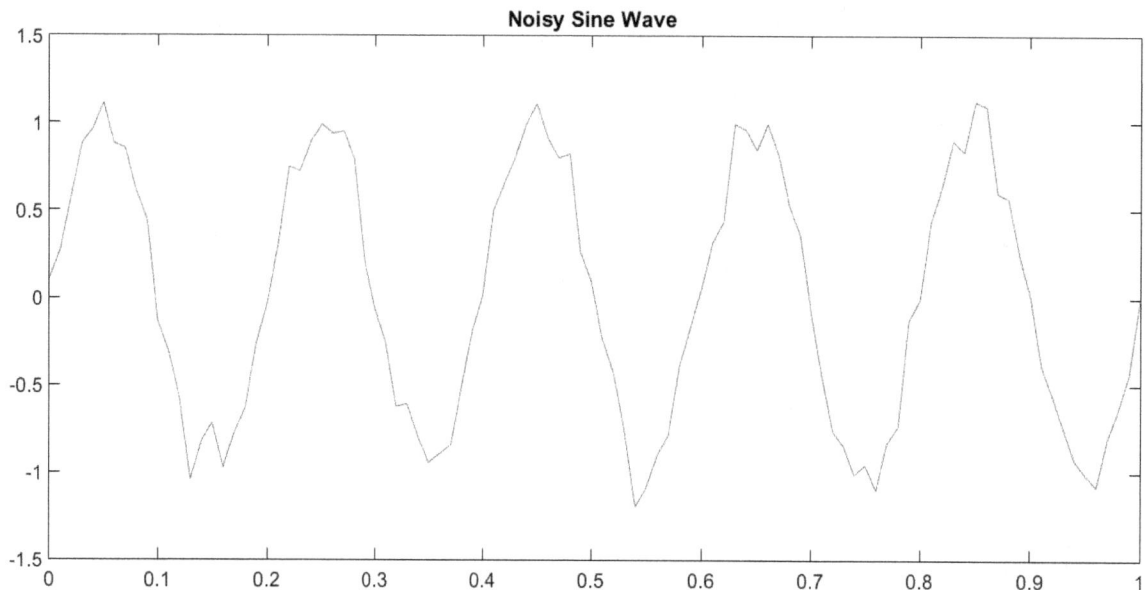

Figure 11.11: *Adding Gaussian noise to a sine wave in MATLAB*

Python:

```
x = np.sin(2 * np.pi * 5 * t) + 0.1 * np.random.randn(len(t))  # Add noise
plt.plot(t, x)
plt.title('Noisy Sine Wave')
plt.show()
```

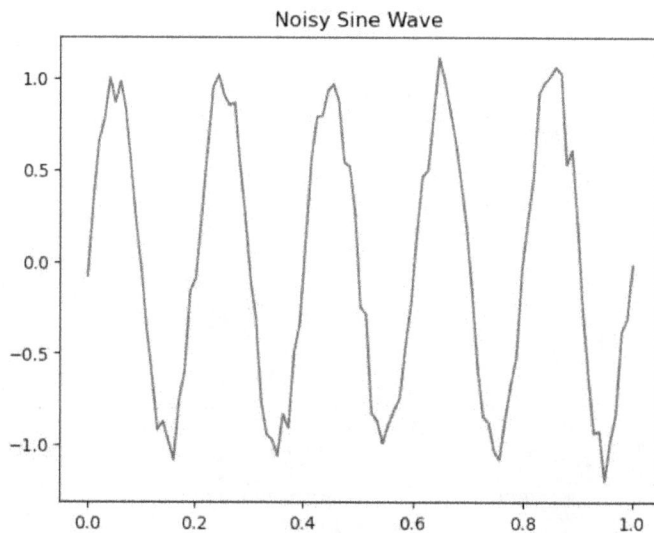

Figure 11.12: *Adding Gaussian noise to a sine wave in Python*

Example 11.11: Compute FFT of a signal

Objective: Compute and plot the FFT of a signal, as shown in *Figures 11.13 and 11.14*.

MATLAB:

```
X = fft(x);
f = (0:length(X)-1)*(1/(t(2)-t(1)))/length(X);
plot(f, abs(X));
title('FFT of Signal');
```

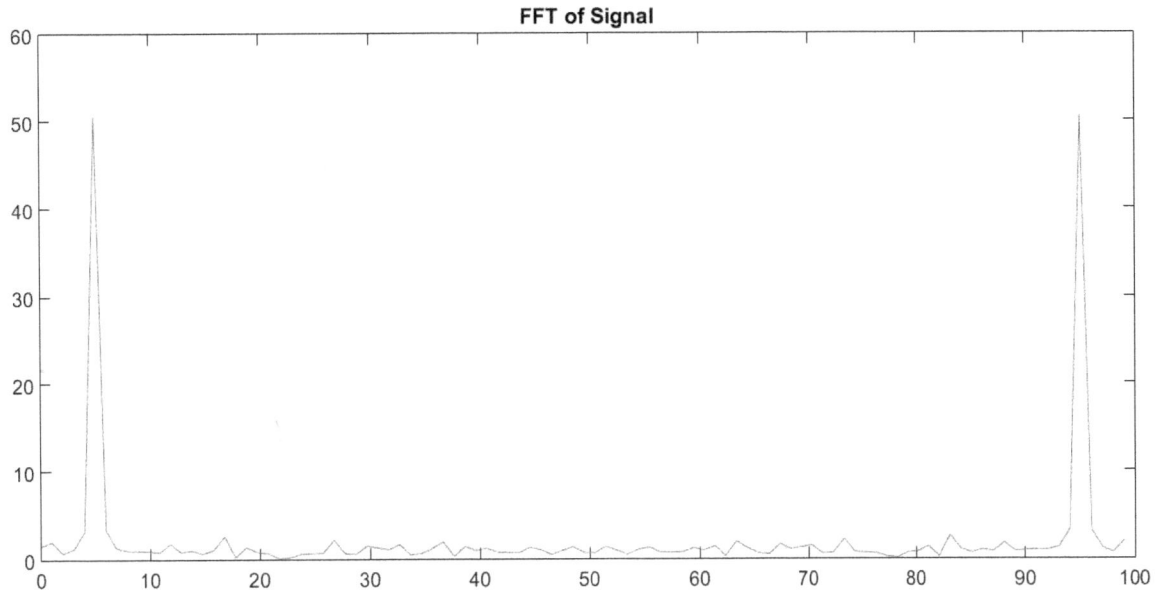

Figure 11.13: *FFT of a signal in MATLAB*

Python:

```
X = np.fft.fft(x)
f = np.fft.fftfreq(len(x), t[1] - t[0])
plt.plot(f, np.abs(X))
plt.title('FFT of Signal')
plt.show()
```

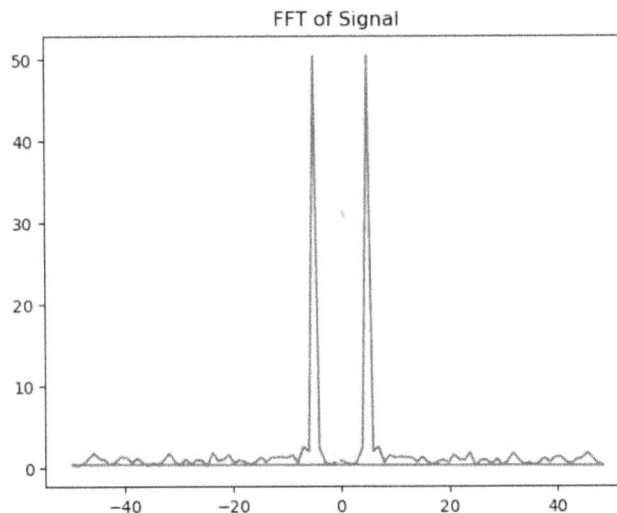

Figure 11.14: *FFT of a signal in Python*

Example 11.12: Apply a low-pass filter

Objective: Apply a Butterworth low-pass filter, as shown in *Figures 11.15 and 11.16,* to a noisy signal.

MATLAB:

```
[b, a] = butter(4, 0.1); % 4th-order filter
y = filter(b, a, x);
plot(t, y);
title('Filtered Signal');
```

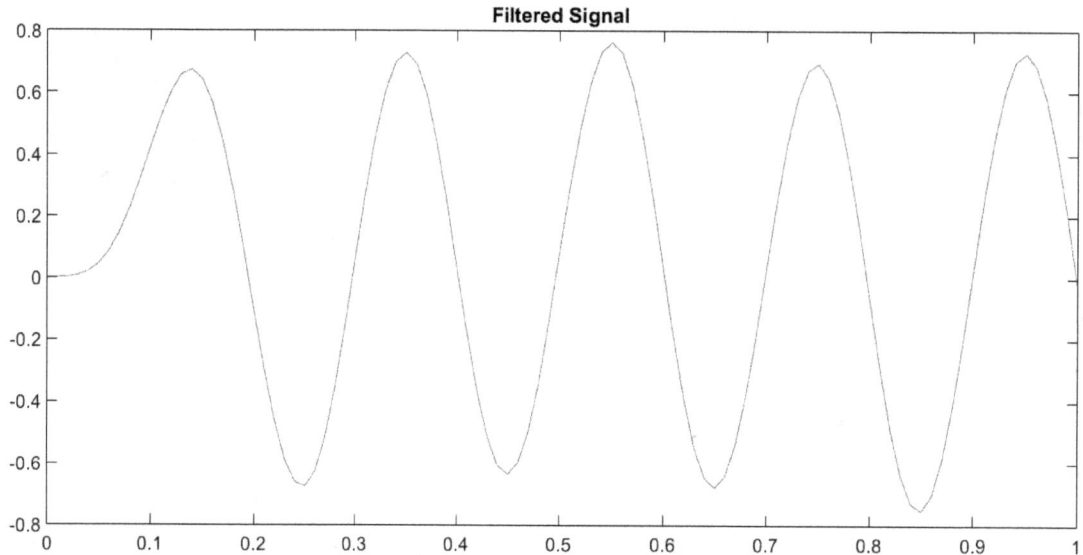

Figure 11.15: Applying a low-pass filter in MATLAB

Python:

```
from scipy.signal import butter, filtfilt
b, a = butter(4, 0.1, btype='low')  # 4th-order filter
y = filtfilt(b, a, x)
plt.plot(t, y)
plt.title('Filtered Signal')
plt.show()
```

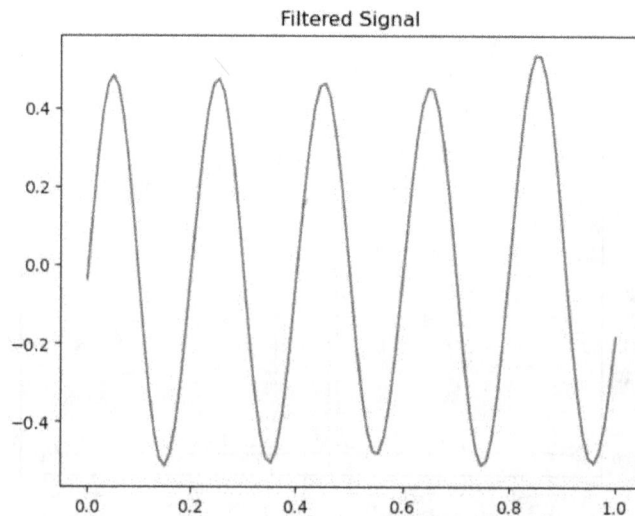

Figure 11.16: Applying a low-pass filter in Python

Example 11.13: Apply a high-pass filter

Objective: Apply a Butterworth high-pass filter to a noisy signal, as shown in *Figures 11.17 and 11.18*.

MATLAB:

```
[b, a] = butter(4, 0.1, 'high'); % 4th-order filter
y = filter(b, a, x);
plot(t, y);
title('High-Pass Filtered Signal');
```

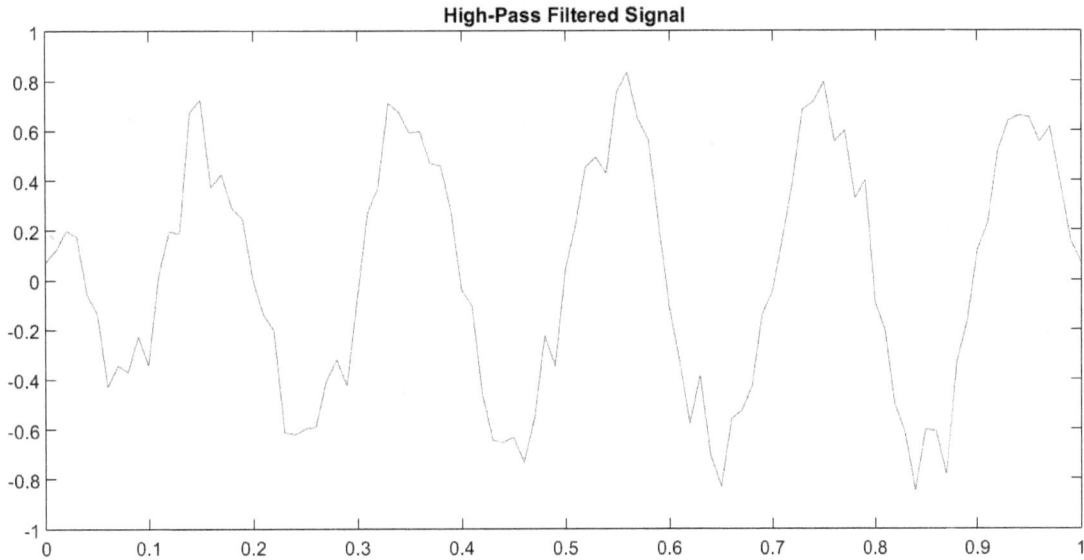

Figure 11.17: *Applying a high-pass filter in MATLAB*

Python:

```
b, a = butter(4, 0.1, btype='high')  # 4th-order filter
y = filtfilt(b, a, x)
plt.plot(t, y)
plt.title('High-Pass Filtered Signal')
plt.show()
```

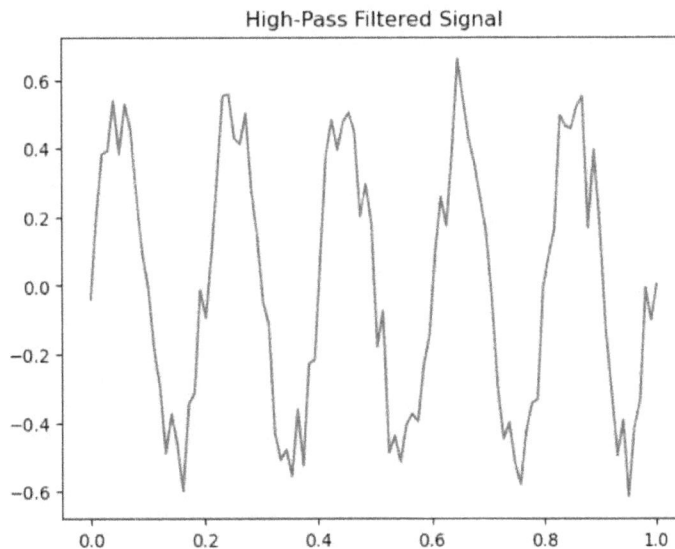

Figure 11.18: *Applying a high-pass filter in Python*

Example 11.14: Apply a band-pass filter

Objective: Apply a butterworth band-pass filter to a noisy signal.

MATLAB:

```
[b, a] = butter(4, [0.1, 0.5]); % 4th-order filter
y = filter(b, a, x);
plot(t, y);
title('Band-Pass Filtered Signal');
```

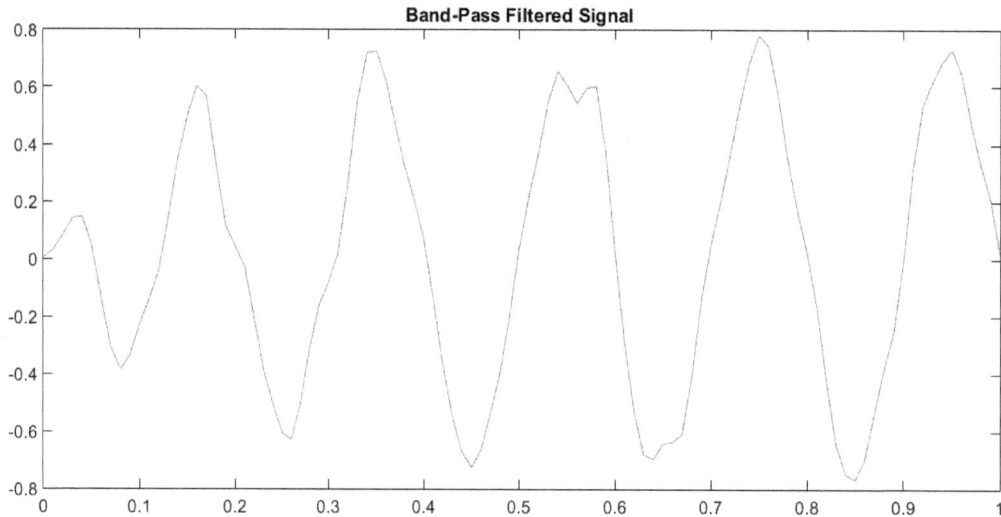

Figure 11.19: Applying a band-pass filter in MATLAB

Python:

```
b, a = butter(4, [0.1, 0.5], btype='band')  # 4th-order filter
y = filtfilt(b, a, x)
plt.plot(t, y)
plt.title('Band-Pass Filtered Signal')
plt.show()
```

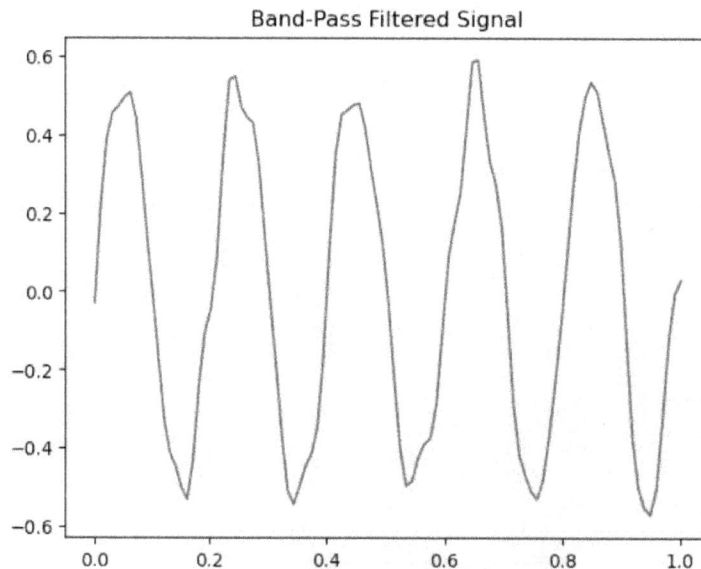

Figure 11.20: Applying a band-pass filter in Python

Example 11.15: Compute **Power Spectral Density (PSD)**

Objective: Compute and plot the PSD of a signal.

MATLAB:

```
[Pxx, f] = pwelch(x, [], [], [], 1/(t(2)-t(1)));
plot(f, 10*log10(Pxx));
title('Power Spectral Density');
```

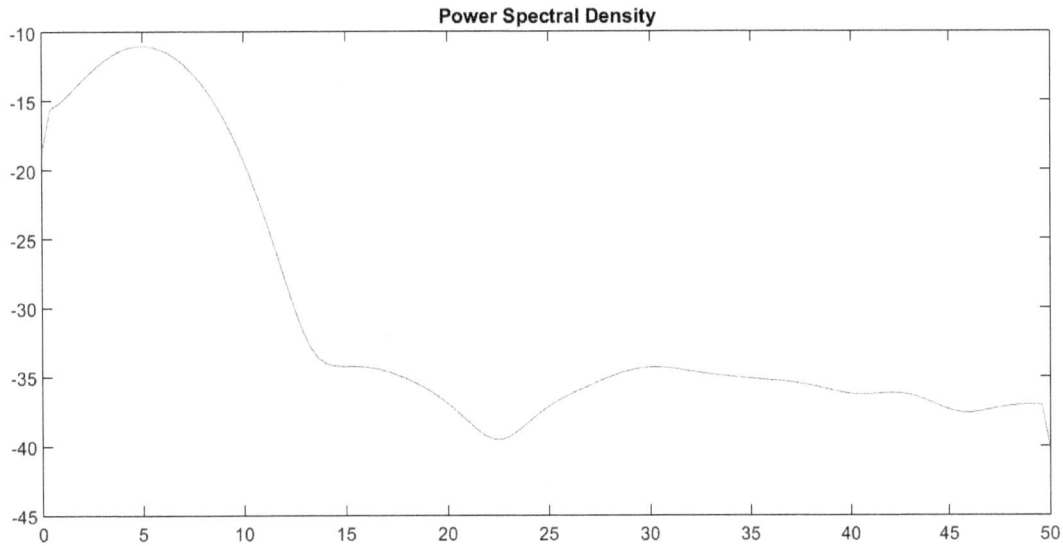

Figure 11.21: PSD in MATLAB

Python:

```
from scipy.signal import welch
f, Pxx = welch(x, fs=1/(t[1]-t[0]))
plt.plot(f, 10*np.log10(Pxx))
plt.title('Power Spectral Density')
plt.show()
```

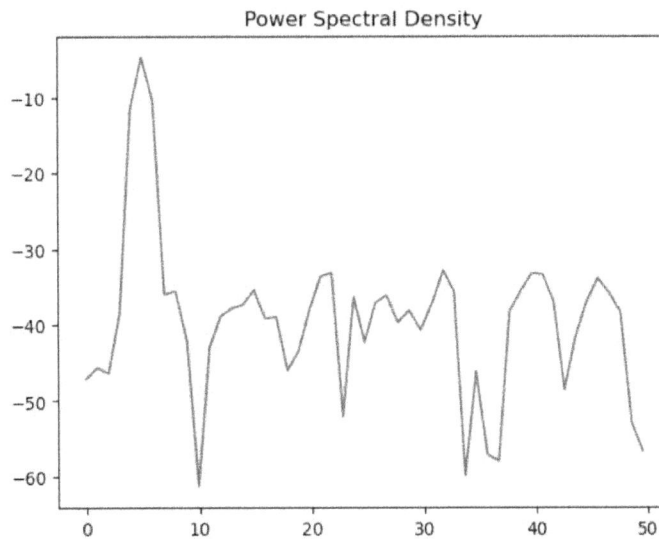

Figure 11.22: PSD in Python

Example 11.16: Resample a signal

Objective: Resample a signal to a different sampling rate, as shown in *Figures 11.23 and 11.24*.

MATLAB:

```
y = resample(x, 1, 2); % Downsample by a factor of 2
plot(y);
title('Resampled Signal');
```

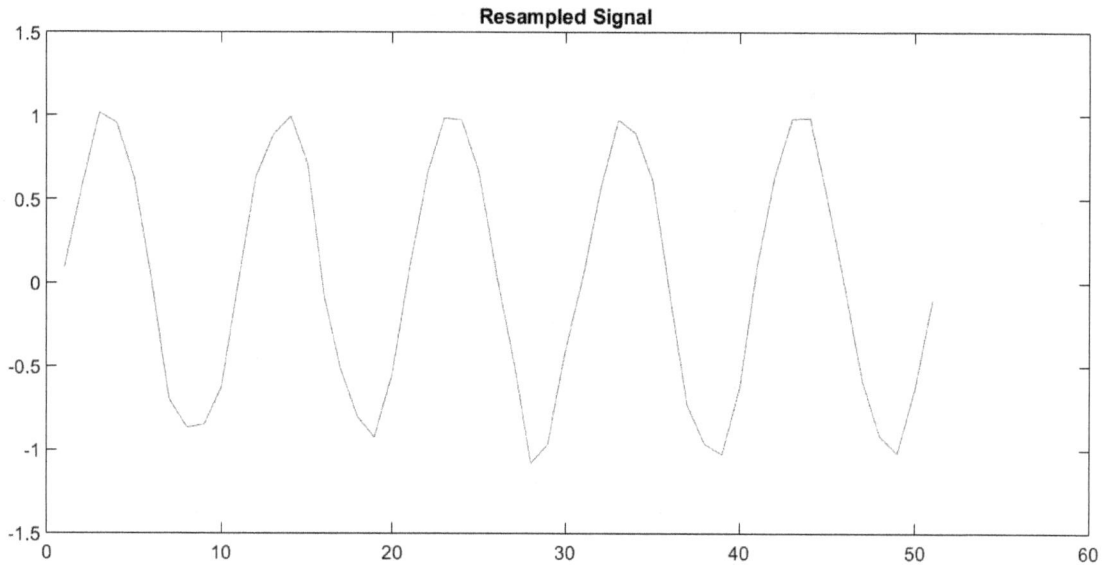

Figure 11.23: *Resampling of a signal in MATLAB*

Python:

```
from scipy.signal import resample
y = resample(x, len(x)//2)  # Downsample by a factor of 2
plt.plot(y)
plt.title('Resampled Signal')
plt.show()
```

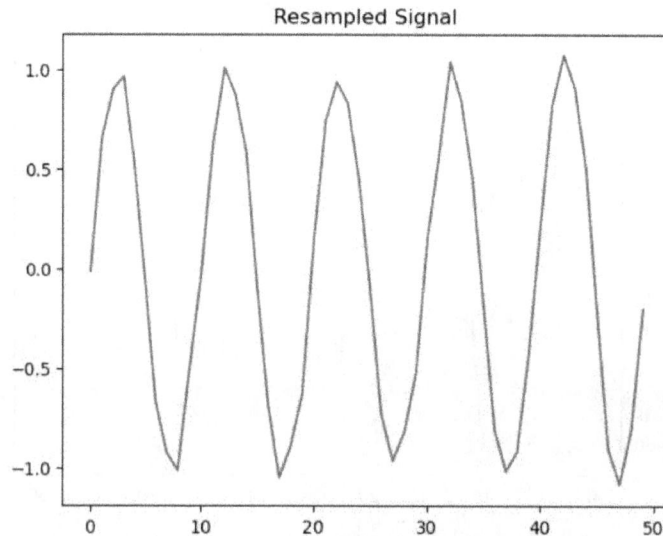

Figure 11.24: *Resampling of a signal in Python*

Example 11.17: Compute autocorrelation

Objective: Compute and plot the autocorrelation of a signal.

MATLAB:

```
[acf, lags] = xcorr(x, 'coeff');
plot(lags, acf);
title('Autocorrelation');
```

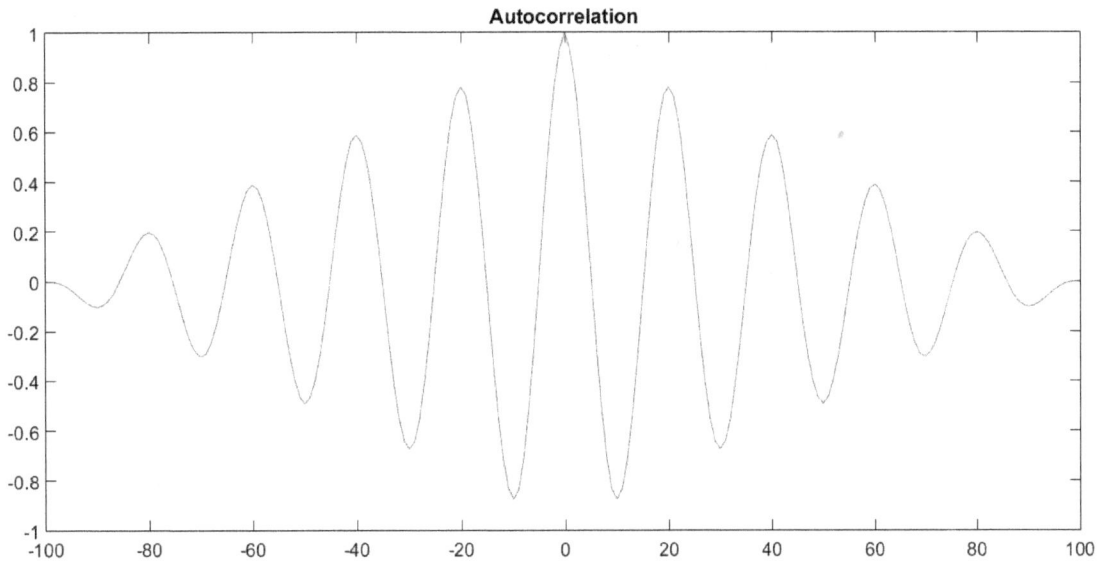

Figure 11.25: Autocorrelation in MATLAB

Python:

```
from scipy.signal import correlate
acf = correlate(x, x, mode='full') / np.max(correlate(x, x, mode='full'))
lags = np.arange(-len(x)+1, len(x))
plt.plot(lags, acf)
plt.title('Autocorrelation')
plt.show()
```

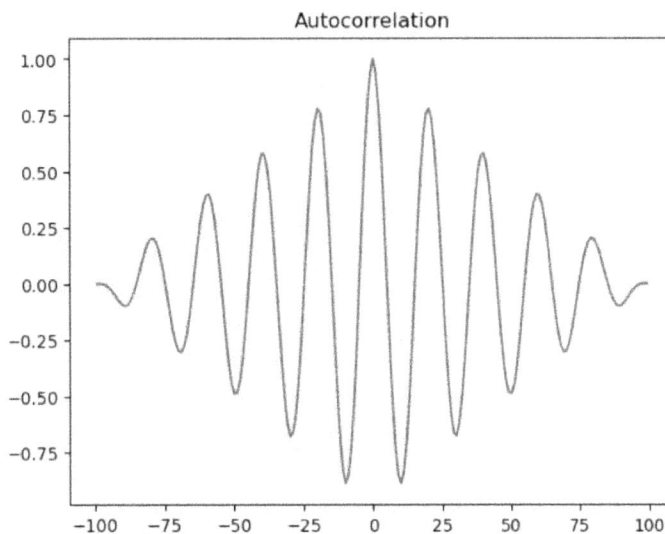

Figure 11.26: Autocorrelation in Python

Example 11.18: Generate a chirp signal

Objective: Generate and plot a chirp signal, shown in *Figure 11.27*.

MATLAB:

```
t = 0:0.001:1;
x = chirp(t, 0, 1, 100); % Chirp from 0 Hz to 100 Hz
plot(t, x);
title('Chirp Signal');
```

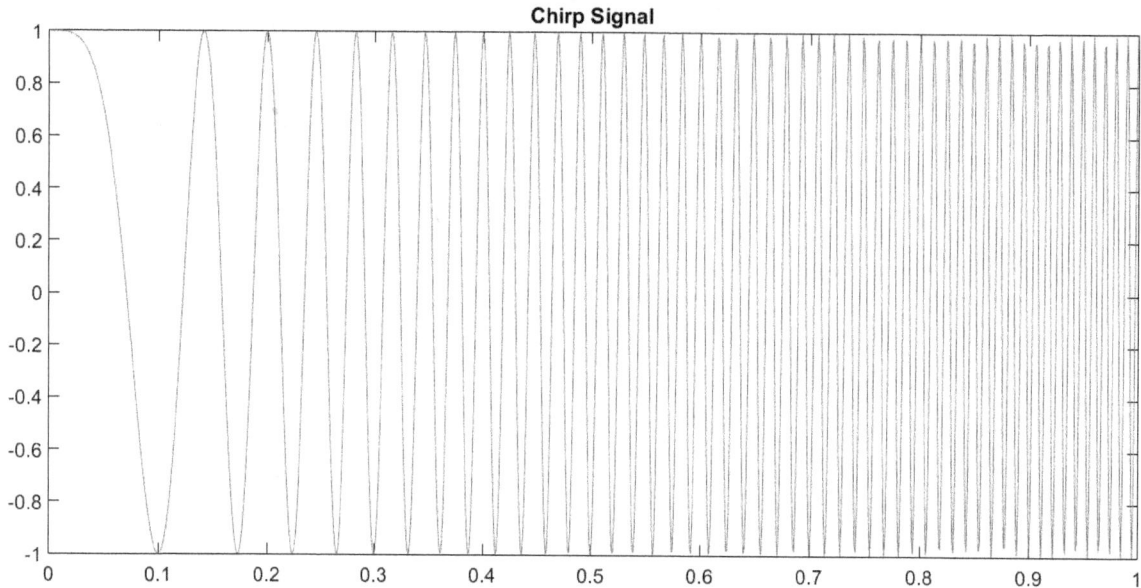

Figure 11.27: *Chirp signal in MATLAB*

Python:

```
from scipy.signal import chirp
t = np.linspace(0, 1, 1000)
x = chirp(t, f0=0, f1=100, t1=1)  # Chirp from 0 Hz to 100 Hz
plt.plot(t, x)
plt.title('Chirp Signal')
plt.show()
```

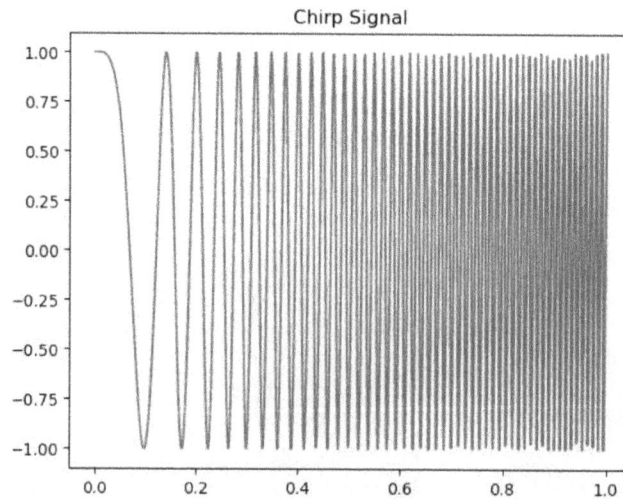

Figure 11.28: *Chirp signal in Python*

11.3.2 Image processing examples

In this section, several examples are discussed to study the comparative behavior of MATLAB and Python regarding image processing. Each example in this section is discussed via MATLAB and Python codes. MATLAB offers an intuitive approach with functions like **imread**, **rgb2gray**, **imgaussfilt**, and **edge**, which are tailored for academic and engineering environments. Python, on the other hand, relies on powerful libraries such as OpenCV and Matplotlib to achieve similar outcomes, though with more coding flexibility and integration possibilities in modern AI and data science workflows. For instance, the **cv2.cvtColor**, **cv2.GaussianBlur**, and **cv2.Canny** functions provide efficient image transformations in Python. Both tools support visualization and preprocessing with high accuracy, making them suitable for research and application development.

Example 11.19: Read and display an image

Objective: Read and display an image.

MATLAB:

```
img = imread('imagefile.jpg');
imshow(img);
title('Original Image');
```

Figure 11.29: Reading and displaying of an image in MATLAB

Note: **In MATLAB, colored image will be generated.**

Python:

```
import cv2
img = cv2.imread('image.jpg')
plt.imshow(cv2.cvtColor(img, cv2.COLOR_BGR2RGB))
plt.title('Original Image')
plt.show()
```

Figure 11.30: Reading and displaying of an image in Python

Note: **In Python, colored image will be generated.**

Example 11.20: Convert image to grayscale

Objective: Convert an RGB image to grayscale, as shown in *Figures 11.31* and *11.32*.

MATLAB:

```
img_gray = rgb2gray(img);
imshow(img_gray);
title('Grayscale Image');
```

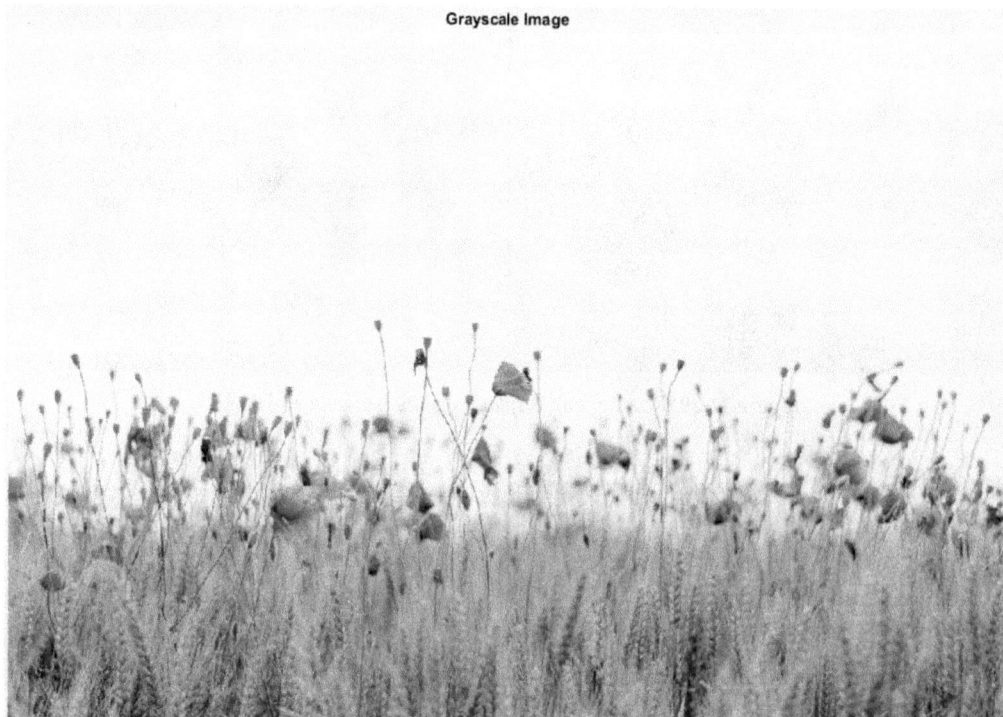

Figure 11.31: Converting an RGB image to grayscale in MATLAB

Python:
```
img_gray = cv2.cvtColor(img, cv2.COLOR_BGR2GRAY)
plt.imshow(img_gray, cmap='gray')
plt.title('Grayscale Image')
plt.show()
```

Figure 11.32: Converting an RGB image to grayscale in Python

Example 11.21: Apply Gaussian blur

Objective: Apply Gaussian blur to an image, as shown in *Figures 11.33* and *11.34*.

MATLAB:
```
img_blur = imgaussfilt(img_gray, 2);
imshow(img_blur);
title('Gaussian Blur');
```

Figure 11.33: Gaussian blur in MATLAB

Python:

```
img_blur = cv2.GaussianBlur(img_gray, (5, 5), 0)
plt.imshow(img_blur, cmap='gray')
plt.title('Gaussian Blur')
plt.show()
```

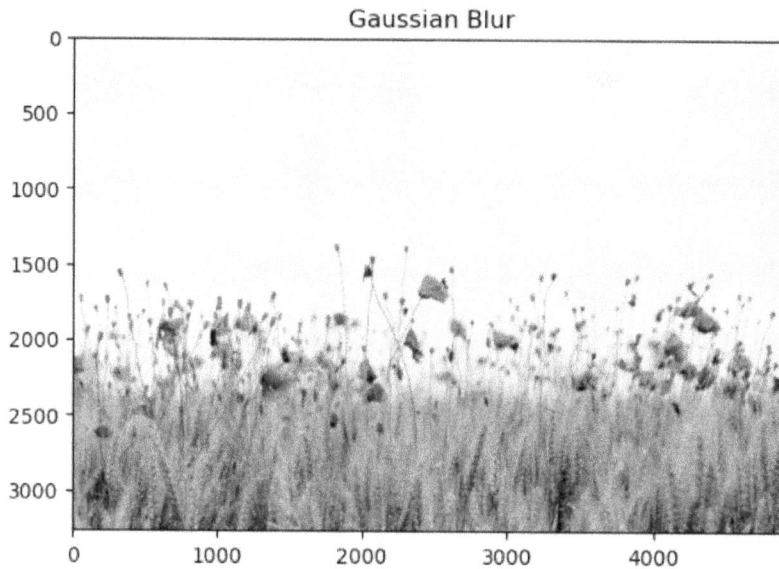

Figure 11.34: *Gaussian blur in Python*

Example 11.22: Detect edges using Canny (See *Figures 11.35* and *11.36*)

Objective: Detect edges in an image using the Canny method.

MATLAB:

```
edges = edge(img_gray, 'Canny');
imshow(edges);
title('Edge Detection');
```

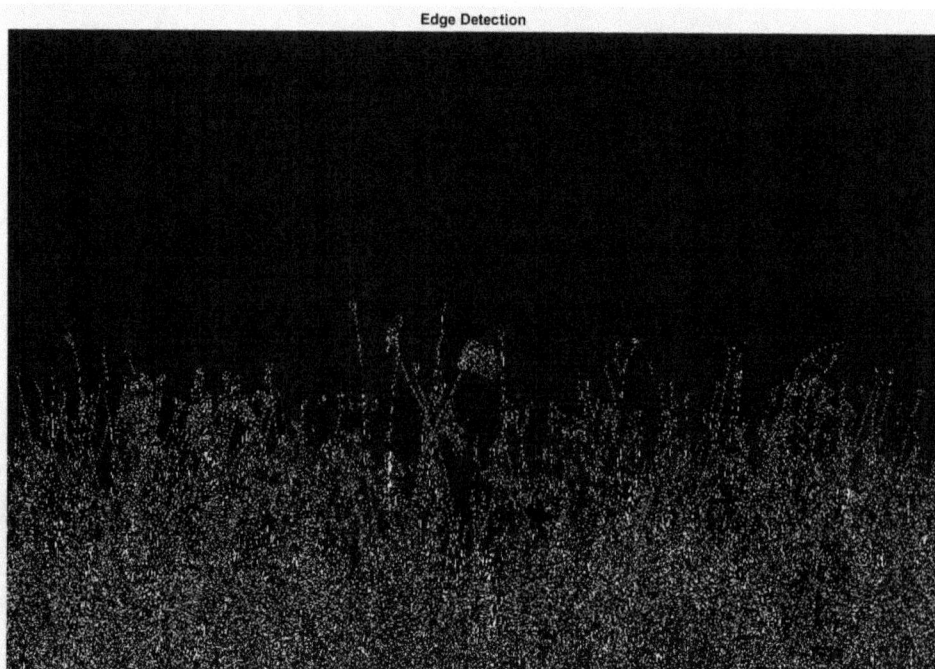

Figure 11.35: *Detection of edges in an image using the Canny method in MATLAB*

Python:

```
edges = cv2.Canny(img_gray, 100, 200)
plt.imshow(edges, cmap='gray')
plt.title('Edge Detection')
plt.show()
```

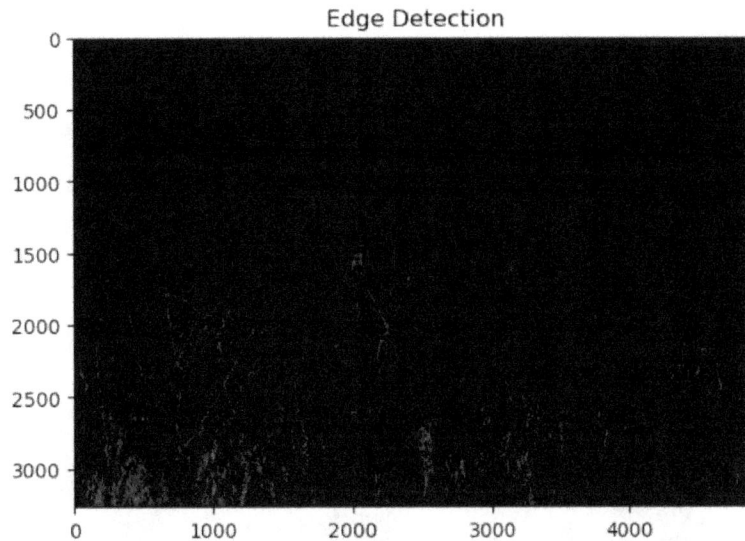

Figure 11.36: Detection of edges in an image using the Canny method in Python

Example 11.23: Apply the histogram equalization (See *Figures 11.37* and *11.38*)

Objective: Apply histogram equalization to an image.

MATLAB:

```
img_eq = histeq(img_gray);
imshow(img_eq);
title('Histogram Equalization');
```

Figure 11.37: Histogram equalization in MATLAB

Python:
```
img_eq = cv2.equalizeHist(img_gray)
plt.imshow(img_eq, cmap='gray')
plt.title('Histogram Equalization')
plt.show()
```

Figure 11.38: Histogram equalization in Python

11.3.3 Advanced applications

Advanced applications in image processing often involve techniques like object detection, segmentation, and feature extraction. This section provides a comparative example of object detection based on color thresholding using both MATLAB and Python. MATLAB leverages the rgb2hsv function and logical indexing to isolate regions within a specific hue range, followed by masking the original image using **bsxfun**. Python achieves the same using OpenCV's **cv2.cvtColor** and **cv2.inRange**, followed by **cv2.bitwise_and** to apply the mask. These techniques are commonly used in real-world applications such as medical imaging, traffic monitoring, robotics, and industrial inspection. The example highlights how each environment can be used to perform complex tasks with relative ease, enabling users to make informed choices based on their workflow and domain requirements.

Example 11.24: Object detection using color thresholding

Objective: Detect objects in an image based on color, as shown in *Figures 11.39* and *11.40*.

MATLAB:
```
img_hsv = rgb2hsv(img);
mask = (img_hsv(:,:,1) >= 0.1) & (img_hsv(:,:,1) <= 0.5);
img_object = bsxfun(@times, img, cast(mask, 'like', img));
imshow(img_object);
title('Detected Object');
```

Figure 11.39: Object detection using color thresholding in MATLAB

Python:

```
img_hsv = cv2.cvtColor(img, cv2.COLOR_BGR2HSV)
mask = cv2.inRange(img_hsv, (30, 40, 50), (80, 255, 255))
img_object = cv2.bitwise_and(img, img, mask=mask)
plt.imshow(cv2.cvtColor(img_object, cv2.COLOR_BGR2RGB))
plt.title('Detected Object')
plt.show()
```

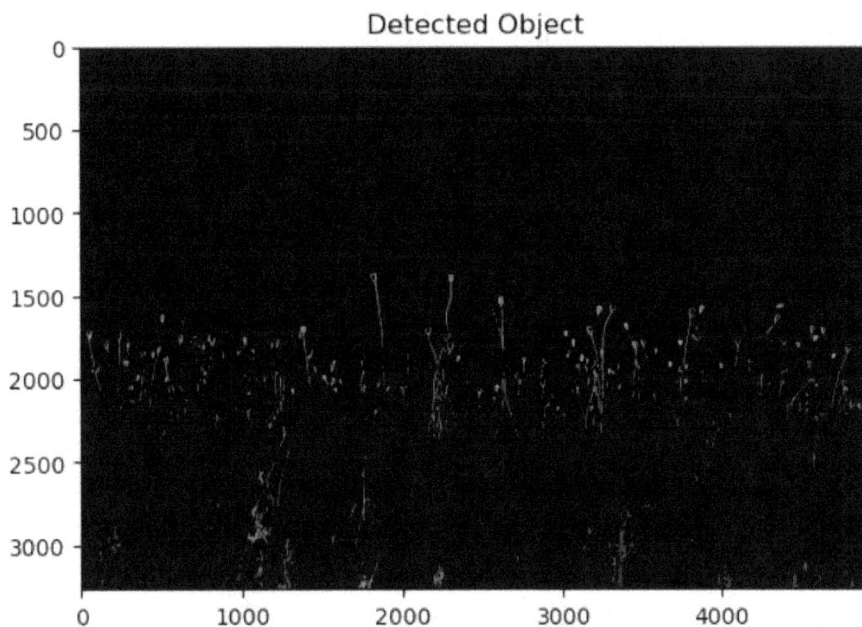

Figure 11.40: Object detection using color thresholding in Python

This section offers examples comparing MATLAB and Python for signal and image processing tasks. Each example includes code snippets and explanations, which enable readers to understand similarities and differences between these two environments.

Conclusion

In this chapter, we explored techniques utilized in signal processing and image processing within MATLAB and Python environments, highlighting their strengths and applications. MATLAB excels in speedy prototyping and mathematical modeling, which offers user-friendly toolboxes for signal and image analysis. Python provides flexibility, scalability, and seamless integration with machine learning and data science frameworks. Through comparative examples, we demonstrated how these platforms may be utilized for tasks such as filtering, Fourier transforms, noise reduction, edge detection, object recognition, and deep learning-based image classification. This chapter focused on the fact that MATLAB and Python are complementary tools, and the choice between them depends on project requirements and the availability of libraries. Via mastering these environments, readers can effectively tackle challenges in fields like telecommunications, computer vision, and medical imaging. This chapter serves as a complete guide for students, researchers, and professionals, providing a robust foundation for further exploration in signal and image processing. The next chapter will provide some insights into the possible case studies in MATLAB and Python for practice purposes for the readers.

Exercises

Signal processing – Conceptual understanding (MATLAB and Python)

1. What is the purpose of signal processing in communication systems?

2. Explain the difference between analog and digital signals.

3. What is the Nyquist sampling theorem and why is it important?

4. Define and differentiate between FIR and IIR filters.

5. What is aliasing in signal processing, and how can it be prevented?

6. How do you compute the FFT of a signal in MATLAB? Give an example.

7. Describe the role of the window function in spectral analysis.

8. What does a spectrogram represent in audio signal processing?

9. How does autocorrelation help in analyzing signals?

10. Explain the concept of convolution and its use in filtering.

Signal processing – MATLAB coding practice

1. Write MATLAB code to generate and plot a sine wave of 10 Hz.

2. How do you apply a low-pass filter to a signal in MATLAB?

3. Use xcorr to compute and plot the autocorrelation of a signal.

4. Write a MATLAB program to downsample a signal by a factor of 2.

5. Generate a chirp signal using MATLAB and plot it.

6. Create a noisy sine wave in MATLAB and apply a moving average filter.

7. Plot the frequency spectrum of a signal using FFT in MATLAB.

8. Use filter in MATLAB to remove high-frequency components from a signal.

9. Write MATLAB code to compute the energy of a discrete signal.

10. Apply a bandpass filter to an audio file in MATLAB and plot the result.

Signal processing – Python coding practice

1. Write Python code to read an audio signal using scipy.io.wavfile.

2. Use matplotlib to plot the waveform and its FFT.

3. Implement a Butterworth low-pass filter using scipy.signal.butter.

4. Write Python code to compute and plot the autocorrelation of a signal.

5. Resample a signal in Python using scipy.signal.resample.

6. Create and visualize a spectrogram using scipy.signal.spectrogram.

7. Generate a chirp signal in Python and visualize it.

8. Apply a moving average filter to smooth a noisy signal in Python.

9. How can you normalize a signal in Python using NumPy?

10. Use scipy.signal.convolve to filter a noisy ECG signal.

Image processing – Conceptual understanding (MATLAB and Python)

1. What is the difference between grayscale and binary images?

2. Explain HSV and RGB color spaces. When is HSV preferred?

3. What is histogram equalization, and why is it used?

4. Define convolution in the context of image filtering.

5. What is the purpose of edge detection in image processing?

6. Describe morphological operations: erosion and dilation.

7. How does Gaussian blur improve image quality?

8. What is thresholding, and how is it used in object detection?

9. What are the main steps involved in the Canny edge detection method?

10. Compare and contrast MATLAB and Python for image processing workflows.

Image processing – MATLAB coding practice

1. Read and display an image in MATLAB. Convert it to grayscale.

2. Apply Gaussian blur using imgaussfilt and visualize the result.

3. Perform edge detection using the Canny method in MATLAB.

4. Write MATLAB code to detect objects using HSV thresholding.

5. Use histeq to enhance the contrast of a grayscale image.

Image processing – Python coding practice

1. Read an image using OpenCV and convert it to HSV.

2. Apply a color threshold using cv2.inRange and mask the object.

3. Perform histogram equalization using cv2.equalizeHist.

4. Detect edges using the Canny algorithm in OpenCV.

5. Apply the Gaussian blur using cv2.GaussianBlur and visualize the output using matplotlib.

Join our Discord space

Join our Discord workspace for latest updates, offers, tech happenings around the world, new releases, and sessions with the authors:

https://discord.bpbonline.com

## CHAPTER 12

Case Studies in MATLAB and Python

Introduction

In this chapter, case studies are provided in MATLAB and Python. This content is provided chapter-wise for the better understanding of the concepts. Readers will gain a full insight of the discussed content in the book via practicing these case studies.

Structure

This chapter covers the following topic:

- Chapter-wise exercises

Objectives

The objectives of this chapter are to provide practical, real-world case studies that illustrate the application of MATLAB and Python to solve complex problems across diverse fields such as engineering, finance, signal processing, and data science. Through hands-on examples, readers will learn how to implement numerical computations, data analysis, and visualization techniques in both environments which enables them to compare their strengths and limitations. The chapter aims to develop problem-solving skills by guiding readers through industry-relevant scenarios, including signal filtering, image processing, financial modeling, and statistical analysis. By working through these case studies, readers will gain proficiency in translating theoretical concepts into functional code, optimizing workflows, and selecting the appropriate tool (MATLAB or Python) for specific tasks. Additionally, the chapter emphasizes best practices in algorithm development, debugging, and performance evaluation, equipping readers with the expertise to tackle real-world challenges efficiently.

Chapter-wise exercises

Chapter 1, Introduction to MATLAB and Python exercises:

- **MATLAB overview**: Describe the main applications of MATLAB in scientific computing and engineering.

- **MATLAB environment**: Explain the functions of MATLAB's toolboxes, workspace, and Command Window.

- **Basic syntax**: Create a MATLAB script to carry out addition, subtraction, multiplication, and division, among other fundamental arithmetic operations.

- **Python introduction**: Examine Python's readability and adaptability in comparison to other programming languages.

- **Python environment setup**: Describe how to install Python and configure an IDE such as Jupyter Notebook or PyCharm.

- **Basic syntax**: Create a Python program that prints "Hello, World!" and carries out simple math operations.

- **MATLAB versus Python**: Compare the basic syntax of MATLAB and Python for arithmetic operations.

- **MATLAB toolboxes**: Research and list three MATLAB toolboxes and their applications.

- **Python libraries**: List the three Python libraries that are necessary for scientific computing, along with their applications.

- **MATLAB Command Window**: Demonstrate how to use the Command Window to execute simple commands.

- **Python REPL**: Describe the Python REPL's function and provide a basic example to illustrate how to utilize it.

- **MATLAB Workspace**: Describe how to view and manage variables in the MATLAB Workspace.

- **Python variables**: Write a Python script to declare and print variables of different data types.

- **MATLAB scripts**: Create a MATLAB script to calculate the area of a circle given its radius.

- **Python scripts**: Write a Python script to calculate the factorial of a number.

- **MATLAB help function**: Demonstrate how to use the help function in MATLAB to get information about a specific function.

- **Python documentation**: Explain how to access and use Python documentation for a given library or function.

- **MATLAB path management**: Describe how to add a directory to the MATLAB path and why it is important.

- **Python virtual environments**: Explain the purpose of virtual environments in Python and how to create one.

- **MATLAB live scripts**: Compare MATLAB live scripts with regular scripts and provide an example of a live script.

- **Python Notebooks**: Describe the advantages of using Jupyter Notebooks for Python programming.

- **MATLAB debugging**: Explain the basic debugging tools available in MATLAB and how to use them.

- **Python debugging**: Describe the use of the **pdb** module for debugging Python code.

- **MATLAB plotting**: Write a MATLAB script to plot a simple sine wave.

- **Python plotting**: Use Matplotlib to plot a sine wave in Python.

Chapter 2, MATLAB and Python Variables and Data Types

- **MATLAB variables**: To define and initialize variables of various data kinds, write a MATLAB script.

- **Python variables**: To define and initialize variables of various data types, write a Python script.

- **MATLAB arrays**: To create a 3×3 matrix and carry out element-wise multiplication, write a MATLAB script.

- **Python lists**: Write a Python script to create a list of integers and perform basic operations like appending and slicing.

- **MATLAB strings**: Demonstrate how to concatenate two strings in MATLAB.

- **Python strings**: Write a Python script to reverse a string and check if it is a palindrome.

- **MATLAB cell arrays**: Create a MATLAB cell array to store different data types and access its elements.

- **Python tuples**: Write a Python script to create a tuple and demonstrate its immutability.

- **MATLAB structures**: Create a MATLAB structure to store student information (name, age, grade) and access its fields.

- **Python dictionaries**: Create a dictionary using a Python script to store and retrieve student data.

- **MATLAB data types**: List the different data types supported by MATLAB and provide an example of each.

- **Python data types**: List the different data types supported by Python and provide an example of each.

- **MATLAB matrix operations**: Write a MATLAB script to perform matrix multiplication and transposition.

- **Python list operations**: Write a Python script to perform list operations like sorting, reversing, and finding the maximum value.

- **MATLAB string manipulation**: Write a MATLAB script to find the length of a string and extract a substring.

- **Python string manipulation**: Write a Python script to count the occurrences of a specific character in a string.

- **MATLAB cell array operations**: Write a MATLAB script to concatenate two cell arrays and access specific elements.

- **Python dictionary operations**: Write a Python script to add, update, and delete key-value pairs in a dictionary.

- **MATLAB structure operations**: Write a MATLAB script to add a new field to an existing structure and update its value.

- **Python tuple operations**: Write a Python script to unpack a tuple and demonstrate its use in function return values.

- **MATLAB data type conversion**: Write a MATLAB script to convert a numeric array to a string array.

- **Python data type conversion**: Write a Python script to convert a list of integers to a list of strings.

- **MATLAB array indexing**: Write a MATLAB script to access specific elements of a 2D array using indexing.

- **Python list indexing**: Write a Python script to access specific elements of a list using negative indexing.

- **MATLAB versus Python data types**: Compare the data types available in MATLAB and Python, highlighting their similarities and differences.

Chapter 3, Basic Operations in MATLAB and Python

- **MATLAB arithmetic operations**: Write a MATLAB script to perform basic arithmetic operations on two matrices.

- **Python arithmetic operations**: Write a Python script to perform basic arithmetic operations on two lists of numbers.

- **MATLAB matrix operations**: Write a MATLAB script to perform matrix multiplication and element-wise division.

- **Python list operations**: Write a Python script to perform element-wise addition and multiplication on two lists.

- **MATLAB logical operations**: Write a MATLAB script to perform logical operations (AND, OR, NOT) on two arrays.

- **Python Logical Operations**: Write a Python script to perform logical operations (AND, OR, NOT) on two lists of Boolean values.

- **MATLAB string manipulation**: Write a MATLAB script to concatenate two strings and find the length of the resulting string.

- **Python string manipulation**: Write a Python script to concatenate two strings and find the number of words in the resulting string.

- **MATLAB built-in functions**: Write a MATLAB script to use built-in functions like `sum`, `mean`, and `max` on an array.

- **Python built-in functions**: Write a Python script to use built-in functions like `sum`, `min`, and `len` on a list.

- **MATLAB matrix functions**: Write a MATLAB script to find the determinant and inverse of a matrix.

- **Python list functions**: Write a Python script to find the sum, average, and maximum value in a list.

- **MATLAB array indexing**: Write a MATLAB script to access specific elements of a 2D array using logical indexing.

- **Python list indexing**: Write a Python script to access specific elements of a list using slicing.

- **MATLAB string functions**: Write a MATLAB script to find and replace a substring within a string.

- **Python string functions**: Write a Python script to split a string into a list of words and join them back into a single string.

- **MATLAB element-wise operations**: Write a MATLAB script to perform element-wise multiplication and division on two arrays.

- **Python element-wise operations**: Write a Python script to perform element-wise addition and subtraction on two lists.

- **MATLAB matrix transposition**: Write a MATLAB script to transpose a matrix and verify the result.

- **Python list transposition**: Write a Python script to transpose a list of lists (matrix) and verify the result.

- **MATLAB logical indexing**: Write a MATLAB script to extract elements from an array that satisfy a specific condition.

- **Python list comprehension**: Write a Python script to create a new list containing only the even numbers from an existing list.

- **MATLAB string comparison**: Write a MATLAB script to compare two strings and determine if they are equal.

- **Python string comparison**: Write a Python script to compare two strings and determine if one is a substring of the other.

- **MATLAB versus Python operations**: Compare the basic operations (arithmetic, logical, and string) in MATLAB and Python, highlighting their similarities and differences.

Chapter 4, Control Flow and Structures in MATLAB and Python

- **MATLAB conditional statements**: Write a MATLAB script to check if a number is positive, negative, or zero using if-else statements.

- **Python conditional statements**: Write a Python script to check if a number is even or odd using if-elif-else statements.

- **MATLAB for loops**: Write a MATLAB script to print the first 10 natural numbers using a for loop.

- **Python for loops**: Write a Python script to print the first 10 natural numbers using a for loop.

- **MATLAB while loops**: Write a MATLAB script to find the factorial of a number using a while loop.

- **Python while loops**: Write a Python script to find the factorial of a number using a while loop.

- **MATLAB nested loops**: Write a MATLAB script to print a multiplication table using nested for loops.

- **Python nested loops**: Write a Python script to print a multiplication table using nested for loops.

- **MATLAB switch-case**: Write a MATLAB script to implement a simple calculator using switch-case statements.

- **Python match-case**: Write a Python script to implement a simple calculator using match-case statements (Python 3.10+).

- **MATLAB break statement**: Write a MATLAB script to demonstrate the use of the break statement in a loop.

- **Python break statement**: Write a Python script to demonstrate the use of the break statement in a loop.

- **MATLAB continue statement**: Write a MATLAB script to demonstrate the use of the continue statement in a loop.

- **Python continue statement**: Write a Python script to demonstrate the use of the continue statement in a loop.

- **MATLAB error handling**: Write a MATLAB script to handle division by zero using try-catch blocks.

- **Python error handling**: Write a Python script to handle division by zero using try-except blocks.

- **MATLAB vectorized operations**: Write a MATLAB script to perform element-wise operations on an array without using loops.

- **Python list comprehensions**: Write a Python script to create a list of squares of the first 10 natural numbers using list comprehension.

- **MATLAB loop optimization**: Write a MATLAB script to compare the performance of a loop-based operation with a vectorized operation.

- **Python loop optimization**: Write a Python script to compare the performance of a loop-based operation with a list comprehension.

- **MATLAB conditional expressions**: Write a MATLAB script to use a ternary conditional expression to assign a value based on a condition.

- **Python conditional expressions**: Write a Python script to use a ternary conditional expression to assign a value based on a condition.

- **MATLAB nested if-else**: Write a MATLAB script to implement a nested if-else structure to check multiple conditions.

- **Python nested if-elif-else**: Write a Python script to implement a nested if-elif-else structure to check multiple conditions.

- **MATLAB versus Python control flow**: Compare the control flow structures (conditional statements, loops) in MATLAB and Python, highlighting their similarities and differences.

Chapter 5, Functions and Scripts in MATLAB and Python

- **MATLAB functions**: Write a MATLAB function to calculate the area of a rectangle given its length and width.

- **Python functions**: Write a Python function to calculate the area of a rectangle given its length and width.

- **MATLAB scripts**: Write a MATLAB script to call the rectangle area function and display the result.

- **Python scripts**: Write a Python script to call the rectangle area function and display the result.

- **MATLAB anonymous functions**: Write a MATLAB script to define an anonymous function that calculates the square of a number.

- **Python lambda functions**: Write a Python script to define a lambda function that calculates the square of a number.

- **MATLAB function handles**: Write a MATLAB script to create a function handle and use it to call a function.

- **Python function objects**: Write a Python script to create a function object and use it to call a function.

- **MATLAB nested functions**: Write a MATLAB script to define a nested function and demonstrate its use.

- **Python nested functions**: Write a Python script to define a nested function and demonstrate its use.

- **MATLAB variable scope**: Write a MATLAB script to demonstrate the scope of variables within and outside a function.

- **Python variable scope**: Write a Python script to demonstrate the scope of variables within and outside a function.

- **MATLAB recursive functions**: Write a MATLAB script to implement a recursive function to calculate the factorial of a number.

- **Python recursive functions**: Write a Python script to implement a recursive function to calculate the factorial of a number.

- **MATLAB function input/output**: Write a MATLAB script to define a function that takes multiple inputs and returns multiple outputs.

- **Python function input/output**: Write a Python script to define a function that takes multiple inputs and returns multiple outputs.

- **MATLAB script organization**: Write a MATLAB script to organize multiple functions and scripts into a single project.

- **Python script organization**: Write a Python script to organize multiple functions and scripts into a single project.

- **MATLAB function documentation**: Write a MATLAB script to add documentation to a function using comments.

- **Python function documentation**: Write a Python script to add documentation to a function using docstrings.

- **MATLAB function overloading**: Write a MATLAB script to demonstrate function overloading by defining multiple functions with the same name but different inputs.

- **Python function overloading**: Write a Python script to demonstrate function overloading using default arguments and variable-length arguments.

- **MATLAB function debugging**: Write a MATLAB script to debug a function using breakpoints and the MATLAB debugger.

- **Python function debugging**: Write a Python script to debug a function using the **pdb** module.

- **MATLAB vs. Python functions**: Compare the function definitions, usage, and features in MATLAB and Python, highlighting their similarities and differences.

Chapter 6, Data Handling in MATLAB and Python

- **MATLAB file reading**: Write a MATLAB script to read data from a text file and display it in the Command Window.

- **Python file reading**: Write a Python script to read data from a text file and print it to the console.

- **MATLAB file writing**: Write a MATLAB script to write data to a text file.

- **Python file writing**: Write a Python script to write data to a text file.

- **MATLAB CSV import**: Write a MATLAB script to import data from a CSV file and store it in a matrix.

- **Python CSV import**: Write a Python script to import data from a CSV file using the csv module.

- **MATLAB CSV export**: Write a MATLAB script to export a matrix to a CSV file.

- **Python CSV export**: Write a Python script to export a list of lists to a CSV file using the csv module.

- **MATLAB Excel import**: Write a MATLAB script to import data from an Excel file using **readtable**.

- **Python Excel import**: Write a Python script to import data from an Excel file using **pandas**.

- **MATLAB Excel export**: Write a MATLAB script to export a table to an Excel file using **writetable**.

- **Python Excel export**: Write a Python script to export a **DataFrame** to an Excel file using **pandas**.

- **MATLAB binary files**: Write a MATLAB script to read and write data to a binary file.

- **Python binary files**: Write a Python script to read and write data to a binary file.

- **MATLAB data parsing**: Write a MATLAB script to parse a structured text file and extract specific data.

- **Python data parsing**: Write a Python script to parse a structured text file and extract specific data.

- **MATLAB data filtering**: Write a MATLAB script to filter data based on specific criteria and save the filtered data to a new file.

- **Python data filtering**: Write a Python script to filter data based on specific criteria and save the filtered data to a new file.

- **MATLAB data transformation**: Write a MATLAB script to transform data (e.g., scaling, normalization) and save the transformed data to a new file.

- **Python data transformation**: Write a Python script to transform data (e.g., scaling, normalization) and save the transformed data to a new file.

- **MATLAB data visualization**: Write a MATLAB script to visualize data from a file using basic plotting functions.

- **Python data visualization**: Write a Python script to visualize data from a file using `matplotlib`.

- **MATLAB data aggregation**: Write a MATLAB script to aggregate data (e.g., sum, average) from a file and display the results.

- **Python data aggregation**: Write a Python script to aggregate data (e.g., sum, average) from a file and display the results.

- **MATLAB versus Python data handling**: Compare the data handling capabilities (file I/O, data parsing, filtering) in MATLAB and Python, highlighting their similarities and differences.

Chapter 7, Data handling in MATLAB and Python

- **MATLAB JSON import**: Write a MATLAB script to import data from a JSON file using `jsondecode`.

- **Python JSON import**: Write a Python script to import data from a JSON file using the `json` module.

- **MATLAB JSON export**: Write a MATLAB script to export data to a JSON file using `jsonencode`.

- **Python JSON export**: Write a Python script to export data to a JSON file using the `json` module.

- **MATLAB XML import**: Write a MATLAB script to import data from an XML file using `xmlread`.

- **Python XML import**: Write a Python script to import data from an XML file using `xml.etree.ElementTree`.

- **MATLAB XML export**: Write a MATLAB script to export data to an XML file using `xmlwrite`.

- **Python XML export**: Write a Python script to export data to an XML file using `xml.etree.ElementTree`.

- **MATLAB database connectivity**: Write a MATLAB script to connect to a SQL database and retrieve data using database.

- **Python database connectivity**: Write a Python script to connect to a SQL database and retrieve data using `sqlite3`.

- **MATLAB data cleaning**: Write a MATLAB script to clean data (e.g., handle missing values, remove duplicates) from a dataset.

- **Python data cleaning**: Write a Python script to clean data (e.g., handle missing values, remove duplicates) from a dataset using `pandas`.

- **MATLAB data merging**: Write a MATLAB script to merge two datasets based on a common key.

- **Python data merging**: Write a Python script to merge two datasets based on a common key using `pandas`.

- **MATLAB data reshaping**: Write a MATLAB script to reshape data (e.g., wide to long format) using `reshape`.

- **Python data reshaping**: Write a Python script to reshape data (e.g., wide to long format) using `pandas`.

- **MATLAB data sampling**: Write a MATLAB script to randomly sample data from a dataset.

- **Python data sampling**: Write a Python script to randomly sample data from a dataset using **pandas**.

- **MATLAB data grouping**: Write a MATLAB script to group data based on a specific column and calculate summary statistics.

- **Python data grouping**: Write a Python script to group data based on a specific column and calculate summary statistics using **pandas**.

- **MATLAB data pivoting**: Write a MATLAB script to pivot data (e.g., create a pivot table) using **unstack**.

- **Python data pivoting**: Write a Python script to pivot data (e.g., create a pivot table) using **pandas**.

- **MATLAB data interpolation**: Write a MATLAB script to interpolate missing data in a dataset.

- **Python data interpolation**: Write a Python script to interpolate missing data in a dataset using **pandas**.

- **MATLAB versus Python advanced data handling**: Compare the advanced data handling capabilities (JSON, XML, databases, data cleaning, merging, reshaping) in MATLAB and Python, highlighting their similarities and differences.

Chapter 8, Plotting and Visualization in MATLAB and Python

- **MATLAB basic plotting**: Write a MATLAB script to plot a sine wave and a cosine wave on the same graph.

- **Python basic plotting**: Write a Python script to plot a sine wave and a cosine wave on the same graph using **matplotlib**.

- **MATLAB customizing plots**: Write a MATLAB script to customize a plot with titles, labels, legends, and grid lines.

- **Python customizing plots**: Write a Python script to customize a plot with titles, labels, legends, and grid lines using **matplotlib**.

- **MATLAB subplots**: Write a MATLAB script to create subplots of sine, cosine, and tangent waves.

- **Python subplots**: Write a Python script to create subplots of sine, cosine, and tangent waves using **matplotlib**.

- **MATLAB bar charts**: Write a MATLAB script to create a bar chart comparing the sales of different products.

- **Python bar charts**: Write a Python script to create a bar chart comparing the sales of different products using **matplotlib**.

- **MATLAB histograms**: Write a MATLAB script to create a histogram of a dataset showing the distribution of values.

- **Python histograms**: Write a Python script to create a histogram of a dataset showing the distribution of values using **matplotlib**.

- **MATLAB scatter plots**: Write a MATLAB script to create a scatter plot of two variables and add a trend line.

- **Python scatter plots**: Write a Python script to create a scatter plot of two variables and add a trend line using **matplotlib**.

- **MATLAB 3D plotting**: Write a MATLAB script to create a 3D surface plot of a mathematical function.

- **Python 3D plotting**: Write a Python script to create a 3D surface plot of a mathematical function using **matplotlib**.

- **MATLAB polar plots**: Write a MATLAB script to create a polar plot of a mathematical function.

- **Python polar plots**: Write a Python script to create a polar plot of a mathematical function using `matplotlib`.

- **MATLAB heatmaps**: Write a MATLAB script to create a heatmap of a correlation matrix.

- **Python heatmaps**: Write a Python script to create a heatmap of a correlation matrix using `seaborn`.

- **MATLAB annotations**: Write a MATLAB script to add annotations (text, arrows) to a plot.

- **Python annotations**: Write a Python script to add annotations (text, arrows) to a plot using `matplotlib`.

- **MATLAB plot export**: Write a MATLAB script to export a plot as an image file (e.g., PNG, JPEG).

- **Python plot export**: Write a Python script to export a plot as an image file (e.g., PNG, JPEG) using `matplotlib`.

- **MATLAB interactive plots**: Write a MATLAB script to create an interactive plot using `plotly`.

- **Python interactive plots**: Write a Python script to create an interactive plot using `plotly`.

- **MATLAB versus Python plotting**: Compare the plotting and visualization capabilities in MATLAB and Python, highlighting their similarities and differences.

Chapter 9, Plotting and Visualization in MATLAB and Python

- **MATLAB advanced plotting**: Write a MATLAB script to create a contour plot of a 2D function.

- **Python advanced plotting**: Write a Python script to create a contour plot of a 2D function using `matplotlib`.

- **MATLAB 3D bar charts**: Write a MATLAB script to create a 3D bar chart comparing the sales of different products over time.

- **Python 3D bar charts**: Write a Python script to create a 3D bar chart comparing the sales of different products over time using `matplotlib`.

- **MATLAB surface plots**: Write a MATLAB script to create a surface plot of a 3D function with custom colormaps.

- **Python surface plots**: Write a Python script to create a surface plot of a 3D function with custom colormaps using `matplotlib`.

- **MATLAB stream plots**: Write a MATLAB script to create a stream plot of a vector field.

- **Python stream plots**: Write a Python script to create a stream plot of a vector field using `matplotlib`.

- **MATLAB pie charts**: Write a MATLAB script to create a pie chart showing the market share of different products.

- **Python pie charts**: Write a Python script to create a pie chart showing the market share of different products using `matplotlib`.

- **MATLAB box plots**: Write a MATLAB script to create a box plot showing the distribution of data across different categories.

- **Python box plots**: Write a Python script to create a box plot showing the distribution of data across different categories using `seaborn`.

- **MATLAB violin plots**: Write a MATLAB script to create a violin plot showing the distribution of data across different categories.

- **Python violin plots**: Write a Python script to create a violin plot showing the distribution of data across different categories using **seaborn**.

- **MATLAB pair plots**: Write a MATLAB script to create a pair plot showing the relationships between multiple variables.

- **Python pair plots**: Write a Python script to create a pair plot showing the relationships between multiple variables using **seaborn**.

- **MATLAB animated plots**: Write a MATLAB script to create an animated plot of a sine wave.

- **Python animated plots**: Write a Python script to create an animated plot of a sine wave using **matplotlib.animation**.

- **MATLAB geographic plots**: Write a MATLAB script to create a geographic plot showing the locations of different cities.

- **Python geographic plots**: Write a Python script to create a geographic plot showing the locations of different cities using basemap.

- **MATLAB custom colormaps**: Write a MATLAB script to create a custom colormap and apply it to a surface plot.

- **Python custom colormaps**: Write a Python script to create a custom colormap and apply it to a surface plot using **matplotlib**.

- **MATLAB Plotly integration**: Write a MATLAB script to create an interactive plot using Plotly.

- **Python Plotly integration**: Write a Python script to create an interactive plot using Plotly.

- **MATLAB versus Python advanced visualization**: Compare the advanced visualization capabilities (3D plots, contour plots, geographic plots, animations) in MATLAB and Python, highlighting their similarities and differences.

Chapter 10, Data Manipulation and Statistical Analysis

- **MATLAB data manipulation**: Write a MATLAB script to perform basic data manipulation (e.g., filtering, sorting) on a dataset.

- **Python data manipulation**: Write a Python script to perform basic data manipulation (e.g., filtering, sorting) on a dataset using **pandas**.

- **MATLAB statistical functions**: Write a MATLAB script to calculate the mean, median, and standard deviation of a dataset.

- **Python statistical functions**: Write a Python script to calculate the mean, median, and standard deviation of a dataset using **numpy**.

- **MATLAB data aggregation**: Write a MATLAB script to aggregate data (e.g., sum, average) by group.

- **Python data aggregation**: Write a Python script to aggregate data (e.g., sum, average) by group using **pandas**.

- **MATLAB data reshaping**: Write a MATLAB script to reshape data (e.g., wide to long format) using **reshape**.

- **Python data reshaping**: Write a Python script to reshape data (e.g., wide to long format) using **pandas**.

- **MATLAB data merging**: Write a MATLAB script to merge two datasets based on a common key.

- **Python data merging**: Write a Python script to merge two datasets based on a common key using **pandas**.

- **MATLAB data pivoting**: Write a MATLAB script to pivot data (e.g., create a pivot table) using **unstack**.

- **Python data pivoting**: Write a Python script to pivot data (e.g., create a pivot table) using **pandas**.

- **MATLAB data sampling**: Write a MATLAB script to randomly sample data from a dataset.

- **Python data sampling**: Write a Python script to randomly sample data from a dataset using **pandas**.

- **MATLAB data grouping**: Write a MATLAB script to group data based on a specific column and calculate summary statistics.

- **Python data grouping**: Write a Python script to group data based on a specific column and calculate summary statistics using **pandas**.

- **MATLAB data interpolation**: Write a MATLAB script to interpolate missing data in a dataset.

- **Python data interpolation**: Write a Python script to interpolate missing data in a dataset using **pandas**.

- **MATLAB data normalization**: Write a MATLAB script to normalize data (e.g., min-max scaling) in a dataset.

- **Python data normalization**: Write a Python script to normalize data (e.g., min-max scaling) in a dataset using **pandas**.

- **MATLAB data transformation**: Write a MATLAB script to transform data (e.g., log transformation) in a dataset.

- **Python data transformation**: Write a Python script to transform data (e.g., log transformation) in a dataset using **pandas**.

- **MATLAB data visualization**: Write a MATLAB script to visualize the distribution of data using histograms and box plots.

- **Python data visualization**: Write a Python script to visualize the distribution of data using histograms and box plots using **seaborn**.

- **MATLAB vs Python data manipulation**: Compare the data manipulation and statistical analysis capabilities in MATLAB and Python, highlighting their similarities and differences.

Chapter 11, Signal and Image Processing

- **MATLAB signal processing**: Write a MATLAB script to perform Fourier Transform on a signal and plot the frequency spectrum.

- **Python signal processing**: Write a Python script to perform Fourier Transform on a signal and plot the frequency spectrum using **numpy** and **matplotlib**.

- **MATLAB filter design**: Write a MATLAB script to design a low-pass filter and apply it to a signal.

- **Python filter design**: Write a Python script to design a low-pass filter and apply it to a signal using **scipy**.

- **MATLAB audio processing**: Write a MATLAB script to read an audio file, apply a filter, and play the filtered audio.

- **Python audio processing**: Write a Python script to read an audio file, apply a filter, and play the filtered audio using **scipy** and **pydub**.

- **MATLAB image processing**: Write a MATLAB script to read an image, convert it to grayscale, and display the result.

- **Python image processing**: Write a Python script to read an image, convert it to grayscale, and display the result using **opencv**.

- **MATLAB image filtering**: Write a MATLAB script to apply a Gaussian blur to an image and display the result.

- **Python image filtering**: Write a Python script to apply a Gaussian blur to an image and display the result using **opencv**.

- **MATLAB edge detection**: Write a MATLAB script to perform edge detection on an image using the Canny method.

- **Python edge detection**: Write a Python script to perform edge detection on an image using the Canny method with **opencv**.

- **MATLAB image segmentation**: Write a MATLAB script to perform image segmentation using thresholding.

- **Python image segmentation**: Write a Python script to perform image segmentation using thresholding with **opencv**.

- **MATLAB object detection**: Write a MATLAB script to detect objects in an image using template matching.

- **Python object detection**: Write a Python script to detect objects in an image using template matching with **opencv**.

- **MATLAB image restoration**: Write a MATLAB script to restore a noisy image using a median filter.

- **Python image restoration**: Write a Python script to restore a noisy image using a median filter with **opencv**.

- **MATLAB image compression**: Write a MATLAB script to compress an image using JPEG compression.

- **Python image compression**: Write a Python script to compress an image using JPEG compression with **opencv**.

- **MATLAB image analysis**: Write a MATLAB script to analyze an image and extract features (e.g., area, perimeter).

- **Python image analysis**: Write a Python script to analyze an image and extract features (e.g., area, perimeter) using **opencv**.

- **MATLAB video processing**: Write a MATLAB script to read a video file, apply a filter, and save the filtered video.

- **Python video processing**: Write a Python script to read a video file, apply a filter, and save the filtered video using **opencv**.

- **MATLAB vs. Python signal and image processing**: Compare the signal and image processing capabilities in MATLAB and Python, highlighting their similarities and differences.

Conclusion

This chapter explored practical case studies demonstrating the real-world applications of MATLAB and Python across engineering, finance, signal processing, and data science. Readers learned how these tools can be used to solve complex problems, from financial modeling and statistical analysis to image processing and signal filtering. Through hands-on examples, the chapter highlighted key differences in syntax, performance, and workflow between MATLAB and Python, helping readers determine the best tool for specific tasks.

Key topics covered included numerical computations, data visualization, algorithm optimization, and debugging techniques. The case studies reinforced essential concepts such as matrix operations, control flow, function handling, and file I/O, while also introducing advanced techniques like machine learning integration and real-time signal processing. By working through these examples, readers gained experience in translating theoretical knowledge into practical solutions, improving their problem-solving skills in technical computing.

Ultimately, this chapter bridged the gap between academic concepts and industry applications, preparing readers to implement MATLAB and Python in research, automation, and data-driven decision-making. The comparative approach provided insights into selecting the right tool for efficiency, scalability, and domain-specific requirements, equipping readers with versatile programming skills for real-world challenges.

Join our Discord space

Join our Discord workspace for latest updates, offers, tech happenings around the world, new releases, and sessions with the authors:

https://discord.bpbonline.com

Index

www.ingramcontent.com/pod-product-compliance
Lightning Source LLC
Chambersburg PA
CBHW061746210326

41599CB00034B/6797